Busoni the Composer

Busoni the Composer

ANTONY BEAUMONT

Indiana University Press
Bloomington

Manufactured in Great Britain

Library of Congress Cataloging in Publication Data

Beaumont, Antony.
Busoni the composer.

"Chronological catalog of Busoni's works": p.
"Catalogue of busoni's transcriptions and cadenzas": p.
Bibliography: p.
Includes index.
1. Busoni, Ferruccio, 1866–1924. Works. I. Title.
ML410.B98B4   1984   780'.92'4   84–47699
ISBN 0–253–31270–1
1 2 3 4 5 88 87 86 85 84

Dedicated to
Stephen Barber
and
Mary Hoffman

Contents

Illustrations

Cover photo: Busoni in Milan, 1912

(between pages 64 and 65)

Grateful acknowledgement is made to the following owners of photographic or manuscript material:

Eric Rosenberg (5,6); Max Reinhart Archive, Binghamton (8,9); Ronald Stevenson (13); Breitkopf & Härtel, Leipzig (17, 29, 34); Library of Congress, Washington DC (39); Hindemith Institut, Frankfurt am Main (23); Theatermuseum, Cologne (24–28); Deutsche Staatsbibliothek, Musikabteilung, Berlin (GDR) (all other illustrations).

Foreword

When Edward Dent published his excellent biography of Busoni in 1933, he made no attempt to write in any detail about the composer's works, explaining that to deal with them 'at all adequately would have required a second volume . . . with extensive musical illustrations and written in a technical style'. I first visualized this book as fulfilling exactly that function—and, to a large extent, it has remained so. In 1970 I planned its overall form and dimensions and set to work, consulting countless manuscripts, press-cuttings and other unpublished material in Berlin, Cambridge, Washington, Winterthur, Zurich etc.

Busoni's literary interests have been of particular significance to me. By referring to the books mentioned in his letters and diaries, or to the source material of his several libretti, one gradually came to realize how predominant a part the world of literature actually played in his work as a composer: one discovered that many of his works, even instrumental compositions, were directly inspired by what he read. Naturally this has often thrown new light on the music. Here I found myself parting company with Dent's initial conception and examining the scores from a literary and philological angle as well as considering their technical aspects. Such analysis is sometimes subjective and I would not always claim, as Dent could, that every statement in this book is 'related to positive evidence'. But from the 'positive evidence' alone emerges a portrait of Busoni as a composer more complete than technical data could ever offer.

Because Busoni is not yet well known as a composer, it seemed essential to provide a basic introduction to his mature works. The book therefore offers an outline of the music's anatomy rather than a dissection of it, an orientation, but nothing which would presume to be the last word. This is supplemented by a large amount of factual information: details of first performances and of the whereabouts of manuscripts have been provided, so far as these are known, as well as the scoring of those instrumental works discussed in the book and the (approximate) duration of each piece. A complete list of Busoni's works is also included: of the 314 pieces catalogued, I have discussed only the last fifty-eight. It is a fond hope of mine that a public better acquainted with Busoni will one day create a demand for a book about the others.

In the interests of homogeneity I have made most of the translations from German, French and Italian myself, even when other versions already existed. Translations by other hands are acknowledged in footnotes as and when they occur.

It remains for me to express my thanks to those who have offered the help and advice without which this book could never have been written. To Philip Radcliffe and Roger Smalley for initial encouragement; to my friend Ronald Stevenson for many insights gained in the course of long conversations; to Dr Karl-Heinz Köhler and Dr Jutta Theurich of the Deutsche Staatsbibliothek in Berlin (G.D.R.); to Dr Rudolf Elvers of the Staatsbibliothek Preussischer Kulturbesitz, West Berlin; to Herr Balthasar Reinhardt in Winterthur and Margaret Cranmer, Rowe Music Library, Cambridge—all of these for unlimited access to archive material. To Gudrun Blom, Christian Ziewer and Heidi Nicolai for their practical help; to Lieselotte and Dr Gerd Sievers in Wiesbaden and to Patrick Carnegy in London for their great help in the decisive stages of writing and publishing. An essay of Erich Heller's, 'Rilke und Nietzsche'[1], and a talk he broadcast in 1971 on *Doktor Faust* have been a considerable influence on my work.

I should further gratefully acknowledge the assistance of:
Frau Christel Benner, University of Hamburg
Herr Wolf-Rüdiger Braun, Cologne
Dr Andres Briner, Zurich
Herr Claus H. Henneberg, Cologne
Claus H. Henneberg, Cologne
Dr Walter Huder, Akadamie der Künste, West Berlin
Herr Walter Labhart-Kieser, Endingen
M. François Lesure, Bibliothèque Nationale, Paris
Herr Reto Melchior, Zurich
Mr William C. Parsons, Library of Congress, Washington
Mrs M. Jansen-Scherchen, Cambridge
Dr Giselher Schubert, Hindemith Institute, Frankfurt a.M.
Frau Hella Sieber-Rilke, Gernsbach
Dr Joachim W. Storck, Deutsches Literaturarchiv, Marbach
Dr Hans M. Wingler, Bauhaus-Archiv, West Berlin
Basler Orchester-Gesellschaft
Tonhalle Gesellschaft, Zurich
Norddeutscher Rundfunk, Hamburg, Music Library
Hochschule für Musik und darstellende Kunst, Frankfurt a.M.

ANTONY BEAUMONT
Cologne, 1984

Chronology

1866   Born in Empoli on 1 April.

1873   Begins to compose; first public appearance as pianist.

1875   Moves to Vienna, enrols at the Conservatoire.

1877   Hears Liszt play and is subsequently introduced to him.

1878   Moves to Graz, later to Klagenfurt.

1879   Studies composition with Wilhelm Mayer-Rémy.

1881   Concludes studies in Graz. Awarded diploma for composition and piano playing by the Accademia Filarmonica di Bologna.

1883   First performance of *Il Sabato del Villaggio* at Bologna. Returns to Vienna.

1885   First visits to Leipzig and Berlin.

1886   Begins work on the opera *Sigune*. Settles in Leipzig. Ever widening activity as concert pianist.

1888   Takes a post as piano teacher at the Musikinstitut in Helsinki.

1890   Marries Gerda Sjöstrand in Moscow. Wins the Rubinstein Prize for Composition and takes a teaching post at Moscow Conservatoire.

1891   Moves to Boston, teaches at New England Conservatory.

1892   Birth of first child, Benvenuto. Resigns teaching post and moves to New York.

1894   Returns to Europe and settles in Berlin. Concentrates largely on a career as virtuoso pianist.

1900   Birth of second child, Raffaello. Master-class at Weimar (repeated the following summer). Completes the Second Violin Sonata (his 'Opus 1').

1902   Conducts the first of a series of concerts in Berlin devoted to contemporary composers. Begins work on the Piano Concerto.

1904   First American concert tour. Completion of Piano Concerto.

1906   Completion of the *Outline of a new Aesthetic of Music*. Takes a piano master-class in Vienna. Starts to compose *Die Brautwahl*.

1907   Composes the Elegies for piano. Growing interest in new compositional techniques.

1909   Death of both parents. Composition of the *Berceuse élégiaque*.

1910   Major American tour; composition of the *Fantasia Contrappuntistica*. Master-class at Basle, where he writes the first half of the libretto of *Doktor Faust*.

1912   Première of *Die Brautwahl*. Composition of *Sonatina seconda*. Acquaintance with the Futurists, growing friendship with Schoenberg.

1913   Appointed Director of the Liceo Musicale, Bologna.

1914   Returns to Berlin; conducts four concerts of his own works. Writes the libretto of *Arlecchino* and, at Christmas, completes the text of *Doktor Faust*.

1915   Settles in New York, but eventually returns to Europe and finds refuge in Zurich.

1916   Completes *Arlecchino*; begins work on the music for *Doktor Faust*.

1917   First performances of the operas *Turandot* and *Arlecchino*. Completion of Bach–Busoni complete edition.

1919   Elected Doctor h.c. at the University of Zurich. A lengthy English visit terminates his refuge in Switzerland.

1920   Returns to Berlin.

1921   Conducts three restrospective concerts. Busoni-number of the *Musik-blätter des Anbruch*. Opens a composition class under the auspices of the Prussian Academy of Arts. First signs of serious illness.

1922   Last public appearance as pianist.

1923   Journeys to Weimar and Paris. Further periods of illness.

1924   Dies in Berlin on 27 July.

1925   First performance of *Doktor Faust*.

Without knowing his music, I believe in it.

Stefan Zweig

Both of these [Liszt and Busoni], with their exceptional, magical powers, were for ever searching for a secret that was never revealed to them, or was only suffered to live in flashes before their eyes for the space of a few moments.

Sacheverell Sitwell

Busoni has a decided gift for composition and also serious tendencies; . . . I could not but regret that [he] in every way did violence to his nature, and strove, apparently, to be German at any price.

Peter Tchaikovsky

Personally, I know that he crystallized my half-formed ideas, stimulated my imagination, and determined, I believe, the future development of my music.

Edgar Varèse

If one only knows Busoni as a musician, one does not know him. (And who knows him as a musician?)

Alfred Einstein

Busoni has been called the prophet of the new music. A better description would be its *conscience*.

Willy Schuh

Section One

The Composer

The Composer

Few characters in recent musical history are so surrounded by paradox and mystery as Busoni. Yet a reasoned and methodical investigation reveals quite a different picture: rarely has a man exerted so precise a control over his own destiny; rarely do we meet an artist so consistent in his beliefs and so single-minded in the pursuit of his goals.

He was born in Empoli, a quiet, rural town not far from Florence, on 1 April 1866. Thus he was born a Tuscan—and, wherever he was, he never considered himself anything else. His father, Ferdinando Busoni, was a travelling clarinet virtuoso of Corsican origin whose nomadic existence bore Ferruccio away from his homeland when he was only eight months old. He and his mother, Anna Weiss, a pianist of part German, part Italian extraction, settled in Trieste which became, for the next few years, a more permanent home. Here it was, at the age of six, that he commenced his studies of piano and composition under the stern, well-meaning but none too expert eye of his father. Already, at the very beginning of his career, he showed equal talent as instrumentalist and composer: at the age of eight, when he played Mozart's C minor Piano Concerto in public, he already had a dozen childish attempts to his credit. In both capacities the young Ferruccio had a natural ability. As a pianist he dedicated his early years to the development of a phenomenal technique, a major influence being his discovery of Liszt. As a composer he worked towards the development of a highly individual style, the chief milestones in which were his discovery and subsequent rejection of Brahms and the eventual establishment of an elective ancestral triumvirate which lies at the root of all his mature works: Bach–Mozart–Liszt.★ At no point along these twin pathways was there any doubt in Busoni's mind that he was primarily a composer. As a child he was exploited by his father as a bread-winning prodigy whose original compositions, or improvisations, added a touch of individuality to his recitals. The audience smiled at the youthful, derivative inventions and applauded politely; the unfortunate little boy devoted his childhood to striving to please patronizing adults, with the result that the man later protested, 'I never had a childhood'. Were it not for his inordinate thirst for knowledge, Busoni would probably have ended, like most prodigies, in obscurity. But he possessed a remarkable ability to begin anew (which astrologers say is a common attribute

★ In 1919 Busoni himself cited 'Palestrina-Mozart-Berlioz' as his threefold lineage.

of those born under Aries) and we can observe several phases of rejuvenation in his life.

At the age of fourteen he began studying composition with Wilhelm Mayer-Rémy (other pupils of whom were Emil Rezniček and Felix Weingartner), who introduced him to the intricacies of counterpoint. Two years later he was admitted to the select Accademia Filarmonica of Bologna, a distinction he was pleased to share with the young Mozart. During this period his music began to free itself from the derivativeness of his juvenilia and, in such pieces as the *Racconti Fantastici* op. 12 or the *Machiette Medioevali* op. 33, a truly inventive spark appears. The young composer was exceedingly prolific—a glance at the list of works at the end of this volume will show that most of them were written before he was twenty. It was at about this time that he began to publish his efforts. The climax of this period was the performance in the Teatro Comunale, Bologna, of a full scale oratorio after Leopardi, *Il Sabato del Villaggio*.

The next step was in a northerly direction—to Leipzig. Busoni was already bilingual. At home, Italian was spoken almost exclusively, but after living in Trieste, where German was the official language, the years spent in Graz, Klagenfurt and Vienna had served to make him fluent (if erratic) in that language. This period in Leipzig was probably the happiest and most settled in his life. At last independent of his parents, he acquired a circle of friends —Henri and the young Egon Petri, Mahler, Delius, Adolf Brodsky among them—and became thoroughly Germanized. Brahms is reported to have said, 'I will do for Busoni what Schumann did for me', and through Brahms Busoni met Hanslick and won his approval. In 1883 Busoni dedicated the Six Etudes op. 16 to Brahms, and his works took on a new solidity of texture and gravity of utterance whose origins were only too clear. When Tchaikovsky met him in 1888 he was full of admiration for the young man's talents but quite appalled at the neglect he had shown of his Italian origins. It was a deficiency which Busoni would have acknowledged, but with regret: in truth, Italian music seemed to him to have reached a point of stagnation and it was only the appearance of Verdi's *Otello* in 1887 and *Falstaff* in 1893 that persuaded him to the contrary.

In 1888 Hugo Riemann, the celebrated music historian, secured Busoni a post as professor of piano in Helsinki. There he met Gerda Sjöstrand, daughter of a Swedish sculptor, and he married her in Moscow two years later. Indeed, it was to Russia that his wanderings now led him, as professor of piano at the Moscow Conservatoire, and as winner of the Rubinstein Composition Prize in St Petersburg, an achievement which set the seal on this second phase of his creative career. He had been working on his first opera, *Sigune, oder das stille Dorf*, the short score of which was completed in 1889. Many of the best ideas from the work were incorporated in the pieces submitted for the Rubinstein Prize, but the opera itself remained unscored and unperformed.

Busoni now embarked on a struggle for mastery of the piano. He continued to compose, but became considerably more self-critical and less self-confident. From now on, his works were often subjected to thorough revisions and were sometimes completely rewritten. He began to make the transcriptions and arrangements for which he has become famous and he also broke his ties of allegiance to Leipzig, spending two years in Boston and New York. In 1894 he returned to Europe and settled in Berlin, which remained his home—with some interruptions—until his death. But it could not be said that his chosen domicile made a German of him. Even after living ten years in the city, he realized that he would never be considered anything but a foreigner, and this was painfully confirmed during the First World War when he approached the German Embassy in Washington for aid in securing concert engagements. The reply came at once, cold and discourteous: His Excellency the Ambassador was unable to give aid to a citizen of a hostile nation. More wounding was the attitude of many Italians, especially in the Press, who also began to treat him as a foreigner. He had become an outsider, left with virtually no choice but to settle in Switzerland and wait out the war.

But for the invitation to return to Berlin, Zurich might have remained his home to the end of his days. He returned because of the new beginning this move offered him and because he saw greater possibilities of reconstituting musical life in Berlin than in Italy. Indeed, his love for his native Tuscany was more an ideal than a reality. The Italy to which he would have returned, and to which he wished to belong, would have had to be the artistic hub of the world it had been during the Renaissance. The true state of the country proved itself, after repeated trials and disappointments, to fall far short of this ideal: the educational institutions were moribund; the public was arrogantly conserva-tive; in the theatres Puccini and the school of *verismo* reigned supreme; in the publishing world Ricordi exercised a virtual monopoly (and Busoni's relations with Tito Ricordi were never very cordial). In Germany things were different. Berlin was a maelstrom of the avantgarde and a breeding-ground for all that was excellent in theatre, literature and painting as well as music; in Oskar von Hase, the head of Breitkopf und Härtel, Busoni found a publisher who supported him as loyally as any composer could hope for; in the concert halls he soon established *his* public and could bring his new works into the world in congenial surroundings. It would have been foolish to ignore these consider-able advantages in favour of returning to Italy, and his one attempted return, to Bologna in 1913, proved disastrous. Circumstances made an exile of him.

Although cosmopolitanism was more or less thrust upon him, it helped him to realize just how provincial were the seemingly majestic borders dividing one country from another and he began to formulate a concept of a universal music, a music that should know nothing of geographical or ethnic distinctions, an art beyond political or religious differences—an art 'Beyond Good and Evil'.

From the publication of his book *Outline of a New Aesthetic of Music* in 1907 to the end of his life, Busoni's one aim was to define the nature of this universal music and to embark on a voyage that would take him as far as possible towards it. He foresaw the form that such a journey would have to take: at the end must come a major work in which the quest would be revealed in allegorical form. Such a work would have to be written for the stage and it was very unlikely that anybody except himself could write the text for it. Furthermore, such a work would have to summarize the essence of all his achievements, hence a preliminary period of totally free experiment would be required. Starting in 1907 with the Elegies for piano, Busoni began to erect the fortifications of his new musical stronghold and as first expression of his theatrical allegory he composed a comedy, *Die Brautwahl*. The hero of this opera, Leonhard, was the first embodiment of his projected autobiographical-mythical figure. Many others were considered for the final all-embracing opera, including Merlin, the Wandering Jew, Don Juan, Dante and Leonardo da Vinci. Finally, after several changes of plan, and in spite of Goethe, he settled on Faust.

Busoni began to develop at headlong pace. He broke down the barriers of tonality and regular rhythmic structures; proclaimed just as vociferously as Schoenberg the emancipation of the dissonance; spoke of the need for machines and new instruments in future music; established a new style of polyphony and advocated new systems of notation, new scales and microtones. Then came the war.

It was a stunning blow which shattered all Busoni's plans and frustrated his every ambition. Yet for a while he fought on. During Christmas of 1914 the text of his great allegorical drama came clear at last and he fled to America with the libretto of *Doktor Faust*— and very little else—in his briefcase. But the war brought a radical change in his musical style, blunting the fierce investigative urge which had driven him for almost a decade, and bringing out a new contemplativeness and sense of compassion. Slowly and painfully he found a way of turning adverse fortune to good effect: he came to realize that the task of synthesizing his experiments had now been forced upon him, perhaps sooner than he would have liked, and that he was now in a position to start work on the score of *Doktor Faust*. In 1919 he wrote to his friend H. W. Draber of the process he now envisaged, not only for himself but for all the musical world:

> Many experiments have been made in this young century; now, from all our achievements—older and newer—it is time to form something *durable* again . . . *Accomplished creation* and the *joy* of making music must come into their own once more. There has been too much brooding and melancholy and subjectivity. Also unnecessary noise.[1]

He evolved a concept which he called *Junge Klassizität* (Young Classicality), and in a note headed 'Ziele' (goals), dated 1920, he enumerated the guiding lines of this final period:

1. Nature: Young Classicality ('perfection')
2. Form: Theatre as universal domain
3. Means: Melody and polyphony
       $\frac{1}{3}$–tones
4. Theory of systematic progress

Much nonsense has been talked about Young Classicality and it is generally confused with neo-classicism. There is a distinction (rather less than fine) between the two: the former is nothing less than an aesthetic of music and music-making, by which an infinite variety of new styles is conceivable; the latter is one of these many new styles. Busoni wrote to Paul Bekker:

By 'Young Classicality' I mean the mastering, sifting and exploitation of all the achievements of preceding experiments: their incorporation in firm and beautiful forms. . . . But this art should be based . . . on a number of ideas which are not yet fully acknowledged . . . the concept of the Oneness of music . . . a final end to motivic working and the recapture of melody as mistress of all voices . . . the casting off of 'sensuousness' and renunciation of subjectivity . . . the reconquest of serenity (Heiterkeit) . . . *absolute* music.[2]

I lay stress on the importance of the word 'Young' in order to distinguish Classicality from conventional classicism'.[3]

In this new objectivity, Busoni would have said, with Leonardo: 'He who is no mathematician should not read me.' And he was delighted to read in an obscure British *Treatise of Music* by Alexander Malcolm, dating from 1721: 'Musick is a Science of *Sounds*, whose *End* is Pleasure.'

With these guiding lines, Busoni set to work to complete *Doktor Faust*. There was very little that occupied him between the summer of 1917 and his death which did not have a direct bearing on the progress of the opera. By now he had reduced his appearances as a pianist to a minimum, based on an exclusive circuit of Berlin, London, Paris and Rome, and he appeared almost as frequently as a conductor. The turmoil of war, however, had left its mark on him and in 1921 he began to feel the first effects of a heart disease which was soon to prove fatal. At the end, only one scene of the opera still eluded him—the vision of Helena—and Faust's closing monologue had to be abandoned at the point where music from that scene should have returned. When Busoni died, on 27 July 1924, although he knew exactly how the opera should finish, he had come no nearer to notating the music for Helena than twelve years before when he had first visualized it. His death itself came almost as a symbolic gesture: his life's work had foundered on the impossibility of writing music to represent the 'unattainable Ideal of Beauty'.[4]

Ten years before, he had written, prophetically:

In the case of a significant artist the first period is one of seeking oneself, the second is that of discovering oneself, while the third and conclusive period often seems to be a new search for the benefit of later discoverers.[5]

Busoni's 'second period' coincided with the turn of the century. His self-imposed process of 'discovering' himself in the first decade of the twentieth century soon led to a significant metamorphosis: whereas as a young musician he had been in close contact with such composers as Brahms, Tchaikovsky, Saint-Saëns or Boito, he now turned his attention to the work of revolutionary figures: Schoenberg, Bartók and Varèse, for example. It would have been foreign to such contemporaries of his as Fauré and Puccini (who both died within a few weeks of Busoni in 1924) to transform themselves so radically, and

one finds little of this desire for renewal in the work of his friends Sibelius and
Delius, nor indeed in that of his greatest contemporary, Richard Strauss.

Dissatisfaction with available means of expression voiced itself remarkably
early in his life: in 1893 we find Busoni calling for new orchestral instruments
—saxophones, cimbaloms, complete families of flutes and oboes, a soprano
bassoon, a sub-contrabass and a bell-machine with a range of six octaves—and
demanding the regular incorporation of other lesser-used instruments into the
symphony orchestra. Twenty years later, when his musical language was
better equipped to deal with such innovation, he even sketched out a few bars
of a piece for such an orchestra, with alto and bass flutes, bass cor anglais (lower
than a heckelphone), 6 cimbaloms (3 *naturale*, 3 *con sordino*), 2 chromatic
harps, pedal timpani and other such rare birds. But it remained speculation. In
1919 he had three bells cast for *Doktor Faust*, to be used in the first production
of the opera at Dresden. It was characteristic that he should write thus to the
foundry:

> I have read in a handbook of musical instruments that there exists an object
> (Chinese or Javanese) which they call a *Bonang*. It consists of 10–12 gongs
> suspended on wires within a frame, which are struck with (covered) wooden
> beaters. Couldn't one build something similar with your plate-bells? That
> would produce a *new orchestral instrument*.[6]

In the *New Aesthetic* he proposed a new division of the octave using sixths of
tones. He devised a notation for it and later even commissioned a New York
instrument builder to adapt an old harmonium to play the new intervals—yet
he never incorporated them in his music. Similarly, in all his orchestral scores,
the most outlandish instruments we ever find are the celesta and the
xylophone, the bass clarinet and the harpsichord. Scarcely innovations!

This was the greatest apparent rift in his personality. But he had his 'theory
of systematic progress' which, in its very slowness and meticulousness, had no
use for potentially senseless irregularities or blind leaps into the unknown. His
actual innovations were subtle and rarely spectacular, for he preferred to
concentrate on the fullest exploitation of those possibilities already existent.
Accordingly he brought about *minor* revolutions such aᴗ the instrumental
technique of the *Berceuse élégiaque* or the harmonic language of the *Sonatina
seconda*. There was not a single turning point in his life which could be
described as a complete break with the past, no major revolution and no
sensationalism. He would strongly have endorsed Schoenberg's dictum that
there was still plenty to be said in C major.

Busoni's encounter with Schoenberg was indeed the most striking of his
relations with younger musicians. The two composers exchanged letters as
early as 1903, but the first significant contact was made in 1909. At this time
both had independently found their way to the emancipation of the dissonance: Schoenberg in one sweeping change with the *Georgelieder* op. 15 and
the piano pieces op. 11, Busoni tentatively (as a composer) in passages of Book
I of *An die Jugend*, but convinced (as a thinker) of the necessity of the step.

Their ways of reaching the same conclusion are symptomatic of their differing approaches to the whole question of creativity. Busoni moved cautiously and wrote that music must begin to seek a path *'upwards'*; Schoenberg had no goals, nor any idea where his probings might lead him. 'My only aim is: to have *no* aims!' he told Busoni[7] and he expressed this same chaotic spirit of revolution in his oratorio, *Die Jakobsleiter*: 'Whether to the right or the left, forwards or backwards, uphill or downhill—one must move on without asking what lies behind or ahead.'

When a copy of the first and second pieces of Schoenberg's op. 11 arrived in June 1909, Busoni realized at once that they confirmed his theories of the new harmony. Without them, the 'Epilogo' of *An die Jugend* (and much of the equally striking music of the following years) would probably never have been written. Busoni in turn sent Schoenberg a copy of his *New Aesthetic* (which had been published two years before) as proof of the brotherhood between them.⋆ 'Your *Outline of a new aesthetic of music* pleased me uncommonly, above all because of its boldness', Schoenberg told him.[8] He also compared their evident concord to the intersection of two circles: 'Sectors of greater or lesser magnitude coincide—but there are the alternate segments which oppose each other.'[9] And, although Busoni prefered a metaphor of tangential circles to intersecting ones, he agreed in principle.

Busoni also played an important part in Schoenberg's return to Berlin in 1911, bringing their friendship to its most cordial point. In the summer of 1913 Schoenberg conducted a private performance of *Pierrot Lunaire* in Busoni's appartment (see Ch. XII); a few weeks later Busoni took up his new post as Director of the Liceo Musicale in Bologna. One of his Italian pupils from that time, Guido Guerrini, recalls:

> For us who considered ourselves advanced in having assimilated the harmonic language of Strauss and Debussy, he revealed for the first time the theories of Schoenberg, also demonstrating their deviations, developments and possibilities.[10]

Three years later, on the point of formulating his ideas of Young Classicality, Busoni still admired Schoenberg. He asked Leichtentritt: 'Have you not realized . . . the painstaking measurements with which someone like Schoenberg . . . writes down an interval?—Any other note would grieve him.'[11] But by now his concept of dissonance had become an essential part of his vision of the 'sounding Universe'; Schoenberg had meanwhile advanced no further since *Pierrot* and the *Four Songs* op. 22, and was not to publish another note for some seven years. Busoni's letter to Leichtentritt goes on to indicate the intimate relationship which he sensed between dissonance and nature:

> It is just as impossible for sounds to be 'wrong' in music as it is for stones, plants or formations in a forest. We just have to learn to discern harmony

⋆ This was not the same copy which Schoenberg later copiously annotated; that was the second edition, which did not appear until 1916.

away from the textbook.—Our goal is this highest stage which will indeed be founded on polyphony (also comparable to the forest).[12]

His last memories of Schoenberg's music were probably of *Erwartung* and *Die glückliche Hand*, compositions whose hysterical investigation of the sub-conscious was no longer in harmony with his serene perception of the voice of Nature. By 1917 Expressionism had vanished from his horizon and by 1918 it had become literally a dirty word for him: the appearance in *Arlecchino* Part II of a curious expressionist animal, Herr Sauberwasser, seems to be a joke at Schoenberg's expense. Had Busoni been aware of his colleague's artistic crisis, he might have been more sympathetic towards him. But, in all fairness, he had warned against the dangers of free atonality as long before as 1911, under the heading 'Anarchy': 'Arnold Schoenberg is attempting it, but is already beginning to turn full circle.'[13]

There is no evidence to suggest that Busoni knew anything of Schoenberg's first dodecaphonic music, nor does it seem likely that he would have been very happy with the sternness of its system. It did, however, signify a turning point in Schoenberg's career very close to the evolution of Young Classicality in his own, and with it Schoenberg also expressed the need for creating 'something durable' again. Indeed, at the close of this saga, the two circles begin to intersect once more: Gerda Busoni asked Schoenberg to complete the score of *Doktor Faust*, which he refused, while Leo Kestenberg offered him the teaching post in the Prussian Academy of Arts left vacant by Busoni's death, which he accepted.

At all times the relationship between Schoenberg and Busoni was nothing less than complex; remarkable for its intensity, for the good intentions of both parties and for their ultimate inability to understand each other. In the way Schoenberg blithely poured scorn on the idea of perfection—Busoni's highest ideal—we can perceive something of that misunderstanding:

> Do you really set such infinite store by perfection? Do you really consider it attainable? . . . I find even God's works of art, those of Nature, highly imperfect. But I find perfection only in the works of joiners, gardeners, pastrycooks and hairdressers.[14]

Busoni saw himself as a spiritual leader who was to guide music into higher, purer realms than it had ever, as yet, inhabited. He felt the world to be in the grips of medieval stagnation and sensed that it was his duty to be the first to proclaim a new Renaissance. Like Hermann Hesse, he could say: 'I was born towards the end of the new era, shortly before the incipient return of the Middle Ages.'[15] And in the commercially orientated, morally blinkered society of the United States he sensed most vividly the oppressive dominance of 'the new Middle Ages' (see *Arlecchino* Part II). In his music there are recurrent references to this state of affairs—intuitively in the *Macchiette Medioevali* and the *Danze Antiche* of his early years, semi-consciously in the *Geharnischte Suite* op. 34, composed in 1895, and as an acknowledged fact in the ever more frequent recourse to Gregorian chant and rough-hewn organum harmonies of his mature music. As one commentator explained: 'He went back to the Middle Ages, because he found there what he wanted—a sense of man's nothingness in the face of his own potentially marvellous future.'[16]

In his writings on aesthetics, Busoni indicated in some detail the nature of this 'marvellous future'. His music takes just the first few steps in that direction, a fact which led Varèse (among others) to detect self-contradiction. Yet Busoni was aware of the slightness of the inroads he had made into the new music and he became preoccupied with handing on the fruits of his endeavours to a coming generation. Hence the importance of his 'theory of systematic progress'. At the end of this long journey, where the 'marvellous future' becomes the present, mankind would attain perfection, and Paradise would be regained. The vision of Helena in Doktor Faust represented the attainment of this perfection. Clearly mankind fell far short of this goal, and therefore the vision appears to Faust only fleetingly and terrifyingly, before vanishing.

Several metaphors for the musical universe represented by Helena are to be found in Busoni's writings: for instance, the image of a great Gothic cathedral or of a mysterious subterranean temple (which we shall come to call Aladdin's Cave). He further employs the metaphor of a garden:

> A composer appears to me as being like a gardener to whom a plot of land of greater or smaller size is allocated for cultivation . . . It falls to the share of this gardener to gather and arrange that portion within the reach of his eyes and arms (his powers of discrimination). Thus even a mighty one, a Bach, a Mozart, will only be able to survey, handle and display a fraction of the complete flora of the earth, a tiny fragment of that paradise-garden which covers the planets.[17]

However, even the garden, he continues, is an inadequate metaphor for it occupies only one plane, while music is an entire universe. His description of this 'Realm of Music' as a region in which all the melodies of the world vibrate simultaneously and eternally is perhaps the closest he came to defining his vision with words. In such a region, time and space have no meaning. Thus he came to formulate a concept which is fundamental to many of his experiments—'die Allgegenwart der Zeit'* (the omnipresence of Time). When music sounds, the temporal world is submerged in the 'sounding Universe' and we are made capable of heightened perception, if only in flashes. Thus the performance of a piece of music is a mystic experience; the concert hall is more of a temple than a place of amusement.

Not for a moment did Busoni imagine that this fantasy 'realm' was attainable

---

* 'I have almost found an explanation for the omnipresence of Time – but I have not discovered why it is that we humans understand time as a straight line from the past to the future, while it *must* be in all directions, like everything in the universe.' (Letter to Gerda, 30 March 1911)

by the ordinary mortal. At the height of his experimental period, in 1909, he asked: '. . . where is the instrument which men would invent and set in motion in order to let the million tongues of Harmony resound? Where is or will ever exist a technique whereby the thousand registers of the World-organ could be rendered playable?'[18]

In his wish to proclaim to the sleeping world a new musical renaissance, Busoni found himself drawn to his great countryman, Leonardo da Vinci. There are several arresting parallels between the personalities of these two artists, affinities which once caused Busoni to remark: 'Perhaps I am mistaken, or do I believe I see some similarities in this figure to my own much smaller one?'[19] First, a simple matter of birth: Empoli and Vinci are no more than five miles apart. Hence Busoni, with his flexible sense of the passing of time, would have found in Leonardo a neighbour, a fellow Tuscan. Both artists had a speculative power far in excess of what they could actually achieve, an instance of which is cited by Kenneth Clark in his famous study of Leonardo: 'His notes on colour perspective . . . include many acute observations in which he anticipated the theories of Impressionism; yet it was not in his nature to incorporate these fine observations . . . in his pictures.'[20] The desire for perfection was, in Leonardo's case, often the reason for his inability to finish a work. Busoni, while not given to leaving work uncompleted, found in Leonardo's diffidence his *alter ego*. One primary source of his knowledge of Leonardo was a lengthy novel by Dimitri Mereshkovsky (*Leonardo da Vinci*), a book closely based on fact. Busoni particularly admired a chapter headed 'The diary of Giovanni Boltraffio' in which he found this appraisal of Leonardo: 'He always strives for the very highest, for the unattainable—for that which a human hand, no matter how great its craftsmanship, will never be able to express.'[21] Vasari, too, writes of Leonardo that 'he was unwilling to look for any human model, nor did he dare suppose that his imagination could conceive the beauty and divine grace that properly belonged to the incarnate Deity'.[22] Thus, in a curious way, it was fitting that Busoni should have left his vision of Helena unfinished. The very fact of its intangibility bears witness to his Leonardo-inspired search for perfection.

Another theme common to both artists was the desire to fly. In Leonardo this fixation took the practical form of observation, experiment and (of course) failure: he made countless sketches of birds in flight, of grotesque machines or attachments for flying. More extraordinary are his aerial views of landscapes and towns: even if he was physically unable to soar into the air, his visual powers could do so. Busoni's wish to fly was entirely in the imagination. Nevertheless, it was in 1903, at the beginning of his period of experiment, that the Wright brothers made their first flight; an achievement which served to convince him that a new Renaissance must now be close at hand, and also to reinforce his view that machines would play an ever-increasing role in the ascent of man, at a cultural as well as practical level. In flying he found the divine attribute of music: 'it touches not the ground with its feet'.[23]

Both artists worked towards their ideals of perfection with the aid of copious sketches and studies, many of them works of art in their own right. Indeed, Busoni's most perfect work, the *Berceuse élégiaque*, is no more than a miniature. Furthermore, both artists used sketches for the expression of considerably bolder material than we find in their major works. There is nothing in Leonardo's finished paintings to compare with his studies of grotesque heads, or with his disturbing outlines of an imaginary natural catastrophe; Busoni's two full-scale operas, his Piano Concerto and *Fantasia Contrappuntistica*, while undoubtedly the focal points of his *oeuvre*, have none of the flights of fancy we find in the first two piano Sonatinas or the second and third orchestral Elegies.

It was on his desire to fly (to soar, to ascend—one need not be too literal) that Busoni's *Weltanschauung**★* was founded and one detects behind this desire a strong inclination to the philosophy of Nietzsche. Although his name is never mentioned in Busoni's letters and occurs but rarely in his published writings, it features in his most important book, the *New Aesthetic*. Not only does this credo of his close with an extensive quotation from *Beyond Good and Evil*, but the whole is also couched in an aphoristic style remarkably close to Nietzsche's own, while the derisive tone in which Busoni attacks ossified musical institutions is strongly reminiscent of similar things Nietzsche wrote about his fellow philosophers. Nietzschean thought is buried deep in the personality of the composer and rises to the surface only at times of dire need—most spectacularly in a passage from Faust's closing monologue which was omitted from the opera when Philipp Jarnach composed the final scene.

If Nietzsche is an invisible ingredient of Busoni's personality, Wagner was to him the equivalent of what physicists today call a black hole. He too is invisible, but his very absence is the cause of a massive output of energy: Busoni's whole creative life was devoted to strong resistance against his gravitational pull, and it is through this resistance that we can best explain his adherence to Nietzsche. Just as the most disparate nations will join forces against a common enemy, so does the aristocratic elegant composer stand shoulder to shoulder with the 'philosopher with the hammer' in their campaign. Even so, there is another major difference between their standpoints: Busoni never admired Wagner, but he sincerely believed him to have attained perfection in his own sphere. Yet this sphere, in his opinion, occupied only a diminutive space in the 'sounding Universe'. Therefore, one had to take pains never to imitate him. *Parsifal* stood as a rare example in the history of music of perfection attained, and Bernard van Dieren assures us that this, as well as *Die Zauberflöte*, was one of Busoni's most treasured scores.[24] Yet *Parsifal* also seemed to offer conclusive evidence that Christianity, if not God as well, was dead. 'The Christian leanings of the piece', Busoni wrote, 'place it . . . at the *end* of an epoch.'[25]

★ Busoni stressed, on several occasions, that he considered it impossible to express *Weltanschauung* through music.

As a mature artist, Busoni was to declare, 'I am no more a Wagnerian than a Christian',[26] and he spoke to Leichtentritt of his 'first instinctive and later rationalized rejection of Wagner'.[27] Yet the struggle to maintain this independence must have been intense. He once explained his dilemma to Egon Petri:

> For quite some time now it has been my cruel, inescapable fate to have been born and brought up, and quite probably also to take my leave, with *Wagner*. How fortunate was a Carl Maria von Weber or even the young Verdi! Is it all conviction? Is there not a silent agreement among thousands who stand and fall only with him, to adhere to Wagner alone? It seems astonishing that a little, contemptible Saxon, with boring music and some strokes of genius, could call an international society of this magnitude into being. One is reminded of that rather restricted Jewish rabbi from Nazareth, who had to suffer for the sake of the extension of the ecumenical power of Rome, and who filled the bill so perfectly.[28]

He envied the younger generation their distance from Wagner: 'Young Zweig here gets angry whenever he hears the word Wagner. This [generation] has it easier than mine, which had to carry Wagner on their shoulders from the cradle!'[29] But he also warned that they would have to find something to replace him:

> . . . the reaction is slowly setting in, eating away at the foundations of this palace in the style of the 1870s. The younger generation (in particular those who are not professional musicians) is apathetically allowing the building to dilapidate. This is happening without hatred or demonstration: with tragic indifference.—Therefore, unfortunately, nobody is taking the trouble to replace the edifice with a new one: and this is where we, who have become 'durch Mit-Leid [*sic*] wissend', have to take action, have to teach.[30]

Busoni spoke of his pride in being the least Wagnerian composer of his generation; the converse is also true—he was the most Nietzschean, far more so than such avowed followers as Richard Strauss (*Also sprach Zarathustra*), Frederick Delius (*A Mass of Life*) and Mahler★ (Symphony no. 3), to name but the foremost. Where the others content themselves with contemplating his seductive outer layer of poetry, Busoni penetrates to the core of the philosophy.

There was certainly much in Nietzsche that he would have rejected, especially in the years of Young Classicality when he spoke of the *Serenitas* he aimed for as 'Neither Beethoven's pursed lips nor the "liberating laugh" of Zarathustra, but the smile of the wise man, of the Godhead.'[31] But in the mythical Faust/Leonardo hero of Busoni's allegorical drama we find a variation of the idealized figure of the *Übermensch*, a variation that is at all times close to the original theme. And in Faust's last words, 'Ich, Faust, ein ewiger Wille', is implicit the *idée fixe* of Nietzsche: 'der Wille zur Macht' (the will to power).

★ We know that Mahler was later to reject the works of Nietzsche.

Busoni's closeness to Nietzsche helps to explain the affinity which he felt towards Rilke, with whom he became acquainted in 1914. One could not exactly say that a friendship arose, for the poet was by that time far too much an isolationist to cultivate friends outside his most intimate circle. But they became allies. Busoni valued Rilke far more than George, Hofmannsthal or the other prominent poets of the age and he dedicated the second edition of the *New Aesthetic* to him, 'the musician in words'. Of Busoni's contemporaries, there is no composer, writer or other creative artist who comes closer to him. The point of contact seems to lie in the nature of Busoni's Faust and of Rilke's Angel.

The Angel is a recurrent figure in Rilke's poetry, developing over the years and reaching final form in the *Duino Elegies*, the poems in which Rilke achieved that which eluded Busoni—a definitive statement of his credo. The Angel appears at the very beginning of the first Elegy:

Wer, wenn ich schriee, hörte mich denn aus der Engel
Ordnungen? und gesetzt selbst, es nähme
einer mich plötzlich ans Herz: ich verginge von seinem
stärkeren Dasein.

Who, if I cried, would hear me among the angelic
orders? And even if one of them suddenly
pressed me against his heart, I should fade in the strength of his
stronger existence.[32]

He recurs thereafter in several passages, of which these lines from the second Elegy are characteristic:*

Jeder Engel ist schrecklich. Und dennoch, weh mir,
ansing ich euch, fast tödliche Vögel der Seele . . .

Every Angel is terrible. Still, though, alas!
I invoke you, almost deathly birds of the soul . . .[33]

In an oft-quoted letter to the Polish translator of the *Elegies*, Rilke explained something of his meaning:

The Angel of the Elegies has nothing to do with the Angel of the Christian heaven (rather with the angelic figures of Islam). . . The Angel of the Elegies is the creature in whom that transformation of the visible into the invisible we are performing already appears completed . . . the being who vouches for the recognition of a higher degree of reality in the invisible.—Therefore 'terrible' to us, because we, its lovers and transformers, still cling to the visible.[34]

---

* Another passage, from the fourth Elegy, is quoted in Chapter XIII.

The Angel's powers of self-transmutation are the goal of Busoni's Faust. The opera charts his development from exceptionally gifted human being to independent, super-human spirit (from man to Angel), which he attains only in his final moments. But Faust also appears in the unpublished drama, *Arlecchino* Part II, where he plays a silent role. Here, confirmation is given of Busoni's intentions: all bow down before Faust, and Arlecchino describes him as 'the one who is able to reach out in a trice beyond the frontiers of Mankind'.

Busoni sees in his Faust the form which he feels mankind must eventually assume; Rilke acknowledges the fearsome superiority of the Angel but himself remains a hypersensitive, mortal man. The difference is merely one of standpoint. Erich Heller has written: 'Rilke is the poet of a world whose philosopher is Nietzsche.'[35] It seems to me that Busoni is the composer of that world.

On the historic occasion of the private performance *chez* Busoni of *Pierrot Lunaire*, one of the guests was Edgar Varèse. He it was, more than any other, who answered the Nietzschean challenge of *Doktor Faust*; the influence of Busoni's thought on him was immeasurable. In Busoni he found that which was so obviously lacking in his first idol, Richard Strauss—a concern for the future of music and for the future of mankind. Listening to Varèse's strident works of the 1920s (*Amériques*, *Arcana* and all the others) one cannot easily believe that their composer owed his allegiance to a man who wrote a fantasy on themes from *Carmen* or a waltz dedicated to the memory of Johann Strauss (both works dating from 1920!). Yet Varèse himself stressed his allegiance and was proud to possess a score of Busoni's *Berceuse élégiaque* dedicated to him, 'L'illustro futuro'. In the 1940s, by which time he had had ample opportunity to change his view, he actually gave a series of lectures in New York devoted entirely to Busoni.

It is not difficult to find the areas in which their ideas coincided. First the search for new means of musical expression and, in particular, new instruments, which haunted Busoni (though without detriment to his compositions) became in Varèse an obsession which forced him to painful years of silence. Even when the advent of electronics opened up completely new worlds of sound to him, it seems he failed to express very much more of his vision with them. In truth, he too pursued an ideal which was 'suffered to live in flashes' before his eyes. Like Busoni, his quest led him to seek intimacy with the forces of nature: in works like *Equatorial* and *Déserts* he expresses, in characteristically volatile manner, the same thought processes as we find (in curiously hybrid form) in Busoni's *Red Indian Fantasy* or (still couched in late Romantic terms) the Piano Concerto. Above all, Varèse and Busoni are also both significant for those works which they never composed.

Part of Varèse's vision was expressed in the words of Paracelsus which he chose to preface the score of *Arcana*—the concept of a star of imagination

'which begets a new star and a new heaven'; another part was expressed in the text he wrote for an opera, the hero of which was an Astronomer who embodied Nietzsche's ideal of the *Übermensch*.

The Greek composer Iannis Xenakis came directly into contact with Varèse in 1958 while working as an architect with Le Corbusier at the World Fair in Brussels to design the Philips Pavilion in which the *Poème electronique* was first performed. However, his affinity with Varèse does not rest with this isolated collaboration: he is a true descendant of that wiry and youthful old man, while his position as aesthetician in the 1950s and 1960s is comparable to Busoni's in the first two decades of the century. There are some striking similarities of outlook here. Xenakis reasserts, for instance, Busoni's hypothesis of the omnipresence of Time: 'Let us resolve the duality *mortal-eternal*: the future is in the past and vice-versa; the evanescence of the present is abolished, it is everywhere at the same time; the *here* is also two billion light-years away. . .'.[36] He also expresses the need for a universal music (which we find simultaneously attempted in the *Telemusik* and *Hymnen* of Stockhausen, in the *Epifanie* of Berio and much of the later music of Messiaen, to cite but the foremost), but warns: 'As it has thus far developed, European music is ill-suited to providing the world with a field of expression on a planetary scale, as a universality, and risks isolating and severing itself from historical necessities.'[37] He reinforces Busoni's notion of a new music based on microtones by returning to the Pythagorean and Byzantine roots of Western music. In calling for a new language based on twelfths of tones, he sees '. . . the syntactical prospects for tomorrow's music, its enrichment, and its survival'.[38] In other words, a genuine progress towards a universal music could well arise through renewed confrontation with the most ancient musical cultures. Busoni expresses this confrontation symbolically through the apparition to Faust of Helena, the classical ideal of perfection; Xenakis expresses it in the language of mathematics.

Where Busoni wrote, 'music was born free and to win freedom is its destiny'[39] (a sentence loudly applauded by Varèse), Xenakis is his echo: 'The space-ships that ambitious technology have produced may not carry us as far as liberation from our mental shackles could.'[40] Finally, both composers speak of the shortcomings of our musical life. Busoni enumerated and bemoaned them in an article written in 1910, entitled 'How long will it go on?'. Since then, the quality of this life has degenerated beyond recognition. Xenakis surely speaks for every musician of integrity when he complains:

> What we are witnessing is an industrialization of music . . . It already floods our ears in many public places, shops, radio, TV and airlines the world over. It permits a consumption of music on a fantastic scale . . . but this is music of the lowest kind.[41]

The figure which Varèse called the Astronomer—whom we trace back to Busoni's Faust—reappears in an 'Open letter to youth' which Stockhausen published in the *Journal Musical Français* on 15 May 1968: 'We are in a time when in certain men heightened consciousness is becoming so strong that they are approaching a higher form of life. Here on this earth.'[42] And when he described his composition *Stimmung* as perhaps representing 'that winged vehicle voyaging to the cosmic and the divine',[43] or when he entitled a piece *Set sail for the sun*, he was reiterating this view.

Yet Xenakis and Stockhausen are just two isolated instances of composers over whom the omnipresent prophetical spirit of Busoni may be seen to hover. Viewing Busoni a mere half-century after his death, one still lacks that historical perspective (which Edward Dent valued so highly, and which Busoni himself humorously derided), without which his true sphere of influence remains partially obscured. Ronald Stevenson, for instance, would deny his influence on the avant-garde of the 1950s and 1960s and finds Busoni's aesthetic 'aligned more with Shostakovich'.[44] But he adds, 'I am sure Busoni would be ultra-critical of the present age'.[45] Vladimir Vogel recently wrote:

> One cannot readily demonstrate that Busoni would have seen a full realiza-
> tion of his anticipations, ideas or intuitions in those electronically produced
> sounds and noises, for instance, which are put out today as 'musical
> art-works'.[46]

If it is attainable at all, the 'full realization' of which Vogel speaks surely still lies in the distant future. Busoni's prime concern was to establish a new and purified attitude to composition—Young Classicality—which could only be brought about through a return to the standards of integrity of the more remote past. Future composers were to build on this solid foundation according to their individual ability and personality. Vogel finds in this simultaneous obligation to the past and to the future a 'conflict': 'But his triumph over it shows evidence of a stature which should make its presence felt for a long time to come as a model of true artistic conscience.'[47]

As will by now have emerged, Busoni's compositions reflect only a part of him—but the most glorious part. Composing played an almost devotional role in his life, and we find that his major works have an air of celebration about them, sometimes verging on the ritualistic, sometimes suggesting an atmo-sphere of carnival. Just as the mayor of even the tiniest Italian community will drape himself in the tricolour of his country before making a speech, so does Busoni—figuratively speaking—put on his best clothes when he composes. One sees it in the calligraphic beauty of his manuscripts, in the quality of paper on which he wrote them, in the expensive limited editions in which they were often first published and, above all, in certain fingerprints common to all his various musical styles.

The most consistent of these is a preoccupation with bells (which Ronald Stevenson has traced back to the acoustical surroundings in which the composer grew up). Festive tolling of bells is already to be found in a piano piece entitled 'Preparazione alla Festa' (from *Una Festa di Villaggio* op. 9); for the early 1880s this bell imitation is quite remarkable (Ex. 1).

Ex. 1

A project for a six-octave bell instrument has been mentioned above, as well as Busoni's idea of a plate-bell instrument. Later, one finds an obsession with glass bells which led him to experiment with the glass harmonica, and there are tintinnabulations high and low in many works of his: three-note glockenspiel chords in the last movement of the Piano Concerto, the eleven mysterious gong-strokes in the 'Erscheinung' from *Die Brautwahl*, the 'Campane di natale' of the fourth Sonatina, above all the many and various bell-effects in *Doktor Faust*. Even Busoni's most popular encore piece, *La Campanella*, belongs to this world. In the random groupings of lighter and darker stones in a wall, in the play of colours in a fire, Leonardo delighted in identifying shapes and figures, real or grotesque, from everyday life; similarly, Busoni's love of bells must have been founded on their complex haze of overtones in which one could pick out any number of themes or chords at random—an earthly representation of the vibrations of the 'sounding Universe'.

One curious phenomenon in Busoni's later works is his use of key: the *Comedy Overture*, both the incidental music and the opera *Turandot*, the Piano Concerto, the *Red Indian Fantasy*, *Die Brautwahl*, the first Sonatina and even *Doktor Faust* are either in or dominated by the key of C.* Exceptions are the *Fantasia Contrappuntistica*, whose D minor was dictated by Bach, and *Arlecchino* which is in A major because A is the first letter of the hero's name. The symbolism of this constant reference to the same key is partly explained in the first four notes of the first Elegy (see Ex. 48), a C major triad followed by an F sharp. The new departures of the music to follow are augured there in simple and telling fashion. In the plain C major cadence at the end of the first Sonatina, the value of that key as the archetype of tonality is stressed once more, coming after pages of intense experiment, as a salutary warning not to reject the achievements of past generations. Schoenberg used the same symbolism to other ends when he posed the question:

Ex. 2

Schoenberg: op. 28, No. 1.

To - nal   od-er a-to - nal?

* Even the atonal *Sonatina seconda* ends with unison Cs.

Another feature which appears regularly in Busoni's mature music is the grouping of works in pairs. There is a Florestan–Eusebius duality in such paring, either depicting a simple male–female relationship (second and first Sonatinas, *Sarabande* and *Cortège*, Divertimento for Flute and Concertino for Clarinet) or a contrast between light and darkness ('Pezzo giocoso' and 'Pezzo serioso' in the Piano Concerto, *Tanzwalzer* and *Toccata*). In the Fantasia after J. S. Bach, written in memory of his father (in F minor) and the *Berceuse élégiaque*, in memory of his mother (in F major) we find the most strongly contrasting pair of all.

Apart from these and other commemorative pieces, isolated works often have a specifically festive function. Since his childhood, it had been Busoni's habit to write short works to celebrate Christmas and the New Year. In his later years, these pieces attain the stature of his finest art.

Set aside from the composition of these smaller pieces came the business of writing major and monumental works. Dent has told us that there was a regular pattern to these occurrences and that each was built up from already extant materials. Although this is a fine idea, except in the case of *Doktor Faust* it cannot be substantiated: with *Sigune* the process was in fact reversed; there are no actual preparatory works for *Die Brautwahl*, where even the sixth Elegy was simultaneously conceived as a piano piece and as a scene in the opera; the *Fantasia Contrappuntistica* was written without premeditation; *Arlecchino* began life as an opera and was then abandoned, the sketches were used for the *Rondò arlecchinesco*, after which work on the opera was eventually resumed. It is unfortunate that Dent put this particular idea into circulation, for it gave a false perspective to much of Busoni's work. Wilfrid Mellers, for example, understood it as 'spiritual stock-taking'[48] and hence based his lengthy critical essay, 'The Problem of Busoni' on shifting sands.

The Piano Concerto sums up a whole decade of achievement in that it expresses the attainment of mastery as an instrumentalist. However, it also closes with a call to begin *anew* as a composer; the *Fantasia Contrappuntistica* stands at the beginning of a period devoted to the study of polyphony, and *Die Brautwahl* is altogether an experimental work. *Doktor Faust* alone is a work of consolidation and synthesis.

Dent's statement can only be justified in more general terms: that Busoni sensed a cumulative progress throughout his whole career, through which every work was implicitly a preparation for the following ones. Describing the *Fantasia Contrappuntistica* as a 'study', Busoni justified himself by explaining, 'Each of Rembrandt's self-portraits is a study; each work a study for the next; every life's work a study for later ones.'[49] He elaborated on the theme ten years later in a letter to his younger son, Raffaello:

The 'Divine Right' is a fairy-tale which the public, that big child, likes to believe.—Even Mozart had to rack his brains. Invention came naturally to him, but 'planning' often caused him to sweat.—Most of his works were composition practice for him. Once, for example, he said to himself he was still rather behindhand with chamber music, so he wrote six string quartets one after the other: for practice. In short, the only object of an artist is *to draw nearer to his goal*; and I believe each one feels within him that the goal is indeed attainable, but *not for him*![50]

As van Dieren wrote: 'He would call an ambitious work of whose value and importance he was well aware, "Sonatina", inferring with esoteric pride that one day he might compose a "Sonata".'[51]

In his letter to Paul Bekker on Young Classicality (quoted on p. 25), Busoni made one statement which calls for closer examination: 'This art should be based on . . . a final end to motivic working [*Thematisches*]'. He was referring to that logical development of small motifs which we associate with sonata form structures from Mozart to Brahms (or beyond), and he called for its 'final end' because he felt that it had become a cul-de-sac. His own methods of developing themes are complex. He approaches the question of musical coherence rather like a chess player. At each stage of the game he carefully calculates the state of play, weighs up the possibilities and finally makes the next move. Of course, many composers think this way but they commit their intermediate calculations to paper (one could take as a random example the concise motivic argument of Brahms's op. 51 quartets). Busoni, on the other hand, only shows us so to speak the completed move. He generally works with longer melodies rather than motifs (and sometimes very long ones) and, as the processes of development which we are accustomed to listen for are absent, his music often seems, at first hearing, to lack organization. Yet growing familiarity yields greater rewards. One discovers ingenious transformations of themes in the manner of Liszt and a host of new techniques, devised intuitively from the material at hand. Once his logic has made itself apparent, one begins to sense the cogency of his forms.

Another point of contact with Liszt is in Busoni's propensity for using themes by other composers. This first manifests itself involuntarily in his two traditional operatic fantasies of the 1880s, but from the Piano Concerto onwards his manner becomes more individual, the material more eclectic. In particular, he seeks melodies that one could justifiably describe as common property: Gregorian or synagogal chant, folksongs, Lutheran chorales (most of which can in turn be traced back to plainsong or folk melody) or Oriental themes (which have wandered in their history as much as the peoples themselves). In using such material—and there is an enormous amount of it in his music—he seeks the voice of Nature; he points to the timelessness of melody (a reaffirmation of the omnipresence of Time) and he indicates his belief in a universal music. Selective use of appropriated material is also characteristic of the music of Mahler, but it is enlightening to observe how both composers, drawing on quite different sources for their materials, create their individual sound–worlds with just as much assurance as those composers who draw entirely on their own resources.

An initially instinctive sense of this universality led Busoni to his activities as a transcriber, taking his cue once again from Liszt. His first works, arrangements of organ music by Bach, date from the late 1880s. Almost at once, their style began to affect his compositions and to bring radical changes in his piano writing. The textures of his Bach arrangements led in particular to the rich sonorities of the Second Violin Sonata and the Fantasia after J. S. Bach. Then the style became more economical, he moved away from Brahmsian chordal spacings towards a leaner, cleaner sound. This was one of the major revelations of the Elegies, whose tonal palette added muted tremolandi, washes of pastel colours and the converse paradoxes of harmonious dissonance and jarring consonance to the techniques he had already perfected. The range of colours in a short piece like 'All' Italia!', and the swiftness with which they change, were novelties: Busoni's new sounds inevitably invited comparison with Debussy, and the fact that both composers owed so much to Liszt only served to confuse the issue.

A comparison between Schoenberg's Piano Piece op. 11 no. 2 and Busoni's concertante transcription of it strikingly demonstrates the state of his elegiac art: the hard, ungracious textures of the original are softened and refined; the dissonances which Schoenberg had proclaimed with such conviction are beautified and—many people would say—trivialized. Certainly Busoni's version deodorizes the music, but it points to his ability to subjugate *any* music to his will.

In 'Nuit de Noël', the 'Berceuse' for piano and *An die Jugend* he came nearer to establishing his individuality and brought his technical control to a peak. Coupled with new, acrid harmonies and free rhythms, the *Sonatina seconda* then became the masterpiece amongst his piano works although, for all its novelty, the shadow of Liszt still stands distinctively over it. One of the first measures of his period of Young Classicality was a turn away from virtuosity. Yet, although the third, fourth and fifth Sonatinas are much less demanding than most of his piano music, the *Red Indian Diary* and the *'Carmen' Fantasy* retain the bravura element, while the *Toccata* shows that there was still plenty of fight in him. It is a work of immense power and energy, authoritative and bitter. To a greater or lesser extent, these are the qualities of all the other late piano works: the Chopin variations, for all their intended charm and good humour, have the same furious drive; the *Prélude et étude* look back to the occult world of the *Sonatina seconda* while sharing the forward impetus of the *Toccata*; in the Albumleaves the more delicate world of the Elegies is re-invoked, but with a new terseness, while the *Perpetuum mobile* and the little known Trills Study (Busoni's last piano work) are glittering, diabolic inventions.

Although his skills as an instrumentalist were devoted entirely to the keyboard, Busoni also acquired a remarkable insight into the orchestra. As a boy he was taught the rudiments of the violin (certainly he learnt enough to write idiomatically for strings) while his father also passed on to him a working knowledge of wind instruments. The technical foundation of Busoni scores is clean, uncluttered texture and virtuosic writing. His mentors in the former were Mozart and Rossini, from whom he learnt the necessity of concentrating on essentials. Thanks to them (and formerly also to Brahms) his orchestras are usually small: only few works call for triple woodwind, none calls for more than five horns, and even *Doktor Faust*, the most lavish of his scores, is modest by the standards of the time. In the question of orchestral virtuosity, his clearest influence is Berlioz (especially in *Turandot*, *Die Brautwahl* and the *Sarabande and Cortège*), and like Berlioz he learnt to think entirely orchestrally. His scores never sound like orchestrated piano music.

In his early years he wrote very little for orchestra: an overture begun in 1876 was left unfinished and the motet (op. 55) 'Gott erbarme sich unser' (1880) would appear to be his first completed piece for larger forces. So it was with relatively little experience as an orchestrator that he presented his *Konzertstück* for the Rubinstein Prize in 1890 and, all things considered, it is a great success. The score is clean, if not particularly imaginative (this can also be said of the following works, the *Sinfonisches Tongedicht* op. 32a and the *Geharnischte Suite* op. 34a). The Violin Concerto is a work of altogether greater stature while the *Comedy Overture*, written a few months later, recalls Mendelssohn as much as Mozart and represents a conscious attempt to break out of the Brahmsian sound-world. There followed a pause of some six years, a period in which Busoni became acquainted with many of the most recent scores of Strauss, Mahler, Debussy, Elgar and others. Then came the Piano Concerto, whose orchestration is masterly, with only a few miscalculations and many original touches. A large orchestra is deployed with reassurance and power. The *Turandot Suite*, written one year later, is simpler in layout and more cunning in its use of conventional resources.

For another four years Busoni wrote no orchestral music at all. When he started to work on the score of *Die Brautwahl* in the spring of 1909 his orchestral style was still close to that of the Piano Concerto. The real breakthrough came in October of the same year with the composition of the *Berceuse élégiaque*. Here he discovered how to restrict his ensemble to the barest essentials, dispensing with bassoons, trumpets and trombones and employing just thirty-eight instruments: the harp plays only harmonics, the celesta plays triads in one simple rhythm, the strings remain muted throughout; only the wind instruments have more freedom, but with total abstinence from virtuosity; the highest registers are avoided, the only percussion instrument (a gong) contributes a mere four soft notes.

The same precepts of economy and intimacy are observed in the *Nocturne symphonique*, the *Song of the Spirit Dance* and the *Sarabande*, while in the other orchestral works of the period 1912 to 1919 (the *Red Indian Fantasy*, *Rondò arlecchinesco*, Clarinet Concertino and *Cortège*) they are combined with more conventional writing. *Die Brautwahl*, when it was first performed in 1912, proved to be an orchestral *embarras de richesse* with elements of the new elegiac style gracing the score at its most mystic moments.

In *Doktor Faust* the refinements of the later years are combined with the dramatic effects of the Piano Concerto and *Die Brautwahl*, together with a new,

'Gothic' quality. Some orchestrations are lifted bodily from the works written as studies for the opera (for example, *Nocturne symphonique*, *Tanzwalzer*), while other interesting comparisons can be drawn between those *Faust* studies orginally written for the piano and their orchestrations in the opera (for example, *Sonatina seconda*, *Toccata*). Another sonic element, the invisible chorus, which had been used rather superfluously in *Die Brautwahl*, comes into its own to intensify the air of magic in the score.

It may seem curious that Busoni wrote no chamber music of note after 1898 and no songs at all between 1886 and 1918. In both cases this was part of the process of freeing himself from his Leipzig background: both forms of music-making evoked worlds of middle-class respectability in which he was not at home, and the shadows of Schumann, Brahms and Wolf loomed too large. If the Goethe songs, which he wrote between 1918 and 1924, reflect a certain reconciliation with that world, it is because other composers had meanwhile demonstrated (especially outside Germany) that the art-song could still be viable in the twentieth century. With songs like the 'Lied des Unmuts' or the 'Zigeunerlied' Busoni achieved forward-looking, unconventional essays.

It was not easy to decide at which point in Busoni's creative development this study should begin. In 1905 he said, 'My existence as a composer only truly begins with the (second) Violin Sonata',[52] but three years later he felt that he had found his entire personality 'at last and for the first time in the "Elegies" '.[53] Four years later still, he wrote of the *Berceuse élégiaque*, 'In this piece . . . I succeeded for the first time in creating an individual sound'[54], and when Hugo Leichtentritt was commissioned to prepare a short biography to celebrate the composer's fiftieth birthday, Busoni was unhappy about any mention of his formative years: 'My early works on your desk. I blush!'[55] If one ignored everything before the Elegies or the Second Violin Sonata, the picture would be considerably less than complete; if one went back to the very beginning, it would become over-cluttered with juvenilia. Furthermore, most of the early works are unpublished and even those which did appear in print are generally almost inaccessible. To draw an analogy with Mozart: there would be little point in writing about the first twenty-four symphonies if the world were still only vaguely acquainted with the last three; there would be little value in an analysis of *L'Oca del Cairo*—no matter how brilliant—if one then failed to do justice to *Don Giovanni*. I have, therefore, resolved to begin *in medias res*, not with the Second Violin Sonata but with three works which preceded it, all of which were performed in the retrospective orchestral concerts which Busoni conducted in 1921.

A further decision, made with some reluctance, was not to linger over the many transcriptions, critical editions and cadenzas which Busoni published. Nor did it seem feasible to touch more than fleetingly on his long and brilliant career as a pianist or on his development as a conductor, from inexpert but enterprising beginnings to a considerable level of assurance and eloquence. In these and other fields there is still plenty to be written.

Section Two

From the Rubinstein Prize
to the
Outline of a New Aesthetic of Music
(1890–1905)

I

Beginnings

Konzertstück op. 31a. Introduzione e Allegro for piano and orchestra. *Dedicated*: to Anton Rubinstein. *Composed*: 1889–90 (completed June 1890). *First performance*: 27.8.1890 (old style 15.8). Concert Hall of St Petersburg Conservatoire. Busoni and the Orchestra of the Russian Musical Society, conducted by Moritz Köhler. *Published*: Leipzig, 1892. PB 1107.* *MS*: 89pp., 34.5×27cm. Deutsche Staatsbibliothek, Berlin. *Arrangement*: for 2 pianos (Busoni) published Leipzig, 1892. KlB 19292. Plate numbers 19291, 19292. *Instrumentation*: 2–2–2–2; 4–2–3–0; Timp.; Str. *Duration*: 20 minutes.

Violin Concerto in D major op. 35a. *Dedicated*: to Henri Petri. *Composed*: 1896–7 (completed March 1897). *First performance*: 8.10.1897. Singakademie, Berlin. Henri Petri (violin) and Berlin Philharmonic Orchestra, conducted by Busoni. *Published*: Leipzig, 1899. PB 1407. *Arrangement*: for violin and piano (Busoni) published Leipzig, 1899. EB 5210. Plate number 22222. *Instrumentation*: 3(Picc.)–2–2–2; 4–2–3–1; Timp., Perc.; Str. *Duration*: 28 minutes.

Comedy Overture op. 38. *Dedicated*: to Wilhelm Gericke. *Composed*: July 1897 and revised 1904. *First performance*: a) original version—8.10.1897. Singakademie, Berlin. Berlin Philharmonic Orchestra, conducted by Busoni; b) revised version—11.1.1907. Beethovensaal, Berlin. Berlin Philharmonic Orchestra, conducted by Busoni. *Published*: (revised version) Leipzig, 1904. PB 1691. *Instrumentation*: 3(Picc.)–2–2–2; 4–2–0–0; Timp., Perc.; Str. *Duration*: 8 minutes.

The opera *Sigune* occupied Busoni intermittently but intensively from 1885 to 1889. He based the work on a fairy-tale by Rudolf Baumbach which was adapted for him by his friends Ludwig Soyaux and Frida Schanz into a libretto stylistically not far removed from 'Des Knaben Wunderhorn'—a folk legend with mysterious, unearthly and bucolic elements.

Diethart, a young stonemason, who is working on the building of a new cathedral, takes a stroll in the forest one summer's day. At noon, a village rises out of the ground and with it the indescribably lovely Sigune. She presents Diethart with a golden ring and then vanishes; the village sinks back into the earth. That night she appears to him in a dream and they pledge a vow of loyalty, but by the following morning the dream is forgotten. Later he marries his betrothed, Lenore, a girl from the town. After the wedding feast, Sigune reappears and Diethart recollects his vow. He joins Sigune in death.

The text was published privately in 1889, under the auspices of Breitkopf und Härtel. Whatever the charm of the story, it is virtually obliterated by the

---

* Where not otherwise stated, the publisher is Breitkopf & Härtel.

clumsy doggerel of the verse and confused by a variety of subsidiary scenes. The complete short score of the opera has survived (it is preserved in the Deutsche Staatsbibliothek, Berlin).

Busoni's next piece was a Concert-Fantasie for piano and orchestra which received its first performance at a Leipzig Gewandhaus concert in January 1890, under the direction of Carl Reinecke. The work was not to the taste of the conservative Leipzig public but was well received by the critics, one of whom commented that the music bore witness '. . . for the most part of independent and captivating invention, and redoubled interest, as the work of an Italian, in its solid nature, suggestive of German ways'.[1] Busoni himself was delighted with the work, particularly with the success of the orchestration. 'It was a highly honourable and uncommon debut,' he wrote to his mother.[2] Three years later he rearranged the work for orchestra alone and renamed it *Symphonisches Tongedicht*.

In April 1890, while visiting St Petersburg for three concerts, he heard of two competitions for composers and pianists to be held there later that year, and resolved to compete in both. Composers were required to submit chamber music and piano pieces as well as a work for piano and orchestra. Busoni's entries for this Rubinstein Prize were the Two Piano Pieces op. 30 (the second of these, *Friedenstanz*, republished in 1914, is adapted from *Signue*), the First Sonata for violin and piano op. 29, and a new *Konzertstück* op. 31a, for piano and orchestra.* He completed the latter towards the end of June, just in time for it to be copied before the journey to St Petersburg in mid August. Only two composers out of the original five arrived for the competition and Busoni won the prize with ease. In the piano competition he took second place, Rubinstein having decided that a Russian should win at least one of the awards. Eugen Raphoph, of the German language *St. Petersburger Herold*, wrote enthusiastically of the young Italian:

> Herr Busoni, who is but 24 years old, can be counted amongst those blessed souls who have at their command, apart from talent, stern application matched with intelligence. Take for instance the Concertstück: fine working-out of themes, brilliant though somewhat noisy scoring, concise and clear form and fairly original piano writing.[3]

It is with the *Konzertstück* that Busoni's career as a composer truly begins. Although Busoni dropped the work from his repertoire after the 1890s, he thought highly enough of it to add two further movements some thirty years later. He also played it for a last time in the third of a series of orchestral concerts in 1921, a series which had historical value as a retrospective of his entire career as a composer.

Influences of Brahms and fainter echoes of Beethoven are detectable in the *Konzertstück*; all is clear-cut, classical and, above all, unpretentious. In its

---

* A further entry was a pair of lengthy cadenzas for Beethoven's Piano Concerto no. 4 in G.

somewhat massive style, the work has a certain kinship with the music of Reger; and indeed Reger, who was for a time quite a close friend of Busoni, published an enthusiastic description of the work in the *Allgemeine Musik-Zeitung*:

> Here Busoni creates out of fullness and profundity alone, and this, combined with the energetic working-out of the great theme, results in a masterpiece, the like of which is no daily occurrence.
>
> The orchestra begins with a sombre introduction whose theme is later much developed . . . The succeeding *Allegro molto* with its main theme (Tutti), which first appears in B flat major, later in D major, the pensive second theme, with the tremendous solo part, the completely polyphonic structure, can without reserve be described as truly great and highly ingenious.[4]

Let us take a closer look at some of the themes. The opening phrase is built out of falling sevenths and rising thirds, material closely akin to some of the principal motifs of *Doktor Faust*:

Ex. 3

A second theme, the sombre melody which Reger mentions, is a rising chromatic figure, related (as Ronald Stevenson has pointed out[5]) to a motif in Carl Goldmark's opera *Merlin*:

Ex. 4

Ex. 5

In 1887 Busoni was commissioned to produce the vocal score of this work and
also wrote a bravura Fantasy for Piano on themes from it. Merlin, the wizard
generally linked with the Arthurian legends, was a figure around whom Busoni
himself considered writing an opera.

   The principal subject of the Allegro molto which follows is taken from Act I
scene 2 of *Sigune*. There, it features in the wedding feast and is sung by Marei,
the landlord's daughter:

Ex. 6

As the merriment of the feast increases, the guests begin to dance. Much of the
music for this 'Invitation to the Dance' has found its way into the extended 3/2
Allegro of the *Konzertstück*. But here there is also the beginning of a fugato,
which is not developed, and much insistence on a little chromatic motif (Ex. 7)
that is often to be found in Busoni's works, even of a much later period (e.g. in
the second bar of Ex. 268):

Ex. 7

   The *Konzertstück* is neither a one-movement concerto following Mendelssohn's or Liszt's models, nor is it a sonata movement; rather, a complex
amalgamation of the two. Busoni's refusal to make use of a stereotyped
symphonic pattern is an indication of his future developments. Already at
twenty-four years of age he had learned how to create an individual entity from
the material at his disposal. The architectural independence of the *Konzertstück*, which transcends the derivative nature of some of the musical language
and orchestration, must have contributed largely to Busoni's continued
affection for this piece in later years.

The Violin Concerto has always been one of Busoni's most popular works. It is
not yet fully characteristic and represents only a passing phase; indeed its
relative popularity may well have given many people a false impression of the
composer. Here we are still in a world dominated by Beethoven and Brahms,
with some passages close in spirit to the music of the young Sibelius.

   Busoni wrote the Violin Concerto during 1896 and 1897 for the violinist

Henri Petri. For a long time leader of the Leipzig Gewandhaus Orchestra and of a well-known string quartet, Petri became a close friend of the young Busoni, while his son Egon (who first learned to play the violin) later became Busoni's pupil and one of his closest friends and assistants.

The three movements of the Violin Concerto correspond to classical convention. Their inner structures, however, which are almost bereft of literal recapitulations, are more complex. Themes are transformed from movement to movement in ingeniously secretive ways—no blatant cyclic methods, no inflation of motto themes into glorious apotheoses, but a much more subtle art. The opening theme, for instance:

Ex. 8

returns fleetingly, just once, in the finale:

Ex. 9

And a wistful fragment in the slow movement:

Ex. 10

becomes the material for a riotous tutti in the finale:

Ex. 11

but again, only once, for six bars. Another characteristic touch is a theme which shifts between major and minor (something that had already been typical of the style of *Sigune*):

Ex. 12

Since the composition of the *Konzertstück*, the most important musical event for Busoni had been the appearance of Verdi's *Falstaff* in 1893. He wrote to his parents:

> Falstaff is—to put it briefly—a highly original work, fresh, spirited, and without doubt
>
> > the best Italian comic
> > opera since the 'Barber'.
>
> And that is not saying little.[6]

Falstaff re-established Busoni's faith in the future of Italian music, and this was immediately reflected in the Violin Concerto. The style of Verdi's last opera can be felt in a few orchestral gestures; for instance, in the way the whole orchestra erupts into an uproarious trill before the main tutti of the first movement, or in the fleeting chromatic scales for violin and flute in the Finale. And the spirit of Italy itself is to be felt in many places, especially in the last movement which, as Busoni wrote, is 'a sort of Carnival'.[7] On the other hand, much of the work is undeniably Nordic in tone. This is perhaps the first composition which breaks with the conventions of what Busoni called 'the Leipzig pattern': since 1890 he had spent two seasons in the United States and had shaken off many old roots. In 1893 he wrote: 'I have become a good deal *less German* and am tending ever more towards cosmopolitanism—is that my salvation? Who knows?'[8] A mixture of Latin and Nordic elements, a tendency to secretive handling of thematic material, a certain fleetingness, an elegiac, melancholy tone alternating with postively plebeian humour—all these facets of the later Busoni are jumbled happily together in the Violin Concerto, but not yet integrated. Nevertheless, the score is, in its own way, cohesive and convincing.

One of the foremost interpreters of the work was Josef Szigeti.* He first met Busoni around 1912, and has left this recollection of the occasion:

> Busoni, in those days mature, aloof, objective, towards his own works as toward everything else, had already gone beyond that stage of his development which had produced the Violin Concerto. One Sunday morning . . . I played it with him in Maud Allan's beautiful studio in Regent's Park, where he was staying at the time, and it was with a half-indulgent, half-proud, 'paternal' smile that he welcomed back his own neglected brain-child with the words, 'Well, I must admit it's a good work, though unpretentious!'[9]

After midnight on 11 July 1897, Busoni sat down and wrote the *Comedy Overture*. By the following morning it was finished. 'Of course nothing is perfect', he wrote to Gerda, 'and this piece will still have to be worked over. But it's not bad, very flowing, and in almost Mozartian style.'[10] The overture is a simple, mostly lighthearted work, an essay in economy of means. The orchestra excludes the heavy brass and makes the lightest use of piccolo, triangle and cymbals. Formally too, it avoids the allusive or elusive techniques of the Violin Concerto and is effectively a clear-cut sonata allegro. All this may give the impression of pastiche, of some dreary *Zopf-Musik*, but the piece is in fact shot through with cunning twists of tonality, humorously baffling and not in the least 'classical'. Setting out in plain C major, Busoni continues adding accidentals until he has arrived at E major within the first minute and, a few seconds later, A flat minor. He then introduces a second theme in A flat major and a third theme in E major.

This restlessness is maintained throughout. In the development section, a quasi-fugato introduces a theme of indeterminate tonality:

Ex. 13

* Szigeti's interpretation of the work, conducted by Busoni's pupil Dimitri Mitropoulos, has been preserved on record.

which is answered neither at the fifth nor at the unison, as all orderly text-book fugue subjects should be, but at the augmented fourth. A passage of unabashed cacophony ensues, followed by a lengthy build-up of a more sinister character: 'Here the dramatic knot is tied which, even in the most harmless comedies, should for a while provoke in the spectator a feeling of uncertainty and thereby apprehensiveness as to a happy ending', explained Busoni in his programme note for the first performance.

With the *Comedy Overture*, the Mozartian spirit is introduced for the first time into Busoni's work and the weightiness of his Leipzig style recedes still further. The piece has always been one of the most popular, for it poses the listener no great problems. Later, Busoni could rate it no more highly than 'très inoffensive'[11] and he produced similar *jeux d'esprit* of greater worth and originality—the Divertimento for flute and Concertino for clarinet, for instance. The simple élan of the *Comedy Overture* was something set aside from the serious business of composing: just as Busoni the pianist would dazzle an audience with an effortless rendering of *La Campanella* at the end of a gruelling recital, the composer also momentarily enjoyed his sheer virtuosity.

The published version of the *Comedy Overture* is a revision carried out in 1904. It appeared together with Mozart's overture to *Die Entführung aus dem Serail*, to which Busoni had added a concert ending. The original version of the *Comedy Overture* was a little too long: even during rehearsals for the first performance, one passage was cut.* When Busoni came to prepare it for publication, he made further cuts, including a lengthy section in 3/4 time towards the close. In this form, the work never threatens to outstay its welcome; it wears a mask of naïve good humour.

The evening of Friday, 8 October 1897 brought the first major consolidation of Busoni's composing career—an orchestral concert in Berlin devoted entirely to his own recent works. The programme consisted of:

1.   *Comedy Overture* (1897)
2.   *Symphonisches Tongedicht* (1893)
3.   Violin Concerto (1897)
        soloist: Henri Petri
4.   *Geharnischte Suite* (1895)

All four works were receiving their first public performances. The critics had mixed feelings. One wrote, 'his works have a simultaneously spellbinding, stimulating and repellent effect'[12], and another found the Violin Concerto 'somewhat dull of invention, fairly arbitrary in form, but compensated to a certain extent by striking, atmospheric and interesting details'.[13] All round approval was expressed of the Concerto's finale—indeed, its success with the public was such that this last movement had to be encored.

---

* In the absence of any traceable manuscripts for the *Comedy Overture*, I have been able to refer to two handwritten string parts of the original version, preserved in the Staatsbibliothek Preussischer Kulturbesitz, West Berlin.

II

In Memoriam

Second Sonata for Violin and Piano, E minor op. 36a. *Dedicated*: to Ottokar Nováček. *Composed*: May 1898 and August 1900. *First performance*: 30.9.1898. Musikinstitut, Helsinki. Victor Nováček (violin) and Busoni. *Published*: Leipzig, 1901. EB 5189. Plate number 22515. *MS*: 36pp., 35.5×27cm. (also MS violin part) Staatsbibliothek Preussischer Kulturbesitz, West Berlin. *Duration*: 32 minutes.

Improvisation on 'Wie wohl ist mir, o Freund der Seele' for 2 Pianos. *Dedicated*: to Marchese Silvio della Valle di Casanova. *Composed*: June–August 1916. *First performance*: 18.12.1917. Tonhalle, kleine Saal, Zurich. Busoni and Ernst Lochbrunner (pianos). *Published*: Leipzig, 1917. EB 4941. Plate number 27971. Later incorporated into Vol. VII of the Bach–Busoni Edition. *MS*: 22p., 35×27cm. Deutsche Staatsbibliothek, Berlin. *Duration*: 12 minutes.

During January and February 1897, with the score of his Violin Concerto all but complete, Busoni set out on a tour of towns in the West of Germany and Belgium. In Elberfeld he met an old Leipzig friend, Hjalmar von Dameck, 'a man of extraordinarily clear understanding and fine irony, cultured, and a philosopher of the best kind'.[1] It was von Dameck, formerly the second violinist of the Petri Quartet, who suggested to Busoni that he should write another violin sonata. The First Sonata op. 29 had been one of the works awarded the Rubinstein Prize; the new Violin Concerto was renewed proof of Busoni's understanding of the instrument.

A year passed, and in the following May the new sonata was composed. Busoni told von Dameck that the sonata 'had succeeded better than almost anything before',[2] and to his parents he wrote, 'I have become much simpler and much more profound'.[3] In emulation of Beethoven, the work was originally entitled 'Sonata quasi una fantasia'; it was dedicated to Ottokar Nováček, one of four brothers, all of whom were musicians. Ottokar was a composer who met with little success—today he is known only for his *Perpetuum mobile*, still occasionally played by virtuoso violinists—yet he composed seriously and ambitiously. Busoni certainly thought highly of his friend's music, for he made a piano transcription of the scherzo from Ottokar's First String Quartet, and later played the solo part in the first performance of his *Concerto Eroico* for piano and orchestra.

The Nováček brothers were carefree Bohemians, bubbling with humour and *joie de vivre*, and close friends of Ferruccio and Gerda. Ottokar himself was only a few weeks Ferruccio's junior and, as Carl Flesch relates in his memoirs, also his chess partner. Unable to make his name as a composer and perpetually beset with financial difficulties, he was obliged to earn his living by playing the viola in Adolf Brodsky's celebrated string quartet. When Brodsky emigrated to the United States in the early 1890s, Ottokar went with him.

It was Ottokar's brother Victor who gave the first performance of the new sonata with Busoni in Helsinki (where Victor was professor of violin at the Musikinstitut) in 1898. On that occasion Busoni must have improvised much of the work, for the rough manuscript score, while notating the violin part in detail, has only a very sketchy rendering of the piano part. The work had already been accepted for publication and a few pages of the fair copy of the score had been written when news came from New York that Ottokar was seriously ill. His condition worsened steadily and, after a year's illness, he died in February 1900. It would seem that the serene melancholy of much of the Sonata had been due to some strange premonition of the tragedy: the work now became a memorial. In the summer of 1900 Busoni gave a master-class in Weimar and here, during August, he completed the fair copy of the Sonata.

Busoni follows classical example by modelling his work directly on an earlier masterpiece, Beethoven's Piano Sonata op. 109—like so many of his compositions it looks to the past and the future simultaneously. Beethoven's external framework is reproduced almost exactly: an opening section of slower and faster tempi is followed by a scherzo section in 6/8 time; the closing movement is a set of variations, some fast and brilliant, others slow and elegiac. Like Beethoven, Busoni chooses the key of E, but his first movement is in the minor throughout, where Beethoven reserves E minor for his scherzo. The theme of Busoni's variations is a chorale-song from Bach's *Notebook for Anna Magdalena Bach* of 1725, entitled 'Wie wohl ist mir'. (The *Notebook* was also the source of the theme for Bach's own *Goldberg Variations*.) Here is the first line of the chorale:

Ex. 14

By transposing the song into E major, Busoni links it with the theme of Beethoven's op. 109 variations: the first four notes of 'Wie wohl ist mir' are to be found in the bass-line of op. 109:

Ex. 15

Beethoven: op. 109

The Sonata opens with a motto theme played by the piano alone:

Ex. 16

The use of such motivic incipits became something of a hallmark of Busoni's mature style. One finds similar openings in the second and fifth Sonatinas, for instance, and in the *Sarabande* op. 51. These mottoes have a quasi-mystical function, they are not unlike the brief quotations which some authors like to place at the head of their works (notably Busoni's revered Villiers de l'Isle-Adam), quotations which contain the essence of what is to follow, often couched in enigmatic terms.

The first movement of the Second Violin Sonata shows the composer at his best; unaffected and subtle, with an unbroken train of thought. An Italianate *cantilena* is modulated by a discipline and logic which never obtrude nor verge towards the pedantic. The entire structure is dominated by a rising minor third figure which is later augmented to become the initial major third of the chorale-song. Two principal ideas—the first in E minor, the second in B flat major—are unfolded with unruffled calm until a cadenza-like transition for the violin leads to a faster middle section in B minor. Towards the close the motto theme makes a brief appearance. There follows a much condensed recapitulation, at the end of which the motto theme returns once again, much altered.

Apart from the *prestissimo* of op. 109, another Beethovenian model for the ensuing scherzo, and one more closely related in mood, is the finale of the 'Kreutzer' Sonata. But where op. 109 has a certain fury about it and the 'Kreutzer' allows itself more relaxed moments, Busoni has produced a thoroughly virile tarantella, earnest at the outset and at the close, at one moment *schattenhaft* (shadowy) but otherwise riotous and ebullient. The opening theme is a transformation of material from the middle section of the first movement, accelerated and rhythmically modified to a point where it is scarcely recognizable as the same idea (a style of metamorphosis which Busoni learned from Liszt). Later, in a passage in the same popular tone as the 'Carnival' of the Violin Concerto, the proceedings threaten to get out of hand: fragments of subsidiary themes from the first movement are thrown about in a mad whirl where more is implied than actually stated. The movement as a whole can be considered as a trial run for the elemental uproar of the tarantella in the Piano Concerto. As it is, the rules of etiquette and good manners which came to be applied to chamber music in the last decades of the nineteenth century are here rudely cast aside.

The silence following the last éclat of the tarantella is broken by a falling minor third, given out by the violin alone, introducing a solemn sequence in C sharp minor:

Ex. 17

Tense, 'crawling' music follows and eventually the main theme of the tarantella is heard, slow and distant, as a reminiscence. Here it is broken into fragments, punctuated by sighs and finally reduced to a long trill. A slow descending scale on the violin leads to the statement of the chorale-song, played first with organ-like richness by the piano alone and then repeated and intensified by both instruments.

The layout of Busoni's chorale-variations closely mirrors that of the variations of op. 109, except for the addition of a long *minore* section. Although the scale of Busoni's movement is larger than Beethoven's, both works inhabit closely related spiritual planes. Variation I, *poco più andante*, is infused with a gentle rocking rhythm in triplets. Variations II and III are in fast tempo; the first *alla marcia*, the second a brilliant perpetuum mobile for the violin. Now comes the *minore* variation, conceived on the lines of a Bachian chorale prelude. Here the theme is considerably transformed and combined with a new motif characterized by three repeated notes:

Ex. 18

In the Fantasia after J. S. Bach, which Busoni composed in 1909 in memory of his father, this figure recurs with greater structural significance and can be identified as a 'death motif'. It is found again in later compositions associated with the death of Faust. The calm of this *minore* variation, underpinned for the most part by a lulling dactylic rhythm in the piano, remains undisturbed. Towards the close a new idea, marked *lamentoso*, is introduced, its hushed conclusion seeming to represent the moment of death itself. The ensuing fugue begins serenely:

Ex. 19

Busoni achieves a monumental build-up: in the fifteenth bar of the fugue the theme is stated *ff* in augmentation, commonly a sign of an impending coda. Here, however, the tension subsides and a new contrapuntal arch of more generous proportions, twenty-six bars, is erected. The augmented theme reappears, finally bursting into an Allegro deciso. C sharp minor is re-established with the music of Ex. 17, now *dramatico, appassionato*, forming the climax of the whole work. All strength then ebbs away and the motto theme, transformed once again, is twice restated:

Ex. 20

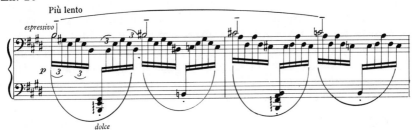

In the coda, marked *più tranquillo, apoteotico*, the last fragments of the chorale-song sink slowly from the upper to the lower reaches of both instruments, laying it, as it were, to rest. The motto theme, *quasi sacro*, pronounces its blessing and the work ends with a simple perfect cadence:

Ex 21

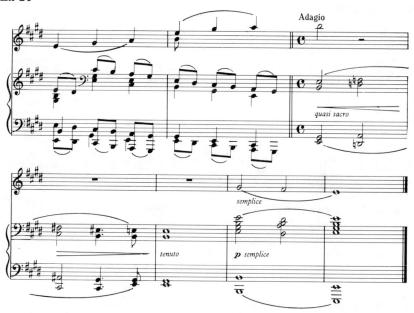

There can be no doubt that this is one of Busoni's finest works. Its antecedents—the contrapuntal language of Bach, the spiritual qualities of late Beethoven, the pianistic textures of Liszt—are clear. That Busoni could transcend these influences to produce a fully cohesive composition is a first indication of his having matured as an artist. Later compositions will again show that thoughts of death and of the world beyond could bring out the best in him.

Fifteen years later, this music was at the centre of a tragic episode strikingly similar to that of Ottokar Nováček. Busoni, as a convinced pacifist, felt obliged to take refuge in a neutral country during the First World War. He eventually settled in Zurich, where he found himself amongst an international colony of distinguished artists in a plight similar to his own. These were difficult times in which to be creative, but work was the only refuge from the horrors of reality. Several projects took shape in Zurich, amongst them the opera *Arlecchino*. Looking around for a new idea, Busoni returned to his Second Violin Sonata, writing at the end of 1915 to Egon Petri:

Would it, in your opinion, be promising to re-shape the Variations on Bach's chorale-song into a concert piece for 2 pianos?—(Some things would have to be added and all the passages related to the two previous movements would have to be removed.)

I find the idea very attractive and well realizable.[4]

The opportunity to carry out his plan arose the following summer. Through the introduction of a mutual friend, Margarete Klinckerfuss, Busoni was invited to be the guest of the Marchese Silvio della Valle di Casanova at his villa San Remigio, near Pallanza on Lago Maggiore. The Marchese had studied the piano with Liszt at Weimar, and later philosophy at the University of Stuttgart. Like Busoni, he was as fluent in German as in Italian, and indeed he published several volumes of poetry in German which were acclaimed by Hesse. He also possessed a valuable collection of Liszt manuscripts, including the *Totentanz*, the Second Hungarian Rhapsody, the Piano Sonata and several songs. A lover of all things German, he held open house at Pallanza for writers and artists, whether German or Italian. Here, together with his Irish wife Sofia, he had designed a large terraced garden on a hill overlooking the lake, and at the top of the hill he built the villa of San Remigio.

It was to this idyllic spot that Ferruccio and Gerda travelled at the end of May 1916—a welcome oasis in wartime. But in fact, Busoni was less interested in the beautiful landscape than in the chance to see the Liszt manuscripts and to have his portrait painted by Umberto Boccioni, the leading painter and sculptor of the Futurist movement. Busoni had befriended Boccioni in 1912 (see Chapter X) and had since been a constant admirer of his work. With the outbreak of war the Futurists had all eagerly enlisted but many of them, confronted with the realities of the situation, were bitterly dis-illusioned. Their faith in the Futurist ideal began to disintegrate and the group gradually split up. (Only Filippo Marinetti, their leader and spokesman, soldiered on and his already suspect Futurist beliefs eventually merged with those of Fascism.)

In 1916 Boccioni was granted one month's leave from the Front. He came to San Remigio to calm his nerves and to paint—he had been unable to produce anything for a whole year. He set to work at once, painting first a still life and two landscapes of the lakeside scenery, then portraits of Gerda Busoni, of the sculptor Riccardo Ripamonti and of Busoni himself. These works constitute the third and maturest period of Boccioni's work, a synthesis of his Futurist and pre-Futurist styles; the 'Portrait of Maestro Busoni' (see Plate 6), now in the Galleria d'Arte Moderna in Rome, is a masterpiece.

Meanwhile, with the help of the Marchese's manuscript, Busoni had prepared a new edition of Liszt's *Totentanz* and, in a very short time, reworked his variations into an Improvisation for two pianos. Contrary to his original idea, he had in fact added material from the first movement of the Sonata. The theme was now preceded by Variations II and III, substantially rewritten, and the whole movement was transformed into a free fantasia. Busoni was particularly pleased with his unusual idea of placing the theme in the middle of the variations—a reversal of the flanking arrangement of the *Goldberg Variations*.

The operations on the music of the Second Violin Sonata do not, however, seem to have been entirely successful. The Improvisation is a hybrid work, neither entirely the new Busoni (for he had changed enormously in the intervening years) nor a straightforward paraphrase of the old. Six years later, in 1922, he came to rework his Chopin Variations of 1884, by which time the gap was more pronounced and, paradoxically, more fathomable. His handling of the two-piano medium is masterful, but in other respects the Improvisation is not on a par with the Second Violin Sonata, whose simple profundity is obscured and distorted.

Apart from a few days' bad weather, it was a pleasant enough time at San Remigio. Busoni described the scene in a letter to the violinist Arrigo Serato:

> Outside rages a primordial storm. In this weather the isolation is complete. Before one's eyes is the blessed lake, inexorable, unchanging, with always the same hills and those little bays and gulfs and the eternal vaporetto going up and down . . . And further away, the war, this war without any purpose and without any result, apart from that of having brought me into the most unpleasant of situations.[5]

Boccioni had insisted on painting the portrait out of doors, so that progress was held up all round. On 23 June, when it was at last completed, Busoni hastened back to Zurich to finish the score of *Arlecchino*, taking the picture with him.

Boccioni returned to his regiment. He was offered an office job but refused it, preferring to remain in active service. On 16 August, riding his horse in the outskirts of Verona on a military exercise, he fell and was severely injured. The following day at dawn, aged thirty-four like Ottokar Nováček before him, he died.* Thus, in the Improvisation on 'Wie wohl ist mir', Busoni's music came to serve, for the second time, as a memorial.

---

* Boccioni's death prompted Busoni to publish the controversial front-page article 'Der Kriegsfall Boccioni' in the *Neue Zürcher Zeitung* on 31 August 1916. As a rule, the neutrality of the Swiss inhibited any explicitly political publications. Busoni's article had an international resonance: reports of it even reached Schoenberg in Vienna, who was then himself moved to draw up a complex peace plan.

III

The Piano Concerto

Concerto per un Pianoforte principale e diversi strumenti ad arco a fiato ed a percussione, opera XXXIX. Aggiuntovi un coro finale per voci d'uomini a sei parti. Le parole alemanne del poeta Oehlenschlaeger danese. *Composed*: 1901–4 (completed August 1904). *First performance*: 10.11.1904. Beethovensaal, Berlin. Soloist: Busoni. Choir of the Kaiser-Wilhelm-Gedächtniskirche, Berlin Philharmonic Orchestra, conducted by Karl Muck. *Published*: Leipzig 1906. PB 1949. *MS*: [390 pp. Deutsche Staatsbibliothek, Berlin] missing since Second World War. *Arrangement*: for 2 pianos (Egon Petri) published Leipzig 1909. EB 2861 (includes revised Cadenza, composed 1909). *Version without chorus*: (1908): unpublished. MS: Property of Mr Daniell Revenaugh. *Instrumentation*: 4 (2 Picc.)–3(C.A.)–3(Bcl.)–3; 4–3–3–1; Timp., Perc.; Chorus (T.T.Bar.Bar. B.B.); Str. *Duration*: 68 minutes.

In the opening years of the century, two major composition projects occupied Busoni: a theatre piece based on Adam Oehlenschlaeger's play *Aladdin*, and a piano concerto. He also began to collect new scores, mostly from younger and lesser-known composers, grouped them into programmes and performed them at his own expense. In this way Berlin witnessed important first performances of works by Elgar, Sibelius, Delius, Debussy, Nielsen and many others, as well as some of Busoni's own works. The gigantic new opuses of Strauss and Mahler were beyond his scope and budget, but he studied their scores avidly. Schoenberg's *Pelléas und Mélisande* came his way too, but had to be excluded for the same reasons. Throughout these years, *Aladdin* was a great source of inspiration to Busoni and his plan to set it to music was only dropped when the text of *Die Brautwahl* was completed in 1906.

The Danish poet Oehlenschlager was born in 1779. As a young man he travelled to Germany and came strongly under the spell of Goethe and Schiller. He wrote *Aladdin* in 1804–5, basing it closely on the tale from the *1001 Nights*, and with it he established himself at the age of twenty-six as Denmark's leading writer. To the fairy tale aspects of the original he added an element of pantheism. It was this nature-mysticism, couched in a language akin to that of Goethe's *Faust*, which drew Busoni to the play. *Aladdin* was in fact written as a counter-pole to *Faust* Part I and the German edition of 1808 was dedicated to Goethe. Oehlenschlaeger wished to show that material happiness can be attained without diabolic intervention; only Aladdin, an innocent youth, can attain the lamp and the undreamed-of riches that it can bring. This is beyond the powers of the wicked magician Nureddin. The magic lamp and ring have a function similar to the flute and bells of *Die Zauberflöte*, and, like Parsifal, Aladdin is the chosen one, the 'guileless fool' who alone may enter the magic grotto and claim the lamp. Nureddin, the North African sorcerer, is comparable to Wagner's Klingsor, while Aladdin, like Tamino, must undergo severe trials before attaining manhood and enlightenment.

Oehlenschlaeger formed this material into a huge work, to be given in two evenings. The first part closes with Aladdin's wedding to the Caliph's daughter, Gulnara. The second part relates how he loses everything, is driven to near madness, regains his wealth and is then driven to the folly of demanding from the Spirit of the Lamp that the egg of the fabulous roc should be suspended from the cupola of his palace. This would mean placing the mother of all things, the Earth itself, in danger of destruction: the Spirit of the Lamp refuses to obey. Finally all is resolved and Aladdin assumes the Caliphate.

Busoni's original plan was to create a composite work of drama, music and magic, reducing the play to one evening and using music only when called for by the action—for song and dance, and portraying scenes of mystery and enchantment. Oehlenschlaeger himself made the first German translation and it was on this version that Busoni planned to base his work. The poet had evidently wished to pander to contemporary German taste and his translation occasionally varies beyond recognition from the original Danish. Unfortunately his unidiomatic and erroneous use of German prevented the play's success.

Only one piece of music ever materialized for *Aladdin*: the chorus with which the play closes (this scene is only to be found in the first editions). Aladdin returns with Gulnara to the magic grotto, bringing the lamp, which he returns for future generations. 'Here is the church of Nature', he says. 'These lofty shapes of metal and stone are the organ pipes through which the voice of the Earth-spirit speaks aloud. Soon they will resound.' And indeed, the pillars of rock, surrounding them on all sides, begin to vibrate, softly at first, then in a mighty crescendo:

> Lift up your hearts to the Power Eternal.
> Draw ye to Allah nigh, witness his work.
> Earth has its share of rejoicing and sorrow,
> Firm the foundations that hold up the world.
> Thousands and thousands of years march relentlessly,
> Show forth in silence His glory, His might.
> Flashing immaculate, splendid and fast they stand,
> Time cannot shake them, yea time without end.
>
> Hearts flamed in ecstasy, hearts turned to dust again,
> Playfully life and death staked each his claim,
> Yet in mute readiness patiently tarrying,
> Splendid and mighty both, for evermore.

Lift up your hearts to the Power Eternal.
Draw ye to Allah nigh, witness his work.
Fully regenerate now is the world of yore,
 Praising its maker e'en unto the end.[1]

Busoni's setting of the 'Hymn to Allah' is simple and homophonic. The opening phrase has two principal motivic features: a repeated chordal progression and a rising and falling semitone motif.

Ex 22

A second setting of these words brings a new idea which Busoni called his 'Church' theme. Here too, in the second bar, we find the rising and falling semitone:

Ex 23

Years later, he recounted how he had first heard this music: 'Once, at sunset, I entered Strasbourg Cathedral. Invisible men's voices rang out':

Ex. 24

'Boys answered from the opposite direction'[2]:

Ex. 25

The 'Church' theme is accompanied by an important motto rhythm:

$\frac{6}{4}\left(\frac{18}{8}\right)$

It is not quite clear when this chorus was written—probably during the winter of 1902. Encouraged by frequent performances of the Second Violin Sonata, Busoni decided to spend the summer at home, composing. His interest now centred on the piano concerto idea and he made a preliminary plan for a work in no less than seven movements:

1. *Prologo*
2. *Pezzo giocoso*
3. *Recitativo strumentale*
4. *Pezzo serioso in tre parti*
5. *Finale all'Italiana e stretta*
6. *Passeggio solenne*
7. *Cantico e Conclusione*

In outline this plan resembles Beethoven's C sharp minor Quartet op. 131 and it appears that, as in the Second Violin Sonata, Busoni was planning to compose according to a proven framework. In the event, he telescoped the sixth and seventh movements into one and the *Recitativo strumentale* was incorporated into the *pezzo serioso*, so that a five-movement form arose.

By the middle of the summer, Busoni could write to Gerda, 'The end of my concerto has now turned out just as I wished—I have almost finished the slow movement. The two scherzos are also sketched out.'[3] The closing *Cantico* was an adaptation of the 'Hymn to Allah' and the *Prologo* was also to use material based on it. The *Pezzo giocoso* had the function of a traditional scherzo, while the *Finale all'Italiana*, as in Mendelssohn's Italian Symphony, was envisaged as a tarantella. A few days later, Busoni sent Gerda a rough drawing of the Concerto, an 'illustration by means of architecture, landscape and symbolism', as he explained:

> The three buildings are the 1st, 3rd and 5th movements, between which come the two 'living' ones: scherzo and tarantella; the first as the nature-play of a magic flower and a magic bird—the second represented by Vesuvius and cypress trees.—Over the *entrance* the sun rises; a seal is fastened to the door of the end building; the winged being at the close is the nature-mysticism of Oehlenschlaeger's chorus.[4]

When the score of the Concerto came to be published, Busoni made use of his symbolic drawing for the title page. A finished version (Facsimile no. 29) was etched by Heinrich Vogeler, one of Germany's leading graphic artists at that time.

Busoni now concentrated on the tarantella, sending Gerda witty reports on his progress: 'The Tarantella will be Naples itself, only a little cleaner', he wrote on 1 August. As the autumn approached, and with it the new concert season, the first sketch was well advanced. It was finished in the summer of 1903. 'I improve upon it every day', wrote Busoni, 'so that I hope to produce as perfect a work as is humanly possible.'[5] A few days later, with the almost indecipherable pencil sketch all but complete, he was due to leave for two

1 (*left*) Busoni with Ottokar Nováček, the dedicatee of the Second Violin Sonata, in 1892. Both artists were at that time in New York

2 (*right*) Busoni in 1898

4   Busoni with the painter Umberto Boccioni, San Remigio, near Pallanza, 1916

3   Busoni in Weimar, August 1900, at the time of the completion of the Second Violin Sonata

5   Oil portrait of Gerda
Busoni by Boccioni, 1916

6   Oil portrait of Busoni
by Boccioni, 1916

7 Busoni in Berlin, *c*. 1901, at the time when he
began work on the Piano Concerto

8 & 9 From Max Reinhardt's production of *Turandot*, Berlin, 1911:
(*left*) Gertrud Eysoldt as Turandot (*right*) Alexander Moissi as Calaf

10   The *Zelten* (Act I, scene 1)
10–12   Designs by Karl Walser for the Hamburg world première of *Die Brautwahl*

11 The *Erscheinung* (Act I, scene 4)

12 The casket ceremony (Act III, scene 3)

13 (*left*) Bernhard Ziehn, the 'Gothic' of Chicago, who drew Busoni's attention to the possibilities of symmetrically inverted harmony
14 (*above, right*) Busoni in Basle, 1910, at the time of the first performance of the *Fantasia Contrappuntistica*

15   Madeline M., for whom the *Sonatina ad usum infantis* was written. The photograph is dated New York, 1918

16 Busoni playing his Dolmetsch harpsichord, *c.* 1912

18 'Ein neuer Schlüssel, ein rostiger Schlüssel: sie arbeiten gleich schlecht.' Pencil sketch by Busoni for *Arlecchino*

17 Alexander Moissi as Arlecchino in the Zurich world première, 1917. Costume by Albert Isler

19　Lola Artôt de Padilla as Turandot,
Berlin, 1921

20　Busoni with Giotto,
Zurich, 1916

21　Busoni at West Wing, Regent's
Park, London, autumn 1919. The
house belonged to the dancer Maud
Allan; it was here that Busoni met
George Bernard Shaw

22　Busoni at the Hôtel Foyôt,
Paris, 1920 with the composer
Charles Marie Widor (l.) and the
pianist Isidor Philipp (r.)

23 Berlin, *c.* 1922 (from l. to r.): Paul Hindemith, Maurits Frank, Busoni, Philipp Jarnach, Licco Amar, Walter Caspar. 'In the twenties Paul Hindemith came to Busoni with his quartet, so as to win him over—as the latter subsequently confided to me with a wink—to his side. It was in vain.' (Letter from Vladimir Vogel to Roman Vlad, 1964)

24 Busoni in Berlin, 1922

25–28 Designs by
Karl Dannemann for
the Dresden world première
of *Doktor Faust*:

25 Vorspiel I and II

26 The ducal park at Parma

27 Tavern in Wittenberg

28 Street in Wittenberg

29 Lithograph by Heinrich Vogeler for the title page of the Piano Concerto, 1904

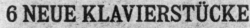

30 Cover of the first edition of the Elegies, 1908, incorporating a design by Busoni

31   Opening of Schoenberg's Piano Piece op. 11, no 2
in Busoni's 'concertante transcription' with pencilled notes by Schoenberg

32 Contrapuntal sketches to *The Art of Fugue* by Wilhelm
Middelschulte and Bernhard Ziehn with comments and additions by
Busoni

33 Sketches for the *Fantasia Contrappuntistica* by Wilhelm
Middelschulte and Busoni

Plan des Werkes

A. Analytischer:

1. Choral - Variationen (Einleitung — Choral und Variationen — Übergang)
2. Fuga I. 3. Fuga II. 4. Fuga III. 5. Intermezzo. 6. Variatio I. 7. Variatio II.
8. Variatio III. 9. Cadenza. 10. Fuga IV. 11. Corale. 12. Stretta.

B. Architektonischer:

34   Busoni's architectural outline of the *Fantasia Contrappuntistica*

35 Busoni's score of *Die Brautwahl*, opening of Act III, part 1

36   Part of 'al Saltarello', the original conclusion to the *Sonatina seconda*

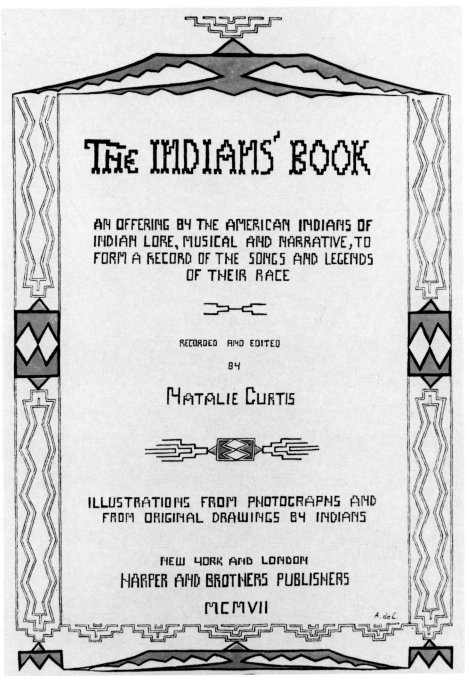

The INDIANS' BOOK

AN OFFERING BY THE AMERICAN INDIANS OF
INDIAN LORE, MUSICAL AND NARRATIVE, TO
FORM A RECORD OF THE SONGS AND LEGENDS
OF THEIR RACE

RECORDED AND EDITED

BY

NATALIE CURTIS

ILLUSTRATIONS FROM PHOTOGRAPHS AND
FROM ORIGINAL DRAWINGS BY INDIANS

NEW YORK AND LONDON
HARPER AND BROTHERS PUBLISHERS
MCMVII

A. de C.

37   Title page of Natalie Curtis's *The Indians' Book*, 1907

38   Closing bars of the 'Carmen' Fantasy

39   Opening of Busoni's setting of Goethe's 'Die Bekehrte'

An Lola Artôt de Padilla
Die Bekehrte
(Goethe)
Andantino tranquillo
Canto.
Bei dem Glanze der Abend-
Pianoforte.
dolce.
-rö — the zog ich still den Wald ent-lang;
Damon saß und blies die Flö — te,
poco rit.....
poco rit.....
B. C.

40 'Die Bekehrte' set as an exercise by Busoni's pupil Vladimir Vogel and published in the November 1921 issue, subtitled 'The struggle for the new style', of a short-lived journal *Faust* of which Busoni was the music editor

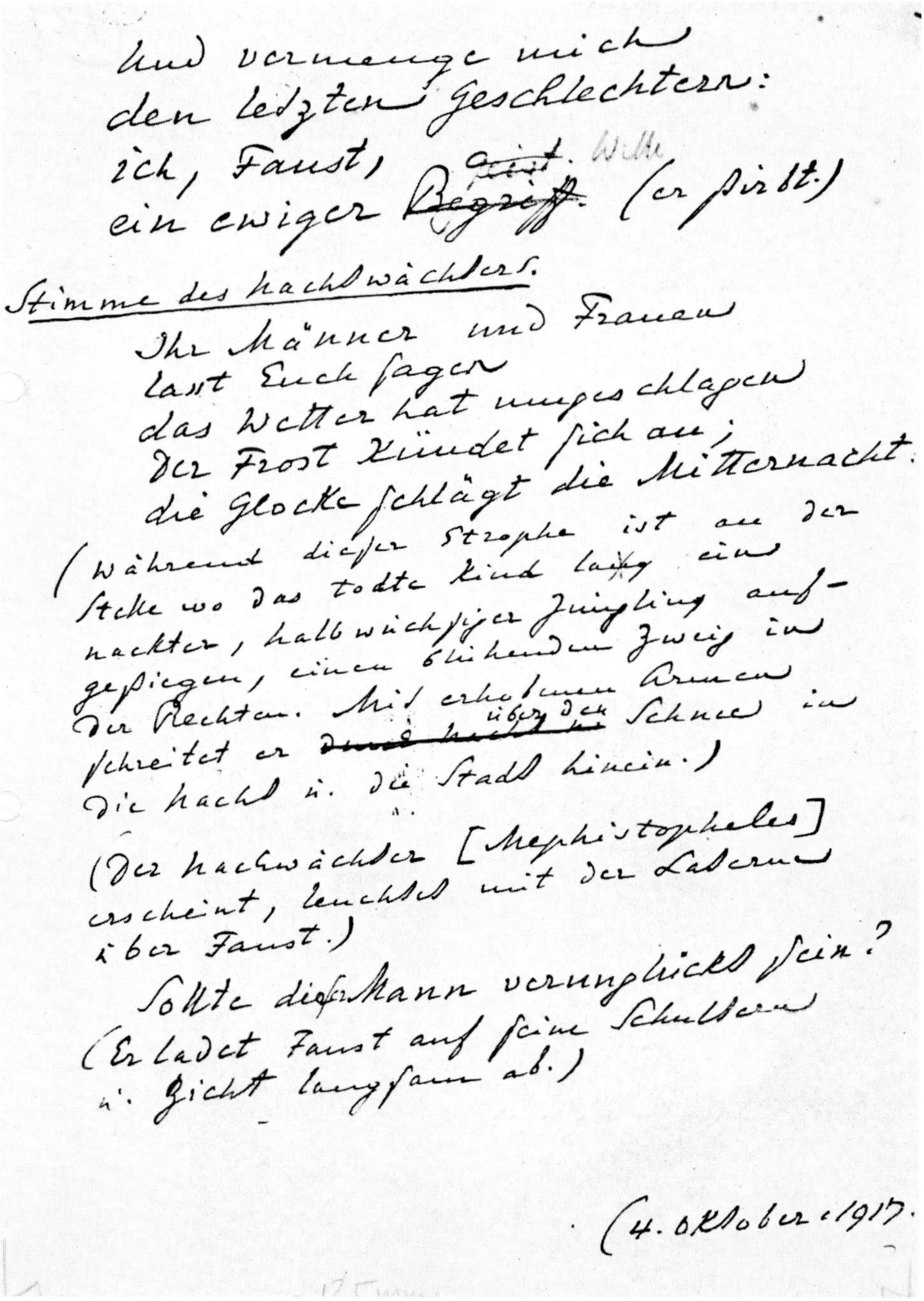

und vermenge mich
den letzten Geschlechtern:
ich, Faust,
ein ewiger ~~Begriff~~ ~~Geist~~ Wille. (er stirbt.)

Stimme des Nachtwächters.

Ihr Männer und Frauen
laßt Euch sagen
das Wetter hat umgeschlagen
der Frost kündet sich an;
die Glocke schlägt die Mitternacht.

(während dieser Strophe ist an der
Stelle wo das todte Kind lag ein
nackter, halbwüchsiger Jüngling auf-
gestiegen, einen blühenden Zweig in
der Rechten. Mit erhobenen Armen
schreitet er ~~durch die Nacht~~ über den Schnee in
die Nacht u. die Stadt hinein.)

(Der Nachtwächter [Mephistopheles]
erscheint, leuchtet mit der Laterne
über Faust.)

Sollte dieser Mann verunglückt sein?

(Er ladet Faust auf seine Schultern
u. zieht langsam ab.)

(4. Oktober 1917.

41 Autograph libretto of *Doktor Faust*, final page

42 Opening of the *Prologo* from an incomplete set of *Notturni*

43 Busoni's grave in West Berlin

concerts in London. What then happened was a turning point in his life: he cancelled the concerts in order to finish the Concerto. It was a situation in which he had never before found himself. Up to that time, composing had taken second place to concert-giving and any serious work had to be done in the summer. With the cancellation of the concerts, Busoni underwent a subtle transformation—from pianist-composer to composer-pianist. The worry about this decision cost him four working days. When Gerda sent him a telegram approving it, he began to work, now at tremendous speed, on a 'great sketch' in ink, in which the solo part is fully written out and the orchestral part written in short score. Within five weeks, on 18 August, this sketch was finished.

Early in September the full orchestral score was begun. In order to save time, Busoni engaged his pupil Leo Kestenberg to write the piano part into the score. After an American tour in the spring of 1904, Busoni resumed work on the fair copy, finishing it on 3 August.

First movement: *Prologo e Introito* In the lengthy orchestral introduction, the opening theme, played by the violas, has a distinctly Brahmsian flavour:

Ex. 26

The rising and falling semitone of Exx. 22 and 23 thus appears at the outset in the first three notes of the work. It dominates large stretches of the Concerto in many forms, often appearing in the guise of parallel triads. The idea, and the ways it is employed, are closely related to the three-note figure:

Ex. 27

which permeates the Second Symphony of Brahms. Likewise, the mood of Busoni's opening is close to the serenity of much of that work's first movement —the serenity of nature.

Almost all the themes in the Piano Concerto are very long. This opening melody, for instance, has an unbroken span of thirty-three bars, after which appears a second motif:

Ex. 28

and soon after, in slower tempo, a phrase whose falling fourth relates it to Ex. 23:

Ex. 29

The length of the themes in the Concerto partially accounts for its immense proportions: their very statement and re-statement is an extended process. After the substantial opening tutti, when the piano enters, pounding out the Aladdin theme (Ex. 22) *sontuoso* (sumptuously), it is now extended to no less than fifty-seven bars, only to give way to a semiquaver figure with the aid of which Busoni modulates to E major. The Aladdin theme is then repeated in this key: the woodwinds take up the melody while the piano, seconded by the strings, surrounds it with extravagant ornament. At this point a striking similarity between Busoni's theme and Wagner's Swan motif (to be found in both *Lohengrin* and *Parsifal*) becomes apparent:

Ex. 30

Ex. 31

(Leo Kestenberg, in a far-fetched interpretation of the Concerto, described this movement as 'the spirit of God moving on the face of the waters'.[6]) The mood becomes stormy, the piano flickers with lightning-like arpeggios, introducing a sequence of variations on the opening theme (Ex. 26). The first, in E major, is for oboe and piano; a second, calling for wide skips on the keyboard, is in F major and a third has a beautiful horn solo. This time the theme is further extended and leads to a soft, fleeting cadenza over a held diminished seventh chord. The coda is heralded by brilliant triple trills on the piano and an *eroico* version of Ex. 28 for the trumpet. The closing bars, in warm C major, recall the end of the first movement of Berlioz's *Symphonie fantastique*, not only in their tonality but also in the *religiosamente* of their prevailing spirit.

Second movement: *Pezzo giocoso* After the calm and stately end to the first movement, the second opens in a mad whirl. Underlying the piano's flying upward runs appears a rapid version of the work's motto rhythm:

This is the motto rhythm's first appearance, a fact of which the listener remains unaware until he is sufficiently well acquainted with the whole Concerto to relate it to the more obvious statement of the rhythm in the *Pezzo serioso*. (These are the involuntary subtleties which a score acquires when the finale is composed first.)

The wild opening of the *Pezzo giocoso* involves three changes of tempo—all abrupt and unrelated to each other—and an orchestral outburst, *giovanescamente* (youthfully). There follows a grotesque episode for piano and 'Turkish' percussion which introduces fragments of a new theme in the bass, surrounded by leaping trill figures. The Turkish music spins ever more wildly until the full orchestra bursts in again, this time with an extended tutti. These thirty-four bars, one unbroken theme, *quasi con brutalità*, exultant and virile, are based on the ♩♪♩ rhythm which, as in Beethoven's Seventh Symphony, dances exuberantly.

From a haze of alternating major and minor chords eventually emerges the melody first hinted at in the Turkish music—an Italian folksong, morose in both harmonization and timbre, featuring the dark lower register of the clarinet:

Ex. 32

A stifled cry of homesickness, intensified by the use of the instrument Busoni heard so often as a child. The melody, with which he seems to have associated the words 'e si, e si che la porteremo', is better known as a Neapolitan folksong, 'Fenesta che lucivi e chiù non luci'.

The nostalgia is brief; the piano spins the folk-tune further into a lithe dance movement in which the tambourine jauntily spells out the motto rhythm, and the ensuing episodes (a shadowy cadenza, an equally mysterious *scherzando*, snatches of the big tutti and a reprise of the Turkish music) culminate in a *Presto* of ever-increasing wildness. 'Fenesta che lucivi' returns, no longer homesick but now stern and admonishing. We hear the Turkish music for a last time and the movement closes as it opened, with the piano's whirling runs, now remote and fantastic.

The 'giocoso' of the title is misleading, for at the heart of this music also lies much sadness. In its juxtaposition of humour—sometimes gentle, sometimes mocking—with more shadowy moments, in its abrupt about turns and its sense of longing for the South, the *Pezzo giocoso* is an incomplete self-portrait.

Third movement: *Pezzo serioso* The second inversion D major chord with which the second movement ended resolves unexpectedly into D flat.* While the two scherzo movements have no firm tonal centre, the three flanking movements are in clearly definable keys: the *Prologo* in C major, the *Pezzo serioso* in D flat major and the *Cantico* in E major (while its coda returns to C major). Thus, those movements depicted in Busoni's picture of the work as buildings have an architectural stability while the scherzos, the natural phenomena, have none.

The *Pezzo serioso* is divided into four sections of unequal length.

1. *Introductio*. Over a baroque quaver figure for cellos and double basses (derived from the first three notes of Ex. 35), the violas and lower wind instruments declaim a jagged invocation:

Ex. 33

forte, recitando

This is answered by a long, dramatic theme for oboes and cor anglais, accompanied by *tremolando* woodwinds and punctuated by rich pizzicato chords. The piano enters musingly, introducing a soft brass chorale. A long pedal A flat leads into the firm D flat major tonality of the second section.

2. *Prima Pars*. The full version of the chorale is now spelled out by the piano.

* The movements of the Piano Concerto are intended to follow one another without a break.

This great theme dates back to *Sigune*,★ where Busoni used it to depict a majestic, newly-built cathedral in twilight. In Act I scene 1, Ulrich, the master-builder, looks up at the great edifice and sings:

Ex. 34

[Behold the cathedral in the evening glow, the slender form through haze and mist.]

The 'Cathedral' theme now found its rightful place in the Piano Concerto, where it complements the 'Church' theme. Its simplicity and the beauty of its mild dissonances are nobly impressive: it represents the twenty years of adolescence and early manhood —years of toil and striving—which were now coming to a close. 'Now the cathedral is built', the piano seems to proclaim: (Ex. 35).

★ The theme first appears in two unpublished piano works written in 1883, an Etude 'en forme d'Adagio d'une Sonate' and an Etude in B flat minor. (Both were intended for a continuation of the set of six dedicated to Brahms in 1883; they are numbered fifteen and sixteen.) The archetypal four-note figure of the theme also dominates the slow movement of the recently published F minor piano sonata (1883), a movement whose formal scheme strikingly anticipates the *Pezzo serioso* of the Piano concerto. We find the *Sigune* theme once more in the unpublished Ballade for piano (c.1894).

Ex. 35

(non forte, ma molto sonoro)

Orchestra and soloist create a sound-picture which exactly reproduces the evening haze of the scene in *Sigune*. All seems to be vanishing into dusk when a sudden crescendo leads to a powerful chord of D flat minor which dies away, leaving a softly vibrating horn triad.

3. *Altera Pars*. F flat becomes E natural and the tonal centre drops to C major. Here the strings at last spell out the motto rhythm while over it the piano hammers out the 'Church' theme. Once again Busoni has created an enormous single phrase, its thirty-one bars forming an unbroken melodic arch. There follows a great climax, an accumulation of all the themes from the *Pezzo serioso* cemented into a massive yet quite unsensuous soundblock. At the apex of this arch-construction the opening invocation theme (Ex. 33) returns, now in close canon. It is a wild and terrifying midnight scene (anticipating the invocation of the Powers of Darkness in *Doktor Faust*) the point of maximum stress being marked by a single tam-tam stroke which caps an already thunderous orchestration. Then all subsides. The piano, and later a solo trombone, reminisce on fragments of earlier themes and the winding quavers from the opening of the movement return. A swirling transition leads to a restatement of the 'Cathedral' theme.

4. *Ultra Pars*. There are three sections. In the first, the woodwinds declaim a new melody:

Ex. 36

tragicamente, molto forte

and another new theme follows.* Marked *Andante idillico*, it shares the D flat

* '. . . A new motif in the coda? Counts as an exception, as my old teacher Rémy used to say.' (From a letter to Hans Huber, 30 May 1918.)

major tonality and veiled scoring of the 'Cathedral' theme, and is formed from a rising-scale motif. In the third section the motto rhythm pulsates inexorably to the end, resolving all the conflicts of this long, complex movement.

The *Pezzo serioso* completes the self-portrait begun in the *Pezzo giocoso*. The juxtaposition of serious and comic elements presented by these two movements was a hallmark of Busoni's personality throughout his career. The 'giocoso' element is always shadowed, if not overshadowed, by the 'serioso': this was already detectable in the tarantella of the Second Violin Sonata. The *Pezzo serioso* gives the impression of an enormous internal struggle; a confrontation of opposing forces and their eventual reconciliation. In its calm closing measures a meditative quality can be detected which recurs in many later works: music of observation rather than of action.

Fourth movement: *'All'Italiana'* 'The Tarantella, following the Adagio, is like coming out of the Forum into a crowded Roman street', wrote Busoni.[7] It is also the most problematical movement of the Concerto, for there was a surplus of material and, even in its final form, the movement is very long—and very loud. The *Pezzo giocoso* expresses a longing for Italy but here the land itself—its commotion and exuberance—is vividly portrayed. All is transitory; the form is episodic, while tonal centres establish themselves briefly, then vanish.

An introduction, building up steadily from *pp* to *ff* over 133 bars, brings fragments of 'Fenesta che lucivi'. Piano and orchestra exchange brief phrases *con brio* and a surprising passage combines the motto rhythm with whole-tone scales:

Ex. 37

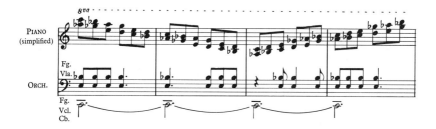

The tarantella whirls on. Even the 'Cathedral' theme is taken up at this wild tempo and chimed out with unseemly gaiety by the glockenspiel. A more gentle moment ensues: a love scene which terminates with an elegant cadence. Fragments of a new folksong begin to form and soon it is given out in full by two oboes. This 'Canzone del Serpentino' has none of the sadness of 'Fenesta che lucivi' (Ex. 38).

Ex. 38

Its delicate humour is rudely interrupted by dissonant trumpet fanfares: it seems that a band of troops comes rushing by in a *passo accelerato*. The tempo continues to increase until an almost diabolic frenzy is built up. At its height comes the 'Vesuvius eruption', as Busoni called it, a climactic tutti in which all the movement's themes are brought together at white heat. The woodwinds and strings scurry through the 'Canzone del Serpentino' while horns and trumpets blare out 'Fenesta che lucivi' *con tutto fiato*. The trombones add the motto rhythm. In its frenzy, the music is not unlike the Witches' Sabbath of Berlioz's *Symphonie fantastique*—with the difference that this is no scene of black magic but rather a wild Dionysian outburst. Closer in spirit is the D flat major whirlwind which comes at the climax of the development section in the first movement of Mahler's Third Symphony; but both Mahler's and Busoni's eruptions probably have a common ancestor in the timpani outburst which opens the recapitulation of the first movement of Beethoven's Ninth Symphony—the forces of nature run for a while amok, reminding man how puny and insignificant he really is.

Piano and timpani now reassert the slow motto rhythm and for a moment the onward rush of the movement is completely halted. Then it starts up again in a final chromatic *stretta*. The piano plays a brilliant cadenza with two brief orchestral interjections and finally the motto rhythm is pounded out with naked force by the entire orchestra. Silence falls, broken only by three soft pizzicato chords, *senza tempo*.

Fifth movement: *Cantico* A drop of a semitone introduces a soft pedal B over all the octaves of the piano, also sustained by various orchestral instruments. This semitone fall induces a feeling of suspense and mystery; it is the same gesture as that at the end of the slow movement of Beethoven's 'Emperor' Concerto. But where Beethoven seeks and soon finds, Busoni protracts his search over forty-three slow bars—a journey into a dimly lit interior. Fragments of the Aladdin theme float by, occasionally illuminated by glittering glockenspiel triads, then engulfed in a strand of melody from the *Prologo*, rising scales in thirds and finally the motto rhythm, softly tapped out by the timpani. This is the most magical moment of the whole work.

In Aladdin's Cave, so the story relates, were trees of metal:

Birds were perched upon them, singing praise to the almighty Creator with their voices . . . And the fruits that hung from these trees were priceless gems of many colours, green and white, gold and red and of other colours. These precious stones radiated with a brilliance that was brighter than the sunshine at midday.[8]

Busoni's music here suggests just such a vast open space, dark and mysterious yet glowing with an extraordinary radiance.

A few years later, in an essay entitled 'The future belongs to melody',* he pointed to the significance of Aladdin's Cave as a specifically musical symbol:

> Immaterialism is the true nature of music, we search for it; we wander through narrow underground passages at the end of which a strange, distant, phosphorescent light gives us a glimpse of the entrance into a magic grotto. Once we have reached the vaulted room of this mysterious nature-palace, we can learn to wing our souls with speech; they will resound in a melody that blossoms and ascends without end.[9]

As the mystic transition comes to an end, scales in thirds begin to undulate calmly in the lower strings and an invisible male-voice choir intones the 'Hymn to Allah'.† It rises slowly and steadily while the orchestra and soloist listen and comment. As it comes to its exultant close—'Praising its maker e'en unto the end'—the piano strikes up the wave-like broken chords from its initial entry in the *Prologo* and the first notes of 'Fenesta che lucivi' rise in a majestic whole-tone scale. A huge orchestral crescendo bursts into the final *Allegro con fuoco*. With cascades of almost banal C major fanfares the work comes to a noisy and brilliant conclusion.

Only four months after the work's completion, the Concerto received its first performance in a concert which also included Busoni's new version of the *Entführung* overture and Ottokar Nováček's *Hymnus*, played by string orchestra. The première provoked two opposing storms in the audience; as one critic reported, rapture on the part of the Busoni circle (which was by this time large and influential in Berlin) and outrage on the part of many others. Between these two extremes, the silent majority shook its head in stupefaction. Dent has given us a taste of the most colourful review of this concert in his biography:

> Noise, more noise, eccentricity and licentiousness provoked yet more noise and had the same effect on us. During five movements we were submerged in a flood of cacophony; a *pezzo giocoso* painted the joys of barbarians lusting in war, and a tarantella the orgies of absinthe-drinkers and common prostitutes . . . It was frightful![10]

Max Marschalk, one of Berlin's leading critics, found that 'One must have an

---

* Mistranslated by Rosamond Ley in her edition of Busoni's *Letters to his Wife* as 'Melody belongs to the future'.
† Note for performers. Busoni stressed that the chorus must remain out of sight.

unshakeable faith in one's own greatness to write music of this kind;'[11] and spoke out strongly against the work. But the critic of the *Deutsche Zeitung* found that there was 'a certain strain of greatness in the work which repeatedly called our attention'.[12] The critic of the *Signale* thought that 'the composer would have done better to stay within more modest boundaries'.[13]

A more recent commentator, the pianist Alfred Brendel, finds the Concerto 'monstrously overwritten'.[14] But the same criticism was regularly made of the music of Mahler until his rediscovery in the 1960s. Today, we have learnt to forgive Mahler his alleged 'sins'—vulgarity, excessive length and over-noisy orchestration; the time will certainly come when Busoni can be forgiven for the same excesses. The Piano Concerto occupies a place close to the earlier Mahler symphonies and the larger tone-poems of Strauss; indeed, in later years Busoni suggested calling the work 'Symphonie italienne'.

The size of the orchestra and the uses Busoni makes of it show how new winds had blown his way in the few years since the Violin Concerto. In matters of harmony as well as orchestration, his intensive study of many of the newest scores paid dividends. His own most original discovery is a new relationship between piano and orchestra. As opposed to the great Romantic concertos, the pianist now no longer emerges as hero; the composer is already dominant over his other self. In the way the fiendishly difficult solo part rarely takes the limelight, Busoni seems to have indicated his new priorities as a musician. Often the piano serves as a vast continuo instrument or takes its place beside the winds, percussion and strings as a separate orchestral register. Sometimes it accompanies a solo orchestral instrument (as in the concertos of Liszt) and frequently it is an orchestra in itself, projecting several strands of colour simultaneously.

Busoni's orchestration, while still creating an entirely Romantic sound-world, shows a new refinement and sureness. In particular the writing for brass is masterful, whether for solo instruments or for the whole group. When the 'Cathedral' theme is first sounded, for instance, the solo trumpet is supported by three trombones and tuba, but these are cunningly mixed with bass clarinet and bassoon to create a full, soft texture, bathing the rich harmonies in light.

In the Concerto, Busoni sums up the achievements of early manhood. With the exception of the mystic music leading up to the 'Hymn to Allah', it points only rarely to the future. In its enormous proportions it constitutes the realization of a youthful dream; it is the great score to which most young composers aspire and hence it signifies the end of an apprenticeship. Later, Busoni liked to call it his 'Skyscraper' concerto; but he also once asked, on an unrelated occasion: 'Why does a skyscraper look wrong? Because its proportions are wrong in relation to the size of men, and because the height of the building is out of scale with the greatness of its conception.'[15] Only one other work of his exploits this mammoth style, the *Fantasia Contrappuntistica*, and there the imagery of the skyscraper is again invoked. His best music is otherwise expressed briefly and concisely, often in elegiac form.

The Piano Concerto terminates with a question mark: the composer leads us the first few steps down the dark corridor towards Aladdin's Cave. Never again did he feel the need to express himself at such length and never again did he write with such lack of inhibition and overt love of life.

IV

The Music for *Turandot*

Turandot, Suite for orchestra op. 41 from the music to Gozzi's fable. *Dedicated*: to Karl Muck. *Composed*: June–August 1905. *First performance*: 21.10.1905. Beethovensaal, Berlin. Berlin Philharmonic Orchestra, conducted by Busoni. *Published*: Leipzig, 1906. PB 1976. *Instrumentation*: 3(Picc.)–3(C.A.)–3(Bcl.)–3(Cfg.); 4–4–3–1; Timp., perc.; 2 harps; Female chorus (unison) ad lib.; Str. *Duration*: 33 minutes.

Verzweiflung und Ergebung [Despair and Resignation]: appendix to the *Turandot suite*. *Composed*: 1911. *First performance*: 26.10.1911. Deutsches Theater, Berlin. Bösendorfer Orchestra, conducted by Oskar Fried. *Published*: Leipzig, 1911. PB 2309. *Instrumentation*: as for the *Turandot suite* (no chorus). *Duration*: 4 minutes.

Altoums Warnung [Altoum's warning]: second appendix to the *Turandot Suite*. [Replacement for the original *In modo di Marcia funebre*]. *Composed*: 1917. *First performance*: 13.1.1921. Philharmonie, Berlin. Berlin Philharmonic Orchestra, conducted by Busoni. *Published* Leipzig, 1918. PB 1976a. *Instrumentation*: as for the *Turandot Suite* (no chorus). *Duration*: (together with the following *Finale alla Turca*) 6 minutes.

Busoni's decision to write incidental music for one of Gozzi's fable-dramas would appear to have been made spontaneously, perhaps with a view to celebrating the hundredth anniversary of the writer's death in 1906. For the space of two and a half months, in the summer of 1905, the idea occupied him to the exclusion of all else. 'I have chosen the fable of the cruel and seductive Chinese (or Persian, God knows) princess Turandot', he told his mother.[1]

Working more or less chronologically through the play he composed short musical numbers wherever called for by Gozzi or wherever his sense of theatre told him that music was called for. He referred to Volume I of the *Geschichte der Musik* by A. W. Ambros as a source of oriental melodies, indiscriminately mixing Indian, Persian and Turkish themes with the limited supply of genuine Chinese material in the book. In this way, thirteen numbers were sketched out and immediately orchestrated. Some of them are melodramas; each of the three riddles is prefaced by mysterious brass chords; Kalaf's solutions to the riddles were originally intended to be sung, although this idea was later abandoned.

There was no immediate prospect of a stage production of the play and Busoni certainly had no intention of trying to organize one in Italy. 'Conditions in the country give no cause for hope', he told his mother.[2] His one concern had been to do the same service for a great Italian classic as Beethoven had for Goethe's *Egmont* or Mendelssohn for Shakespeare's *A Midsummer-night's Dream*. As he later pointed out, Italian straight theatre, overshadowed by the country's powerful operatic tradition, had never had this intimate relationship with serious music.

Gozzi's play differs considerably from the operatic version by Simoni and Adami which Puccini set to music two decades later. In the interests of clarity, both here and in the discussion of Busoni's subsequent *Turandot* opera, there follows an account of the plot.

Act I The curtain rises on a scene depicting one of the city gates of Peking. A number of shaven heads on stakes are placed over the gate. Kalaf enters and recognizes Barak, his former servant. Both are living incognito: after the defeat of Kalaf's father at the battle of Astrakhan, Barak fled and eventually arrived in Peking, where he assumed the name of Hassan and took a wife, Skirina. Kalaf fled with his parents, disguised as beggars; they came to the court of King Keikobad. The King was defeated in war with the Chinese Emperor, Altoum; his daughter Adelma, it is said, was drowned. Kalaf wandered further with his parents until they finally arrived at Peking. Barak tells him of the haughty Princess who offers riddles to her suitors whom she beheads if they cannot answer them. Kalaf has heard the gruesome story but always taken it for a fable. Ismael, servant of the Prince of Samarkand, rushes in. His master has just been executed, he groans, and he hurls the fateful portrait of Turandot to the ground. Kalaf picks it up and is at once enraptured. On the city wall appears the blood-spattered executioner who adds a new head to the display over the gate. Kalaf resolves to undergo the trial by riddles. He gives Barak a purse of gold and rushes off.

Act II (The great hall of the imperial Divan.) Truffaldino (chief eunuch), Brighella (head page), and a crowd of servants are hastily preparing the hall for the reception of the new suitor. Accompanied by eight doctors, his secretary Pantalone and his chancellor Tartaglia, the Emperor Altoum now enters. He questions his courtiers, who answer him in Venetian dialect, telling him of the new trial. Kalaf is led in; he refuses to reveal his name. Despite the discouraging words of Altoum and the courtiers, he is firm in his resolve, 'Death or Turandot'. The Princess, veiled, enters, attended by her servants Adelma and Zelima, with slaves and eunuchs. She immediately feels a stifled love for Kalaf; Adelma recognizes in him her father's former servant. Tartaglia stutters his way through a reading of Turandot's decree, after which she herself pronounces the riddles. When she comes to the third, her hatred mounts and she unveils herself to dazzle Kalaf with her beauty. Shaken for a moment, he regains his presence of mind and guesses correctly: the powerful beast that rules the seas is the Lion of San Marco, the symbol of Venice. Turandot demands new riddles, refuses to marry, threatens to kill herself—all in vain. Finally, Kalaf poses her the riddle of his identity.

Act III (A room in the harem.) Adelma reveals her hatred of Turandot, who then enters with Zelima. She takes counsel with her servants as to the solution of Kalaf's riddle.

Kalaf and Barak are discovered in front of the palace by three of the Masks. They escort Kalaf back to his quarters and order Barak to be off. Timur, Kalaf's father, appears and recognizes Barak. He tells him of the death of his wife; they are discovered by Truffaldino who escorts them at sword-point to Turandot.

Act IV (The harem.) Bound to a pillar, Barak and Timur are questioned by Turandot. First she offers them gold, then threatens torture and death. All is in vain—the Princess herself still feels a secret sympathy for the unknown prince. Adelma promises to prise the secret from him. Altoum informs Turandot that a messenger from a far-off land has brought him the name. He entreats her to surrender, but she refuses, declaring that she will triumph at dawn.

In another room in the palace, Brighella warns Kalaf to beware of ghosts. Three nocturnal phantoms visit him—Skirina, Zelima and Adelma—each in turn cunningly seeking to trick him into revealing his name. The scene is interrupted by a comic interlude in which Truffaldino places a mandrake root under the pillow of the sleeping Prince. Adelma tries to persuade Kalaf to flee with her. In despair, he unwittingly reveals his name.

Act V (The great hall.) Kalaf, Altoum and the courtiers await the arrival of Turandot. Both she and her entire retinue arrive in mourning. She proclaims Kalaf's name and dismisses him, but he draws a dagger and tries to stab himself. She prevents him, and declares her love. Adelma, realizing that her hopes of winning Kalaf are shattered, snatches the dagger, but Kalaf wrests it from her. Altoum frees her from her slavery and restores to her the kingdom which her father had forfeited. Turandot calls upon the men in the audience to applaud her capitulation.

The legend of Turandot is ancient and its exact origins are uncertain. The earliest known version is related by the Persian poet Nezami (1141–1202).[3] It is set in Russia and is the fourth tale from his collection known as the *Haft Peiker* (The Seven Pictures) of 1197. There are no riddles as such; instead, the Prince and Princess of his story exchange symbolic gifts. The tale has none of the macabre and tragic aspects of later versions. In their place, Nezami's exquisite poetry draws on a wealth of images to express the magical way in which two souls predetermined for each other must finally be united. The unknown Prince is the chosen one who alone has the powers to storm the fortifications of the Princess's castle. Goethe observes predetermination in all of Nezami's lovers:

> They are matched to each other through presentiment, destiny, nature, custom, inclination or passion, which places them in a close relationship; but then they are separated through whim, obstinacy, coincidence, necessity or force, then equally miraculously reunited.[4]

The mysterious balance of forces between the two characters forms the basis for all later versions of the story.

In following generations, the tale was re-told by several Persian writers, some of whom set the story in Greece. The thirteenth-century poet Lari was the first to move the fable to China and hence to coin the name Turandot, for *Turan* is the Persian word for China, while *doht* means daughter, hence daughter of China. Later the legend made its way to Europe in a collection of oriental tales published in 1710 by Pétis de la Croix with the title *Les mille et un jours*. The version of la Croix is extremely long and involved. Gozzi concentrated on the second half of the tale, introducing the necessary background from the first half in the opening narrative of Barak. The minor characters in the play, Barak, Adelma among others, are Gozzi's invention, but his most striking innovation was the idea of introducing the Masks.

Carlo Gozzi (1720–1806) has attained a new fame in the twentieth century through the various operas based on his plays: with Prokofiev's *The Love of Three Oranges* and Henze's *König Hirsch* ('King Stag'), for instance, as well as various settings of *Turandot*. Yet, when Busoni wrote his incidental music, the playwright was virtually forgotten, especially in Italy where no edition of his works had been published since 1802. Through the advocacy of his score, Busoni was one of the first to restore Gozzi to his rightful place in literary history. An aristocratic adventurer and, theatrically speaking, an amateur, Gozzi turned to play-writing in order to defend the old *commedia dell'arte* traditions against the incoming vogue of servant–master comedies with their undercurrent of social unrest, which had found their Italian champion in Goldoni. As D. Nevile Lees has written:

> He made a stand for the drama of large Imagination at a time when Goldoni was conquering the city with the drama of little Actuality. He stood out against the intrusion of Realism on the stage.
> . . . It is a world in which everything can and does happen except the rational. It is a land of paradoxes, of the comic and supernatural, of the impossible come true.[5]

Gozzi chose the Turandot story in answer to the challenge of those critics who had asserted that his style was only suited to magical happenings. In his reworking of the ancient tale he silenced his critics at a stroke. The Masks fitted in perfectly: according to Busoni, the *commedia dell'arte* figures 'cast a bridge from the Venetian public into the imaginary Orient and thus destroy the illusion of reality'.[6]

With his love of the supernatural in the theatre, Busoni could well have chosen one of Gozzi's more extravagant fables such as *King Stag*. His reasons for preferring the more worldly *Turandot* are not at once obvious. One factor, however, stands out: the Princess is a symbol of unattainable beauty, or of beauty attainable only through supreme sacrifice—a theme we have already observed in the figure of Sigune and shall find again in the Helena of *Doktor Faust*. Kalaf, on the other hand, the 'chosen one', is of the same pedigree as Tamino, Parsifal, Aladdin and even Edmund Lehsen (from *Die Brautwahl*). The relationship between Kalaf and Turandot can be likened to that of an immovable object confronted by an irresistible force. Kalaf and Turandot are symbols; the riddles, like the trials of fire and water in *Die Zauberflöte*, are the essential life-and-death ordeals through which, and only through which, the Ideal can be attained. Given that the two lovers initially represent opposite poles, their eventual union seems to indicate a paradoxical destruction of established values: the point where the immovable object is united with the irresistible force would seem to foretell, metaphysically speaking, the beginning of a new world.

There was also a more concrete reason for Busoni's choice of *Turandot*: he wished to win back for an imaginary Italian stage a play that had been thoroughly Germanized by Schiller and Weber. In 1801, Schiller adapted Gozzi's play for the Hoftheater at Weimar. Many German writers had a very high regard for Gozzi, notably Goethe, E. T. A. Hoffmann and Schlegel; yet Schiller had to pander to the taste of his public, to whom the intervention of the *commedia dell'arte* figures no longer seemed credible. The result was a somewhat humourless, even prudish approach—he omitted, for instance, the scene of Truffaldino's nocturnal adventure with the phallic mandrake root— despite which, the function of the Masks in the play was still ungraspable to the public, while the contrast between the elevated tragedy of Turandot and Kalaf and the antics of the Masks seemed to disturb rather than entertain. Julius Körner, who produced the play in Dresden shortly after its Weimar première, hoped to solve this problem by asking Schiller to find Persian names for the Masks. The problem, however, lay elsewhere: as Karl Vollmoeller later wrote, 'The four masks, Gozzi's beloved ad-libbers, suffocated under the weight of the iambic pentameter.'[7] Their wings were clipped, making impossible the improvised flights of fancy on which their existence depended.

Schiller himself outlined the change in taste in the forty years since Gozzi had written his play: 'The figures have the appearance of marionettes operated by wires; there is a certain pedantic stiffness running through the whole thing which will have to be overcome.'[8] It was precisely this marionette-like quality in Gozzi which found favour once again a century later. The significance of the marionette and of the mask as strong means of theatrical expression came to be realized. Love of the mask is the third and probably most important reason for Busoni's sudden and apparently unmotivated homage to Gozzi.*

In 1870s the child prodigy Busoni had been championed in the Viennese press by two distinguished music critics, Eduard Hanslick and August Wilhelm Ambros. The latter is chiefly remembered for his *Geschichte der Musik*—his life's work, a study of such thoroughness that the four volumes he lived to complete, beginning from the dawn of civilization, progress only as far as the seventeenth century. Vol. I, which deals with the earliest known music (India, China, Nubia, Ancient Greece and Byzantium), is the source for Busoni's *Turandot* music. There is scarcely any thematic material in the score that cannot be traced back directly or indirectly to one of the numerous musical examples in Vol. I of Ambros's *Geschichte*. Having written the incidental music for *Turandot* entirely for his own amusement, Busoni took two practical steps. He began to look for a German theatre interested in reviving the play in its original version, and he created a suite of eight movements for concert use.

---

* The renaissance of the marionette in the twentieth century is more fully discussed in Section Five, Ch. XIII.

The first movement, 'Die Hinrichtung, das Stadttor, der Abschied', is made up of three separate pieces from the original score, opening with the music for the executioner's procession which features an ostinato on the timpani:

Ex. 39

The large orchestra is deployed in small groups, forming unusual mixtures of timbre. A subtle distinction is drawn, for instance, between the sound of flute-piccolo and oboe–piccolo octaves, and the unison of cor anglais and bassoon in its highest register evokes the timbre of some weird, forgotten oriental reed instrument. One by one the various instrumental groups enter. The pace quickens as the horns pronounce Kalaf's theme, adapted from an Arabian muezzin call (Ambros, p. 105)*:

Ex. 40

The movement closes with a boisterous tutti depicting Kalaf's love-intoxicated rapture.

In the second movement we are introduced to 'Truffaldino'. The incessant semiquavers of the introduction suggest the bustle on stage as he orders his servants about. There follows a *Marcia grotesca*, brilliantly scored for wind band and percussion.

'Altoum', third movement, suggests the gentle dignity of the old Emperor. His main theme is a Turkish song (Ambros, p. 110) of which the historian wrote, 'This sounds . . . almost like European music.' A fanfare which opens and closes the movement is derived from a Persian melody (Ambros, p. 109).

'Turandot' is the most extended movement of the Suite and offers a complete tone-picture of the icy beauty, divided into four sections which could be subtitled: 'Cruelty—Passion—veiled Beauty—unveiled Beauty'.[9] Turandot's theme is one of Ambros's few original Chinese melodies, the second of a group (pp. 34–5) which have dominated *Turandot* scores in Western music. The first was used by Weber (and later symphonically metamorphosed by Hindemith) and the third later became Puccini's Turandot

* Page references to Ambros are based on Volume I of the second edition of his *Geschichte der Musik* (Leipzig, 1880).

theme. The melody which Busoni chose is described by Ambros as 'amazingly ugly'!:

Ex. 41

The cruelty of the Princess is suggested by a wailing motif with fluctuating triadic harmonies, while her passion is depicted in a stressful tutti. In the play, the Princess is at pains not to reveal her love for the Prince; in the orchestra, of course, it can be given full rein. The 'veiled Beauty' is portrayed by an exquisite pianissimo version of the Turandot theme in canon, which employs the full orchestra. As she removes her veil, there is a dazzling fortissimo reprise of her 'passion' music.

The fifth movement, 'Das Frauengemach', is scored for an ensemble of two flutes and two harps, with a few triangle strokes and even fewer notes for trumpet and timpani. Dent observed a similarity here to the trio for two flutes and harp from Berlioz's *L'Enfance du Christ*, a comparison which Busoni was glad to endorse. This little composition poses a riddle:

Ex. 42

The main theme is none other than the Elizabethan melody 'Greensleeves', conjuring up an unlikely vision of Merrie England. What is this theme doing in legendary China? There has been no lack of ingenious attempts to answer this question. Dent assumes that Busoni was unaware of the melody's English origins and had somehow understood it to be Italian. Ronald Stevenson has established that Busoni saw the tune in a famous sixteenth century manuscript by William Ballet when he visited Trinity College, Dublin in 1903, and has also pointed out that the song was originally connected with public executions. However, this seems to offer only a partial solution to the riddle. Quite possibly, the significance of 'Greensleeves' lies in the colour green and its symbolism. Busoni did in fact know the title and origin of the song. When he finally received confirmation that *Turandot* was to be staged in Berlin with his incidental music, he noted in his diary (9 October 1910): 'At home. A look back and hope. "The lady with the green sleeves"'* And the riddle is taken further in the handsome cover illustration which Emil Orlik produced for the orchestral score: the red, black and gold of the lithograph are supplemented by a fourth colour, purely to give Turandot a garment with long, flowing *green* sleeves.

Green is the colour of envy or the colour of nature. In Schubert's *Die schöne Müllerin* it is an ambiguous colour; at one moment 'die liebe Farbe' and at the next 'die böse Farbe'. In *Die Brautwahl* it is the colour of youth (Lehsen's

---

* This last in English.

painting is described as 'die grüne Kunst') and of death (Thusman contemplates suicide—'der grüne Tod'). For Nezami, it is the colour of '. . . the paradise maidens and the angels in heaven. Green is the colour of the cypress tree and of the seed in the fields and, of all things, the soul needs green most of all, which brings fire to the eye and which is the melody of all increase and the sign of all growth.'[10] In Nezami's *Seven Pictures*, each of the tales explains the symbolism of clothes of a certain colour. Thus, in his Ur-Turandot, the Prince wears red—first as a symbol of mourning for the death of the Princess's suitors and later as a symbol of good fortune.

Busoni's brief innocent-sounding composition grins like a sphinx: 'Greensleeves' seems to embody 'that which the soul needs most of all'.

The next movement of the Suite, 'Tanz und Gesang' (with female chorus), uses a long Arabian melody (Ambros, p. 111) which, 'simultaneously warns of idle harem-life and cruelty'. A brief middle section in D flat major uses an Indian melody (Ambros, p. 70), in which he heard 'the merriment of dancing young girls'. The melody, in 6/8 time, is remarkably similar to 'Greensleeves'. As a whole, the 'Tanz und Gesang' is not one of Busoni's most distinguished inventions, lapsing into a literal kind of orientalism that he was elsewhere at pains to avoid.

Not so the seventh movement, the 'Nächtlicher Walzer'. This is a brief, powerful and original invention in which oriental scales are used to create strange haunting harmonies. The first part is a violent and sinister outburst, while the second part spins the same material into a seductive waltz melody, depicting the nocturnal spirits which 'slip through the keyhole' into Kalaf's room in the palace. The main theme, here in its brief and dissonant first version:

Ex. 43

is later extended to form an unbroken melody of forty-one bars. The movement has two alternative endings. The first closes simply in waltz rhythm; the other changes to 2/4 time and introduces a few snatches of Truffaldino's music. This is the point in the play where he creeps into Kalaf's room clutching his mandrake root.

The 'Marcia funebre', with which the last movement opens, brings back two ideas from earlier pieces, Turandot's theme and the executioner's drumming, against a contrasting ostinato on muffled drums and lower strings. A tutti statement of the Turandot-theme leads via an unexpected modulation to C major. The ensuing 'Finale alla Turca' is a bright rococo dance, reminiscent of the *Comedy Overture*. As in that piece, the theme is pulled through many keys before finally arriving back at its starting point. On the closing page even the 'riddle' chords and the executioner's motif join in the dance.

'One would not only require an élite theatrical company for the production, but also great opulence and excellent taste in the design of costumes and scenery,' wrote Busoni.[11] He accordingly offered the idea to Max Reinhardt, who gladly accepted it. A production was scheduled for 1907 and Emil Orlik (who had recently returned from a two-year journey to the Far East and was considered the leading German expert on chinoiserie) was to design the sets and costumes. The production was held up by two principal obstacles: the lack of a usable translation and Busoni's steadfast refusal to change a note of the score, let alone reduce the orchestration. Eventually Karl Vollmoeller, a young poet and member of the George circle in Berlin, made a new translation and adaptation for the Deutsches Theater and, despite the horrifying expense of the orchestra, the production opened on 26 October 1911. It met with only moderate success, although some critics commented on the extraordinary topicality of the play, coming as it did only a short time after the fall of the last Chinese imperial dynasty. Opinions about Busoni's music and its aptness for the theatre were varied. The critic of *Der Tag* observed bluntly: 'it certainly has great qualities, but it is concert music not theatre music'.[12] The *Berliner Zeitung*, on the other hand, found that 'it fits the action on the stage precisely. This is real Chinese music, half refined, half primitive.'[13] There was much praise for Reinhardt's production as well as for the designs of Ernst Stern (Orlik had been unable to collaborate). Yet the play only had a short run; costs of the orchestra were high, and it was overshadowed by more popular items in the repertoire. A guest at one of the performances was Puccini and it was his later recollections of the spectacle that persuaded him to make use of the subject himself.

The only other production of the play with Busoni's music was staged by Sir George Alexander in the St James's Theatre, London in 1913. Johan Wijsman (the dedicatee of the 'Berceuse' for piano) made an arrangement of the score for theatre orchestra without the composer's consent.* The reduced version sounded terrible and, as the producer had needed more music than was available, pieces by Rimsky-Korsakov and Saint-Saëns were interpolated. Busoni only discovered this state of affairs in the course of the opening night, with the result that he left the theatre in a rage after the second act and later tried to instigate legal proceedings against the director. 'I have coined the following aphorism', he wrote grimly to Gerda, 'Theatre pieces should be

---

* This score recently turned up in a second-hand music shop in Birmingham and is now the property of the composer Giles Swayne. In the absence of the original MS, it is the only surviving version of Busoni's original incidental music.

written but not performed (my expectations in this respect are high).'[14]

There are two appendices to the *Turandot Suite*. At Reinhardt's request Busoni composed an entr'acte between Acts IV and V, entitled 'Verzweiflung und Ergebung', which expresses Kalaf's fluctuating emotions at this point in the play. His despair as guards lead him to the Divan yields to an 'oriental philosophical resignation'. Strengthened in spirit, he enters the hall of judgement calmly and decisively.

The opening half of the piece is one of the finest passages in all of the *Turandot* music. In an expansion of the violent opening of the 'Nächtlicher Walzer', several themes from earlier movements are reintroduced: the executioner's drumming, Kalaf's theme, the seductive 'Nächtlichen', Truffaldino's theme and other fragments are welded into a quasi-symphonic unity. Off-stage trumpets open and close the scene, heralding the dawn. The second half, the 'Ergebung', is given over to a lengthy oriental melody solemnly declaimed by three trombones. This Indian *Terana* is also taken from Ambros (p. 69) and Busoni's setting highlights the 'inward and quiet expression of noble feelings' which the historian heard in it. A brief coda, *poco più agitato*, closes the piece with defiant C minor gestures.

The second appendix, 'Altoums Warnung', was composed six years later, for concert use. Busoni had recently completed his *Turandot* opera (see Ch. XV), in which he had made use of most of his incidental music but also added some new material. One of the new numbers, Altoum's second aria, was based on the Albumleaf for Flute and Piano, composed in 1916. Busoni subsequently incorporated this music into the *Turandot Suite*, where it replaces the *in modo di Marcia funebre* of the eighth movement. The Albumleaf is scored for solo trumpet with a discreet but sonorous accompaniment; a new transition passage leads to the 'Finale alla Turca'. It was this version of the finale which Busoni chose for his performance of movements from the Suite in the second of his 1921 retrospective concerts, and therefore it would appear to be the definitive version.

Busoni's use of original oriental melodies for *Turandot* is moderated by the great pains he took to avoid conventional theatre-exoticism of the *Land of Smiles* variety. His is a more generalized orientalism, closer to the gypsy music of Liszt, with its lightly spiced harmonies and exotic scales, invoking some distant realm of make-believe. Indeed, the melodies he used would hardly be considered ethnologically acceptable today, for Ambros's sources were of doubtful authenticity or reliability. The historian was, however, at pains to point out the affinities of his melodies from India or Arabia to European music, and Busoni, putting theory into practice, uses them in this spirit. His score directly mirrors Gozzi's synthesis of oriental flavour, classical form and homespun Italian humour. The way in which these elements were integrated was aptly described by Dent: 'Just as the decorators applied would-be Chinese detail to French rococo or Italian baroque forms . . . so Busoni lets us see a

Mozartian framework underneath the polychromatic brilliance of his strange harmonies and yet-stranger melodies.'[15] Busoni read Dent's review and wrote to express his delight at feeling himself for once understood.

If there is any criticism to be levelled at the splendid *Turandot Suite* it is this: it demonstrates, as did the *Comedy Overture*, how easily composing could come to Busoni. The music is often a little facile, perhaps too unambitious. Except for the purging of some lingering elements of Romanticism, the score represents no positive progress since the Piano Concerto. Yet, for Busoni it was essential to develop from one work to the next and those works in which he was emotionally most stretched are also his best. He was a man whose heart and head were so completely at one that a strong intellectual motivation was essential to the fabric of feeling in a composition. The relatively low-keyed intellectual stimulus afforded by the *Turandot* project accounts for the lack of tension one can sometimes sense in the score. But it is, above all, music that seeks to please.★

★ Note for performers. The *Turandot Suite* is a little long for concert use, especially if one includes 'Verzweiflung und Ergebung'. The following sequence is suggested:

I	'Die Hinrichtung, das Stadttor, der Abschied'
II	'Truffaldino'
IV	'Turandot-Marsch'
V	'Das Frauengemach'
VII	'Nächtlicher Walzer'
	'Verzweiflung und Ergebung'
	'Altoums Warnung'
VIIIa	'Finale alla Turca'

In this form the Suite would last approximately twenty-eight minutes. For the 1921 retrospective concert, Busoni conducted Nos. IV, VI ('Tanz und Gesang'), 'Altoums Warnung' and 'Finale alla Turca'. Apart from the disadvantage of requiring a female chorus (although ad lib), this is a curiously unrepresentative selection. It is mentioned here in the interests of completeness: its duration would be approximately sixteen minutes.

Section Three

Outline of a New Aesthetic of Music

Outline of a New Aesthetic of Music

Outline of a New Aesthetic of Music *First edition completed*: November 1906. *Published*: 1907 by Schmidl Verlag, Trieste. *MS*: last known owner Gisella Selden-Goth. *Second edition* (revised and enlarged) *completed*: 1915. *Published*: 1916 by Insel Verlag, Leipzig. Inselbücherei Nr. 202. *Dedicated*: to Rainer Maria Rilke. *MS*: (partly printed, partly handwritten) Deutsche Staatsbibliothek, Berlin.

At the head stands a quotation from Busoni's drama *Der mächtige Zauberer* (based on a short story by Gobineau):

> . . . I wish for the Unknown!
> What I already know is limitless. I want to go
> Still further. . .

(A second quotation, from 'Ein Brief' by Hugo von Hofmannsthal, describes a search for a new language 'in which perhaps I would some day answer to an unknown judge in the grave'.)*

In his preamble, Busoni regrets that none of the achievements of past composers 'lead *upwards*', then explains his denial of the historical perspective of music. 'The absolutely modern does not exist—only things which have come into being earlier or later.' He unifies the aim of all the arts as 'the imitation of nature and the representation of human feelings'. Music, however, is a child compared with the other Western arts, he continues, a mere four hundred years old, a child, moreover, that 'floats on air'. But the freedom and irresponsibility of this child have been disavowed by the 'law-givers'. 'Music was born free and to win freedom is its destiny.' Music can express itself without visual or verbal aids: an imitation of painting or of poetry, in other words programme music, is without validity. What then are the aims of music?

There follows an account of the misunderstanding of the term 'absolute music': not a thing of fixed, traditional forms and well-ordered counterpoint, rather a creation liberated from all material limitations. Beethoven, for instance, did not quite attain this absolute music, 'but he divined it', just as many other composers, even the 'much slighter' Schumann, came closest to it in moments of transition and introduction. Bach's organ fantasias (but not his fugues) could be inscribed 'Man and Nature'—but Bach and Beethoven represent only the beginning and should not be considered unsurpassable, especially as regards the problem of form versus freedom. Wagner, on the other hand, is unsurpassable because he himself achieved and completed everything within his own 'circle'.

Programme music is too limited in gesture, too provincial, to have anything in

---

* Passages in () brackets are those added in the English edition of 1911; passages in [] brackets first appeared in the second German edition of 1916. Hofmannsthal's quotation was printed at the close of the English edition; it comes from his so-called 'Chandos-Brief', published in *Der Tag*, Berlin, 18–19.10.1902.

common 'with that music which pervades the universe'. Likewise, theatre music too often merely repeats that which we see on the stage, instead of interpreting 'the states of *mind* of the persons of the action'. Busoni upholds the recitative–aria construction of classical opera as a fair way of giving music its place in the action, the corruption of the aria form itself having finally brought the style into disrepute. [Music-theatre should rely on the 'Incredible, Untrue or Unlikely'—*verismo* theatre cannot last. The opera of the future should use music only where it is indispensable—especially in the portrayal of the supernatural or the unnatural. Thus, either as a magic mirror (*opera seria*) or a comic mirror (*opera buffa*). The actor should 'play' and not feel; the spectator should think and not 'believe'. But the greatest hindrance to such a plan is—the public itself; for half the effort required for the comprehension of a work of art must come from the public.]

What is the relationship between notation and interpretation? What is definitive: the signs which composers write down, or the inspiration behind the signs? This leads Busoni to explain the purpose of the transcription. A composition is the transcription of the composer's original idea; the performance of the work is also a transcription. But no transcription can destroy the original, 'for the musical art-work exists before it sounds and after it has died away, complete and intact'. Variations are also nothing more than a series of arrangements of the original theme: strange that they should find favour with those who scoff at transcriptions!

Busoni now examines the German word *musikalisch*, a word which has no equivalents in Italian or French. Strictly speaking, he concludes, the only 'musical' person is the singer, for he himself *sounds*. But a 'musical' person has come to mean one who has an understanding of the rules. 'When shall the buoyant child cease at last to be "musical"?', he asks.

(Feeling in music should never be hysterically exaggerated but only so far expressed that 'everyone should stop, look and listen'. Feeling on a large scale is often mistaken for lack of emotion. One must learn to hear lengthy passages as part of an even greater whole. Feeling is born of six 'graces'—Taste, Style, Economy, Temperament, Intelligence and Balance. Out of these elements emerges Individuality.

The 'Apostles of the Ninth Symphony', however, should not confuse taste with profundity. Nor should depth of feeling be confused with weight.—'In the so-called "Champagne Aria" in *Don Giovanni* lies more "depth" than in many a funeral march or nocturne.')

'The function of the creative artist consists in making, not in obeying laws.' Busoni tempers his remark by adding that 'an intentional avoidance of the laws cannot masquerade as creativity'. The true creator makes new laws without premeditation.

(Routine should be avoided. It 'transforms the temple of art into a factory'. Too much routine acts as a curb on the imagination and hampers the artist's ability to stretch out his hand and grasp one of the countless strands of melody that have been waiting in readiness for him since the beginning of time.)

Busoni calls for respect for the pianoforte, especially for its one great and unique possession, the pedal, whose effects and colours remain unexhausted. 'Let us experiment with *sensible* irregularities.'*

[The hindrance to true creation lies in our musical instruments, with their innate and unalterable properties. We must take all possible steps to create an 'abstract sound, a

* The passage beginning 'Respect the pianoforte!' was replaced in the 1916 edition by the following paragraph.

technique without hindrance, an unlimited world of tones'. Looking far into the future, Busoni sees such a breakthrough as leading to the collapse of all musical cliques and the first full flowering of the art in the entire history of music. In turn, decay will set in and the symbols will lose their purity. . . .]

For the time being, one of the greatest gifts in our music is that of silences—rests and pauses. In the tension between two movements, the great interpreter can capture something of the true essence of music.

The penultimate section of the book is devoted to an evaluation of our harmonic system. Drawing attention to the limitations of tonality—'in a sphere where no dissonances can possibly exist!'—Busoni calls for infinite graduations of the octave, for freer use of the established twelve semitones, for divisions of the scale in new ways (he has worked out 113 possible new 'modes') and for divisions of the whole tone, for practical purposes, into sixth-tones.* He proposes a notation for this new scale of micro-intervals and quotes a report on Thaddeus Cahill's early electronic organ, the Dynamophone, with which such scales were for the first time made possible.

In the concluding paragraphs, Nietzsche comes to the surface, with a lengthy quotation from *Beyond Good and Evil*, a region which Busoni, the collector of Buddhas, identifies with Nirvana. 'I could imagine a music whose rarest magic should consist in its complete divorce from Good and Evil—only that its surface might be ruffled, as it were, by a longing as of a sailor for home, by certain golden shadows and tender frailties.' Such is the essence of Nietzsche's prophecy. Busoni has endeavoured to point some ways to the very portals of such a musical art: 'It may be that we must leave Earth to find that music.'

In the period often described as The Radical Years, the decade immediately preceding the First World War, there was a general progression in all the arts—and particularly in music—to remove the last remaining constraints of the nineteenth century. Busoni's constant process of self-rejuvenation was intensified by this new liberal *Zeitgeist* and led him, in 1907, to publish his eloquent plea for the loosening of all shackles, without which music would never be able to indulge in its greatest joy, to float on air.

At first his *New Aesthetic* was read only by a small, élite circle. Carlo Schmidl, who published the first edition, was an old family friend whose firm in Trieste was small and little known. The handsomely produced volume, which also contained two of Busoni's opera libretti, *Der mächtige Zauberer* and *Die Brautwahl*, was printed in Berlin and evidently circulated largely through the author's own efforts. Yet the small circle of initiated who read the book received it with delighted approval. Ernest Newman described it as containing 'a few calm proposals that deserve the name of revolutionary if ever any did',[1] while Dent noted that Busoni, 'however much he may enjoy scandalizing the pedants, is no friend of the anarchists'.[2] Paul Bekker wrote a lengthy and

---

* To Schoenberg's challenge regarding these 113 scales, 'Can he name them?', one can reply that two sheets are preserved in the East Berlin Busoni archive, in which the 113 scales are systematically notated—and later extended to 145, including some double-octave scales.

sceptical appraisal, but concluded, 'You lovable dreamer . . . you float on the clouds and intoxicate yourself with aetherial perfumes. But how I prefer your sparkling fables and flickering lantern pictures to the sober reasonings of our professional aestheticians.'[3]

Busoni soon felt the need to revise the text, to express himself more fully and clearly in certain matters. In 1909 he prepared several new short sections for a second edition which Schmidl intended to publish. This version never appeared.* In the introduction Busoni asserted: 'This little book . . . contains the seed for a revolution. Had it been read, and read with faith—the revolution would have been born.'

In 1910 followed another new contribution, a beautiful short essay entitled 'The Realm of Music':

> Come, follow me into the realm of music. Here is the barrier which separates the earthly from the eternal. Have you loosened your fetters and thrown them away? Then come. . . . Here there is no end to astonishment but yet we feel ourselves from the beginning at home . . . And now the *sound* makes itself manifest! Countless are its voices, compared with them is the whisper of a harp a fearful din, the blaring of a thousand trombones a mere chirrup.
>
> All, yea all melodies, heard or unheard, resonate together and at once, carry you, entwine themselves round you, brush against you—melodies of love and sorrow, of spring and winter, of melancholy and high spirits —are themselves the feelings of a million beings in a million epochs.[4]

Although subtitled 'Epilogue to the New Aesthetic', this essay has never been incorporated into any new edition of the book. The other additional material was published, however, when Schirmer of New York brought out the English translation in 1911. Four short essays were included in an appendix. Two translations were rejected in the desire for perfection (one of them by Dent, who was dissatisfied with his own attempt) and it was Theodore Baker who finally solved the problems caused by Busoni's intentionally antiquated German style.

As in Europe, the book, published on 1 March 1911, met with enthusiasm from the initiated and scepticism from many others. Busoni's former pupil Natalie Curtis wrote of 'a few words disclosing a view from the mountain top',[5] while a Los Angeles critic was heard to exlaim, 'But these people just want to amuse their readers!'[6] Writing to Dent, Busoni explained the need for the revisions: 'The last 5 years have made a man of me at last.'[7]

Yet even now, he felt that total clarity had not been achieved and his increasing insight was also matched by a feeling that too few people had read his book.

In March 1914 Rilke paid a brief visit to Berlin and was introduced to Busoni by a mutual friend, Magda von Hattingberg, a pianist from the group of adoring females which always surrounded Busoni (the 'caryatides' as Dent

* The MS of the 1909 amendments is in the Deutsche Staatsbibliothek, Berlin.

described them). Her brief but intense friendship with Rilke led her to publish a vapidly sentimental novel, *Rilke und Benvenuta*, in which she freely distorted or invented facts for their expressive effect. However her description of this unique meeting seems to ring true:

> Busoni . . . greets Rilke with a cordiality enchanting in its Latin respectfulness. In the way the two men shake hands it is as if two worlds were greeting each other . . . Busoni fiery, spirited, life-affirming, a man who likes to laugh, who is childlike and superstitious, Rilke shy, reserved, full of life's wisdom, serious and anxious, profound and calm, with a humour that only occasionally shines out. . . .
>
> After dinner we drank black coffee in the library, the conversation came round to Marcel Proust and his new book, *Du côté de chez Swann*. . . . At the close, Busoni mentioned that he particularly loved the Piccola marina from the 'Neuen Gedichte', and so Rilke read us the poem. He spoke it by heart, as only he can speak. . . . Two men, two worlds, had understood one another.[8]

Shortly after this meeting Rilke read a copy of the *New Aesthetic* which Busoni had given him and he wrote to his publisher in Leipzig, Anton Kippenberg:

> Dear friend, I have taken to my heart a very, very beautiful book which probably has also for you an assured future. . . . It is called 'Outline of a new aesthetic of music' (a musical counterpart to van de Velde's 'Amo')—a series of comments based on innermost experience and complete conviction. I think that such consciousness of music is otherwise only to be found in the letters of Beethoven.[9]

Kippenberg's reaction was positive and plans were made to incorporate the book into the *Inselbücherei*, a highly popular series of paperbacks, carefully chosen for their educational content.* Partly due to the outbreak of war, publication was held up for two years. Busoni, faced with the problem of revising his text, felt inclined to write an entirely new book. Eventually he found a way of satisfactorily combining the older and newer material. The revisions of 1909 were supplemented by the important passage on the theory of opera, originally published in the *Vossische Zeitung* on 23 March 1913. Several composers and writers, including Rezniček, Nikisch and Gerhard Hauptmann, had replied to the question, 'What do you think of the future of opera?' (Richard Strauss wrote, 'I would answer your questionnaire about the future of opera if I had even the faintest notion of this future'.) Hence the second edition of the *New Aesthetic* appeared towards the end of 1916, bearing the dedication:

In admiration and friendship for
Rainer Maria Rilke
the musician in words

* The first of the series was Rilke's own *Die Weise von Liebe und Tod des Cornets Christoph Rilke*.

Ten years after its original conception, the book was at last available to a wider public.

The quotations which open the book are Janus-faced: Hofmannsthal's 'Letter from Lord Chandos'—an essay of radical importance to many writers at the turn of the century in its expression of the artist's inability to progress any further within the limits of known languages—is countered by Gobineau's vision of the unlimited 'Unknown', of an underground passageway leading either to Aladdin's Cave or to self-destruction. Together, the quotations explain Busoni's call for the composers of the new century to venture out in search of a transcendental language.

The most important passages of the book are undoubtedly the opening and closing sections and those on law-making and law-giving. The description of music as a radiant child, whose joy is 'to follow the line of the rainbow and to break sunbeams with the clouds' is an Art Nouveau standpoint, debatable in the light of more recent composers' recourse to the considerably older musical cultures of Ancient Greece, India and the Far East in their aim to expand to an 'outside-time' music, as Xenakis calls it—a universal music which we can identify with the *ultimate* aim of the *New Aesthetic*.

Rilke's comparison of the book to Henry van de Velde's *Amo* shows that he valued it primarily for its definition of music's place in Art Nouveau. Van de Velde, father of the new architecture and precursor of the Bauhaus movement, was a Belgian who set up a workshop and taught in Weimar. For a time he wrote profusely, hoping to further his cause, but later he dedicated himself entirely to his handwork. *Amo* was published as no. 3 of the *Inselbücherei* in 1912. It shows that van de Velde, like Busoni, was grappling with the problems of the creative artist in a godless world: 'At a time when everything threatened to abandon us, when in earlier times men fell to their knees and irresistibly declared the "Credo", we have found on our lips an "Amo" ', he explains in his preface. He bewails a society which has come to believe in things it does not love, or no longer loves, and he formulates three articles of faith. Here, as craftsman, he comes closest to Busoni:

> Evolve the form and construction of all objects only as defined by the strictest logic and by their raison d'être.

> Adapt and subordinate these forms and constructions to the fundamental application of the material that you employ.

> And should the wish inspire you to beautify these forms and constructions, succumb to this desire only insofar as the rights and essential appearance of these forms and constructions can be observed and maintained.

Both books arose out of deep-seated misgivings concerning the art of the immediate past; they proclaim new technical ideals and formal principles. Busoni, however, never makes use of the word beauty and his chief concern is not the present but the future. When, in 1918, van de Velde came to read

Busoni's book, he recognized that there were basic differences of approach. He later recalled in his memoirs: 'I found that what I meant by "construction" did not correspond with that concept which Busoni characterized as typically modern in contemporary musical composition.'[10] Nevertheless, Busoni's 'child' theme, his Art Nouveau dream, returns at the end of almost every section of his book, while the condition that a piece of music should be beautiful seemed to him to be self-evident.

He first expressed his 'child' idea in a letter to Gerda in 1904:

> There must be a reason why music developed so late *as an art*. Maybe because it does not find its models ready-made in Nature as the other arts do and the first impulse—to imitate—cannot arise . . . Music is most *closely* related to Nature, *but not in its forms, rather in its essence.*[11]

The origin of his attack on the 'Apostles of the Ninth Symphony'—a passage which, as we shall see, later caused him extreme difficulty—is a letter to Egon Petri (dated 6.9.1905) headed 'Polemical national letter to E.P.':

> Are the Germans musical? Technically adroit? Artistically feeling? Profoundly sensitive? Nonchalant conquerors of the depths?—Music, a bird on the wing, if it remains in German regions, is in danger of ending up in a cage. And the Germans will become museum janitors.

It is the child's ability to soar, to float on air, that brings us away from Art Nouveau and specifically German problems and points more directly to the future of music. Leo Kestenberg finds this true understanding of music's ability to float 'only in our modern existentialist world' and quotes the philosopher Karl Jaspers to illuminate his theory:

> The fall from certainties, which were anyway illusory, will become the ability to float—what seemed a chasm will become the zone of freedom—apparent nothingness is transformed into that from which true existence speaks to us.[12]

Busoni proclaims the new freedom to be won for music in the Nietzschean era—this is what makes the *New Aesthetic*, even today, undiminished in its power and integrity. It is, arguably, the *Also sprach Zarathustra* of the musical world, a musical prophecy aptly making use of an almost biblical style.

The publication of the second edition had drastic consequences. Busoni's criticisms of the Germans—made in all innocence ten years previously—and especially his comments on their 'musicality', were much resented, coming from a foreigner in time of war. One of the first press reactions came from the young critic Hans Mersmann. He expressed his horror at the easy availability of the book (which now cost only fifty pfennigs): 'In the position it now occupies, distributed in thousands amongst the widest strata, I consider it to be dangerous in the highest degree.'[13] He drew attention to certain illogicalities, summing the book up as '. . . a denial of our existing music and the rejection of its form, its means of expression, its system and, in part, its content'.[14] An even more bigoted article appeared in the *Neue Musik-Zeitung* a few months later, the kernel of which was: 'Were we at peace, hundreds of supporters would unquestioningly praise his prattling as revelations of the newest and highest esprit. . . . We must do all in our power against the slandering of the music of our greater masters.'[15]

Hans Pfitzner now stepped into the fray with a lengthy counterblast, *Futuristengefahr* (The Danger of Futurism).[16] The publication of this essay coincided with the preparations for the world première of his masterpeice, *Palestrina*, naturally a suitable occasion for a composer to utter aesthetic proclamations. Pfitzner's pamphlet is typical of its creator; sometimes amusing, often long-winded, nationalistic in the worst sense of the word. He tries hard to stir himself to wounded pride, taunting Busoni with 'a penetrating incomprehension of the Germans in music which oozes out of all pores of the book'. He condemns the quotation of Nietzsche's warning against German music with an artless argument: Nietzsche's desertion of Wagner proves that he 'had never understood [his] depth and beauty'. He upholds the melodic genius of Lortzing and proclaims: 'It is illogical to talk of the aims of art at all. Art has no purpose and no aims.' Quoting Busoni's criticism of all previous music, that none is directed 'upwards', he interjects, 'What does that mean?'; Wagner, on the other hand, is upheld for 'striving for the heights'! Finally he shrugs his shoulders: 'Let come what must. Whether what is to come is beautiful is another question; and whether it will be more beautiful than what we already have is a question which *moves* us.' He registers amazement at Busoni's belief in the future, at the same time misunderstanding it. 'Remarkable! He doesn't believe in the extant, only in the non-existent!'

Reading *Futuristengefahr* today, its hostility seems mild, embedded as it is in lengthy parentheses and tortuous explanations. But its tone touched Busoni to the quick: Pfitzner spoke for all musical Germany. (Curious that he should have chosen Palestrina, an Italian, for the leading role in his magnum opus!) In an open letter to the *Vossische Zeitung*, Busoni made it clear that he had no intention of making any personal attacks in the *New Aesthetic*, nor did he subscribe to any particular artistic sect. 'Futurism, a movement of the "present", has no relation to my arguments', he wrote.[17] In the certainty that Pfitzner's attack was based on misunderstanding, he reiterated his main theme: 'From the "magic child" music, I hope for the undreamed-of, for which I "yearn": the all-embracing and the super-human.' He voiced his deep disappointment in private, telling his friend Vianna da Motta: 'Germany is always turning out lesser Martin Luthers, men who seem in the eyes of the people bold reformers, but who are basically quarrelsome, rigid sectarians.'[18]

Heading the courageous few who supported the book at this time was Paul Bekker, the music critic of the *Frankfurter Zeitung* and Germany's leading avant-gardist. It would be doing Busoni an injustice, he wrote, to take an opposing view:

Its value lies entirely in its suggestive powers, for the strength of which Pfitzner himself offers the best proof through the fact that he has published an extensive refutation . . . Pfitzner speaks of the 'danger' of Futurism. Art is threatened by one danger only: it is called Stagnation.[19]

The saddest aspect of this bitter controversy is that both sides propose several identical opinions. In *Palestrina* Pfitzner sets out his artistic creed, looking back some 400 years to what he saw as the beginnings of Western music; Busoni looked forward into the indeterminate future, to some moment of highest perfection.

In the pivotal scene from Act I of *Palestrina*, nine Masters appear to the composer and spur the unwilling man to new activity:

The last note is still missing
In the resounding chord.
You are to sound it

is their command. It is exactly this search for the last word that the Dervish expresses in Busoni's *Der mächtige Zauberer*:

What I already know is limitless. I want to go
Still further.

In the same sense, the nine Masters explain:

The circle of the most high is full of longing
For the one who will complete it.

While Busoni, in the epilogue to *Doktor Faust*, later expressed the hope that:

. . . rising on the shoulders of the past
Mankind will close the circle at the last.★

And the final word of Palestrina's vision, just as that of Busoni at the opening of *Doktor Faust*, is 'Frieden', 'Pax'. The cause of this controversy was the war and its isolating influence on the nations.† 'How alien and unfamiliar is man to man', says Palestrina, while Arlecchino comments dryly, 'What is the Father-land? A squabble in one's own house.'

The reasons for this particular squabble, therefore, were purely temporary. There was only one basic disagreement: Pfitzner, unlike Busoni, lived in fear of the future:

★ 'vollendet sich der Reigen'—literally 'the round-dance ends'. But the word 'Vol-lendung' also means perfection. Dent's translation, 'Mankind will reach his heaven at last', seems to me too free and I have taken the liberty of altering it.

† Busoni often stressed that he had completed the libretto of *Doktor Faust* on 26 December 1914; curiously enough, just one day earlier, on Christmas day, Pfitzner had finished scoring the second act of *Palestrina*.

> Who can say
> if the world is travelling paths undreamed of,
> and if what seemed eternal will be
> > gone with the wind?—
> A bleak thought it is—scarcely graspable

is Palestrina's sad comment.

The storm died down as quickly as it had arisen. Hans Mersmann now attributed the whole controversy to the differing personalities of the two composers: 'an antithesis of country and race'.[20] It had also to be admitted that Pfitzner had expressed himself none too well, that his book had certain weaknesses and self-contradictions; Busoni remained 'the great perplexer'.[21] In 1930 the same Mersmann wrote that Busoni's writings 'bring forth perceptions and demands whose meaning has only now become completely clear to us'.[22]

Even Busoni himself was later proud of, or amused at, the influence of his book. Speaking of Pfitzner's 'trench-warfare misinterpretation' he later found himself 'simultaneously angered and satisfied to observe the effect which my teachings have had, even if the results were somewhat obtuse'.[23] His derision of the up-and-coming young Hindemith for instance, had a strange paternality about it.* 'I could do everything the "young ones" do, but they couldn't do what I can', he told Gisella Selden-Goth. 'But they fail to mention that I played an active role in their efforts and that the circulation of my little Aesthetic to a certain extent occasioned them (even if through misunderstanding).'[24]

Pfitzner continued to indulge in polemic, attacking Paul Bekker's influential book on Beethoven in an essay entitled 'The new aesthetics of musical impotence'. This was in turn answered by Berg in his well-phrased but inconclusive retort, 'The musical impotence of Hans Pfitzner's "New Aesthetic" '. Only under the hail of such cudgel-blows was it possible to drag Busoni's unfortunate 'child' into the twentieth century.

And an inhospitable century it proved! In 1934, Pfitzner's *Futuristengefahr* was hailed in Germany as 'a book written from beginning to end in the spirit of the Third Reich'[25]; at the same time, Busoni was dismissed as a man whose 'split personality' made him unfit to be a leader. Woe to the artist without a clearly coloured ideological banner. Busoni does not fit into any such neat pigeon-hole: this has never ceased to perplex.

---

* While the twenty-one year old Hindemith pencilled into his copy of the *New Aesthetic* (against the quotation from *Beyond Good and Evil*): 'It is extraordinary that Busoni can stand it here on earth at all.'

Section Four

The Radical Years
(1907–15)

V

Elegies

Elegies. 6 new piano pieces. 1. 'Nach der Wendung' (Recueillement). *Dedicated:* to Gottfried Galston. *Composed:* September 1907. *Duration:* 4 minutes. 2. 'All'Italia!' (in modo napolitano). *Dedicated:* to Egon Petri. *Composed:* September 1907. *Duration:* 6 minutes. 3. 'Meine Seele bangt und hofft zu Dir. . .' (Chorale Prelude). *Dedicated:* to Gregor Beklemmischeff. *Composed:* (?) October 1907. *Duration:* 7 minutes. 4. 'Turandots Frauengemach' (Intermezzo). *Dedicated:* to Michael von Zadora. *Composed:* November 1907. *Duration:* 3 minutes. 5. 'Die Nächtlichen' (Walzer). *Dedicated:* to O'Neil Philipps; *Composed:* December 1907. *Duration:* 3 minutes. 6. 'Erscheinung' (Notturno). *Dedicated:* to Leo Kestenberg. *Composed:* November 1907. *Duration:* 6 minutes. *First performance:* (all six) 12.3.1908. Beethovensaal, Berlin. Soloist: Busoni. *Published:* Leipzig, 1908. EB 26042–6, 26052. *MS:* 45 pp., 34×27cm. Deutsche Staatsbibliothek, Berlin.*

'Nuit de Noël'. Esquisse pour le piano. *Dedicated:* to Frida Kindler. *Composed:* December 1908. *Published:* Paris, 1909. Durand et Fils. D&F 7298. *Duration:* 4 minutes.

'Berceuse' pour le piano. *Dedicated:* to Johan Wijsman. *Composed:* June 1909. *First performance:* March 1910. Choralionsaal, Berlin. Soloist: Leo Kestenberg. *Published:* Leipzig, 1909. EB 3053. *Arrangement:* for 2 pianos by Emil Debussman (1961). Published Wiesbaden, 1961. MS. *MS:* 4 pp., 34×27cm. Staatsarchiv, Leipzig. *Duration:* 4 minutes.

The Elegies and 'Berceuse' were later republished together as Elegies. 7 new piano pieces. Leipzig, 1909. EB 5214.

The *New Aesthetic* had elevated Busoni, for better or for worse, to the role of a leader of Germany's musical avant-garde. In that era (the zenith of what Hesse scornfully called the 'feuilletonistic age') he was now in a highly exposed position, a fact of which he was well aware. Every new composition would be avidly awaited, on the one hand by the blood-lusty opponents of the new, on the other by those eager to show themselves up-to-date.

After the *Turandot Suite* there followed, not surprisingly, a period of

---

* The MS of 'Die Nächtlichen' was published in facsimile in *Musica Viva*, Brussels, Rome, London, Zurich, April 1936, No. 1.

compositional silence lasting some two years. When Busoni finally came to reap the first fruits of his new insights, he did so not with any bold and extended major work but with a series of piano pieces of modest proportions and generally delicate character. He began work on the new pieces in the autumn of 1907 while living in Vienna, where he had taken over a master-class at the Conservatoire. Between his frequent concert tours he took the opportunity to become friends with Gustav Klimt and to cultivate many new acquaintances, notably with the Secessionists. Although Vienna was no longer considered the centre of the musical avant-garde, a position firmly occupied by Berlin, Busoni revelled in the fresh spirit he found there in the other creative arts.

By mid-November he had completed five pieces; when he wrote to Gerda, telling her with great enthusiasm of his new achievement, he was still referring to them under the general title 'Nach der Wendung' (After the Turning).[1] He told Egon Petri that the music seemed to be 'the most mature' he had as yet achieved.[2] During the course of December he added a sixth piece (the 'Nächtlichen'), retitled the collection 'Elegies' and completed the fair copy on 1 January 1908. One particularly revealing point emerges from a preliminary list of titles which Busoni had drawn up: the second piece was originally to represent a 'Neuer Flug' (new flight). The piece, however, was never written; as yet he remained earthbound. By coincidence, it was only two weeks after the completion of the Elegies that the Wright brothers made their first European flight 'not accidentally, without a balloon, but purely mechanically', as Busoni enthused to Gerda on 16 January 1908, '. . . the answer at last to Leonardo's question, then also to the questions and hopes of the whole world'.[3]

In their final sequence, the Elegies alternate between completely new work and transcriptions of older pieces. Busoni stands at the frontier of *terra incognita*. Poised for the journey yet reluctant to depart, his situation was comparable to that of the exiled Ovid: 'Ter limen tetigi, ter sum revocatus.'[4] For in the six Elegies, Busoni thrice touches his stylistic threshold and is thrice called back. When one appreciates the agony of his situation, the significance of the third and largest piece, 'Meine Seele bangt und hofft zu Dir. . .', becomes clear. The chorale prelude summons up emotions of fear and belief ('Angst und Glauben'—Busoni actually wrote these words on the manuscript): belief in the future, in the ability of mankind to ascend, and the unnameable fears aroused by the prospect of this ascent. Although the chorale prelude is the climax of the Elegies, these emotions, in varying forms, run through all six pieces, providing a slender unifying thread. As further expression of his belief in the future, Busoni dedicated each piece to a promising young pianist; and, as justification of his accompanying fears, it should be mentioned that two of these six young men died in obscurity, one took his own life only three years later and the other three made careers of some repute—foremost of all, of course, Egon Petri.

An elegy is literally a song of lamentation. It was this exact translation from the Greek which Rilke had in mind when he proclaimed the principal theme of his *Duino Elegies* as *Klage* (lament). Busoni applies the term more freely, referring back to the elegiac verse form favoured by many of the poets of ancient Rome, revived with fervour by the Latin poets of the Renaissance and revisited once more by Goethe in the passionate love-poetry of his *Marienbad Elegie* and *Römische Elegien*. For Busoni the elegy is a term more suggestive of poetry than the naked title *Klavierstück* which Schoenberg, for example, preferred. Busoni suggests more an overall colouring than any specific or established form: these are his watercolours, while he still reserved the use of oils for his larger canvasses. In a letter to Vianna da Motta he complained of the German 'lock, stock and barrel concept' of elegies as lamentations. 'A German should at least know his Goethe', he continued, 'and are this prodigy's "Roman elegies" songs of lament? Practically the opposite.'[5]

In later years, Busoni grouped six of his orchestral pieces together to form a second set of Elegies. Of these, three are true songs of lamentation (*Berceuse élégiaque, Song of the Spirit Dance* and *Sarabande*), while the other three (*Nocturne symphonique, Rondò arlecchinesco* and *Cortège*) are quite diverse in tone. There is also an Elegy for Clarinet and Piano, a wistfully amorous cantabile. These elegies are neither linked stylistically nor in expression; all they have in common is their brevity—none exceeds ten minutes—and a certain subdued quality of gesture and tone colour. They call the listener to intense, inward concentration. These are works of solitariness and contemplation.

When Rilke reached the elegiac final phase of his career, he announced it in a poem, 'Wendung' (Turning):

Werk des Gesichts ist Getan,
tue nun Herz-Werk . . .

Work of sight is achieved,
now for some heart-work . . .[6]

When Busoni published his piano pieces 'Nach der Wendung', he too looked inwards. The Elegies represent his 'heart-work'.

'Nach der Wendung' (Recueillement): from the opening four notes of the first Elegy we sense how a new subtlety is brought to the play of note against note; from the first phrase in its entirety Busoni's new use of tonality as a fluid, ever-changing component takes the ground away from beneath the listener's feet. The mild disturbance of C major occasioned by the F sharp in the second bar is made to carry its influence through until F sharp major is momentarily established, only to vanish again just as quickly (Ex. 44).

Ex. 44

The architectural axis of this short piece is formed from the tension between C and F sharp; a power-struggle in miniature between the remotest notes of the scale. (Exactly the same struggle, on a large scale, is fought out in Bartok's opera, *Duke Bluebeard's Castle.*)

In the filigree work that follows, the sighing fall of a semitone from bar 6 of Ex. 44 becomes a leading figure. Groups of triplet semiquavers rise in kaleidoscopic washes of triads from the lower to the higher regions of the keyboard. The opening theme is repeated in the bass, in G major, accompanied by more conventional broken-chord figuration, after which a muffled climax is reached in a third statement of the theme, this time mid-way between C and F sharp, in A major. There is a further development of the sighing motif, *en affaiblissant,* in which the most complex harmonic implications of the piece are achieved. Over an indistinct wash of semiquaver sextuplets, *mormorando,* the theme is again stated in G, breaking off with a recitative-like gesture. In the closing bars, Busoni alternates F sharp and C major triads over a regularly descending chromatic bass-line. Finally, F sharp major comes to the fore and the piece closes with muted chords in that key. Curious spacing results in an unsettling effect, however: the overtone of the low sixth in the bass completely unbalances the resonance of the chord, making it sound virtually dissonant:

Ex. 45

There is no definable form in this piece, yet a concealed, dream-like logic holds it together. It is, in the literal sense, a reverie. And, in its introverted play of tonalities, it seems to pose the questions of the six pieces while offering no solution to them.

'All'Italia!' (in modo napolitano): the first Elegy carries on at a point where the later piano works of Liszt left off. To the unworldly and pallid colours of 'Unstern!' or 'Nuages gris' Busoni adds his own new harmonies, his distinctive tonal fluctuations. In the second Elegy the debt to Liszt is again apparent, but in a different way. 'All'Italia!' is in fact a re-working of the Italian elements of the Piano Concerto. But where the two scherzos of the concerto were infused with youth and vivacity, latter-day echoes of Liszt's brilliant tarantella from 'Venezia e Napoli', the second Elegy comes closer to the two late pieces which Liszt entitled 'La lugubre gondola', premonitions of Wagner's funeral in Venice. In the opening bars this line of descent virtually takes the form of a quotation:

Ex. 46

Ex. 47

True, some of the music in the Piano Concerto is already tinged with sadness, but in the second Elegy the *Tristia* of the exiled Ovid seem to acquire new relevance. The music sounds like a lament for a landscape lost perhaps for ever, the opening is dark and subdued; when the folksong 'Fenesta che lucivi' enters, it does so with an unexpected discord (Ex. 48).

Ex. 48

Nevertheless the texture gradually lightens. The theme is repeated three times in successively more complex and dramatic forms. In the Piano Concerto it had been simply harmonized; now each main note is a new key-centre so that the melody is clothed in a blur of spiralling triads.

The 'Canzone del Serpentino' appears as a brilliant F sharp major round-dance, much of the music being taken over almost literally from the Piano Concerto. Then it fades out and, over an F sharp pedal point, a long theme based on the 'invocation' from the *Pezzo serioso* appears. A few bars of the opening major–minor waves return, now more calmly, and the piece closes unexpectedly, illogically even, in B flat major, with a gentle Italianate cadence.★

★ Note for performers. A revised version of the second Elegy exists which was never published. While practising it for a concert in Zurich in 1917, Busoni had to write to Egon Petri in Berlin for a copy of his alterations, a fact which seems to indicate the greater authenticity of this later version. On p. 20(14), at the end of the fourth bar, the following bars are added (in the absence of a more reliable source I have noted them from Petri's recording of 1938):

Ex. a

This leads directly into the final section (Andante). For the further alterations I am

'Meine Seele bangt und hofft zu Dir. . .' (Choralvorspiel): the third Elegy is the centrepiece of the set and in every way the most progressive. Busoni uses the Lutheran chorale, 'Allein Gott in der Höh sei Ehr', generally stating it in the minor key rather than in its original major. The contrasting emotions of fear and belief, expressed in the title, are immediately juxtaposed in the opening bars. Three intervals in double octaves—a third, a fifth and an octave—are presented like pillars, then echoed quietly; a declaration of faith followed by an anxious echo:*

Ex. 49

Ängstlich (fearfully) is the marking over the ensuing music: crawling chromatic scales in the bass and pathetic rising figures in thirds. The chorale, in contrast, is now fully and confidently stated in Lydian A major over a rocking E flat pedal point, the harmonies resulting from the combination of two keys a tritone apart being here taken one step further than in the first Elegy. A new section, which takes the rising third from the opening as the basis for a passage marked *implorando*, grows from a soft beginning to ever more impassioned gestures. The piano texture expands dramatically; the chorale is split into stuttering triplets while a bass-line in broken octaves rises ever higher. A double octave run, *crescendo ed accelerando*, leads to the climax of the section, marked *in höchster Angst* (in greatest fear). The opening minor third motif now serves as the basis of a dark, phantom-like broken chord which rises in quick

* Note for performers. Two years after composing the Elegies, Busoni altered the R.H. notes in bars 4–6. He wrote to Petri on 19.7.1909, asking him to observe this amendment:

Ex. d

remarking, 'The line is more perfectly expressive in this way. Also it is more "beklemmisch".' (A pun on the name of the dedicatee, Beklemmischeff, and the German word *beklemmt* [anxious].)

---

grateful to the late Prof. Gordon Green who was a pupil of Petri. 'At the Tempo I there is a G sharp added to the first (R.H.) chord making it: (b) and the second (L.H.) chord is altered to: (c).—The next bar is the same, and the following bars are respectively one and two octaves higher. . . . Knowing Petri as I did, I feel sure that he would not play any version of Busoni's which did not have the composer's authority.' (Extracts from a letter to the author, 12.9.1977.)

succession over four octaves:

Ex. 50

This third-based harmony is then augmented to form a dominant ninth chord.
The atmosphere thus becomes calmer and the chorale returns as a barcarolle.
In one of the most deeply felt moments of the Elegies, a gentle left-hand figure
is introduced into the swaying rhythm of the chorale—music composed in
exquisite pastel shades:

Ex. 51

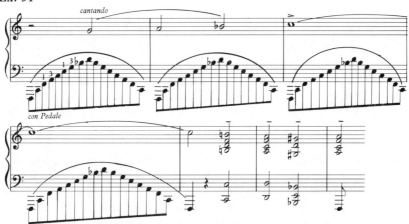

But the drama of the piece is not yet ended. The left-hand figure of Ex. 51
becomes stormy and the lines of the chorale are reduced to brief, sighing
phrases (*gemendo*—groaning). The final bars pose no solution to the conflict; B
minor triads disturb the closing G minor chords like unresolved doubts and
even the final D major chord, sonorously spaced as it is in its *ppp* dynamic,
seems more like a question mark than a full stop.

The third Elegy poses anew Beethoven's question, 'Muss es sein?'—but here
there is as yet no comforting 'Es muss sein' in answer. Through a chorale
prelude with its roots in Bach and its piano textures directly inherited from
Liszt, Busoni stages an unfinished autobiographical drama in the stream-of-
consciousness style of the twentieth century.

'Turandots Frauengemach' (Intermezzo): The origins of the two *Turandot*
elegies were evidently quite prosaic. Max Reinhardt had originally accepted
Busoni's score and Gozzi's play for production in 1907, indeed he had
tentatively scheduled New Year's Eve as the date for the opening night.
Busoni's publishers immediately began to press him to produce a piano

arrangement of the incidental music for rehearsal purposes. Unfortunately, he was quite unable to undertake any such routine job—had he not written 'routine transforms the temple of art into a factory'?—and if he ever undertook a work of transcription he found himself inevitably modifying, improving and modernising the original. He began indeed to rethink his *Turandot* music in pianistic terms, but far from producing a piano score for theatre repetiteurs, he turned his innocent 'Frauengemach' into a brilliant virtuoso piece, remaining faithful to the original text but demanding considerable agility from the player.*

The layout of the music on the piano is ingenious. At one point the pianist's five fingers themselves give rise to new, unusual scales:

Ex 52

and Busoni's pianistic principle of avoiding unnecessary jumps is here applied in drastic fashion, confusing to the eye but uncommonly practical to the hands. He also relishes the ambiguity of key afforded by the melody of 'Greensleeves'. Here it is never committed to E minor or G major but always hovers somewhere between the two. The close, with streams of G major arpeggio figures, is then suddenly and impishly interrupted by a chord of E major.

'Die Nächtlichen' (Walzer): while 'Turandots Frauengemach' adheres quite closely to the text of the orchestral version, 'Die Nächtlichen' is a completely free fantasia on the original 'Nächtlicher Walzer'. This is the Elegy in which Busoni most thoroughly exploits his concept of new scales. However, he does not simply choose one or two of his 113 modes and apply them doggedly throughout the piece—that would be too simple and unsubtle. Rather, he drifts imperceptibly from one scale pattern to another, using the ambiguous properties of his harmonies to smooth the way. This can at once be seen in the opening phrases. The first two bars seem to be in traditional A minor. Then the B flat of the third bar seems to imply G minor (and the ensuing notes in the right hand would appear to confirm this); but there is a disturbing C sharp, and the F sharp/C sharp fifth in the bass causes the momentary suggestion of F sharp major (Ex. 53).

This bewildering process is continued throughout the piece. The harmonic

---

* Although the orchestral and piano versions are largely identical, some bars have been cut and other material has been added or altered.

rhythm is varied considerably, however, and is sometimes slow enough to mislead the listener into believing that a stable key-centre has been established. Yet this is never the case. In the last seven bars Busoni hovers between B major

Ex. 53

and C minor, the result being that, by the end, the two keys seem to have lost their individual identities and have merged into one colour:

Ex. 54

Added to this fleeting play of tonalities (and the two examples above have been chosen for their relative simplicity) comes a rapid tempo and an almost exaggerated remoteness. This is perhaps the quietest waltz ever written: the dynamic range extends only from *ppp* to *p*. One appearance of the main theme, marked *un poco pesante*, is the loudest moment, but even this comes within a *pp* framework. The melodic material of the piece is also somewhat slender. All these factors combine to create an effect of distance and fragility. Placed immediately after the imposing 'Meine Seele bangt und hofft zu Dir. . .' and the readily enjoyable bravura of 'Turandots Frauengemach', the piece is overshadowed. It belongs in the company of the first and sixth Elegies. Then it would be easier to appreciate it for the fine study in filigree that it is.

'Erscheinung' (Notturno): The final Elegy is a study for *Die Brautwahl* and was written for the scene in Act I part 1 of the opera where a vision of the heroine, Albertine, appears at the window of a deserted tower in Berlin's Spandauerstrasse. (See the following chapter.)

With its mysticism, conjured in typically Hoffmannesque manner out of Biedermeier surroundings, this is one of the scenes that most appealed to Busoni in *Die Brautwahl* and it is also one of the most eloquent passages in the score. There are two long themes; the first a warm, Italianate cantilena, marked *amoroso*, the second more slow-moving, based on wider intervals and accompanied by a fluttering figure which (by inference from other scenes in the opera) can be interpreted as nervous heartbeats (Ex. 55).

Ex. 55

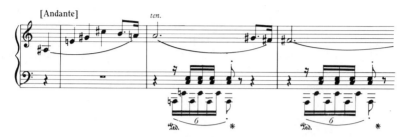

Between these two themes appears a leitmotiv from the opera, one of the few passages in Busoni's music which exploits whole-tone scales. He criticized Debussy for making too frequent and unvaried use of whole tones; this passage seems to be a demonstration of how the uniform colour of the scale can be gently tinged with other shades:

Ex. 56

Both themes return in more complex, exalted forms after which the coda introduces two new elements, a richly harmonized chorale-like melody over an A pedal-point and rapid right-hand scales. The chorale brings a hint of warmth and reassurance after the nervousness of the rest of the piece, recalling the more dramatic struggle of the third Elegy. Yet at the same time the scales in the right hand diverge ever further from the tonality of the chorale and eventually contradict it, creating what Leo Kestenberg, the dedicatee of this piece, has described as a 'magic-fantastic' effect.[7] The contradictory harmonies—at the close C major against D flat minor and D flat major against D minor—resolve into A minor and the heartbeats of Ex. 55, thrice repeated, have the last word.

An alternative ending, only to be used if the Elegies are played as a set, reintroduces the opening theme of 'Nach der Wendung', now marked *visionario*.

The first performance of the Elegies, in March 1908, drew hostile comments from the critics though all were entranced by 'Turandots Frauengemach'. It was probably a mistake to introduce all six to the public at one sitting. August Spanuth's review in the *Signale für die musikalische Welt* is so typical of the lordly attitude of the feuilletonists that it seems worth quoting at some length:

[Busoni] conducts, composes, agitates etc. He is one of those restless spirits who are never satisfied with what has been achieved, who can never call a halt. . . . He is something of a born opposer of the Establishment and when that for which he strives with all his power, a new aesthetic of music, is established and recognized, Busoni will become its irreconcilable opponent. . . .
Busoni's six elegies were a veritable source of dismay, with the exception of the fourth, which bears the title 'Turandots Frauengemach'. He who knew something of Busoni's strivings for a new harmonic system and of his belief that he has already achieved new tonalities through curiously built scales, could certainly perceive a structural logic and an aesthetically ordered system of sound deployment in these pieces; but the novelty seekers will have found as little 'music' here as the normal, naïve listener. . . . No, no and no again, these were not the inspirations of a man ahead of his time, these were simply calculations. . . . What a weird creature, for instance, is the 'waltz' entitled 'Die Nächtlichen'. I trust they aren't 'All-Nächtlichen'.[8]

Two months later Busoni observed, 'I have now experienced on several occasions that [the Elegies] appear infinitely more simple to the *reader* than to the *listener*', but he found this no reason to deprecate his new compositions. 'In these pieces', he continued, 'I am in fact particularly proud of the form and clarity. For instance, the structure and proportions of the "Erscheinung" seem to me exemplary.'[9] And five days later, in equally positive tone, 'the Elegies signify a milestone in my development. Almost a transformation. Hence the title, "nach der Wendung".'[10]

After completing the Elegies, Busoni concentrated on the composition of *Die Brautwahl* and during 1908 he worked intensively on the short score, finishing it at the beginning of December while on tour in England. His next composition, 'Nuit de Noël', is not strictly speaking an elegy—Busoni classifies it merely as a sketch—but it comes stylistically close to the Elegies in its introspectiveness and its ebb and flow of tonality. Quite possibly 'Nuit de Noël' was intended as a personal thanksgiving for the completion of the music of the opera and as a plea for strength to continue with the full score; at any rate, the little piece introduces us to an important aspect of Busoni-lore: that of ritual. His attitude to Christmas and New Year was pre-Christian; he looked upon the festivities as symbolic of rebirth and of new beginnings, of a time where the overriding universal emotion was that of hope. At this time of year he would shed the air of a *grand seigneur* to become a child once again. He had found this same transformation in Liszt: 'from demon to angel—from the first bravura fantasy "sur la Clochette" . . . to the childish mysticism of the "Weihnachtsbaum", *wherein lies that final naïvety which is the fruit of all experience*, resonating so exotically across into a "bessre Land"'.[11] In its rusticality and lengthy dissonant ostinatos, 'Nuit de Noël' acquires a certain rough-hewn simplicity akin to that of Liszt's entrancing late piano suite.

Commentators have seen the work as an attempt to emulate Debussy and Ravel, but they have probably been led astray by the French title and by the sheer look of the music on paper (the work is scarcely ever played). Apart from an occasional dominant ninth chord, or a passage in whole tones, there is nothing in the least 'impressionistic' about the piece. The title refers back to the Noëls of the French *clavecinistes*, while the dissonant style of much of the music is softened by an atavistic element—

Ex. 57

and by a reference to the old Sicilian Christmas carol, 'O Sanctissima' (itself a cosmopolitan tune, well known in Germany as 'O du fröhliche'). All in all, 'Nuit de Noël' is a merry affair, opening with an imitation of lightly falling snowflakes, later introducing bell effects and passages marked for timpani and for trumpets, returning finally to its opening simplicity. The long trill which runs through Ex. 57 recurs in the coda, after which a perfect cadence closes the proceedings *avec solennité* in C major.

Six months later, in June 1909, followed the 'Berceuse' for piano, which Busoni was later to republish as the seventh Elegy. 1909 was in fact one of his great years of abundance as a composer (only to be equalled by 1918 and 1921); a time when he had at last found his bearings in the new world of sound towards which the Elegies point the way.

The 'Berceuse' opens with a rocking left-hand figure spread over four octaves:

Ex. 58

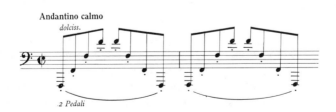

It is as if we were once again in the dark passageway leading towards Aladdin's Cave, for these F octaves are a distant echo of the B natural octaves which introduce the last movement of the Piano Concerto. (They also look back further to the unison F in all octaves of the piano with which Beethoven opens the last movement of the 'Hammerklavier' Sonata.)

Upon this ostinato Busoni introduces a simple, slow-moving theme (cf. Ex. 81) whose twice repeated rising minor third is identical to that of the 'Hymn to Allah' (cf. Ex. 22). The rhythm of this theme implies a sense of movement towards the second beat of each bar and this coincides with the rise and fall of the octave ostinato to form a gentle ebb and flow sustained almost throughout but varied in intensity. This flow creates a sense of timelessness in what is actually a very short piece. We find this same static feeling in a short orchestral piece written at almost exactly the same time as the 'Berceuse'—Schoenberg's 'Farben' (No. 3 of his Five Orchestral Pieces).

The harmonies spread out in irregular motion from the pure F major of the opening, their contour determined by freely moving lines to form what Busoni later described as 'polyphonic harmony'.[12] Only one interlude interrupts the flow, a passage of bitonal investigation:

Ex. 59

The undulating music resumes and with it reappears the opening theme, now more emphatic. An almost Schoenbergian use of fourth chords occurs:

Ex 60

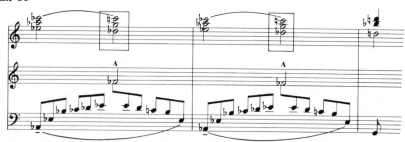

An abrupt halt to the proceedings is the cue for a brief coda. A swaying figure, slowly syncopated between the left and right hand, expands and vanishes like the ripples on the surface of water briefly disturbed.

Like the more forward-looking of the six Elegies, the 'Berceuse' is composed in a stream-of-consciousness style. It has an embryonic air about it; there is a lack of transition and a sense of imbalance. Nevertheless, it succeeds in penetrating one stage deeper into Busoni's universe of tones and affords a tantalizing glimpse of a new world.

Busoni seemed aware that he had not said the last word on this piece; his first idea was to transform it into a composition for violin and piano for his friend Arrigo Serato. Later in the year he changed his plan and produced his masterpiece, the *Berceuse élégiaque*. Whatever its formal deficiencies, there was no denying the further change of style reflected in the 'Berceuse'. 'On the first hearing . . . my friends were greatly startled', wrote Busoni. 'I, however, considered it one of my most successful piano pieces.'[13]

VI

Die Brautwahl

Die Brautwahl: a musical-fantastical comedy based on the tale by E. T. A. Hoffmann. *Dedicated*: to Gustav Brecher. *Composed*: February 1906 to October 1911. *First performance*: 13.4.1912. Stadtheater, Hamburg. Conductor: Gustav Brecher; producer: Siegfried Jelenko; designer: Karl Walser.

Kommissionsrat Voswinkel (baritone)	Hermann Wiedemann
Albertine, his daughter (mezzo-soprano)	Elisabeth Puritz-Schumann
Thusman (buffo tenor)	Willi Birrenkoven
Edmund Lehsen (lyric tenor)	Otto Marak
Baron Bensch (grotesque tenor)	Eduard Lichtenstein
Leonhard (baritone)	Robert vom Scheidt
The Jew Manasse (bass)	Max Lohfing
A servant of Voswinkel (tenor)	Fritz Windgassen
An invisible chorus	

Published: Berlin, 1914. Harmonie Verlag. *Vocal score*: (Egon Petri) published jointly by Harmonie Verlag and Breitkopf und Härtel, 1912. EB 5313. *MS*: 883pp., 35×26.5cm. Deutsche Staatsbibliothek, Berlin. *Instrumentation*: 3(3 Picc.)–3(C.A.)–3(Bcl.)–3(Cfg.); 4–3–3–1; Timp., Perc.; Harp; Celesta; Str. Stage music: 1–2–2–2; 2–0–2 cornets–0–0; Timp., Perc.; Organ; Harpsichord; Bells; solo cornet. *Translations*: Italian (two versions) by Giovanni Trampus (Br.u.H.) and Augusto Anzoletti (unpublished).

Orchestral Suite from Die Brautwahl op. 45: *Dedicated*: to Curt Sobernheim. *Composer*: 1912 (completed August 1912). *First performance*: 3.1.1913. Beethovensaal, Berlin. Berlin Philharmonic Orchestra, conducted by Oskar Fried. *Published*: Leipzig, 1917. PB 2347. *Instrumentation*: as the opera (without stage music). *Duration*: 27 minutes.

Grausige Historie vom Münzjuden Lippold [The gruesome history of Lippold the Jew-coiner] for baritone and orchestra. [Intended as op. 55 no. 1]. *Composed*: February–March 1923. Unperformed. Unpublished. *MS*: 23pp., 33×26cm. Deutsche Staatsbibliothek, Berlin. *Instrumentation*: 2 (Picc.)–2(C.A.)–2–2; 4–2–3–0; Timp., Perc.; Harp; Str. *Duration*: 6 minutes.

Act I part 1 The curtain rises on the Zelte, a fashionable promenade in Berlin's Tiergarten. The time: late afternoon on a summer day around 1820. A wind-band is playing the Hebrews' March from Rossini's opera *Moses*, no doubt for the benefit of the

predominantly Jewish clientèle at the open-air restaurant. Voswinkel is having difficulty with his cigar. Edmund offers him one of his own and he gladly accepts, singing
the praises of the barbarous races who have enriched mankind with their tobacco.
Inviting Edmund to join him at his table, he introduces his daughter Albertine. She
recognizes the young man as Lehsen the painter, whose work she has already admired.
The two are left alone. As dusk falls Albertine sings a stanza of Fouqué, which develops
into an extended duet: the two have fallen instantly in love. Voswinkel returns and all
three leave the now almost deserted park. Suddenly Leonhard appears in the gathering
gloom. Edmund, who shows the greatest promise as an artist, is under his protection,
he explains. At all cost, he must direct this new development with Albertine to a
favourable conclusion.

The scene changes to the old Rathaus in the Spandauerstrasse. Thusman is hurrying
home, for he is late and he detests unpunctuality. Suddenly he notices Leonhard
hammering at the door of the clock-tower and sighing woefully. It strikes eleven and a
figure appears at an upper window: it is Albertine. This is a vision, Leonhard explains,
that only appears on the night of the autumn equinox. By the following spring, the girl
at the window will have become the happiest bride in all Berlin. Leonhard persuades
the unwilling Thusman to follow him.

Act I part 2 A dimly-lit wine cellar. The old Jew Manasse is seated alone at a table.
Enter Leonhard and Thusman, who declares that he intends to get married. 'What?'
storms Manasse, '*you* marry? Much too old and ugly!' But Thusman has a weapon to
counteract his unbecoming age and bearing: Thomasius's book of manners, published
in 1710. He quotes from it at length, finally provoking a vivid curse from the old Jew.
Leonhard recounts the tale of Lippold the Jew-coiner, who was put to death in 1572 for
forging gold coins with the aid of a magic file. Thusman interrupts: he had recognized
the girl at the tower window as Albertine and *she* is the bride he intends to woo.
Leonhard feigns anger. 'Be warned', he threatens, 'you are mixed up with curious folk
here', whereupon his face changes into a fox-head. Manasse takes a large radish out of
his pocket and cuts it into slices. In his hands they become gold ducats. Leonhard takes
them and they vanish in sparks. The two magicians play ever more wildly until
Thusman, his hair standing on end, rushes off, their laughter echoing in his ears.

Act II part 1 A room in Voswinkel's house, early the following morning. The
Kommissionsrat is admiring a new portrait, painted by Lehsen, depicting him as a
wealthy businessman. Thusman bursts in and gives a sorrowful account of his
escapades the previous night. He saw Albertine in the Rathaus tower, he says, dancing
with a stranger to raucous music. He too began to dance, danced ever faster and finally
fell unconscious. Plain drunkenness, expostulates his future father-in-law reprimand-
ingly. Leonhard and Manasse magicians?—impossible: the government would never
grant a licence for such a trade. Manasse enters somewhat menacingly to announce that
his nephew, recently elevated to the nobility, is pressing for Albertine's hand. He begs
Voswinkel to consider the proposal, then takes his leave. The crestfallen father forgives
Thusman his carousal and begs him to marry his daughter.

Act II part 2 Another room in Voswinkel's house. Albertine is singing her Fouqué
song, accompanying herself at the harpsichord. Lehsen is painting her portrait—or at
least, pretending to. As they fondly embrace, Thusman enters. There is an icy silence.
When Lehsen has finally mastered his anger, he takes a brush and paints a broad green

stain over Thusman's face. Enter Voswinkel. Insults now fly in all directions. Just as Lehsen is about to revenge himself, Leonhard appears, stunning all to silence. Unless Thusman withdraws his suit he shall, as punishment, remain green for ever, he threatens. The confusion quintet that follows is interrupted by the return of Manasse with his nephew, Baron Bensch. The latter makes repulsive advances to Albertine, but Leonhard catches the despairing girl in his arms and claps his hands three times. All the others begin to dance until they sink back exhausted. Manasse, cursing Voswinkel with financial ruin, storms off with Bensch. Leonhard consoles the lovers.

Act III part 1 We hear the post-horn of a coach leaving the city. As it fades into the distance, the curtain rises on the Froschteich [Frogpond] in the Tiergarten. Thusman, his face green as ever, is lying in misery under a tree. So great is his dismay that he decides to throw himself to the frogs and die a 'green death'. He throws his wretched Thomasius into the water and is about to follow it himself when Leonhard suddenly appears and stops him. Thusman is almost out of his wits and panics when Leonhard tries to lead him back into the city, but the magician passes a handkerchief over his face and all trace of the green stain vanishes. Despite all Leonhard's warnings, his resolve to win Albertine, now restored, stands firm.

Act III part 2 In the Voswinkel household things are not running smoothly. The Kommissionsrat gives vent to his annoyance, whereupon Leonhard, the very object of his anger, suddenly enters and outlines three dangers: 1) Lehsen is repainting the portrait to depict Voswinkel as a bankrupt and intends to display the new version at the banking house in the Jägerstrasse; 2) Thusman is contemplating suicide. If he dies, Voswinkel must be held morally responsible; 3) Manasse and his nephew have every means at their disposal to bring about Voswinkel's financial ruin, as they had threatened. Leonhard suggests a trial by caskets to settle the dispute. The idea is stolen from *The Merchant of Venice* observes Voswinkel dourly, but eventually he agrees.

We discover Albertine in a state of nervous collapse: her future decided by a lottery? Only one ray of hope still glimmers—Leonhard seems trustworthy. She sinks into a trance, in which Leonhard appears and consoles her, then reveals Lehsen's future. In a vision we see the painter at work on a great Italian altarpiece. Invisible voices, accompanied by organ music, sing the words 'Deus et ars et natura, vera sunt Trinitas'. The vision vanishes and Albertine awakes refreshed.

Epilogue The trial of the caskets; a room in Voswinkel's house. The three suitors appear, Lehsen dressed for a journey. Voswinkel outlines his plan and all declare themselves in agreement. Albertine enters and the ceremony begins, though not before the suitors have lavishly sung her praises. Thusman opens the first casket. His prize is a magic book which will turn in a trice into any title he wishes for. Bensch wins an empty leather bag which Manasse recognizes with horror as the very magic coin-bag for which he had sold his soul. He chases his nephew out of the house. Lehsen opens the third casket and wins his bride. All has turned out for the best. Leonhard makes an imperious gesture: 'Off to Rome!'

Beside impressive collections of Cervantes and Faust literature, rare early editions of Hoffmann, and secondary literature about him, formed a mainstay of Busoni's library. Indeed E. T. A. Hoffmann exerted a lifelong fascination upon him which can be traced back at least as far as his character piece for piano, 'Klein Zaches', composed at the age of sixteen (no. 2 of the *Racconti Fantastici* op. 12). Later Busoni became an acknowledged Hoffmann authority and in 1914 he wrote a foreword for an edition of the *Phantastische Geschichten* (it was, however, only ever published as a separate essay). His involvement became almost morbid; some years later Egon Petri recalled, in conversation with Dent, that Busoni 'became at one time so absorbed in E. T. A. Hoffmann that he came really to believe that he was a reincarnation of him'.[1]

Stage adaptations of Hoffmann's short stories have not been so numerous as might be expected; the problems of translating his volatile style into terms suited to the more cumbersome apparatus of the theatre are considerable. While his writings have often been an inspiration to librettists, it is undeniable that their effect remains greatest in their original form, whether on the printed page or read aloud. Only then does unfettered imagination, their most vital quality, have full play.

Busoni was well aware of this. He considered it impossible, for instance, to set Hoffmann's greatest work, *Der goldne Topf*, to music on the grounds that the story itself contains so many descriptions of imaginary music. 'Where music of supernatural effect is described, actual music can never be its equal', he explained.[2]

In the case of *Die Brautwahl* this did not apply, but there were other problems of equal magnitude to be solved. Nevertheless, Busoni had cogent literary reasons for choosing this piece and these seem to have blinded him to the considerable practical difficulties to be overcome. For in Hoffmann he found a striking identity of ideals and insights.

Nowhere is this more apparent than in the *Serapionsbrüder*, Hoffmann's last major publication, a collection of twenty-eight short stories linked by the commentaries of the partly fictitious 'brothers'. Each of these stories represents an attempt to write according to the so-called Serapiontic principle. As set forth in the first tale, *Der Einsiedler Serapion* (Serapion the hermit), this is an ideal which anticipates Busoni's concept of the omnipresence of Time. 'Time is just as relative a concept as number', says the hermit, and he leads his entire life in blithe disregard of the accepted conventions of time and place, speaks of meetings with Ariosto and Petrarch and imagines that the south-German forest in which he lives is the desert beyond Alexandria. So convincing are his arguments that those who at first question his sanity are soon led to doubt their own more conventional beliefs.

Die Brautwahl comes closer to the Serapiontic ideal than almost any other tale in the anthology; the petit-bourgeois society of Berlin in Hoffmann's time is constantly being disrupted and mystified by happenings which cannot be explained in rational terms. Such a society attributes these things to drunkenness, madness or, at best, reverie. Yet the reader is left to ponder for himself the question: where does the dream begin and reality end?

One great merit of the Serapiontic principle is that it can be used to transfer mythical ideas to modern times. The crux of this argument is expounded by Hoffmann himself:

The Jacob's ladder upon which one wishes to ascend into higher spheres must have its foot firmly planted in life, so that each of us can climb it. Climbing ever higher, if one then finds oneself in a fantastic world of magic, one can believe that this world actually is part of life and is in fact the wondrous, most delightful part of it.

Therefore, he continues, the reader will profit more from a story set in familiar surroundings than, for instance, from the tales of the *Thousand and One Nights*. To the Persians of the Middle Ages, he points out, those tales of cobblers, tailors, dervishes and merchants were taken from their immediate surroundings and fulfilled exactly this enriching function in their daily lives. The cogency of Hoffmann's argument must have persuaded Busoni to abandon the Orient in favour of Berlin. Although he worked on the idea of Aladdin up to 1906 and also wrote *Der mächtige Zauberer* around this time, he never composed any music for them—or for his operetta, *Frau Potiphar*, the text of which he wrote in 1909, drawing on the same biblical story which Strauss and Hofmannsthal later used in *Die Josephslegende*.

In Hoffmann's writings on music and the theatre in the *Serapionsbrüder*, Busoni again found an echo of his own thoughts: 'Music is surely the mysterious language of a distant world of the spirit, whose miraculous strains resound within us, awakening an elevated, intensive existence', writes Hoffmann in 'Der Dichter und der Komponist'. The sentence could almost come from Busoni's *New Aesthetic*. Hoffmann's ideals of *opera buffa*, expounded in the same dialogue, were the guiding lines for Busoni's own libretto:

In opera buffa, the Romantic aspect [of tragic opera] should actually be replaced by a fantastic element . . . and the spirit of adventure which besets the characters should have as miraculous an effect upon us as if some poltergeist had entered our lives and were driving us irresistibly into his world of delectable banter.

The practical difficulties of transferring *Die Brautwahl* to the stage are manifold. They lie primarily in the question of language. Hoffmann's dialogue, largely unaltered in Busoni's libretto, reflects in minutest detail the modes of address used by all classes and kinds of people in the Berlin of his time. As a study in the history of spoken language it is as intricate as Hofmannsthal's use of Viennese dialects in *Der Rosenkavalier*. The problem is that Hoffmann's characters are generally loquacious people, often somewhat pedantic in their manner of speech. This can be endearing in written form but is never-ending when sung. As an example, here are Voswinkel's opening lines:

So! That was the last one! Did I spend all that time and energy ordering the cigaros from Hamburg, just so that the wretched things should annoy me? Simply dreadful! How can I now enjoy my walk in any reasonable way, or make profitable conversation? It's simply dreadful!

Busoni has cut only very few words from Hoffmann's original. The whole situation, however, could be played with a minimum of text, even if the result is linguistically rather dry:

Kommissionsrat (*struggling to light a cigar*): Drat it!
That ruins my whole afternoon!

Even this text is dispensable; mime could be used, leaving the music to express the whole affair. As it stands in the score, Voswinkel's struggle with his cigar lasts almost sixty seconds—a long time to make a small point.

This style persists almost throughout. The polished phraseology and bourgeois grandiloquence of the language may be amusing, but it reduces the pace of the action considerably; more seriously, it undermines the effect of intended moments of breadth. At times it leads to incomprehensibility; in condensing the novella into a libretto, some passages of the narrative had to be abbreviated. Occasionally Busoni seems to have overlooked the fact that his audience was unlikely to be as familiar with Hoffmann's tale as he was. For example, when at the end of Act II part 2 Manasse curses Voswinkel, he exclaims, 'May . . . the Dalès infest your palace and eat up your goods!' Hoffmann explains to the reader in a parenthetical narrative of some 400 words what the Dalès actually is (a monster who literally eats his victims out of house and home). In the opera the point remains unexplained and the sentence becomes virtually meaningless. Busoni was too much slave, it appears, to his delight in Hoffmann's language, too inexperienced as an opera librettist, to make a success of his difficult task.

In his overall handling of the structure of the drama, however, and in the adjustment of the original to serve new purposes, Busoni has been highly successful. Whatever the problems of pace or language, he has divided the action into a series of atmospheric tableaux, has ensured that each scene contains contrasts, moments of tension and relaxation, surprises, climaxes and, at each curtain-fall, a satisfying *envoi*. Yet here we come to the other major problem of the libretto: its excessive length. The sequence of Hoffmann's opening scenes is reversed, allowing them to be telescoped together, and a dialogue between Leonhard and Lehsen has been cut, but otherwise every detail of the story (which covers sixty-six closely printed pages in the standard German edition) has been retained. The result is a comedy of epic proportions and with a serious core—a Berliner's *Rosenkavalier*, perhaps. Running uncut for three hours, it remains an opera for *aficionados*, scarcely a work to draw the crowds.

In *Die Brautwahl* even Thusman, the pedantic minor official, is led into a dream-world out of which he escapes only with the greatest of difficulty; Hoffmann's Serapiontic principle intrudes even on the lives of those completely lacking in imagination. However, the tale also has its private satirical side, for all the characters are modelled on real people. Of course this aspect of the piece is primarily of academic interest to later readers and Busoni made no attempt to adhere to it except in the case of Leonhard the goldsmith. There can be no doubt as to the identity of his prototype. 'The only Berliner living in 1819 with whom Leonhard has any traits in common', wrote Hans von Müller, 'was Hoffmann himself'.[3] If we postulate that Busoni, with his intuition of reincarnation, reassumed this identity, *Die Brautwahl* can be viewed as an autobiographical—and hence allegorical—work. At the close of Hoffmann's story, Edmund leaves for Rome. He does write to Albertine, but his letters grow more infrequent and less passionate. At this point the story breaks off. Busoni ends instead with the unison call, 'nach Rom!'. But he has also conjured up the fantastic vision of the altarpiece, an indication of the masterwork to come—an episode which does *not* occur in Hoffmann. The autobiographical purpose which Busoni sensed in writing the opera is thus made clear: the altarpiece can be seen to stand for Aladdin's Cave, for the goal towards which future generations must strive. Hence that final cry, 'nach Rom!', has none of the exile's homesickness which we sometimes sense in Busoni's references to Italy; it is closer in spirit to that very same cry at the end of the second act of *Tannhäuser*, a call to pilgrimage, a prayer for salvation.

Hoffmann compiled his story from a variety of sources. For the characters of Manasse and Leonhard he went back to an old history of Berlin, the *Microchronologicon* by Peter Hafftiz, written in 1595. It contains a detailed description of the execution of Lippold, a Jewish coiner who was suspected of using witchcraft in pursuit of his profession. In 1577 he was tortured and burned at the stake in Berlin's Neue Markt. The saga relates that, while the flames were at their height, a huge rat jumped into the fire—the evil demon who had assisted the old Jew. The chronicle also mentions a certain Swiss goldsmith, Leonhard Thurneisser zum Thurn, who lived from 1530–95 and was rumoured to be an alchemist. These two figures are the prototypes for the *revenants* in *Die Brautwahl*.

It was characteristic of Hoffmann that his quotations from this ancient chronicle are precise and unaltered and it was due to this precision that he lit upon his other chief source for the tale, namely Shakespeare's *Merchant of Venice*. The play, having also been first published in the 1590s, was directly contemporary with the *Microchronologicon* and in the figures of Shylock and Lippold he found the embodiment of the mythical Wandering Jew, whom he called Manasse. Shakespeare's Portia then became the prototype for Hoffmann's Albertine and hence arose the notion of the three suitors. (It was no coincidence that Shakespeare's play was enjoying a successful run in Berlin in 1819, when the story was written.)

According to von Müller, the Manasse of Hoffmann's tale is a caricature of the actor who played Shylock in Berlin, one of the greatest theatre personalities of his age and a close friend of Hoffmann's, Ludwig Devrient. Edmund Lehsen is modelled anagrammatically on the painter Wilhelm Hensel (1794–

1861), who in 1829 married Fanny Mendelssohn. In 1818, Hoffmann saw some of Hensel's large allegorical paintings in an exhibition and subsequently drew him into the story in order to poke fun at the 'grüne Kunst' of the young artist.

Central to the action is the battle of wits fought out with grim humour by the two *revenants*; the conflict between good and evil which is a recurring theme in Hoffmann's stories (see, for instance, 'Der goldne Topf' or 'Nussknacker und Mausekönig'). In *Die Brautwahl* the two ancient enemies are both workers in gold, Leonhard the master-goldsmith and Manasse the false coiner. The scene of magic at the end of Act I scene 2 illustrates their divergent attitudes to the noble metal: Manasse cuts a radish into slices which become gold coins, but Leonhard transforms the metal into blinding flashes of light—an allegory of true creativity versus falsification. For Leonhard is the epitome of the benevolent genius in whom Busoni saw the only hope for the perfection of Art. Clearly the concept is derived from Nietzsche, but it was Bernard Shaw, wrestling with the same problems of world salvation in his metabiological pentateuch, *Back to Methuselah* (1921), who expressed most succinctly the function of such an omnipresent creature: '[Men] will live three hundred years, not because they would like to, but because the soul deep down in them will know that they must, if the world is to be saved.'[4]

This is the visionary skeleton around which the opera is built. It may seem curious that Busoni chose to express such matters in a comedy. Yet, when a lady friend remarked that he was far too serious a person to write an *opera buffa*, he countered with an aphorism: 'Humour is the fruit of the Tree of Seriousness.'[5]

Work on the music of *Die Brautwahl* occupied Busoni intermittently from the beginning of 1906 until autumn 1911. Here is a brief chronology of the various stages in the accomplishment of his project:

1906 By February the first draft of the libretto was complete and work was begun on a short score. The first musical sketch (which was not incorporated into the score) bears the date 2.2.1906. The libretto was finished on 22 June, by which time the music for the opening scene of Act I was almost completely sketched. At the end of the summer, on holiday in Trent, Act II part 1 was written.

1907 Little was added to the work of the previous year. The two scenes which had been begun in 1906 were completed. In December the 'Erscheinung' was written.

1908 In April Busoni wrote: 'Our old friends Thusman and Leonhard are waking from their hibernation, stretch, yawn and turn over again before getting up altogether.'[6] Work now proceeded at great speed. Act III part 1 was followed by Act II part 2 during May. By 26 June the short score was complete up to the end of Act III. The Epilogue (originally Act IV) was finished in England; the last page of the short score is signed '1.2.3 December, Hull–York–Doncaster'.

1909 Work on the orchestration began at the end of March. Act I part 1 was finished on 16 July. The rest of the year was devoted to the composition of a number of smaller works in quite different styles (see Ch. VIII).

1910 On tour in the USA Busoni met Arnold Dolmetsch in Boston who demonstrated a harpsichord to him. Delighted by the instrument, he at once decided to use it in the opera for Albertine's song in Act II part 2. After completing the *Fantasia Contrappuntistica* on 1 March, Busoni resumed work on the full score, finishing Act I part 2 on 11 July. Act III part 1 followed in October. During the course of the year arrangements were made with the Stadttheater Hamburg for the first performance and a contract to publish an engraved full score, vocal score and libretto was signed with the recently founded Harmonie Verlag. Egon Petri undertook the preparation of the vocal score.

1911 During the course of the year the full score was completed: Act III part 2 on 12 January (in Chicago), the Epilogue on 14 June, Act II part 1 on 28 July and Act III part 3 (later to become the second half of part 2) on 22 October. Meanwhile disaster struck; having underestimated the cost of producing such an enormous score the publishers decided to postpone publication. Busoni, however, continued to send material to the engravers. The results were unpleasant: Busoni found himself in debt by over 10,000 Marks (a considerably larger sum at that time than now), and Harmonie began a protracted legal tussle with him.

1912 As a result the vocal score was not ready in time for the critics and public at the first performance in May.* The publisher Cassirer, however, brought out a luxurious edition of the libretto illustrated by Karl Walser's designs (some of them hand-coloured) in an edition limited to 200 copies, signed by both composer and designer. In August, Busoni completed the *Brautwahl Suite* and produced a shortened version of the opera for the second production (Mannheim, 1913).

The important point that emerges from this chronology is the position *Die Brautwahl* is seen to occupy in Busoni's *oeuvre*. It constitutes a link between the music before and after the writing of the *New Aesthetic*: some of the score comes closer to the Piano Concerto in idiom, some is related to the more forward-looking of the Elegies. The opera thus serves as a stylistic compendium of Busoni's development between 1902 and 1909. As Dent wrote after the first performance: 'Those strange experiments in melody and tonality which puzzled the readers of the "Elegies" contributed largely to the imaginative effect of the whole.'[7] And Bernard van Dieren (who, like Dent, travelled to Hamburg for the world première) went so far as to claim: 'When something perplexing is found in the more portentous of his shorter compositions, it can nearly always be elucidated by reference to the conversational treatment of comparable material in "Die Brautwahl".'[8] Yet in the transition from short

* The world première took place not on 12 May, as cited by Dent and others, but on Saturday, 13 May.

score to full score almost nothing was altered, despite the fact that the three years between the completion of the two brought a radical development in Busoni's style; while he was penning the almost atonal passages of the first Sonatina he was still struggling to finish a work in a style he had already abandoned. This consideration, together with the crippling financial loss involved in the preparations for the first performance (not to mention the enormous amount of time required for the completion of such a score) indicates the grim determination with which Busoni, perhaps still slightly ashamed of his failure to finish *Sigune*, brought his first opera into the world.

He was adamant that the score of the opera should be carefully worked out, that there should be no empty moments. 'There is invention in every bar and that is how it should be, right to the end', he wrote after sketching the opening scene[9], and he reiterated this ideal the following summer, speaking of his 'steadfast conviction that every bar must have something to say.'[10] Naturally he had little use for leitmotiv technique and therefore he sought other ways of achieving structural unity. The guiding principle he evolved—and one which became exemplary for many twentieth-century composers—was that of breaking up the dramatic action into sections which could be set to music in quasi-symphonic forms. A second principle, analagous to Hoffmann's system of quoting from already extant material, is that of working all manner of 'extraneous' music into the score. Busoni's quotations have two opposing effects on the music: such numbers as the Rossini march and the German dance by Mozart at the beginning of the opera accurately specify the period in which the piece plays; the use of synagogal chant, plainsong and German folk-dance imposes upon these Biedermeier surroundings a certain sense of timelessness. The Serapiontic principle is thus applied to the music. As a third means of diversifying the score, Busoni devised separate styles of vocal writing for each character, which remain unique to them throughout the piece:

> For the diction and inflexion I have taken it into my head not only that each character should have his own way of talking but also that this should be modified according to the feeling or temperament of the moment; thus scope is given for meaningful melody.[11]

According to Busoni's vocal disposition of the roles, we have three tenors (Lehsen, Thusman and Bensch), two baritones (Leonhard and Voswinkel) and one bass (Manasse). The young hero has, of course, to be a lyric tenor, but the quasi-heroic fermatas and exposed high notes in his part reflect a certain degree of caricature on Busoni's (and Hoffmann's) part. Thusman's multi-coloured role is a gift for a talented *tenor buffo*, while the young Baron Bensch has little to say for himself, being always overshadowed by his uncle. Voswinkel and Leonhard are cast in the most natural register of the male voice, the former in order to portray his commonness, the latter to emphasize his function as the true hero of the drama. Manasses's *basso profondo* drones through the opera with a grotesque blend of malevolence and sarcastic humour. From his earliest years, Busoni had always preferred the mezzo-soprano and baritone voices to all others, for he suffered a lifelong phobia for primadonnas and tenors. The role of Albertine was therefore conceived for a mezzo-soprano, but in fact the tessitura of the part is entirely that of a soprano. The radiant voice of the young Elisabeth Schumann graced the first production.

A few months before completing the opera, Busoni wrote to H. W. Draber about the problems of writing stylishly and credibly for voices:

> Only Mozart and Verdi have up to now found the true 'Cadenzare' of their texts.—It incorporates many factors: mood, tempo, pitch, chiming in with a response, the support, discrete falling back or complete silence of the orchestra, changing the subject of the conversation, expressing a parenthesis and what know I. 'Falstaff' is the absolute model collection of such things. I can think of hundreds of examples. In 'Der Rosenkavalier' I found not a single one.[12]

Act I part 1 opens with a lively introduction, reminiscent of the style of the *Comedy Overture*. Oily chromaticisms and bizarre orchestral colours point to the more sinister aspects of what is to come. The scene that follows is built in the form of a suite:

1. *Alla marcia* (Rossini, 'Moses' March)
2. Lied (in praise of tobacco)
3. *Tempo di menuetto vivo* (Mozart, German Dances, K. 600)
4. Duet-Lied (Fouqué's poem; love-duet)
5. *Allegretto quasi marziale* (reprise of No. 1).

The most substantial movement, the love-duet, introduces us to two themes which occur frequently:

Ex. 61

Ex. 62

The two lovers sing in fresh, intense and gently exaggerated tones; Voswinkel, on the other hand, while struggling to give the impression of a man of the world, often lapses into a more vulgar style, betraying the *parvenu* in him. This is particularly noticeable in his extended Lied which concludes with a patronizing imitation of American negro music, in an effort to pay tribute to the plantation workers who have made his cigar so pleasurable.

The scene continues with the appearance of Leonhard. His monologue, a free fantasia in alternating slower and faster tempi, illustrates the amalgam of humour, seriousness and magnetic power in his personality. The scene changes. (Evidently Busoni intended a magic transformation here, in which 'a Rathaus is built out of tents'.) The orchestration of the bridging scherzo is particularly vivid; three piccolos emit Berliozian shrieks and there is a long trill for muted violins which we meet again at the close of the Sarabande in *Doktor Faust*.

Thusman's entrance together with the ensuing vision of Albertine and finale, is built in the form of Scherzo, Adagio and Allegro. The 'Erscheinung' itself is an ostinato, dominated by eleven gong-strokes and underpinned by a pedal A throughout. The whole-tone motif (cf. Ex. 55) runs through the entire scene, its symmetrical harmonies suggesting some cabbalistic mystery too remote for Thusman to grasp:

Ex 63

The effect of the 'Erscheinung' music, even in the abbreviated form in which we hear it in the opera, is overpowering; the strokes of the gong resonate through the scene with an unearthly power. Earlier, the love-duet of Albertine and Edmund already had an overdimensional, impressionistic effect in relation to its surroundings. This further ascent into mystic realms, stage-managed by Leonhard for the benefit of the uncomprehending Thusman, presents a sharper contrast to the well-ordered world in which the opera otherwise seems to play. Nearly every scene features such a 'Serapiontic' moment.

One particular theme is often associated with Thusman:

Ex. 64

He sings with a mixture of naïvety and pedantry, his grotesquely high-pitched voice often cracking into falsetto at moments of particular stress.

Act I part 2 The orchestral introduction, which Busoni based entirely on old Jewish melodies, paints a dark picture of Manasse. The rest of the scene is written in the form of a gigantic brightly-coloured scherzo, the only relief from this uninterruptedly fast and piquant invention coming in Leonhard's ballad, 'The gruesome history of Lippold the Jew-coiner'. This is one of the most striking passages: a recitative-like introduction sets the scene during which Manasse becomes restless, calling 'leave the dead in peace'; but Leonhard goes on to describe the magic book which Lippold used 'to outdo his lord with hellish tricks'. Even as he sings, the orchestra begins to flicker with light, brilliantly depicting the flames licking round the stake:

Ex. 65

The ensuing scene of magic, from which Thusman flees, uses music from the fourth *Scène de Ballet* (composed in 1892) and from the introduction to the opera, building it into an uproarious climax. Throughout these long scenes there are countless points of subtle thematic development, splendid ensembles and virtuoso examples of the art of orchestration. In Dent's opinion: 'His score is remarkable not for the wonderful instruments he uses, but for the wonderful things he makes the ordinary instruments do.'[13]

Act II part 1 The introduction depicts Thusman's further adventures in the night of the equinox, with a noisy *Spuk- und Wirbel-Walzer* which is practically athematic, and a distant Prussian march (*quasi marcia brandenburghese* noted Busoni in his libretto) which suggests the ensuing day-break, perhaps the arrival of the police to restore law and order (Ex. 66).

Ex. 66

The curtain rises and we hear a gentle *aubade* as Voswinkel muses on his successes. Thusman's ensuing narrative, 'The unlikely disclosures of privy council secretary Thusman', is in three sections: March—Waltz—March. As he recounts his hair-raising experiences the music of the introduction returns, now including Albertine's theme (Ex. 61). Finally, in horrified tones, he describes how he awoke to find himself in the saddle of the great statue of the Kurfürst (return of the Prussian march)—a delightful and characterful caprice.

Voswinkel begins to upbraid his future son-in-law in vehement but common tones (the impotent scorn of the *nouveau riche* merchant is close to that of Faninal in *Der Rosenkavalier*). He is interrupted by three menacing knocks at the door. Manasse enters to the accompaniment of a sinister version of one of his synagogal themes. As the conversation turns to his Austrian nephew, Benjamin von Bensch, we hear appropriate strains of the Kaiser Hymn coloured by a distinctly Oriental bass-line:

Ex. 67

Manasse departs and there is a brief reconciliation duet for the two old school friends (still to the music of the *Wirbel-Walzer*, for Thusman is not quite himself yet), after which the curtain falls.

Act II part 2 This is the most complex scene of the score. It opens peacefully with an extended duet for the two lovers: Albertine plays a gentle neo-baroque invention on her harpsichord, then sings the poem by Fouqué, first heard in Act I. Sweet reminiscence of their first meeting reintroduces the Rossini march which opened the opera and their growing enthusiasm is expressed in a cool sequence of chords in fourths, rising to an intense but unsentimental moment:

Ex. 68

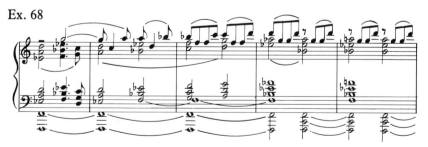

when, with a falsetto yelp, Thusman appears.

There are angry words between Thusman and Albertine; Lehsen brandishes his paintbrush, smearing a green stain over Thusman's features—'The privy council secretary flies into a rage and becomes green in the face'.[14] Voswinkel enters and his amazement at Thusman's 'eccentric complexion' turns to rage as the situation becomes clear to him. Leonhard's arrival makes up a quintet which in turn is interrupted by the entrance of Manasse and his repulsive nephew. Now Leonhard assumes the role of dancing master and whips up another ferocious waltz. At its height, Manasse launches into his curse, 'like a furious beast, but not without a certain majesty'. It is a formidable outburst and, as an extra fire and brimstone gesture, his cry is echoed by an off-stage chorus.

After 'Jewish fury' comes 'Christian consolation' and the scene ends with a peaceful waltz-coda.

Act III part 1 Dent describes the lengthy off-stage cornet solo with which this scene opens as a dissertation on old-fashioned German romanticism. Its relevance to the action may indeed seem abstruse, but it is Busoni's indirect way of expressing the loneliness of the scene which follows, inspired no doubt by the distant solo horn which opens the final scene of Verdi's *Falstaff* and so tellingly evokes the solitariness of Windsor Forest by moonlight.

Thusman has become an outcast. However, he does find some company to console him—his new green brothers, the frogs. Note-clusters lovingly depict the frogspawn:

Ex. 69

And, as Thusman staggers to the edge of the pond, his mind bent on suicide, his frog-like hops are cannily depicted by the bassoons:

Ex. 70

Leonhard appears, and his vision motif is now transformed into a funeral march. As the infernal green paint is washed away, the motif makes another mysterious appearance. Thusman expresses his joy in a polacca and here the vision motif is even drawn into the dance. Busoni has a surprise in store: a sizeable quotation from his *Comedy Overture*, but with the original phrases of four bars condensed to three. The scene, perhaps the best proportioned and certainly one of the most inventive in the opera, closes as it opened with distant post-horn fanfares.

Act III part 2 This was originally conceived in two sections and, for purposes of analysis, this division is best retained.

Section one deals with the lengthy dialogue between Voswinkel and Leonhard, in which is born the idea of the caskets. The whole scene is underlined by a *moto perpetuo* (marked *Stürmisch und zornig*), fragments of which return at the end of each paragraph of the discussion. The opening virtuoso figure for the violins, perhaps depicting the Kommissionsrat's rage:

Ex. 71

is soon joined by a more jaunty figure:

Ex. 72

The curtain rises on Voswinkel's choleric monologue. Leonhard outlines 'The Three Dangers' in the form of a set of variations, or rather quasi-variations, each of which brings back small motifs associated with the figures mentioned—Lehsen and his picture, Thusman and the frogs, Manasse and his curse of bankruptcy. In an agitated coda Leonhard hastily settles the matter of the caskets.

Section two brings the strongest music in the entire opera. As Busoni himself remarked, the situation at this point is no longer comic and he rose to the challenge of this culminating scene with rare eloquence. The score is built on a rhythmic ostinato:

over which is superimposed an *agitato* version of one of the vision motifs (Ex. 55) and a new motif which Busoni borrowed from Carissimi's oratorio, *Jephtha*:

Ex. 73

Carissimi

Heu, ____ heu mi – hi fi – lia __ me - a!

'Her situation,' he wrote, '(that of a daughter betrayed and sold by her father) is to an extent parallel.'[15] The following extract, Albertine's first entry, combines all these various elements:

Ex. 74

She sinks slowly into a trance (muted trumpets play the Jephtha motif over fluttering triad figures) and Leonhard appears. In an extended cantilena he reveals his true identity to her. 'As for Edmund', he continues, 'behold, here stands his future!' In the church vision which now appears, Busoni reaches the cathartic moment of the opera, an awe-inspiring superimposition of sonorities—off-stage chorus, organ and a complex, flickering orchestral texture— over which towers the triumphant voice of the goldsmith. Just as the final *Cantico* of the Piano Concerto follows the noisy vulgarity of the tarantella, we are plunged abruptly from boy-meets-girl domesticity into the depths of a great Gothic mystery. The music is also finer than the *Aladdin* chorus, with a subtler harmonic palette, and its irresistible forward drive (matched on stage by a steady crescendo of light) results in a structure of considerable power, of lofty sensuousness. The musical materials are simple in the extreme: Albertine's theme (Ex. 61) is answered by phrases of plainchant; parallel organum-like chordal blocks are surrounded in the orchestra by impression-istic halos of overtones, creating even in a dry theatre acoustic the effect of the wide-open spaces of an echoing cathedral. 'One can find all my youthful recollections of Catholic atmosphere here,' wrote Busoni.[16] The music of this vision dwarfs the entire opera.

Epilogue The scene is divided into two parts: 'Cheerful' and 'Mystical'.

Cheerful
- Prelude
- Arrival of the suitors (first)
- (second)
- (third)
- The father's speech (to I.II.III.)
- Agreement (Quartet—also conclusion of the Prelude)
- Terzet of the suitors

[Entrance of Albertine]

Mystical
- Ceremony of the opening of the caskets
- The three caskets (first)
- (second)
- (third)
- Quartet-scherzo for the remaining characters ('all has turned out for the best')
- Leonhard carries Edmund off to Rome.[17]

The opening of the caskets takes the form of a theme and three variations. 'I myself only noticed it subsequently and found it the correct reaction', wrote Busoni. 'Naturally: variations in the fantastic sense.'[18]

In Busoni's mature works one often finds a somewhat disconcerting freedom in the use of traditional nomenclature, a breaking away from slavish appli-cation of established forms while nevertheless retaining their names. He was thereby putting views expressed in the *New Aesthetic* into practice. In a letter to Robert Freund he wrote: '*I am a worshipper of Form!!* . . . but I reject *traditional* and *unalterable* forms and feel that every idea, every motif, every individual thing demands a form related to that idea, to that motif, to that thing.'[19] Thus, paradox as it may appear, Busoni here writes 'variations' that are thematically unrelated. It is this kind of musical 'chess playing' which places his work beyond the reach of traditional academic analysis.

After the elevated music with which Act III came to an end, the Epilogue runs the risk of bathos, particularly in the comic terzet of the suitors. The most imaginative passage is the beginning of the casket ceremony, an elaborate orchestral interlude with curiously remote harmonies and delicate shades of chiaroscuro orchestration (cor anglais, bass clarinet and celesta all playing leading roles). Once again Busoni uses an invisible chorus to add to the mystery of the proceedings, although admittedly there is a law of diminishing returns in such an effect. Nevertheless, when Edmund opens the third casket, the six-part off-stage chorus, joined later by the voices of the two lovers, presents a fine idyllic picture, also bringing the beautiful music of the love scene (Ex. 68), previously so rudely interrupted, to its rightful conclusion. The final quartet and envoi return to the *buffo* spirit of the opening of the scene and the score closes with a musical depiction of convulsive laughter.

In the theatre, where its effect on first hearing is somewhat abstruse and where many of the subtleties of Busoni's fine score are inevitably lost, *Die Brautwahl* has never been truly accepted. It is an opera which becomes more endearing the more one hears it. In Hamburg it received a highly prestigious world première which drew critics and musicians from all over Germany (and indeed from further afield as well). Yet the reception was cool and it ran for only four performances. The general impression was of a work for connoisseurs, lacking that streak of crudity which, frankly, makes for effective music-theatre. Max Marschalk put the problem in a nutshell: 'His best work is not strong, but fine and artistic. But for the stage, only strength will do!'[20] One of the Hamburg critics, although personally very impressed by the work, expanded on this problem more wittily:

> . . . and this is supposed to be an Italian? Where are the arias, where are the melodies rolled in schmalz and butter which an Italian opera composer is surely bound by an unwritten rule to write? Is there no opera-police to remind Herr Busoni of his obligations to his fatherland under this law?[21]

Of course, the enormous length of the opera was also, justifiably, a cause for displeasure. Paul Bekker took exception to the almost uninterrupted scherzando of the score: '. . . [the music] laughs ceaselessly in order to stimulate us to laugh.'[22] Bernard van Dieren explains:

> The intimacy of detail . . . becomes in its totality responsible for dimensions that must frighten any producer, and test even the patience of a sympathetic audience . . . It is a score to be savoured bar by bar, but . . . with all its *leggierezza*, it shows enough of the Beethovenian *patte du lion* to become somewhat of a trial to any but the most determined enthusiasts.[23]

Yet, van Dieren writes, Busoni had considered calling the work an operetta!

For the second production, a year later in Mannheim, Busoni produced a new and abbreviated version of the score. The cut material alone would amount to a very respectable short opera, he grumbled, yet there was no doubt that the work benefited from such severe pruning. Even now it never really caught the public's imagination and, up to the time of writing, the opera has enjoyed only a very small number of stage productions. Two reasons for this neglect must be held to Busoni's account: the impossibility of translating a highly characteristic literary work into theatrical terms without completely re-thinking it for its new medium, and the over-demanding role to be played by an audience in such a piece.

Busoni prefaces his score with a quotation from Tieck's *Gestiefelte Kater*: 'If you are to take pleasure in this, you must lay aside all your so-called education and become children again, so as to enjoy all in a childlike spirit.' And in his *New Aesthetic* Busoni had also stated that half the effort required for the comprehension of a work of art must come from the public. Busoni seems to be expecting too much: every one of his stage works departs radically from operatic convention in one direction or another—that in itself is only laud-able—but he never seems to have realized the futility of wishing to 'pro-gramme' the theatre audience; he always seems to have expected a public just as well-read and just as quick of understanding as himself. Only in *Doktor Faust* did he hit upon a theatrical language that speaks to all.

Dent places *Die Brautwahl* alongside such pieces as *Euryanthe* or *The Trojans* as a work that will always find its admirers on account of the beauties of the score, even if it never wins a regular place in the repertoire. And Busoni, viewing the opera from a perspective of ten years, later asked: 'Does my "Brautwahl" with its 700 pages of full score achieve more than "Figaro" with its six accompanying wind instruments?'[24]

The financial fracas surrounding the publication of *Die Brautwahl* gave rise to a host of unpleasant occurrences in which H. W. Draber took most of the dealings with lawyers into his own hands and the banker Curt Sobernheim, a close friend of Busoni's, struggled in vain to achieve a satisfactory settlement. However, the scandal had one positive outcome: the publication of an orchestral suite from the opera. Even if the original purpose of the *Brautwahl Suite* was nothing more than an attempt to make good some of the financial loss incurred, Busoni carried out the project with inspiration and produced one of his most splendid works, and an ideal companion piece to the *Turandot Suite*.

Rather than simply selecting a few favourite passages from the opera, Busoni singled out five aspects of the score—ghostly, lyric, mystic, Hebrew and cheerful—and devoted to each of these a self-contained movement. The ghostly music begins with Leonhard's transformation scene in Act I part 1, then jumps to the frantic dance at the end of Act II part 2. Finally, we hear a portion of Thusman's *Wirbel-Walzer*, vanishing into thin air. The lyric music follows at once and is devoted entirely to the two love scenes, introducing an extended *scène d'amour*, in many ways comparable to that of Berlioz in *Roméo et Juliette*—not, however, in calour; Hoffmann's Prussian lovers lack the intense passion of Shakespeare's young Italians. The third movement stands alone, devoted to mystical happenings. It opens with music from the casket scene followed by the 'Erscheinung', and closes with Leonhard's music of consolation at the end of Act II part 2. It is, in effect, a musical portrait of the goldsmith. The Hebrew music is devoted correspondingly to Manasse. We hear the introduction to Act I part 2, an extended version of 'The Ballad of Lippold the Jew-coiner', and finally a passage from his curse. The cheerful music follows without a break, describing a circle around the whole opera. It opens with the prelude to Act I part 1, jumps to the scene of conjuring in the wine cellar and closes with the last bars of the Epilogue.

Where necessary, vocal lines have been transferred to orchestral instruments, otherwise we hear the score exactly as it is in the opera. Hence, in the Suite, one can concentrate undividedly on the orchestral score and observe how lovingly—and ingeniously—it is written. The music takes its place in the concert hall as naturally as if it had been conceived for it and shows that Busoni's score is effectively complete without the visual element, even without the vocal element. The imagination can be stimulated by the music in just the same way as by Hoffmann's prose; it seems to be 'absolute music'. This may be a rare compliment to Busoni's imaginative powers, but it was the damnation of the opera.

Another sad tale of *Die Brautwahl* remains to be told. In February 1923 Busoni made a new version of 'The Ballad of Lippold the Jew-coiner' for concert use, intending it as a companion piece to his newly composed 'Zigeunerlied'. The vision of the lonely Wandering Jew still haunted him. He wrote a new introductory recitative which includes the following lines:

Two hundred and fifty years later
the story is taken up once more
in the light-hearted play of the Brautwahl.
The old man turns up once again:
his activities expand in Berlin today
as *maître de finances*,
procurer and forger,
as blustering monster—

Busoni was simply implying a continuation of the ageless fairy-tale into modern times. Unfortunately Wilhelm Guttmann, the baritone for whom the piece was written, viewed the matter more prosaically and declared that the text was anti-Semitic. Certainly, for anyone unacquainted with the composer's private world of myth and make-believe, it appears so. Guttmann resolutely refused to sing the ballad, and it remains to this day unpublished and unperformed.

'Strano mondo', wrote Busoni to Dent, 'sorprendente mentalità. Oremus.'[25]*

---

* 'Strange world, surprising mentality. Let us pray.'

VII

Epitaphs

Fantasia after J. S. Bach [for piano]. *Dedicated*: 'Alla memoria di mio padre Ferdinando Busoni, morto il 12 Maggio 1909.' *Composed*: June 1909. *First performance*: 16.10.1909. Bechstein Hall, London. Soloist: Busoni. *Published*: Leipzig, 1909. EB 3054. Later incorporated into the Bach-Busoni Edition, Vol. IV. *MS*: Deutsche Staatsbibliothek, Berlin. First four pages missing. *Duration*: 9 minutes.

Berceuse élégiaque [First Elegy for orchestra], op.42. The man's cradle-song at his mother's bier. Poésie for sixfold muted string quartet, three flutes, one oboe, three clarinets, four horns, gong, harp and celesta. In Memoriam Anna Busoni, neé Weiss,† 3.Oct.MCMIX. *Composed*: October 1909. *First performance*: 21.2.1911. Carnegie Hall, New York. New York Philharmonic Orchestra, conducted by Gustav Mahler. *Published*: Leipzig, 1910. PB 2147. *MS*: 19pp., 36×27cm. Deutsche Staatsbibliothek, Berlin. *Instrumentation*: 3–1–3(Bcl.)—0; 4–0–0–0; Perc.; Harp: Celesta; Str.(6–0–6–6–6). *Arrangements*: (1) for two pianos (Egon Petri) ca. 1910. Unpublished. MS. Property of Mr Daniell Revenaugh; (2) for chamber ensemble (Erwin Stein, incorrectly ascribed to Schoenberg) ca. 1922. Instrumentation: fl., cl., harmonium, pfte., 2 vn., vla., vc., cb. Published Wiesbaden, 1965. PB 3894. Plate number Wb. 666. MS: Schoenberg Institute, Los Angeles. *Duration*: 8 minutes.

Ferdinando Busoni died in May 1909 after protracted illness. Early in the following month, in the space of three days, his son composed the Fantasia after J. S. Bach in his memory (the original title was Fantasia on motifs by J. S. Bach), immediately after the 'Berceuse' for piano. Stylistically the two pieces could scarcely be less alike. The 'Berceuse' is entirely an original work; the Fantasia introduces us to a new genre of composition, the *Nachdichtung*. This almost untranslatable term, meaning neither paraphrase nor transcription, implies a reconstruction of an original text in another language or style. As with the word elegy, it is noteworthy that Busoni chooses a literary term for his work; it points to the poet in him as well as the bibliophile.

Although the Fantasia makes use of three separate organ pieces of Bach, almost half the work is original material. The Bachian elements are transformed in much the same way as the original themes in a Lisztian operatic fantasy. There is therefore ample justification in considering the Fantasia a composition in its own right.

It opens with a distant murmur of F minor, the tonic gently ringing out as

the foundation for steadily rising figuration. Fragments of a chorale theme
emerge and disappear. The bass falls to D flat and the rising waves of
semiquavers slowly penetrate to the higher registers of the piano, establishing
pure and luminous A flat major. In this short prelude the progressions of the
whole piece, both emotional and tonal, from profound grief to reconciliation,
from F minor to A flat major, are briefly exposed.

In the ensuing music:

Ex. 75

appear the three repeated notes which we have already identified, in the
Second Violin Sonata, as a 'death motif'. A cadenza, *non brillante*, represents
the culmination of this restrained outburst. The music comes almost to a halt:
there is a tolling of bells, based on the death motif, then silence.

The Bach chorale setting, 'Christ, du bist der helle Tag' follows, with full
organ-like sonority, the sigh of the death motif interrupting each line:

Ex. 76

Busoni unfolds the opening variations on this chorale from the Chorale
Partita BWV 766. His own contributions are restricted to editorial marks of
phrasing and expression, occasional added octave doublings and even less
frequent alteration of notes. The first variation is marked *parlando*.* Some

---

* Note for performers. Busoni suggested scoring this austere variation for cor anglais
and bass-clarinet: perhaps a useful indication of the tone colours the pianist should
seek.

years later Busoni vividly described this music, with its sparse second voice, 'as if stuttering and interrupted by sighs, in the language of a soul begging for consolation.'[1]

Busoni now interpolates a free adaptation of the Fughetta on 'Gottes Sohn ist kommen' (better known as 'In dulci jubilo') BWV 708, from the Kirnberger collection of chorale settings. Bach's twenty-two bars are amplified to forty and although the material used is largely original, Busoni has dismantled the entire fughetta and reassembled it in a totally different way. (A detailed comparison of the two versions makes a fascinating compositional study.) The introduction of this more soothing chorale brings another distant memory of the Second Violin Sonata:

The almost exultant *ff* climax of Busoni's fugal interlude breaks off and sinks through A minor back to F minor. There follows an ingenious transcription of the last variation of BWV 766 in which independent material is progressively introduced until, near the close, a modulation to A flat major leads to the work's sonorous climax. An imperceptible transition is effected to the Chorale Prelude 'Lob sei dem allmächtigen Gott' BWV 602, from the *Orgelbüchlein*, enhanced by multiple octave doublings and transposed. Once again, the chorale melody is reminiscent of 'Wie wohl ist mir':

Ex. 79

A brief return to a phrase from 'Christ, du bist der helle Tag' brings a reminder of former grief, and the tears of Ex. 75 flow once more. Finally, in a passage marked *riconciliato* (reconciled), bells ring out, enveloping a phrase from BWV 766 in F major arpeggios. *PAX EI!* reads an inscription over the music. In the last two bars the death motif makes a last appearance, peacefully in F major and then *mancando* (failing) in F minor.

One can image that in his last years Ferdinando Busoni had often accused his son of modernity. As a sign of respect for his father, Busoni returns to a style not far removed from that of his pre-elegiac works. For 1909 the Fantasia is, by any standards, old-fashioned and, compared with Busoni's other works of this nature, unusually open in its show of emotion. Busoni wrote to his mother, herself seriously ill: 'The piece dedicated to the memory of Babbo is written from the heart and all those who have heard it were moved to tears, without knowing of its intimate destination.'[2] His young friend Gino Tagliapietra was able to play the piece to the old lady in her home in Trieste shortly before her own death a few months later.

When Busoni himself played the Fantasia in public for the first time, in London, the critic of *The Times* grasped the function of the *Nachdichtung* at once (this was a recital devoted entirely to transcriptions, of Bach, Beethoven, Paganini and Liszt): 'The piano was used to interpret and translate, not merely to reproduce.'[3]

On 3 October 1909, Anna Busoni died. Despite regular but painful visits and more frequent letters, Ferruccio had kept his distance from his parents for many years. His marriage to Gerda had, for a time, strained his relationship with his mother to breaking point. Yet when she died it was as if some insufferable loss had occurred, as if a wound had been inflicted that could never heal. Some years later he wrote to his friend Arrigo Serato: 'I have never overcome the grief which I felt at the loss of my mother. I believe it will remain the most profound event in my life.'[4]

At the time of her death he was reading a collection of essays by Thomas de Quincey, the *Suspiria de Profundis*. This succession of 'dream visions' is a sequel to the famous *Confessions of an English Opium-eater*, writings of rarified and exotic beauty which give expression to moods of grief clearly identifiable with Busoni's own. On 4 October, as news arrived from Trieste of the old lady's death, he noted in his diary, 'Our Lady of Sighs'.* The reference is to the dream vision from the *Suspiria* entitled 'Levana and our ladies of Sorrow'.[5] Levana, de Quincey tells us, was 'the Roman goddess that performed for the new-born infant the earliest office of ennobling kindness'—the pagan goddess of childbirth. In his opium-inspired dreams the author had seen Levana. She was accompanied, he tells us, by three sisters, the ladies of Sorrow, for 'Levana often communes with the powers that shake man's heart; therefore it is that she dotes upon grief'. It was the second of these sisters, Mater Suspiriorum, Our Lady of Sighs, who became Busoni's muse in his bereavement. She gave vent to her grief only in muted tones: 'Murmur she may, but it is in her sleep. Whisper she may, but it is to herself in the twilight. Mutter she does at times, but it is in solitary places that are desolate as she is desolate, in ruined cities.' And she was the comforter of the outcast, of the wanderer, the visitor of every woman 'sitting in darkness, without love to shelter her head, or hope to illumine her solitude'. 'Finiteness much harder to determine than infiniteness', wrote Busoni in his diary that same day. His thoughts echoed the profound conclusion of de Quincey's meditations on birth and death: 'Death we can face, but knowing as some of us do what is human life, which of us is it that without shuddering could (if consciously we were summoned) face the hour of birth?'

* in English.

Apart from de Quincey's essay there was another literary influence on the *Berceuse élégiaque*, that of Oehlenschlaeger's *Aladdin*. While he was writing the play, the poet's own mother had died. He gave form to his grief in a touching and eloquent scene, actually one of his most important additions to the original *1001 Nights* story. Aladdin is driven virtually mad at the news of his mother's death, coming as it does in the midst of his other great misfortunes. Sitting in pathetic isolation on his mother's grave, he makes as if to rock her in a cradle and intones a lullaby of such poignancy that even the stoic Danish language seems moved:

> Visselulle nu Barnlil!
> Sov nu sødt og sov nu længe!
> Skjøndt din Vugge stander stil,
> Uden dun og uden Gænge.

> Sleep my baby, sleep in peace,
> do not let yourself be woken,
> though your cover has no fleece
> and the rockers long were broken.[6]

Inspired by these texts, Busoni seems to have fallen into a kind of pre-Raphaelite trance, turning his mind back to the little piece which he had written earlier that same year. As he recalled:

> . . . my spirits returned to the strange mood of the Berceuse; I took up the composition again, penetrated deeper into it and conceived the extended orchestral arrangement of the little work. In the intervals between some London concerts I was compelled to write the score, frequently working until deep into the night, in order to free my mind of it.[7]

For the first twenty bars of his new orchestral version, Busoni follows the text of the 'Berceuse' for piano. The left-hand rocking octaves are divided between basses, cellos and violas (all muted) and the main beats of the bar are lightly marked by the harp. Thus an intangible surging movement is formed (Ex. 80).

The opening right-hand motif of the piano version, a rising minor third, is orchestrated in veiled colours: each note has a different timbre, each is doubled by two or three wind instruments so that no single tone colour stands out.

Ex. 80

These are the half-shades in which Our Lady of Sighs 'whispers to herself in the twilight'.

Ex. 81

Busoni then repeats the opening in a new setting. Individual colours begin to emerge; the theme is given to a solo oboe (later joined by two flutes) and is newly harmonized with a descending series of seventh chords sustained in the lower strings. The rocking rhythm of the opening is maintained by clarinet and bass-clarinet, forming a pre-echo of the similarly elegiac opening of Berg's Violin Concerto (Exx. 82 and 83).

Ex. 82

Ex. 83

It would appear that this remarkable parallel has been overlooked by Berg scholars. There is little doubt that Berg knew the *Berceuse élégiaque*—probably also the version for chamber ensemble discussed at the end of this chapter—and it may well have been on his mind while writing his concerto 'to the memory of an angel'.

The blur of bitonality of the 'Berceuse' for piano (see Ex. 59) is slowed down to half tempo in the *Berceuse élégiaque* and out of the former combination of F major and A flat minor triads now emerges a melody. It cannot stray from its parent keys and thus its effect is static and melancholy:

Ex. 84

A third reprise of the main theme follows, the most complex section of the score, the perpetual rocking rhythm intensified by a rising and falling triplet figure in the violas. The theme reaches its highest tessitura and widest-flung harmonies, in turn provoking the triplet figure to a more dramatic variant. For a moment the mood is agonized, then the three flutes climb chromatically in triads. It is a gesture comparable to the moment of death in Strauss' tone poem

Death and Transfiguration. Here all remains veiled and remote, there is none of the sick-room realism of the Strauss, but perhaps the upward motion of the flutes symbolizes the departure of a soul from a body.

The oscillating bitonal music returns, now in more disjointed form; celesta and harp chords overlap* in combinations of A major with C minor, E major with G minor, while isolated fragments of melody are again extracted from the notes of this harmony. In the most impassioned phrase of the piece, the F of B flat minor and the F sharp of D major are stretched out into a leap of an augmented octave:

Ex. 85

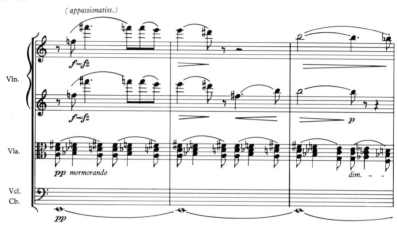

Finally the wave motion from the close of the 'Berceuse' begins to spread out, the harmonies, based on the rising minor third of the opening melody, become smoother and more static. The bass line, swinging at first in semitones, opens out into whole tones, then thirds, finally fourths and fifths. At the same time the harmonies in the upper strings also begin to oscillate, until the entire spectrum is filled out. Solo wind instruments introduce brief reminiscences of the few slight melodic motifs of the piece; the rising minor third figure sounds for the last time, high in flutes and clarinets, like a plaintive cry. The waves in the strings subside. In the closing bars a skeleton of the berceuse-rhythm is

* Note for performers. Confusion arises in the *Berceuse élégiaque* about the notation of the harp and celesta parts. The harp harmonics are notated as they sound, contrary to standard practice, and Busoni has indicated this fact in the score. However, the celesta part is also notated *at sounding pitch*, calling for some low notes only available on German (Schiedmayer) celestas. This octave transposition makes a radical difference to the tone colour of many passages.

Furthermore, it should be noted that the last bars call for a gong and not a tamtam, as is usually used. Busoni knew the difference between these intruments very well, indeed he possessed his own 'splendid' Chinese gong (as he wrote in a letter to a Swiss bell-foundry, 30.5.1919). With the correct instrument, the effect of a muffled and distant funeral bell is unforgettable.

divided between harp and celesta; a gong, the only percussion in the score, strikes softly three times—an echo of the death motif.

The *Berceuse élégiaque* is half as long again as the original 'Berceuse'. Their relationship is that of a finished painting to a crayon sketch—even if the outcome, in the spirit of the Elegies, is a watercolour. Busoni seems to have conjured up with the greatest precision the sound fantasy world suggested by his reading of de Quincey. Master of orchestration that he was, he never again quite achieved the refined *chiaroscuro* of this work. Noteworthy is the fact that each separate instrument is listed in the title. The thirty-eight players build layers of sound like the finest of tissues; the most sensitive ensemble playing is demanded, for every single note has its exact place in the sound-picture.

Where the Fantasia after J. S. Bach was written partly out of a sense of respect and filial piety, the *Berceuse élégiaque* is a composition of spontaneous intensity; the compulsive grasping and setting down of a vision. It is the closest Busoni ever came to a precise account of a dream and, for that reason, it is his most perfect work. Had it been given to him to recount to us larger portions of his musical dream, he would probably have become the most significant composer of his age.

The *Berceuse élégiaque* was completed on 27 October 1909. So novel was the score that Busoni felt he could not dare to publish it without having first heard it, 'inasmuch as it contains a number of singular harmonic and instrumental combinations which have not yet been approved'.[8] For once in his life he undertook a menial task—he wrote out the orchestral parts—and on 1 November Henry Wood granted him half an hour's rehearsal time with the Queen's Hall Orchestra to try out the new work. Bernard van Dieren was present and recalls the bewilderment of even the admirers: '. . . there was a noticeable embarrassment on all sides at the strange, impressionistic sound'.[9] Yet Busoni was satisfied and the score was published the following year. When Oskar Fried played the work through with the Berlin Philharmonic in 1910, a similar scene of astonishment and disbelief occurred. Hugo Leichtentritt recorded that:

> Neither the conductor nor the players knew what to do with the strange piece which evoked the barely suppressed mirth of the orchestra and Fried's great embarrassment. Its polytonality, its collisions of major and minor triads, its strange enervated harmony, its symphony of sighs appeared altogether novel in 1910.[10]

Not until 1911 did the work receive its first performance. Gustav Mahler, impressed by the *Turandot Suite* which he had conducted the previous year, accepted it for one of his New York concerts. For 21 February 1911 he had planned a concert of Italian music. Apart from the *Berceuse élégiaque* the programme featured works by Sinigaglia, Martucci and Bossi (though pride of place went to Mendelssohn's 'Italian' Symphony!). Of Busoni's work, the critic of the *New York Times* wrote: 'It is a gruesome work in a modern composer's most modern manner. However, it was applauded and Mr Busoni, who sat in a box with Mr Toscanini, rose to bow his thanks.'[11] 'The piece is effective and I still almost believe that it will attain a sort of popularity', reported Busoni to Gerda,[12] as well as mentioning Toscanini's great admiration for the piece. (Some years later the maestro made a private recording of it with the NBC Symphony Orchestra.)

A few days later, the Italian programme was due to be repeated. Mahler was forced to cancel due to ill-health and Spiering, the orchestra's concert-master, took over the direction of the concert, except for Busoni's work, which was led by the composer himself. Mahler, a dying man, was never to conduct again. It is one of those curious quirks of fate that the birth of the *Berceuse élégiaque*, itself a meditation on birth and death, should be intimately connected with the death of a great composer.

By 1912 the Berlin public finally took the *Berceuse élégiaque* to its heart. On 19 January of that year it occupied the central position in a concert promoted by the Berlin Gesellschaft der Musikfreunde devoted entirely to Busoni's music. (It was flanked by Stock's orchestration of the *Fantasia Contrappuntistica* and by the Piano Concerto.) Writing in the journal *Pan* the following month, Busoni explained, 'in this piece . . . I succeeded for the first time in creating an individual sound and in dissolving the *form* into *feeling*'. He also launched an attack on those who had found in the work an imitation of Debussy: 'I feel myself to be at the beginning—and Debussy has reached his conclusion.'[13] More productive would have been a comparison with the late works of Fauré. His song-cycles *La Chanson d'Ève* and *Le jardin clos* date from around this time and are arguably his finest works, inhabiting a dream world closely related to Busoni's. Fauré declared his satisfaction with these late songs, allegedly, in having turned feeling into form.

Busoni's greatest strength had always been his Latin instinct for form; Fauré, throughout his career as a composer, had always been more successful in shorter works with finely differentiated flavours, notably piano music and songs. 'Form into feeling' or 'feeling into form'; both composers actually imply the same triumph of technique; each had, in his own way, at last achieved that elusive balance between form and feeling which makes a masterpiece.

One of those present at Busoni's Berlin concert in January 1912 was Schoenberg, who had recently left Vienna and settled in Berlin-Zehlendorf. The day after the concert he began to keep his so-called 'Berlin Diary' and he noted: 'Up to now I had not cared for Busoni's compositions. But I liked the "Berceuse" yesterday. Downright moving. Deeply felt.'[14]

When Josef Rufer produced a catalogue of Schoenberg's posthumous manuscripts in 1957, great interest was excited by his discovery of a transcription of the *Berceuse élégiaque* for nine instruments—flute, clarinet, harmonium, piano, string quartet and double bass. The ensemble is typical of the many transcriptions made for the Society for the Private Performance of Music which Schoenberg founded in Vienna in 1918. As Rufer mentioned in the catalogue, the MS was not in Schoenberg's hand, but it was tacitly assumed that it was nevertheless his work. The score was published in 1965 and has since been performed perhaps more frequently than the original version.

Schoenberg's transcriptions are unfailingly remarkable for their refinement and attention to detail, proof of his astounding ability to 'hear' a score and to recreate its sonorities with much smaller forces. Yet in this arrangement the original sound picture has been distorted or over-simplified too often. In the first bar, the low F of the harp, which in the original gently marks the pulse of the rhythm, is given to the double bass pizzicato; where the original note makes a subtle inflection, the transcription inevitably coarsens the effect, destroying the dream vision of the score before it has even unfolded. Disappointing too is the close, where no attempt has been made to depict Busoni's gong strokes. When Schoenberg wrote for harmonium he was always careful to indicate the registration, manner of attack and phrasing required; likewise his directions for piano pedalling are always unambiguous—in a Schoenberg score nothing is left to chance. Yet here the harmonium part is virtually bereft of performing instructions, while the first bar of the piano part bears the vague marking *con Pedale*. Hastiness could not have been to blame, for we know that Schoenberg always worked extremely rapidly—even an unfinished fragment such as the Three Little Pieces for chamber orchestra of 1910 is committed to paper with all necessary details.

It therefore comes as no great surprise to learn that this transcription is not the work of Schoenberg at all. Jutta Theurich, curator of the Busoni archive in East Berlin, has established its authorship beyond any reasonable doubt and set down her discoveries in a thesis on Busoni and Schoenberg (see Bibliography). In the Berlin archive she came across a letter from Hans Stuckenschmidt, written in 1923, asking permission to play the transcription in a concert he was organizing in Hamburg with Josef Rufer. He states that this version was made, at Schoenberg's suggestion, by Erwin Stein. Stein's transcription is certainly worthy of performance (nowadays one would probably substitute an electronic organ for the harmonium). However, for a true picture of one of the unique compositions of our century and of Busoni's undisputed masterpiece, there can be no substitute for the original.

VIII

New Beginnings

An die Jugend. A sequence of piano pieces. 1. 'Preludietto, Fughetta ed Esercizio'. *Dedicated*: to Josef Turczinski. *Composed*: June 1909. *Duration*: 5 minutes. 2. 'Preludio, Fuga e Fuga figurata' (study on J. S. Bach's *Well-tempered Clavier*). *Dedicated*: to Louis Theodor Gruenberg. *Composed*: July 1909. *Duration*: 4 minutes. 3. 'Giga, Bolero e Variazione' (Study after Mozart). *Dedicated*: to Leo Sirota. *Composed*: July 1909. *Duration*: 4 minutes. 4. 'Introduzione e Capriccio' (Paganinesco). *Dedicated*: to Louis Closson. *Composed*: August 1909; Epilogo. *Dedicated*: to Emile R. Blanchet. *Composed*: August 1909. *Duration*: 7 minutes. *First performance*: (except no. 1 and 'Epilogo'): 16.10.1909. Bechstein Hall, London. Soloist: Busoni. *Published*: Leipzig, 1909 by Jul. Heinr. Zimmermann. Z 4755–4757 and Z 4781. All four later republished by Breitkopf und Härtel, EB 4944–7. No. 2 later incorporated into the Bach–Busoni Edition, Vol. IV; no. 4 later incorporated into the *Klavierübung*, second edition, Book 10 (without 'Epilogo').

Sonatina [no. 1, for piano]. *Dedicated*: to Rudolf Ganz. *Composed*: August 1910. *First performance*: 30.9.1910. Musikhochschule, Basle. Soloist: Busoni. *Published*: Leipzig, 1910 by Jul. Heinr. Zimmermann. Z 4951. Later republished by Breitkopf und Härtel, EB 4948. *MS*: 15pp., 35×27cm. Deutsche Staatsbibliothek, Berlin. *Duration*: 10 minutes.

1909 was a year of intense creative activity for Busoni. After the New Year's gesture of the 'Nuit de Noël' he had, as usual, to wait until the end of the concert season before he could devote himself uninterruptedly to composition. The summer and autumn then brought forth:

1. 'Berceuse' for piano (5 June)
2. Fantasia after J. S. Bach (8 June)
3. 'Preludietto, Fughetta ed Esercizio' (end of June)
4. 'Preludio, Fuga e Fuga figurata' (3 July)
5. 'Giga, Bolero e Variazione' (13 July)
6. Concertante transcription of Schoenberg's Piano Piece, op. 11 no. 2 (26 July)
7. 'Introduzione e Capriccio' (early August)
8. 'Epilogo' (end of August)
9. *Berceuse élégiaque* (27 October).

He also wrote the new passages for the projected second edition of the *New*

Aesthetic, several transcriptions of Bach chorale preludes, the libretto for a musical comedy, *Frau Potiphar* (which remains unpublished), and around 100 pages of the full score of *Die Brautwahl*. His highly complicated 'Organic Piano Notation' also dates from the summer of 1909 (the MS sketches bear the date 25 September).

In the last week of July, one day before the Schoenberg transcription was made, Louis Blériot became the first man to fly across the English Channel. It truly seemed that mankind would now begin to climb heavenwards. That might even dissuade a few people from spending their precious hours practising scales and arpeggios; as Busoni remarked jestingly, 'it is to be hoped that the younger generation will be diverted from piano playing through this new (flight-)path'.[1] Apart from the two pieces marking his personal bereavements, all his music that year was directed emphatically towards the younger generation. *An die Jugend*, which was originally visualized as an extended series of piano pieces, consists of four volumes and an epilogue, compiled from transcribed and original material.

Volume 1: 'Preludietto, Fughetta ed Escercizio' The first volume of the sequence (entirely original work) is a curiously uneven miniature suite, ranging from almost naïve simplicity to moments of considerable complexity. Although the opening pages are within the reach of any pianist of modest ability, the writing becomes progressively more virtuosic, the final Esercizio being a true bravura piece.

The Preludietto is based on an ostinato rhythm of alternating triplets and duplets: ♪♪♪ ♪♪ In a tender childlike theme in A major, Busoni combines this lulling rhythm, gently rising and falling, with a single line of melody, delicately drawn. With a few deft turns he shifts in and out of A major, reaching a small climax which is in no definable key at all. The single line is now expanded to parallel chords and the fourth chords, which he had so eloquently exploited in *Die Brautwahl*, appear once more:

Ex 86

[Andantino tenero]

The ensuing Fughetta continues in this peaceful spiritual mood, the C major subject imbued with a distinctly pastoral character yet also possessing inherent chromatic instability. Without overstepping the bounds of classical fugal exposition, Busoni here creates a minor masterpiece of 'free tonality'.* (Ex. 87).

*We shall use the term 'free tonality' to describe Busoni's harmonic style from 1909 onwards, as it expresses his identity of aims and opposition of means to those of Schoenberg.

Ex. 87

D flat major has been established (though via unexpected paths), but is at once put in question by the E double-flat and C flat in the first bar. By a process of gradual shifting, a return to C (major or minor) is subtly effected, during which the two intermediate bars are neither in the one key nor in the other. These four bars demonstrate in simple form the tonal no man's land which Busoni explores.

The Esercizio is also experimental. The right hand plays in 4/4 time throughout, while the left hand maintains a *quasi Valse* rhythm in opposing 3/4. Although the left hand stays quite firmly in A flat major, the right hand is based strictly on whole-tone harmonies, first in single strands and later chordally. In the middle of the piece a cadenza briefly interrupts the waltz rhythm; the two hands then wend their independent ways until the right hand shoots off into space, leaving the left still waltzing. A strangely amorphous composition with a sardonic humour, the Esercizio seems to be poking fun at the Impressionists by tying firm keys to the whole-tone scale. In the last two bars, traditional tonality celebrates a brief, undemonstrative victory.

Like the 'Berceuse', these three little pieces are embryonic. But we can also recognize the bud from which a finer work, the first Sonatina, was later to grow.

Volume 2: 'Preludio, Fuga e Fuga figurata' This is a study based on the D major Prelude and Fugue from Book I of *The Well-tempered Clavier*, strictly speaking a transcription and a supplementary study. The Fuga figurata is the realization of an idea which had occurred to Busoni while preparing his edition of Book I of the '48', in 1894, an extended combination of the music of the Prelude with the subject of the Fugue (Ex. 88).

An ingenious touch comes at the end of the Prelude: the note values of the Fugue are doubled, implying an exact tempo relationship, and, by carrying

Ex 88

directly through without a break, Busoni reinforces the agogic nature of the fugue theme:

Ex. 89

Incidentally, this short extract gives some idea of the meticulous care which he lavished on his transcriptions. The fugue theme is divided between the hands, thus imparting extra power and rhythmic precision to the opening semiquaver motif as well as effecting the editiorial crescendo which has been added. Here, in brief, is an illustration of the simple but effective pianistic innovation Busoni brought to Bach's keyboard music, also of his fastidious indications of phrasing and note-lengths. His Bach editions help to open the eyes even of those already well acquainted with the music to beauties or subtleties that may otherwise have gone unobserved.

Shortly before the close of the fugue, Busoni interrupts the action with a cadenza based on the opening of the Prelude, which leads directly into the Fuga figurata. The hair-raising contrapuntal feats of this study are achieved with considerable elegance and even humour. We experience the composer's thrill at achieving the near-impossible.

Volume 3: 'Giga, Bolero e Variazione' Mozart is the 'subject' of the next volume, which opens with a free transcription of his 'Kleine Gigue' for piano K.574. The original texture is thickened, the repeats (which are written out) are varied by octave transpositions and the whole is adorned with markings of phrasing and articulation. The Giga is followed by a transcription of the courtly fandango from Act III of *Le Nozze di Figaro*, transposed from A minor to G minor. Busoni stipulates that the new crotchet must equal the previous dotted crotchet and, as the limits of tempo are therefore very fine, he takes the unique step of adding a metronome mark. He has rethought the entire texture in pianistic terms. Towards the end he also includes a disguised reference to the theme of the Giga:

Ex. 90.

(ORIGINAL)

It was a favourite pastime of his to work out contrapuntal combinations of unrelated themes: he could do so with the same ease with which others can solve crossword puzzles. As in the Fuga figurata, he combines the themes here more out of playfulness than in the search for any deeper significance.

The Variazione is a brilliant reworking of the Giga in duple time. Mozart's already curious harmonies are distorted even further, creating dazzling moments of free tonality. Rhythmically too, the assymetries implied by Mozart are taken up and developed. At the height of the complexities the following vertiginous passage occurs:

Ex. 91

Tonality is at no point abandoned—it is simply made to spin. Likewise, where many a composer would have barred this passage 5/16, 5/16, 6/16, 2/4 —as it actually sounds—Busoni respects the classical convention of regular barring while at the same time freeing himself of its fetters. The 'message' of this music is clear: the Variazione performs the considerable feat of creating a completely new and individual language from elements latent but unexplored in Mozart.
Volume 4: 'Introduzione e Capriccio' (Paganinesco); 'Epilogo' A slow introduction, for left hand alone, is taken from Paganini's Caprice no. 11 in C major. The faster middle section that follows (for both hands) comes from the Caprice no. 15 in E minor. The piece is rounded off with a cadenza followed by a boisterous reprise of the opening theme, now in E major. As a composition this is by far the simplest of *An die Jugend*. Busoni has adapted his originals, without any radical alterations or clever contrapuntal devices, in a brilliant Lisztian manner. In place of any compositional problems he concentrates his

attention here on the technical possibilities of piano playing.

After the Bach, Mozart and Paganini transcriptions, the Epilogo is entirely original work. The opening:

Ex. 92

depicts a journey, spread over some 300 years of musical history. The first six notes all belong to the classical scale of E flat minor, but then the notes C and D are interpreted as the beginning of a whole-tone scale and, by transposing the opening motif accordingly, the tonality is opened up, lifted off the ground to culminate in a sequence of symmetrically moving chords with tonal allusions and atonal effect. This one bar symbolizes the meaning of the entire cycle: that the new must grow out of the old, 'rising on the shoulders of the past'. Classical tonality leads to free tonality and that, in turn, points to remote and unknown regions.

In the following music tonality is briefly re-established, then a flurry of whole-tone scales, marked *fantastico*, reminds one of the Esercizio from Volume 1; the fugue theme from that work reappears. Busoni repeats it in three different ways, each pointing to a new technical possibility. There is a chromatic-expressionist version:

Ex. 93

a bitonal setting:

Ex. 94

and a harmonization in streams of triads:

Ex. 95

Yet the close is a simple I-III-V-I cadence in C major, recalling the even plainer
I-V-I cadence (Ex. 21) with which the Second Violin Sonata ended. Thus, not
only does the Epilogo point to the future, it also makes the autobiographical
nature of the series clear by indicating the progress of a decade. At no point in
the wide-ranging spectrum of harmonic techniques unfolded in these bars does
Busoni compromise his search for the absolutely beautiful. The Epilogo is, in
an undemonstrative way, one of his masterpieces.

Confronted at one hearing by these five totally different pieces the listener is
likely to be puzzled. For *An die Jugend* is indeed intended as a cyclic work. The
clue to their unity lies in a cryptic entry in Busoni's diary. On 5 October 1909,
two days after his mother's death, he noted, 'An die Jugend! The source of the
palimpsest'. As with the entry of the previous day—'Our Lady of Sighs'—the
inspiration comes from de Quincey's *Suspiria de Profundis*.

   A palimpsest is the word for a manuscript of parchment or vellum whose
original inscription has been erased so that it may be reused, a practice which
arose in the Middle Ages due to a general shortage of parchment. The result
was that many an ancient Greek or Byzantine manuscript was later overlaid,
perhaps with a theological tract or a monastic legend. The erasure of the
original was not always complete and in the early nineteenth century chemists
discovered a way of making the former inscriptions visible once more. In an
essay entitled 'The Palimpsest of the Brain' de Quincey compares the ineradic-
able inscriptions of generations to the memory processes of the human brain.
He also comments on the passage of a work of literature through the ages:

   What would you think, fair reader, of a problem such as this: to write a book
   which should be sense for your own generation, nonsense for the next;
   should revive into sense for the next after that, but again become nonsense
   by the fourth; and so on by alternate successions, sinking into night or
   blazing into day?

Busoni sees this concept as corresponding to the history of Western music. The
seemingly random anthology of compositions and transcriptions which com-
prises *An die Jugend* is intended to make us aware of the omnipresence of Time.
All that is needed is an effective stimulating agent to free us from everyday

temporality. De Quincey used opium, Busoni music, to achieve this freedom. (Berlioz, in the *Symphonie fantastique*, had recourse to both!)

To emphasize the historical thread in *An die Jugend* the pieces are carefully chosen for their special relationships to one another. Bach is the Alpha and Liszt the Omega of the classics, as Busoni wrote: 'the two make Beethoven possible'.[2] To represent the Alpha he went back to one of his earliest Bach editions.

Mozart composed his 'Kleine Gigue' during a brief visit to Leipzig in May 1789. In the Köchel catalogue, the piece is described as an 'entry in the visitors' book' in which Mozart had 'payed homage to . . . the *genius loci*'.[3] And as a further direct link with Bach, it should be mentioned that Mozart, in an age where Bach had already seemingly 'sunk into night', had transcribed fugues from the '48' and added his own preludes to them.

The Bolero from *Figaro* is not by Mozart at all. It is a piece that truly belongs to the eternal calendar of music: the same dance can be found in Gluck's ballet *Don Juan* as well as in several zarzuelas. Its origins are lost in an uncertain Spanish past.

Another dance which also appears in Gluck's *Don Juan* is the traditional theme for variations, the so-called 'Folies d'Espagne' or 'La Folia', long attributed to Corelli. This is where we arrive at Liszt (and with him Paganini— the two are inseparable in the history of music), for Liszt's Spanish Rhapsody opens with variations on 'La Folia'. Another of the old Spanish melodies in that work appears (in half tempo) in the posthorn solo of Mahler's Third Symphony.★ These are confusing travels in time; but it is a game one can play for hours and, the more one plays it, the more one begins to perceive the truth behind Busoni's vision of music as living proof of an Eternal Calendar.

At the time of composing *An die Jugend*, Busoni received from Schoenberg copies of his first two piano pieces op. 11, sent in the hope of having the master perform them. The package arrived in Berlin only a few days after the completion of the Giga, Bolero e Variazione and Busoni hailed the pieces as an outstanding achievement. Nevertheless, he felt unhappy about the style of their piano writing and, after musing over them for five days, produced his *konzertmäßige Interpretation* of the second one. On the same day he wrote to Schoenberg, outlining his criticisms but tactfully making no mention of the transcription. However, an unpublished letter to Gerda written the same day tells the whole story:

> I came so far with Schoenberg's pieces that I *transcribed* one of them. I thought I could detect the grain of goodness in them and held his piano writing to blame for the shortcomings which I sensed . . . It has thus become

★ Busoni explains some of these ramifications in his article 'Wert der Bearbeitung', first published in 1910.

a *very* special piece with a certain significance; one step *further* than the *Elegies* and the *Berceuse*.[4]

Only when Schoenberg replied in defence of his composition did Busoni tell him of his experiment but, as his colleague was at that time without a publisher, he made the gallant suggestion of publishing both the original and transcribed versions of the piece in his *An die Jugend* series. It would nicely have brought his chain of transcriptions up to date. Not surprisingly, Schoenberg was horrified at the suggestion and replied:

> It is impossible for me to publish my piece together with a transcription which shows how I could have done it better. Which thus shows that my piece is *imperfect*. And it is impossible to try to make people believe that my piece is *good* if I simultaneously indicate that it is *not good*.[5]

The idea was abandoned and original and transcription were eventually published separately. Whatever the merits of Busoni's transcription, his friendly and professional criticism drew from Schoenberg some of the finest letters he ever wrote about his art.

With *An die Jugend* the deliberately confusing nature of Busoni's titles reached a critical point. Bernard van Dieren gives a clear exposition of the problem:

> Every musician has seen so many pieces 'für die Jugend' that he may be excused for believing that these simply constructed movements were meant for childish brains and fingers. Busoni intended them as visionary sketches of aspects which, in his belief, music was to assume and dedicated them to Youth which would see the full growth. . . . One must admit that he did not resist the temptation to leave possibilities of confusion. It points to a didactic strain in his mind which avoided the danger of pedantry by an impish sense of humour.[6]

Certainly, this sense of humour was not shared by his publishers, with whom he had recently signed a lucrative contract. Oskar von Hase wrote to him to express his delight at the forthcoming pieces, which he hoped would reach a wide public. When the manuscripts arrived at the office in Leipzig and he tried them at the piano, his pleasure soon vanished. After a few pages he discovered that only a virtuoso had any chance of grappling with their problems. In view of the diminished market that this implied, he felt obliged to offer Busoni a lower fee for each piece than originally agreed. Busoni, wishing to avoid conflict on financial matters, responded by taking the manuscript back and offering it instead to other leading publishers—without success. Finally the small Leipzig firm of Julius Heinrich Zimmermann accepted it.

Like the Elegies, the five works which comprise *An die Jugend* are dedicated to young musicians. The two composers of the group, Gruenberg and Blanchet, both made something of a name for themselves, although their works have not stood the test of time. (Gruenberg later wrote an opera, *Die Götterbraut*, on a libretto by Busoni.) The pianists, Turczinski, Galston and Closson, suffered varying fates—but none attained the highest ranks.

Shortly before completing *An die Jugend* Busoni wrote a foreword to it which was only published twelve years later:

> My love belongs to the young and shall always belong to them. Their impossible plans, their open-minded questions, disarming criticisms, defiant contradictions and fast-beating hearts—they turn the earth over and sow new seed in it.
> . . . Very fine, but unfortunately optimistic. Youth is mostly conservative and its promise is often deceptive. . . . The 'best' stand alone in every generation.[7]

One sees how Busoni's high ideals were in fact tempered by an almost cynical realism. Yet some were able to perceive these ideals, as for instance the American critic (probably Leichtentritt) who reported on the first Berlin performance of *An die Jugend*: 'He is the Nietzsche of the musical world', he wrote, 'a born "gruebler", whose mental processes are investigative, ruminative, cogitative.'[8]

The following year, after completing the *Fantasia Contrappuntistica*, Busoni continued to 'grueble' with the music of *An die Jugend*. He had never played his own original contributions to the series in public; in August 1910 he remodelled them into his first Sonatina.

The work opens with a new theme which, like the beginning of *An die Jugend* itself, gives the impression of childlike simplicity. Its gentle, pastoral lilt in 3/8 time anticipates a certain mood that one finds recurrently in the music of Hindemith:

Ex. 96

The opening of the *An die Jugend* Preludietto follows, though much revised. Over the triplet–duplet rhythm of the original now float brief phrases based on

Ex. 96 and later a theme from the Epilogo. The Fughetta theme is also incorporated:

Ex. 97

In the next section the 3/8 theme returns in the right hand while the left hand maintains the triplet–duplet rhythm in 2/4 time. A smooth transition leads to the exposition of the Fughetta, which appears unaltered. A newly composed link of one bar, a whole-tone scale, introduces music from the Esercizio. Here the original is enhanced by the addition of the theme of the Fughetta:

Ex. 98

The whole of the Esercizio is reworked in this way. At the point where the right hand shoots off into space, the pedal is held down throughout. Out of the agreeable haze of dissonance appears a fragment of Ex. 96, this time ushering in the music of the Epilogo. This final section is taken over unaltered from *An die Jugend*.

Thus the Sonatina is scarcely a new composition, more a task of setting the house in order. The idealism of the composer occasioned the original sequence of obscurely linked pieces, the practicality of the performing artist then refashioned the material into a more usable and effective concert piece. *An die Jugend* and the first Sonatina make severe demands on the pianist. The first performance of Volumes 2–4 of *An die Jugend* in London moved one critic to write: 'Unable to find pianoforte works sufficiently difficult and all-embracing to display his marvellous technical gifts, Mr. Busoni has evidently been compelled to adapt existing compositions to his own requirements.'[9] And its publication provoked an article in the *Allgemeine Musik-Zeitung* entitled 'Can piano playing be any further developed?'.[10]

Although the Sonatina begins and ends with charming and simple music, it entices the listener into unknown and disquieting regions: 'The contents of the piece have nothing to do with that which one had previously expected of a sonatina; they rather lead us into inaccessible territory,'[11] wrote one of the Swiss critics at the first performance. A second, led astray no doubt by the use of whole-tone scales, found that the work classified Busoni as a 'modern Impressionist'.[12] Reviews of the first Berlin performance three months later provoked an explosion from the composer: nobody seems to have understood the work. 'The Sonatina has been panned here', he wrote, 'the mildest critics found it an imitation of Debussy!'[13] Even a more recent commentator, H. H. Stuckenschmidt, exaggerates the significance of Busoni's use of whole tones; they were only one of many new possibilities to be fully explored; at no time did he wish to identify himself with any school of composers, least of all with the so-called Impressionists.

In his collection of press-cuttings only one review of the Berlin performance has been preserved, in which the critic seems genuinely to have grasped the significance of the Sonatina:

> Certainly this description has not been selected without real justification, but probably also not without a slightly ironical undercurrent of thought. A 'Sonatina' means a piece for beginners, and in this Sonatina the composer may have regarded himself as the beginner or founder of a new system of harmonies.[14]

The forty-four-year-old composer still delighted in being called a beginner. And of his many new beginnings, this period of experiment was the most exciting. Four years later he was to write, 'Couldn't one make it clear to the critics that dissonances *don't exist*? That the term cacophony has no meaning any more?'[15] And during the frenetically productive summer of 1909, when this phase began, he exclaimed with joy, in a letter to Egon Petri: 'Simply on the *piano* and with *12 semitones* one could progress infinitely; and how much further with a new tone-system and an orchestra! But what a technique and what a long life one would need for that!'[16]

IX

The *Fantasia Contrappuntistica*

1. Grosse Fuge: Contrapuntal Fantasy on J. S. Bach's last and unfinished work [for piano]. *Dedicated*: to Wilhelm Middelschulte. *Composed*: January to March 1910. *Published*: privately New York, 1910 by Schirmer. Limited edition of 100 copies printed on van Gelder paper, signed by the composer. Plate number 22004. *MS*: 22pp., 35×26cm. Deutsche Staatsbibliothek, Berlin.

2. Fantasia Contrappuntistica. Edizione definitiva: Preludio al Corale 'Gloria al Signore nei Cieli' e Fuga a quattro soggetti obbligati sopra un frammento di Bach [for piano]. *Dedicated*: to Wilhelm Middelschulte. *Composed*: 1910 (completed June 1910). *First performance*: 30.9.1910. Musikhochschule, Basle. Soloist: Busoni. *Published*: Leipzig, 1910. EB 3491. Later incorporated into the Bach–Busoni Edition, Vol. IV. *MS*: 52pp., part printed, part handwritten. 35×26cm. Deutsche Staatsbibliothek, Berlin. *Duration*: 25 minutes.*

3. Fantasia Contrappuntistica. Edizione minore: (Chorale Prelude and Fugue on a fragment by Bach) [for piano]. *Dedicated*: to Richard Buhlig. *Composed*: July 1912. *Published*: Leipzig, 1912. EB 3829. Later incorporated into the Bach–Busoni Edition, Vol. IV. *MS*: 20pp., 35×27cm. Deutsche Staatsbibliothek, Berlin.

4. Fantasia Contrappuntistica for 2 Pianos: *Dedicated*: to James Kwast and Frida Kwast-Hodapp. *Composed*: June 1921. *First performance*: 16.11.1921. Beethovensaal, Berlin. Egon Petri and Busoni. *Published*: Leipzig, 1922. EB 5196. Plate number 28713. *MS*: last known owner Frida Kwast-Hodapp. *Duration*: 26 minutes.

Transcriptions by other hands:

1. Fantasia Contrappuntistica: Transcribed for *organ* by Wilhelm Middelschulte (1911). *Published*: Leipzig, 1912. EB 3612.

2. Fantasia Contrappuntistica: Newly transcribed for *organ* by Helmut Bornefeld (1955). *Published*: Wiesbaden, 1962. EB 6342. Plate number Wb. 495.

3. Fantasia Contrappuntistica: Transcription for *double string orchestra, piano, harps and celesta* by Antony Beaumont (1971). *Dedicated*: to Ronald Stevenson. *Published*: Wiesbaden, 1977. MS.

* Cf Egon Petri's LP recording. Other performances have lasted as much as ten minutes longer.

At the end of 1909 Busoni and his wife set sail for the United States. On 22 December he noted in his diary, '"SS Barbarossa". Seven passengers, a menagerie'; and the following day, as they got out to sea, 'Seasick *after all*. Nasty weather'. Christmas was celebrated under these forlorn circumstances.

As the year turned, he settled down to work. The task at hand was a critical edition of *The Art of Fugue* for his planned complete edition of the keyboard works of Bach. On 1 January he jotted down an initial thought in a note-book: 'Out of the preceding 14 forms one could make up a *set of variations*, append the "completed" *Fuga a 3 Soggetti* as a (concertante) finale and perhaps create a prelude out of the dubious Chorale.' He also occupied himself with Bach's unfinished final fugue and, in order to study it more closely, began to copy it out, adorning it with analytical notes.

Soon SS *Barbarossa* docked in New York and work on the *Art of Fugue* project was set aside as he embarked on a gruelling recital tour. 15 January found him in Chicago, where he met an old friend from his Leipzig days, the composer and theorist Bernhard Ziehn, as well as one of his pupils, the organist Wilhelm Middelschulte. His meeting with these two sober, dedicated contrapuntists, practising their art in the shadow of the twenty-storey Chicago skyscrapers, inspired him to write an article for the musical journal *Signale*, entitled 'The Gothics of Chicago'. He defined Gothic art as:

> . . . that art in which delight in delicacy combines with the possibilities of power, feeling combines with fantasy, strict calculation with mystical belief. . . . It is a preponderantly Teutonic or Frankish art . . . and [César] Franck is the name, significantly, of a later representative of its symbols and forms.[1]

He also briefly described a 'new polyphony' which Ziehn had demonstrated to him; a technique in which melodic lines were combined in a strictly symmetrical way, without any prime regard for the resulting harmonies. Classical fugal principles demand the alteration of the notes of a theme where inadmissible harmonies would otherwise result. Ziehn taught that the themes should retain their original intervallic structure, whatever the resulting harmony might be. From the wealth of inversions and transpositions applicable to any given motif, entirely new and unexpected harmonies arise.

A sheet of examples of this technique which Ziehn gave Busoni (and which was later passed on to Petri) serves to illustrate it simply but succinctly enough. A chromatic theme:

Ex. 99

is combined with its inversion one semitone higher to form the following:

Ex. 100

This example is particularly striking in that the theme, containing nine of the twelve semitones arranged in a flawless inner structure of motif and inversion, as well as Ziehn's manner of manipulating it, are direct precursors of dodecaphonic technique.

The composer had suddenly ceased to become primarily a seeker, he had become a chooser: where previously he had looked for harmonically viable combinations of themes, any motif now threw out a vast number of polyphonic possibilities.

The conversation at this meeting also came round to *The Art of Fugue*. It was generally known that Bach had planned to complete the work with a mighty quadruple fugue, but there was some doubt as to the identity of its fourth subject. Ziehn confirmed what Busoni and others had long suspected: that the missing subject was none other than the principal theme of the whole opus itself. He wrote down the combination of the four subjects:

Ex. 101

and followed it with some new combinations of the themes according to his principles of 'symmetrical inversion'.* Busoni took the sheet with him and began experimenting with the new technique by adding some attempts of his own. Four days later he wrote to Gerda from Minneapolis, 'I am studying counterpoint again, for which Chicago has greatly stimulated me'.[2] By the end of the week he had achieved eighteen separate 'essays' on the first three of Bach's subjects, varying in length from four to thirty bars. It suddenly became clear to him that he could use this material for a completely novel completion of Bach's fugue; on 29 January, back in Chicago, he drew up an initial plan for the whole piece.

Further essays on all four subjects followed, from Milwaukee, Toronto and Buffalo. By then a new fragment of sixty bars had been formed, as well as some freer material visualized for a fantasia to precede the fugue. During a brief

---

* Ziehn (1845–1912) published a number of articles and books on piano playing, harmony and counterpoint. His major work is *Canonical Studies*, the book quoted by Busoni in his edition of Book II of the '48'. It was published, with an introduction by Ronald Stevenson, in London, 1976, by Kahn & Averill.

return to New York, where Gerda had remained the whole time, he told her of his plans and added some more material, drawing now on other themes from *The Art of Fugue*. From Cincinatti he wrote to tell her:

> I have changed the plan of the Fantasia Contrappuntistica. I shall do *without* the introductory Fantasie and rather bring all the fantasy-material into the fugue. It will be like something between C. Franck and the Hammerklavier Sonata, but with an individual nuance.[3]

During a visit to St Louis he noted the progress he had made so far: he had visualized the overall form in 'chapters', composed three variations, selected the material for the remaining sections and conceived the idea of incorporating a cadenza into the main body of the work. This cadenza was composed the following day in Kansas City and the ensuing fourth fugue was added one day later. On 26 February Gerda left New York on her way back to Europe; the same day Busoni wrote to H. W. Draber: 'Do you know B. Ziehn's principle of the symmetrical inversion of harmony? It produces—when applied to polyphonic writing—quite surprising sounds, and leads me one step further.'[4]

Four days later, 1 March, the work was completed in New Orleans and the fair copy was ready some five days after that. When one considers the enormous distances Busoni covered almost daily on his tour, the constant changing of hotel rooms and environment, not to mention the recitals he played in each city,* it seems amazing that any time or energy could be left for composition at all. But by dividing the great fugue into 'chapters' he had devised a rapid and economical way of working.

The new work, to which Busoni gave the ambitious title 'Grosse Fuge', was engraved and printed by Schirmer of New York in time for his birthday on 1 April, in a presentation edition of 100 copies on handmade paper.

The 'Grosse Fuge' opens with a rising fifth, D–A, thrice repeated. Bach's fugal fragment then runs uninterrupted (though considerably altered) to its close, after which Busoni works out the first three fugue subjects in detail and follows them with an intermezzo, three variations, a cadenza, a fourth fugue (which introduces the 'missing' fourth subject) and a final Stretta. The 'Grosse Fuge' is, in effect, an original composition; Busoni wrote of it, 'It occupies the same place amongst piano fugues as my Concerto amongst piano concertos'.[5]

On the train from St Louis to Denver he conceived the idea of orchestrating the great fugue—a plan which he himself never found time to execute. He also had the idea of adding the third Elegy, 'Meine Seele bangt und hofft zu Dir. . .' as a prelude. After returning to Europe, he performed this simple operation in June 1910, reintroducing the chorale theme as a reminiscence before the final Stretta. The extended version, which he considered to be 'one

---

* His programme on this tour (thirty-five concerts in four months) generally consisted of Beethoven's 'Waldstein' Sonata, the Brahms Paganini Variations, Chopin's B minor Sonata, Schumann's 'Abegg' Variations and a group of Liszt pieces—plus five or six encores.

of the most significant works of modern piano literature',[6] was entitled
Fantasia Contrappuntistica. This *edizione definitiva* consists of:

1. Chorale-Variations (on 'Allein Gott in der Höh sei Ehr')
2. Fuga I
3. Fuga II
4. Fuga III
5. Intermezzo
6. Variatio I
7. Variatio II
8. Variatio III
9. Cadenza
10. Fuga IV
11. Chorale
12. Stretta

Of the four fragments which Busoni received from Ziehn as a starting point,
only the first was incorporated and the authorship of these bars was acknowledged in a footnote. In adapting the third Elegy to its new purpose a few small
cuts and amendments were made, while all German marks of expression were
now either expunged from the score or translated into Italian.

As the chorale prelude dies away, the rising fifths which had opened the
'Grosse Fuge' sound in the bass while a gentle three-part invention winds its
way, *intimamente e indugiando*, above it. Fragments of the first subject of the
fugue are juxtaposed with three strettos on the inversion of the BACH motif.
As the last of these rises to a climax, the first subject itself now enters in the bass
con molta importanza, signalling the beginning of Fuga I. The theme is enlarged
and interpreted: each successive long note, for instance, is graduated into a
diminuendo, while the last notes are accompanied by a sighing phrase in
parallel falling sixths. Here is the whole passage from the end of the introduction to the last note of the first subject:

Ex. 102

Busoni underpins Bach's exposition with an almost continuous low pedal D, enveloping the music in shadow. The ensuing episodes are also freely handled. In one of them a chain of rising fourths is taken as the cue for a suave ascent to the higher reaches of the keyboard, where the entire structure comes to an ethereal *piano* climax. In Bach's original, the moment of greatest tension comes much later, just before the end of Fuga I, with the last statement of the subject in the bass. Yet when we come to this point in Busoni's version, we find the entry marked *sotto voce* and it marks the beginning of a gradual diminuendo. Thus the whole structure of Fuga I is reshaped to form a symmetrical arch. Likewise, the entire musical content has been reassessed: the stark outline of the theme is frequently softened with chromatic passing notes, while longer notes are often filled out with ornament.

In Fuga II the longer notes of the theme are punctuated by muted and dissonant references to the chorale:

Ex. 103

In one later passage Busoni introduces an anticipation of the BACH motif as well as further fragments of the chorale (these latter in smaller notes):

Ex. 104

Ex. 105

A subsequent entry of the second subject is raised an octave and marked *quasi flauto*; as in Fuga I some thematically irrelevant passages are cut (one an episode of three bars, the other of six). Thus on the one hand Busoni colours the score, interpreting it for the modern grand piano and even going so far as to suggest appropriate tonal shades; on the other he subtly reshapes the polyphonic argument.

Fuga III introduces the BACH theme, marked *pensoso*. The original is scarcely altered here; only a few passages are displaced by an octave in order to achieve a gloomier texture, while one bass entry is raised two octaves to become the soprano voice. A delicate touch of homage can be sensed in the way Busoni reduces the tempo shortly before the last bars that Bach lived to complete.

The rising D–A fifth rings out three times like a call to new achievement, introducing the combination of the three subjects with which Bach's fragment actually breaks off:

Ex. 106

From this starting point, and with the aid of Ziehn's symmetrical inversion, Busoni assembles a panoply of tense, tersely argued counterpoint. The play of theme against theme unleashes a stream of harmonic surprises, as in the last three bars of the following example. Here theme I in diminution and stretto is combined with theme II; later theme III (BACH) appears in parallel major thirds, together with its inversion. (The middle note of the final left-hand chord should by rights be A flat. The G is probably pianistic licence.):

Ex. 107

The tension mounts steadily, almost unbearably, finally resolving through a sequence of grinding dissonances onto a D major chord.

The ensuing Intermezzo brings a large-scale relaxation in the overall structure of the work, placed at the point of equilibrium between two great

sonorous masses; a point which seems to defy the laws of gravity. And indeed
the music now appears to leave the ground in passages marked *misticamente*★
and *visionario*. Two transpositions of the BACH theme are symmetrically
combined to produce an esoteric sequence of chords:

Ex. 108

Finally, the music dissolves into a haze of trills, fading to a single strand. The
Intermezzo is a perfect example of Busoni's concept of Gothic art: 'strict
calculation' is combined with 'mystical belief'.

Variation I continues in this rarefied mood, a distant two-part invention
without any apparent tonality. With a gradual expansion to four-part texture
and the establishing of D flat major comes a note of reassurance, a flush of
warmth, something of that 'longing as of a sailor for home' which Busoni had
quoted from Nietzsche in the *New Aesthetic*:

Ex. 109

Variatio II takes as its subject the BACH theme (actually a rhythmical
variant of it which later becomes a fifth fugue subject). In imitation of the
Canon alla Decima from *The Art of Fugue*, the texture breaks into eddies of
triplets. At the outset of Variatio III these suddenly assume the outlines of
theme II, while the new variant of theme III is joined by a jaunty version of
theme I (Ex. 110).

Tension builds up in a passage analogous to the end of Fuga III. Where the
former had come to a majestic full close, the Variatio is precipitated into the
sudden outburst of the Cadenza. Counterbalancing the Intermezzo, this is also
a 'floating' part of the overall structure. Rippling arpeggios based largely on
chords in thirds conceal within themselves the BACH theme in inversion, the

★ In the version for two pianos the marking *misticamente* is replaced by *occulto*.

Ex. 110

harmonies forming a link with the third-based broken chords of the chorale prelude (cf. Ex. 50). A transition passage, *senza agitazione*, brings with it a curiously subdued atmosphere in which, for the first time in the whole work, a chordal progression is repeated.

Fuga IV begins in the remote key of B flat minor, using material from Contrapunctus II of *The Art of Fugue*. By choosing music so closely related to the opening Contrapunctus, and hence to the 'missing' fourth theme, Busoni creates a feeling of closing the circle, the first sighting of land in his great fugal voyage. Suddenly and dramatically the key changes to D minor and the fourth theme thunders out in the bass. Now follows the contrapuntal climax of the whole work. A mass of stretto entries in six-part polyphony (slightly simplified in the solo piano version for reasons of playability) forces the tonality momentarily down to C sharp minor then disperses in a chain of falling trills. Only the BACH theme forges on in the shape of an ostinato figure deep in the bass; the chorale theme returns, distant and ethereal.

The concluding Stretta is based on the final section of Bach's Contrapunctus XI, his extended Fuga a 3 Soggetti. The threefold rising fifth, the first call to attention, returns *fff* in double octaves. A series of chords of increasing amplitude—tonic triad, minor ninth and dominant fifteenth—finally resolves into unison Ds. This penultimate chord, the most complete dominant:

Ex. 111

closes the circle of D minor with a last reference to the third-based harmonies of the chorale prelude, indeed to the rising third with which the piece began.

Busoni was at once concerned to point to the feeling embedded in this immense form and to explain this form in visible terms. He accordingly adorned the score of the 'Grosse Fuge' with a picture of a ship with five sails, enclosed within a decahedron.*

'The ship'—which represents the fugue itself—'moves over the difficult waters with five taut sails', he later explained,[7] confirming that he had deliberately added a contrasting fifth subject to Bach's four. Yet the ship signifies more than just the contrapuntal element of the Grosse Fuge. We have already noted that work on the piece was begun at sea; in the composition itself there was occasion to speak of a 'great fugal voyage', even of the 'longing as of a sailor for home'. Busoni implies that the ship represents a journey to a new world.

In the score of the *Fantasia Contrappuntistica*, the symbol is intensified by the superimposition of a cross.

In his edition of Book II of the '48', Busoni writes of polyphonic composition as 'a thought process which strives for the heights (vertical) brought into effect through the services of an art with four strands (horizontal)'. Recognizing in this idea the sign of the cross, he is swift to add 'the ground-plan of a cathedral!', and he continues:

It is not the fugue as a practical end in itself but the ideal importance of its motivating forces with which the contemporary composer seriously reckons: with the aid of these forces he is fully enabled to form his ideas skilfully and exhaustively, to speak the language of *his own* age.

* The ten sides of the decahedron correspond to the ten parts of the work: four fugues, three variations, intermezzo, cadenza and stretta.

The first performance of the new work was given before an audience of receptive young musicians. Busoni spent the whole month of September 1910 giving master-classes at the Conservatoire in Basle, regularly punctuating his teaching programme with recitals designed to illustrate the history of piano literature. The final concert was devoted to his own transcriptions and original works, an occasion on which both the *Fantasia Contrappuntistica* and the first Sonatina received their first performances. The critics of Basle, taken aback by these novelties, seemed unable to pronounce a verdict. One observed that:

> For some people this kind of music has an intoxicating effect, for others a bewildering effect which makes them nervous. A third group, one can call them the clairvoyants, sees in it a sort of 'look into the future'. Who knows? Ideas have long been fermenting in various quarters which point to the advent of something new and unheard of.[8]

One more qualified to comment on the work was the scholar-pianist Donald Tovey, who himself made a brilliant attempt to carry out Bach's original plan and completed the fragment in a style closely matched to that of Bach himself. He assumed that Busoni's intentions must have been similar to his own and therefore found an unwarrantable break in style (as did many lesser critics). Tovey was scarcely likely to sympathize with Busoni's solution, a composer's visionary attempt to build a new house on established foundations. Yet, whatever Busoni's intentions, the problem persists: do the spirits of Bach and Busoni harmonize in the *Fantasia Contrappuntistica*, or do they lock in perpetual combat?

The question is best answered with an architectural analogy: next to the charred remains of the Kaiser-Wilhelm-Gedächtniskirche in West Berlin, an entirely new church in a contemporary style has been erected. It is an achievement notable not so much for its beauty as for its meaning. An overt lack of stylistic unity accentuates the historical significance of the landmark. In this spirit, Busoni utilizes Bach's majestic fragment, his last will and testament, as the starting point for a musical voyage of discovery. The *Fantasia Contrappuntistica* is the forerunner of such works as Hindemith's *Ludus Tonalis* or the Preludes and Fugues of Shostakovitch—otherwise it stands like a skyscraper, isolated, massive and imposing yet not without a certain element of ugliness.

Busoni himself found one deficiency in his new work: 'It is too tightly corseted'.[9] While polyphony played an essential part in his music thereafter, he never again deployed the new-found techniques so exclusively or severely.

The *Fantasia Contrappuntistica* exists in several alternative versions. In 1911 Wilhelm Middelschulte made a transcription for organ and Frederick Stock, conductor of the Thomas Orchestra (later renamed the Chicago Symphony), made one for full orchestra with organ obbligato. (These will be discussed below, together with other versions not by the composer.)

In the summer of 1910 Busoni wrote a simplified and expanded version of the fugue for didactic purposes. In 1912 he composed a new chorale prelude to precede this fugue and published the two pieces as an *edizione minore* of the *Fantasia Contrappuntistica*. The terms *versio definitivo* and *versio minore* are actually borrowed from the technical jargon of the book world and point once again to the philologist in Busoni. (One would describe Goethe's *Urfaust* as a *versio minore*, while *Faust* Parts I and II is the *versio definitivo*.) Busoni's new version is a compositional study not intended for performance. Several such studies, on a smaller scale, are appended to his Bach editions. Presented with a variant of the fugue, the student can observe its compositional processes more closely. While the *versio definitivo* of the *Fantasia Contrappuntistica* is technically only within the reach of a virtuoso pianist, the textures of the *versio minore* are radically simplified, bringing the work within the range of any moderately talented player, while the sections extraneous to the fugal argument, the Intermezzo, Cadenzas and Variations, are omitted.

The *versio minore* is introduced by a completely new chorale prelude, the completion of an abandoned preliminary sketch for the third Elegy. After a calm exposition of the chorale in a network of flowing quavers there follows a pianistically more demanding variation—a study in two contrasting dynamic levels:★

Ex. 112

A second variation, *più segretamente* in G minor, combines the chorale in various ways with the BACH motif. In the closing section all these elements are ingeniously combined, the final bars containing an allusion to the third-harmonies of the original Elegy. The prelude can be performed on its own (it would make an interesting appendix to the Elegies) and an alternative ending is provided for this purpose.

Busoni's own contrapuntal extensions to the fugue are simplified but otherwise unaltered, except in Fuga IV, which is extended from the original

★ This music later found its way into *Doktor Faust* (cf. Ex. 282).

fifty-six bars of the *versio definitivo* to eighty. Yet Busoni refrains from exploiting all the combinations of the four themes made possible with Ziehn's technique, sacrificing his delight in the new polyphonic language to his sense of proportion. The final cadential flourish is a classic example of symmetrical harmony:

Ex. 113

The seven-volume Bach–Busoni Edition was published in 1920 (see Chapter VXIII), Volume IV of which included both the *versio minore* and the *versio definitivo* of the *Fantasia Contrappuntistica*. Busoni made a small revision in the last two pages of the latter, producing an editorial nightmare: an alternative reading of a definitive text (all modern reprints are based on this later version). As he explained, in a letter to the pianist Frida Kwast-Hodapp, the amendment was pianistically superior. Together with her husband (and former teacher), James Kwast, she had been touring extensively with the Improvisation for two pianos on 'Wie wohl ist mir' and was now hoping for further duo works for their repertoire. She suggested the *Fantasia Contrappuntistica*. 'The piece is a disproportionate task for ten fingers,' admitted Busoni, 'whereas divided between twenty it would be easy and transparent for player and listener alike.'[10]

A year elapsed before he found time to study the problem more closely. In June 1921, he quickly carried out his plan, incorporating all his *arrières pensées* on the work and adapting it in the spirit of his post-war ideals of clarity and synthesis. He had been fascinated by the possibilities of two-piano texture for many years, discussing them at length in his edition of Book I of the '48' in 1894. Moreover, Bach himself had indicated the possibilities offered by the medium in his contrapuntally enriched version of Contrapunctus XIV for two harpischords.

The chorale preludes of the two earlier versions are now amalgamated and a certain amount of new material is added. The opening octaves are presented in dotted rhythm and followed by a new brief outburst based on the BACH motif: (Ex. 114).

Abrupt changes of direction exploit a spectrum of emotion ranging from resignation to anger, from tenderness to violence. Finally, a hushed octave passage ushers in Fuga I (Ex. 115). Now the theme is no longer stated *con molta importanza*, as in previous versions, but *tranquillissimo*; where previously it had appeared bold and aggressive, its effect is now serene and reassuring. This new transition to the great theme is comparable to that mysterious moment in

Ex. 114

Beethoven's Ninth Symphony when the cellos and basses softly intone the 'Freude' theme.

Ex. 115

The textual revisions in the rest of the work are less extensive. There are a few cuts and transpositions; Busoni avails himself of all the opportunities afforded by the twenty fingers at his disposal to make lucid that which, even in the hands of a brilliant performer, had formerly been obscure. Now one can concentrate entirely on the content of the music.

As an aid to this concentration, Busoni furnishes the score with an architectural ground-plan. The Chorale Variations, Intermezzo, Cadenza and Stretta are depicted as dividing stages between groups of arches; three tall ones depicting the first three fugues, three lesser ones the variations, and one massive single arch the fourth fugue. The flanking sections (except the Chorale Variations) are cast by the arches into a half-shadow in which one can sense the Gothic and occult mysteries implied in the corresponding music.

As Busoni revealed to Hugo Leichtentritt, this plan was not entirely his own invention. It was based on the outline of the great west entrance of the Palace of the Popes at Avignon. Busoni's design diverges from the original but is nevertheless identifiable—one could describe it as a 'transcription' of the building (see Facsimile 34).

The Palace is so vast that it completely dwarfs its surroundings. It is the Gothic equivalent of a skyscraper, not in its height but in its super-human proportions. Where the pre-war 'Grosse Fuge' was created under the shadow of the American skyscrapers, resulting in a work of stark defiant modernity, Avignon now presents a visible link with the past. And, just as the post-war *Fantasia Contrappuntistica* takes an indestructible landmark on the desolated map of Europe as its symbol, the music of Bach no longer stands in the score as a challenge nor as the foundation on which composers were to build further and higher; but as a temple of refuge for lost souls, as a lighthouse in troubled waters. Even before the war, Rilke had sensed in the gigantic Palace this authoritative and welcoming symbol of refuge (had it not been built at a time when the Eternal City was devoured by heresy and secular strife?). Thus in Rilke's novel, *Malte Laurids Brigge*, we find the Palace of the Popes described as 'an utmost emergency body for the homeless souls of all'; this would appear to be its significance in the new score of the *Fantasia Contrappuntistica*.

The version of 1910 belongs entirely to the New World; even Ziehn's technique of symmetrical inversion could be described as a system of 'unlimited possibilities'. The version of 1921, on the other hand, is the work of a man uprooted from his old ways of life, endeavouring to make straight that which had become crooked. The alteration of notes was minimal; the change in the work's meaning radical. The Avignon plan is an exhortation to the interpreter to look beyond the *blanc et noir* of his piano keys to the inner meaning of the music.

Although Busoni tended to consider the *Fantasia Contrappuntistica* as a work for piano—he himself performed it quite frequently—he had in fact conceived it without any specific instrument in mind. While the part-writing of *The Art of*

Fugue is so arranged that it lies comfortably for a keyboard player, Busoni's work is not in the least considerately written. Transcriptions of the work were therefore amply justified. The composer himself had seen the inherent orchestral possibilities but never found time to exploit them; therefore he was content to authorize Frederick Stock to produce an orchestral version in 1910–11.

The new version included an important solo organ part, played by Middelschulte at its first performance (during a festival of modern music in Dortmund, 21 August 1911); Busoni was entranced. 'What the layman understands by "music of the angels" was brought into being', he wrote. 'Stock's orchestral arrangement', he continued, 'is un-mystical and, for my taste, lacking in fragrancy and transparency, though in some parts brilliant work.'[11] A Dortmund critic, B. Friedhoff, wrote: 'I could not rid myself of the impression that "two souls" abide in this work, as if two regions of expression which could never be fused into a unified work of art are in confrontation.'[12] Busoni's sardonic reaction was the comment that a Dr Friedhof (graveyard) 'has tried to *bury* my Fantasia'.[13]

Despite Busoni's mixed feelings about Stock's score it received several further performances. Schoenberg and Webern were both present at a performance in Berlin on 19 January 1912 conducted by Oskar Fried. In a letter to Busoni, Schoenberg voiced his criticism of Stock's efforts (orchestrating Bach was later to become a speciality of his):

> I couldn't really enjoy the fugue because of . . . the unbelievably inappropriate instrumentation. During the concert I said to Webern: 'One never hears the leading voices but only the theme.' The performance and the instrumentation had an equal share of the blame for that. For it is naturally the subsidiary voices in a fugue which produce the unifying contrasts. Exclusive bringing out of the main theme gives the impression of great erudition but never the sense of a piece of music. I almost think that the theme should appear mostly as an accompaniment to the subsidiary voices. The theme, so to speak, as a basic colour, as a neutral background, upon which the design, its forms and colours, should stand out. But when the background stands out (!!!) then everything else is overshadowed. All atmosphere, all flow, all contrast is destroyed.—Nonetheless, I could sense the broad outline and the expressive powers . . . of this work—which I already knew through reading the piano version. And above all the contrapuntal art![14]

When Busoni finally came to conduct Stock's orchestration himself, for the Royal Philharmonic Society in London, something of a scandal occurred at the rehearsal (Dent describes the occasion in detail in his biography). The work was withdrawn from the programme and that version has never been played again since.

Middelschulte's arrangement for organ is a much finer piece of work, carried out in close consultation with the composer. Although it is as demanding for the organist as the original is for pianists, courageous players still perform it from time to time. Certain distinct advantages are gained through the sustained tone of the organ which clarifies the polyphony and projects the great climaxes with increased force. Only the chorale prelude, which is idiomatically written for the piano, loses its flexibility, calling as it does for incessant changes of registration.

A more recent organ transcription is that of Helmut Bornefeld, made in 1955 and first performed in 1957 (together with Reger's Fantasia on BACH). Feeling that composers had neglected the organ in the general advance of instrumental techniques, Bornefeld made a number of transcriptions of piano works, including music by Bartók, Mozart, Brahms and Dvořák. He based his Busoni transcription exclusively on the text of the version for two pianos, using modernized notation in which barlines play a subsidiary role. It is a well-made transcription but it seems regrettable that Bornefeld did not choose some other works of Busoni for his organists' crusade. He describes Middelschulte's version as 'old fashioned': certainly it was conceived for the large romantic organ, complete with crescendo pedals and all the necessary paraphernalia, and is not easy to play on modern instruments. But it has the composer's blessing. If Bornefeld had arranged the fourth and fifth Sonatinas, or made a version for solo organ of the great chorale prelude from *Doktor Faust*, he would have done organists a greater favour.

Finally, modesty shall not prevent me from mentioning my own orchestration of the *Fantasia Contrappuntistica*, which calls for double string orchestra, piano, celesta and two harps. Like Bornefeld, I have generally used the text of the two-piano version, but reopened some of the cuts in the fugues and reverted to the *versio definitivo* for some passages which were too overtly pianistic in the later reading. The use of strings has the dual function of providing the sustained, unpercussive sonority necessary for the clear articulation of the polyphony, and of securing a variable but uniform tone colour. The instrumentation acknowledges a debt to Bartók, of course, but it was stimulating to discover that his *Music for Strings, Percussion and Celesta* had by no means exhausted the possibilities of this rare and wonderful medium. In its string-garb the *Fantasia Contrappuntistica* takes its place more distinctly in the tradition of 'great fugues': Mozart's Fugue in C minor K.426 (originally for two pianos) and Beethoven's 'Grosse Fuge' (as well as the finale of the 'Hammerklavier' Sonata) are shown to be its forbears. It also looks forward to the first movement of Bartók's *Music for Strings*, a fugal movement written in precise accordance with Bernhard Ziehn's symmetrical techniques.

Several unpublished orchestrations exist of the *Fantasia Contrappuntistica*. Ronald Stevenson once wrote of his ambition 'to pay a small homage: to make a version of the Great Fugue—a transcription into electronic music'.[15]

With the adoption of Ziehn's symmetrical inversion, Busoni showed how polyphony could be freed from classical harmonic shackles and formed into a new language which, however dissonant, would at all times be absolutely logical. The ruthlessness of his first experiments in this language (described by himself as 'corsetedness') was a necessary measure against the anarchy of free atonality.

Busoni proved one important point for himself, and for everyone: counterpoint was a relevant modern weapon. In later compositions, he wrote, '. . . "melody" will have to rule autocratically and that final "polyphony" will then appear in a perfected state, which shall be a sublimation of Bach's art.'[16]

X

The Occult

Sonatina seconda [for piano]. *Dedicated*: to Mark Hambourg. *Composed*: June–July 1912. *First performance*: 12.5.1913. Concert Hall of the Verdi Conservatoire, Milan. Soloist: Busoni. *Published*: Leipzig, 1912. EB 3828. Plate number 27311. *MS* sketches: Deutsche Staatsbibliothek, Berlin. *Duration*: 8 minutes.

Nocturne symphonique [Second Elegy for orchestra] op. 43. *Dedicated*: to Oskar Fried. *Composed*: October 1912–July 1913. *First performance*: 12.3.1914. Beethoven-saal, Berlin. Berlin Philharmonic Orchestra, conducted by Busoni. *Published*: Leipzig, 1914. PB 2345. *MS*: 24pp., 35×27cm. Breitkopf und Härtel, Wiesbaden. *Instrumentation*: 3(Picc.)–2(C.A.)–3(Bcl.)–3(Cfg.); 3–0–0–0; Timp., Perc.; Harp; Celesta; Str. (12–12–8–6–6). *Duration*: 7 minutes.

The orchestration of *Die Brautwahl* caused an interruption of almost two years in Busoni's creative output, giving him a valuable opportunity to consolidate the intensive searchings of 1909 and 1910. In 1912, when he began to compose again, the effect of this enforced silence was manifested in the form of a new leap further into the unknown. This phase of creativity was dominated by three important factors: the arrival of Schoenberg in Berlin, the rise of the Futurist movement and a growing preoccupation with occultism.

In the autumn of 1911, a letter signed by Busoni and four other musicians was published in the Berlin journal *Pan*, inviting pupils who wished to study with Schoenberg to submit their names to the editors. The appeal was successful and Schoenberg moved to Berlin in October of the same year. Busoni's important concert on 19 January 1912 afforded the two composers the opportunity to meet (evidently for the first time) and occasioned an unusually flattering letter from Schoenberg (quoted in part on p. 175). Busoni in turn paid him the compliment of attending one of his lectures and a concert of his more recent works.

The concert took place on Sunday, 4 February 1912 in the Choralionsaal at noon. A small and select public listened to the world premières of *Das Buch der hängenden Gärten*, the Six Piano Pieces op. 19 and Nos. 1, 2 and 4 of the Five Pieces for Orchestra, in a transcription by Erwin Stein for two pianos, eight hands, as well as some earlier songs. Among the performers were Anton Webern and three of Busoni's pupils: Eduard Steuermann, Louis Closson and Louis T. Gruenberg. In the audience apart from Ferruccio and Gerda Busoni was the critic M. D. Calvocoressi, who later reported Busoni's 'great interest' in Schoenberg's 'experiments'.[1] Busoni himself, writing in *Pan*, recorded his mixed feelings:

> A daring harmony, the point of which is blunted by its continuous use—short-breathed phrases—frequent drawings of breath and listening back—naïvety in almost barbarous measure. And on the other hand so much unaffectedness, clear-sightedness and honesty.[2]

The concert had re-established Schoenberg's presence in Berlin. For a short period he and Busoni dominated the musical avant-garde of the city like demigods. Their relationship was not unlike that of Leonhard and Manasse in *Die Brautwahl*, founded on the sympathy of kindred spirits, but tempered by misunderstanding and a certain degree of mistrust. Busoni described Schoenberg's music as experimental, yet this music offered confirmation of many of his own insights and now encouraged him to go further with his own self-styled 'experiments'. The strongest vibrations of concord between the two arose on a philosophical plane: 'In the lecture I said . . . that the future form of mankind will be the genius', noted Schoenberg. 'That seemed to please Busoni greatly.'[3]

The Futurist philosophy was a yet more radical expression of this view:

> Courage, valour, rebellion shall be the essential elements of our poetry.
> Why should we have to look over our shoulders when we wish to burst the mysterious gates of the Impossible asunder? We already live in the Absolute, for we have created eternal, omnipresent speed.

These are two of the eleven clauses of F. T. Marinetti's Futurist Manifesto, published on the front page of *Le Figaro* on 20 February 1909. Under his leadership the group—numbering amongst its members the painters Boccioni, Carrà, Balla, Severini and Russolo, and supported by Apollinaire and d'Annunzio—ventured to exhibit their works for the first time in February 1912. On 5 March the exhibition opened in the Sackville Gallery, London, on the second stage of an ambitious European tour. Busoni, visiting England for concert engagements, saw this explosive exhibition in its third week. He recognized at once the qualities of Boccioni's work and also found some praise for Carrà and Severini. 'Unfortunately I can see that these people too will become "old-fashioned" ', he wrote.[4] Yet he was so impressed with Boccioni that, when the Futurists exhibited in Berlin in April–May 1912, he bought his enormous picture, 'The Rising City'.

Despite strong misgivings, he was carried along for a while by the impetus of this new youthful and dynamic movement, especially as it was an entirely Italian venture which seemed to augur well for the future of the arts in his native land. Yet his brush with the Futurists was fleeting, he was suspicious of any idea so ostentatiously promoted as the *dernier cri*. In *Mafarka*, Marinetti's most important book, the tale is told of a negro futurist Superman who begets an immense son, Gazurmah, an 'invincible and gigantic bird with great, flexible wings, made to embrace the stars'.[5] Like Busoni, the Futurists shared Leonardo's desire to be able to fly.

For a few days in April 1912, Dent was a guest of the Busonis and on one occasion he noted in his diary: 'Marinetti and Boccioni called—they talked very hard and B. listened very patiently.'[6]

Here we have a lively picture, in very few words, of Busoni's actual relationship to Futurism.

The music of 1912–13, the *ne plus ultra* of Busoni's experimentalism, is dominated most strongly neither by Schoenberg's art nor by the Futurists but by his own obsession with occultism, an interest shared by many at that time. Sartre has described how, before World War I:

> . . . the West was dying of suffocation . . . Since it had no visible enemies, the bourgeoisie enjoyed being scared of its own shadow . . . there was talk of spiritualism and ectoplasm, the other World was there, the more to be feared because it was not mentioned.[7]

Writing to Petri, Busoni drew his attention to an article in *Meyers Konversationslexikon* (a German domestic encyclopaedia): 'It discusses <Occultism> with great seriousness; worth reading'.[8] He speculated on the possibility of using clairvoyance for seeing not only into the future but also into the past: 'like a Marconi telegraph station that can reach equally far in all directions'.[9] He also wrote to his American friend, Harriet Lanier, confirming his belief in extra-sensory perception. It was at this time that he formulated his hypothesis of the omnipresence of Time.

In the *Sonatina seconda* the marking *occulto* appears for the first time in Busoni's music. On 29 July 1912, by which time the piece was virtually finished, he noted with evident satisfaction in his diary: 'At night the Boccioni in the music room acquires a strange, ghostly appearance in the fairy-tale light that seeps in from the square below.' Such a picture of the composer, seated alone in a darkened room—perhaps at the piano—contemplating the shadowy Buddhas and the speckled tornado of colours thrown out by a huge painting on the wall, somehow evokes most vividly the mystic and abstruse world towards which his speculations were drawing him. Table-tapping, hypnotic suggestion and the consultation of mediums were symptoms of a society on the brink of collapse, the society so accurately depicted in Thomas Mann's *The Magic Mountain*. Busoni approached the difficult topic with a certain detachment: for him it was a research project, an attempt to penetrate deep into the soul of that mythical figure—be he Leonardo, Dante or Faust—who was to be the hero of his master-work. Evidently he felt the need to contemplate the world beyond before attempting to search for the absolute, for the music 'beyond Good and Evil'.

At the end of May 1912, after a hectic concert season, Busoni returned to Berlin. The summer lay free for composition. A single page of sketches from the end of that month, entitled '6 Préludes', begins with a Schoenbergian broken fourth-chord:

Ex. 116★

and a theme:

Ex. 117

At this stage it was not certain for which medium the intended new work was to be written—the sketch contains both piano fingerings and notes for orchestration—but it soon became clear that a second Sonatina was taking shape. By 22 June a first draft was ready and on 25 June the work was seemingly completed. 'Two to one=Boy to Girl' noted Busoni in his diary that day, meaning that the first of his sonatina-children may be the more supple and delicate, but the second had been born virile and aggressive. Three days later, after spending six hours on the first fair copy, he noted, with fine understatement, that he had 'come harmonically further than before'.[10] This first draft was finished the following day, concluding with a brilliant *al Saltarello* which repeated and developed much of the preceding material. Busoni must have quickly sensed the break in style which this movement implied, for the *Sonatina seconda* is otherwise bereft of literal recapitulations and the material does not lend itself to dance rhythms. A new, brief coda was sketched out and the form finally came clear on 8 July. By mid-August the manuscript was with the engraver, bearing a dedication to the pianist Mark Hambourg.

The very appearance of the music on the printed page proclaims it as revolutionary and its harmonic language prompted Busoni to take the unique step of describing the work as 'senza tonalità'.[11] There are lengthy passages without barlines and a novel method of notation is employed, whereby an accidental refers only to the note which it directly precedes. Yet most of the passages without barlines can be written out in 6/4 time—as they later appear in *Doktor Faust* and as they sound—and the new notation serves to confuse

★ The musical examples from the *Sonatina seconda* have been rewritten in traditional notation.

rather than clarify. (Breitkopf's engraver was baffled by the manuscript and Busoni had to add an explanatory note to the score.) The real innovations of the work lie not in its appearance but in its sound and, more specifically, in its form. The stream-of-consciousness structure of the Elegies is brought to perfection here and one will search in vain for logical developments. There are links between some of the thematic ideas and there is a certain cross-referencing of material, but the overall impression is of a free fantasy.

The most immediately striking music comes in the first section. The opening bar, an unaccompanied motto theme, *parlando*, spans over two octaves:

Ex. 118

Based almost entirely on the harmony of Ex. 116, the ideas of Exx. 117 and 118 are then elaborated with venomous bravura, *Il tutto vivace, fantastico, con energia, capriccio e sentimento*. Over a murmuring accompaniment appears a full statement of Ex. 117, which we shall call, with hindsight, the students' theme:

Ex. 119

Ronald Stevenson has shown how the second part of this theme, with its jagged, ever-widening leaps, is in fact a distant echo of a motif from Carl Goldmark's opera *Merlin*:[12]

Ex. 120

A little cell of parallel major seconds wells up into a chromatic ascent over five octaves and at its peak the Merlin theme is thrown into the air like a shower of sparks, then forcefully hammered out in the bass. The students' theme now appears in its original guise (Ex. 117), *opaco*, and is then repeated *triste lamentoso* to the accompaniment of a long trill, a passage whose desolate effect is further stressed by intrusions of the first three notes of Ex. 118. A cadenza finally runs headlong into the final section of this first movement, *con fuoco, energicissimo*, nine of whose eleven bars are occupied with a vigorous ostinato, over which emerges a new version of the students' theme in canon, marked (in the sketches) *agonizzante*:

Ex. 121

There are also two appearances of the *Merlin* theme at this frantic pace, after which the movement finishes abruptly with three crashing chords. Apart from the first bar (Ex. 118), which was added later, this movement was conceived and hastily written in one uninterrupted flow—an unrestrained and spontaneous outburst. The music surges forwards—violent, chaotic, unstable—a sonic counterpart to that dynamic jumble of men, horses, factories and water which constitutes Boccioni's 'Rising City'.

In contrast to the block harmonies and wide-ranging homophony of the first movement, the substance of the second, which follows without a break, is an extended contrapuntal invention on a falling semitone motif:

Ex. 122

As preface, there are two atmospheric episodes. The first, which is the nerve centre of the entire work, is a combination of this 'fugue' theme (Ex. 122) with the rising major seconds of Ex. 118, both harmonized in triads:

Ex. 123

In his sketches, Busoni described this passage as the '3-mal. Akkord', the same name Mozart gave to his Masonic chords in *Die Zauberflöte*; indeed, Busoni's mystic device is centred, like Mozart's, on E flat major. The tempo marking of this passage is further confirmation of Busoni's intentions: *Lento occulto*.

The second episode takes a motif made of the highest three notes of Ex. 116:

Ex. 124

and spins it, with the aid of symmetrical counterpoint, into a canon. The resulting string of unresolved dissonances is the most overtly experimental passage in the whole work, after which the beginning of the fugal movement sounds in comparison like a return to terra firma. Here symmetrical counter-point is formed out of the opening semitone of Ex. 122, which soon splits into two voices: the motif and its mirror image. The canon theme returns and Ex. 122 is also extended by a further pentatonic phrase. The following three bars illustrate a combination of all these elements:

Ex. 125

Sostenuto

A semblance of tonal stability is subsequently achieved by the setting up of pedal points, first on F sharp then on E flat, later on B natural. But this stability is short-lived and a reintroduction of the opening fourth-chord harmony brings with it a restatement of the motto theme, *quasi Violoncello*. In imitation of the cadenza in the first movement, a passage of bitonal triplets follows which uses exactly the same combination of keys as the 'Berceuse', F major and A flat minor (cf. Ex. 59). Motif and mirror image return, as in Ex. 125, and the contrapuntal argument is resumed. It soon fades, however, leaving only the theme, shrouded in the mystery of the '3-mal. Akkord'. The canon formed from Ex. 124 returns, inverted and abbreviated. A subdued round of counter-point over a B flat pedal leads into a reprise of the students' theme, which marches slowly away, terminating in the falling sevenths of the *Merlin* theme. The closing leap in sarabande rhythm, marked *estinto*, plunges us into the deepest abyss of this disturbing work:

Ex. 126

Ten years later, Busoni confirmed that the *Sonatina seconda* had been expressly conceived as a study for *Doktor Faust*. On 5 September 1912 he began work on the second of these preparatory works, originally intending it to be a third Sonatina. The material for this new piano work came from another sketch for the intended '6 Préludes'. In moments snatched between London engage-ments he wrote playfully to Petri of his progress on 8 October:

> The third Sonatina seems to have the character of a butterfly . . . at any rate, it is undergoing a metamorphosis, has for the moment assumed the form of a

caterpillar, is feeding on smuggled half-hours and crawling up the trunk of the orchestra-tree.

Four days later the fragment emerged from its chrysalis in full orchestral glory, bearing the working title 'Deuxième élégie pour orchestre'. Soon the title was changed to *Nocturne symphonique* and the work was planned to consist of a slow opening (already well advanced) proceeding via a recitative to a march in ternary form, then to a closing section with 'all five melodies united and spun out' over a pedal point. In this final section an important role was to be played by the glass harmonica, the instrument which E. T. A. Hoffmann thought probably the nearest in sonority to the music of the spheres and which 'has in the deepest matters so wonderful an effect on our souls'.[13]

The music Busoni here conceived would seem to be the very music which he visualized for the appearance of Helena in *Doktor Faust*, and which tantalized and eluded him for the rest of his life. Its literary inspiration undoubtedly comes from Mereshkovsky's *Leonardo* romance; a scene from this book that particularly fired Busoni's imagination was a courtly entertainment provided by Leonardo for Ludovico Sforza, Duke of Milan. The artist had devised a system of crystal spheres from which music emanated: 'Curious, soft, uncommonly sweet tones . . . that mysterious music . . . of which the Pythagoreans tell us. Special glass bells, invented by Leonardo, operated from a keyboard, emitted these sounds.'[14]

By the time Busoni left London only eighteen bars of orchestral score of the *Nocturne* had been completed. Work was resumed later in the month in Russia. On 16 November Busoni wrote from Moscow to his former pupil Irma Bekh: 'Yesterday—at last!—I felt a fresh breeze on my MS, the pages seemed to ripple and there was a springtime rustling amongst them.—How often has one thus been deceived!'[15] On 18 November he met that other master of the occult, Alexander Scriabin, in St Petersburg. Busoni, who found Scriabin's earlier music 'une indigestion de Chopin',[16] respected the 'heroic aspirations'[17] of his last years. Only a few months later, Scriabin composed his Ninth Piano Sonata (the 'Black Mass'), a work by which Busoni is said to have been 'charmed'![18] Shortly after Scriabin's death, Busoni wrote: 'He was most admirable in regard to the fact that he never felt satisfied with his achievements.'[19]

Whether Scriabin's ideas had any real influence on him or not, progress on the *Nocturne symphonique* was slow and it was temporarily abandoned in favour of the *Red Indian Fantasy*. Eventually, on 6 July 1913, the fair copy was completed. Passages quoting the students' theme from the *Sonatina seconda* were removed at a late stage; the marches were never written, nor does a glass harmonica feature in the score. The work, as planned, would have amounted to a three-movement symphony, yet despite the absence of recognizable symphonic characteristics in the final form, Busoni left the title unchanged. 'The Nocturne symphonique, after definitive checking and reading through, seems to me to possess its own kind of perfection', he wrote,[20] as he sent the work to the press.

If not symphonic in the traditional sense of the word, it is even less a nocturne after the manner of Chopin or Field. Here the word is used to imply a picture of a clouded night-sky, an essay in dark colours and swirling mists. The work falls into three sections: a Sostenutissimo in 12/8 time, an Adagio in 3/8 and an Allegretto tranquillo in 3/4, this closing section being under-pinned throughout by an E flat pedal-point. The effect of this undisturbed triple time, combined with a progressively decreasing tempo throughout the piece, is to give the impression of focussing ever more closely on a distant object.

The first section falls into six parts:

1. (12 bars) A number of themes are presented (for the opening theme see Ex. 262), all notable for their dark colouring and flowing rhythms. A falling seventh:

Ex. 127

is of motivic importance throughout the work.

2. (4 bars) A faltering lyric theme in a high register over a G flat pedal:

Ex. 128

3. (5 bars) *Tranquillo*. A long, winding theme in a low register with a rich filigree accompaniment. This music was the first inspiration for the work:

Ex. 129

4. (8 bars) Begins in a benevolent E flat major, undermined however by the presence of the sinister opening theme in the bass. A dramatic wide-spanning theme for the violins, echoed by woodwinds, restores the original nervous tension.

5. (4 bars) A decorated version of No. 2.

6. (6 bars) A highly dense agglomeration of previous materials, myriads of trills; the climax of the work. A D flat pedal is established, out of which the second section emerges.

As the Adagio opens, the web of polyphony is curiously changed, as if a temperature had been attained at which melody melts. Out of the resulting limbo a new shape slowly begins to rise; at its peak a solemn recitative-like theme, for three solo stringed instruments in unison, adds an element of the grotesque to the nightmarish atmosphere of the music:

Ex. 130

Three horns softly intone the 'benevolent' theme of the first section, resolving on a pure chord of E flat major (the Masonic key once again), which dominates the complex free tonality of the score.

An E flat pedal-point, tolling in the bass like a funeral bell, announces the opening of the final section. A stately cortège of woodwinds in unison moves steadily onwards, with a spectral semiquaver accompaniment in the strings. In the coda, *più tranquillo*, the winding theme of the opening (Ex. 129) returns in altered form and the ghostly procession finally comes to rest on a question-mark; a chord neither major nor minor but nevertheless E flat:

Ex. 131

This is by far the most complex of Busoni's orchestral compositions. The polyphonic harmony of the 'Berceuse' is further exploited and, just as in the *Sonatina seconda*, the only stability arises from occasional pedal points. In this bleak and dissonant language the few moments when simple triadic harmony comes briefly to the fore are particularly striking.

The most radical aspect of the score is Busoni's use of instrumental timbres, which are broken down into indeterminate colours by a complex process of doubling and mixing. Especially arresting is the scoring of Ex. 128: the theme is played an octave above the written pitch by first violins divided into four, doubled by celesta; the *loco* notes are played by three flutes and a horn which combine into a single timbre, sweet but undefinable; the whole is supported by a G flat tremolando for second violins and violas, out of which emerge two muted horns and harp with a menacing tolling figure. A fleeting vision, it passes and does not return—indeed, no sonority in the score is used more than once.

While the *Sonatina seconda* is the more radical of Busoni's two 'occult' works, the *Nocturne symphonique* is the more refined; a composition 'woven with nerve fibres'.[21]

This new language had certain limitations: it was difficult to incorporate faster music without causing a break in style; no longer could one engage in the deft manipulations of key which had been the essence of free tonality up to that time; despite the precise polyphonic calculations involved, the public would be bound to dub such music impressionistic.

In the spring of 1913 Busoni gave a series of eight piano recitals in Milan, designed to cover the entire literature from Bach to the present day. This major undertaking, the 'Octomeron' as Busoni called it, was his most auspicious contribution to Italian musical life since his childhood. At the final recital, on 12 May, devoted entirely to his own compositions, he ventured to perform the *Sonatina seconda* in public for the first time. Writing to Egon Petri he recorded:

> Remarkable evening yesterday. After the 2nd Sonatina something like an uproar arose at the back of the hall, Condottiere Marinetti engaged in fisticuffs with some of the rebels, from the artists' room I heard squabbling voices, one very loud one which repeatedly bellowed 'Fuori!' [Get out!] —But all ended with roses and bouquets, and a *cenacolo* attended by distinguished men and beautiful women . . . Toscanini, Bossi . . . the Futurists Marinetti and Boccioni . . . the composer Sinigaglia . . . also Borgatti, Italy's Wagnerian heldentenor, who presented me with nothing less than a golden laurel wreath—all these were present as well as many others.[22]

Typical of Busoni that he should first perform his quasi-Futurist new work in his native land; typical of an era when *Le Sacre du Printemps* and Berg's *Altenberg Lieder* were shouted down that the public should accord the great and respected Busoni a similar reception.

The circumstances of the first performance of the *Nocturne symphonique* were very different. In the spring of 1914 Busoni promoted four concerts of his own works in the Beethovensaal, Berlin. The second orchestral concert, on 12 March, consisted of:

> Suite from the opera, *Die Brautwahl*
> *Fantasia Contrappuntistica* (version for solo piano)
> *Berceuse élégiaque*
> *Nocturne symphonique* (first performance)
> *Red Indian Fantasy* (first performance)

All but the last work were conducted by Busoni himself; in the *Fantasia Contrappuntistica* and the *Red Indian Fantasy* he was the soloist.

As with the 'Octomeron' in Milan, these concerts showed Busoni at the peak of his fame and energy. Three of the four concerts were completely sold out; all

were the scenes of enthusiastic ovations. Leichtentritt, who wrote the programme notes, spoke of the new works as 'stages on the way towards musical
terra nova' and explained the language of the *Nocturne symphonique* with these
words:

> Voice is not countered by voice, nor instrumental groups countered by one
> another, but note by note, each separate instrument against every other.
> Different chords are often superimposed, major and minor sound
> simultaneously, unexpected chords frequently collide.

Most of the Berlin critics, while unable to deny Busoni's personal success,
viewed these developments with their customary scepticism. Yet, in their very
rejection of the *Nocturne symphonique*, some came close to comprehending it.
Walter Dahms, for instance, considered the work 'Chaos, disintegrated music,
protoplasma',[23] while Georg Schünemann dryly observed, 'We experience in
this music a parallel to Futurist painting'.[24] Max Marschalk wrote more
positively while sensing, in a remarkable flash of intuition, the ultimate
purpose of the work:

> Such music is to be greeted not only as a valuable human and artistic
> statement, but also as an experiment which extends the expressive possibili-
> ties of music and passes on new technical aids to a coming generation.
> Studies like . . . this Nocturne have such a self-contained effect and are in
> themselves so perfect, that we will always be glad to encounter them as the
> utterances of an outsider, self-assured and spirited, amongst living com-
> posers . . . We would like to think that Busoni is now occupied with forging
> the sword which he can later wield, so that he can prove to us with a large,
> serious work that he is truly one of the elect.[25]

Busoni himself was pleased with the work. After the first orchestral rehearsal,
on 4 March, he noted in his diary: 'Have achieved what Schoenberg strives for
in his best moments.'

But he must soon have become aware of the danger of 'suffocation' in the
spheres he had penetrated with the *Sonatina seconda* and *Nocturne symphonique*.
These are the most forward-looking works of his entire output; he never
rejected them and later he was able to re-immerse himself in their language in
order to incorporate them into *Doktor Faust*. Yet he never attempted anything
of the kind again. One thing is certain: neither the unstable world of free
atonality nor the speculative world of the occult opened any new paths which
seemed to lead 'upwards'. It became clear that the search would have to take
other directions and Busoni's thoughts now turned to Nietzsche's vision of
'. . . a supra-European music which holds its own even before the brown
sunsets of the desert, whose soul is kindred to the palm-tree and knows how to
roam and be at home among great beautiful solitary beasts of prey'.[26]
The next works breathe the clean air of folksong, Red Indian folksong.

XI

The Indians' Book

Red Indian Fantasy op. 44 (Fantasia—Canzone—Finale) for piano and orchestra. *Dedicated*: to Natalie Curtis. *Composed*: April 1913 to February 1914. *First performance*: 12.3.1914. Beethovensaal, Berlin. Busoni and the Berlin Philharmonic Orchestra, conducted by Alexis Zdislaw Birnbaum. *Published*: Leipzig, 1915. PB 2346. *MS*: 96pp., 35×27cm. Staatsarchiv, Leipzig. *Arrangement*: for 2 pianos (Egon Petri) published Leipzig, 1915. EB 4773. Plate number 27686. *Instrumentation*: 2(Picc.)–2(C.A.)–2–2; 3–2–0–0; Timp., Perc.; Harp; Str. *Duration*: 22 minutes.

Red Indian Diary: Book One. Four studies [for piano] on motifs of the North-American Indians. *Dedicated*: to Helen Luise Birch. *Composed*: June–August 1915. *Published*: Leipzig, 1916. EB 4837. Plate number 27881. *MS*: 16pp., 35×26cm. Deutsche Staatsbibliothek, Berlin. *Duration*: 11 minutes.

Song of the Spirit Dance op. 47. Book Two of the *Red Indian Diary*. Study for string orchestra, six wind instruments and timpani. [Third Elegy for Orchestra]. *Dedicated*: to Charles Martin Loeffler. *Composed*: August–December 1915. *Published*: Leipzig, 1916. PB 2452. *MS*: 23pp., 35×26cm. Deutsche Staatsbibliothek, Berlin. *Arrangement*: for 2 pianos (Mario Feninger, 1964) published Wiesbaden, 1966. MS. *Instrumentation*: 1–1–1–1; 0–1–1–0; Timp.; Str. *Duration*: 5 minutes.

Since 1891 Busoni had been a frequent visitor to the United States. Lengthy American tours had dominated his concert schedule in 1904, 1910 and 1911. Occasionally he had serious reservations about the value of these marathon journeys, but they brought him into contact with people and places far removed from his European environment.

In March 1910 Mahler conducted the *Turandot Suite* at a concert in New York. In the audience was Natalie Curtis-Burlin, a young lady who had studied harmony with Busoni in 1893. In honour of the occasion she presented her former teacher with a copy of her recently published *Indians' Book*.

Born in New York in 1875, she had begun her career as a pianist. While visiting Arizona she became acquainted with the Hopi Indians and became fascinated by their folklore and way of life. Unbelievable as it may now seem, at that time the Indians were forbidden to sing traditional songs or perform old ceremonies. Regardless of the restrictions, she began to collect songs and legends from the various North American tribes and in 1907 she published her collection, interspersed with photographs and traditional designs, in a handsome 550-page volume. As a result of her endeavours the Indian music was sanctioned by the government and steps were taken to revive and preserve it. To emphasize this official recognition, her book was prefaced by a facsimile of a letter from Theodore Roosevelt: 'These songs cast a wholly new light on the depth and dignity of Indian thought, the simple beauty and strange charm —the charm of a vanished elder world—of Indian poetry.' In the same year, Edward S. Curtis (unrelated) published the first volume of a monumental photographic collection. This was a considerably more costly and ambitious enterprise which took thirty years to complete. Here too, Roosevelt provided a few words of introduction, speaking of 'that strange spiritual life . . . from whose innermost recesses all white men are forever barred'.[1]

It was above all this mysterious barrier between the cultures that so fascinated the American folklorists and resulted in a spate of photographic and other ethnographical research publications. Natalie Curtis's musical anthology looks slight, for instance, beside the work of Frances Densmore, whose publication, *The Music of the North American Indian*, embraces fourteen volumes and appeared over a span of forty-six years, between 1910 and 1956. Edward and Natalie Curtis both count among the leading pioneers in this field; in the renewed interest in Red Indian culture during the 1960s their major publications have been reissued (that of Edward, however, in radically abridged form [2]). Of course, the world knows the Indians—through the books of Karl May and the endless stream of blood-lusty Wild West films. But the folklorists painted a very different picture. They knew that a centuries-old untarnished culture was in danger of destruction. *The Indians' Book* was assembled and published 'in the hope that [it] might help to revive for the younger generation that sense of the dignity and worth of their race which is the Indians' birthright, and without which no people can progress'. And one of Edward Curtis's most telling and poignant pictures is entitled 'The Vanishing Race'.

It was the Indians' mysticism and other-worldliness that appealed most strongly to Busoni. In a letter to Gerda he noted:

> The Indians are the only cultured people who will have *nothing to do with money* and who dress the most everyday things in beautiful words. How different is a business-man from Chicago by comparison. He knows Roosevelt as 'Teddy', the Indians know him as 'our great white father'.[3]

Reading the fairy-tales in Natalie Curtis's book, he discovered for himself a world that rivalled the fantasy of the *1001 Nights* in poetry and exoticism. He began to plan a work, or series of works, based on their music. Miss Curtis had notated the melodies quite scrupulously but many seemed too foreign for his purposes. He therefore wrote to the 'Song-Maiden', as the Indians called her, asking her to suggest those melodies which she thought capable of greater expansion. By the following year he had formed a vague idea for a theatre piece:

It would be ridiculous to make a symphony on the Leipzig model out of the
Red Indian melodies (like Dvořák) . . . I thought I would first write *one or
two scenes* based on *actual* ceremonies and actions (very simple) in one act
and link them with one of the 'eternal' stories: mother, son, bride, war,
peace—without any *raffinement*.[4]

But this idea was replaced a few days later by a new one, '(very uncertain and
visionary) . . . for an Indian Rhapsody for piano and orchestra'.[5] Busoni left
the United States three weeks later with his vision reinforced by the new
insights he had gained into the spirit of the old America. 'I understood this
country now as never before', he said to Natalie Curtis shortly before his
departure.[6]

On 2 April 1913, the day after his forty-seventh birthday, he began to sketch
the new piece, giving it the working title 'Concerto secondo'. During the
summer of that year he worked at it intermittently and on 19 August he was
able to write to the 'Song-Maiden' that the first movement had that day been
completed.

On a sheet of manuscript paper dated 6 August 1913 he noted down all the
themes which he intended to use, as well as several that never found their way
into the finished work. Their generally pentatonic nature proved a greater
stumbling block than he had foreseen. 'The Indian melodies are not very
fruitful or productive', he told Gerda. 'I will have to graft in quite a lot of my
own.'[7] Contemplation of this unwieldy material gave rise to some penetrating
observations on the nature of melody:

Absolute melody: a series of repeated, rising and falling intervals which,
rhythmically articulated and set in motion, contains within itself a latent
harmony and renders a state of mind; which can exist independent of a text
as expression, and independent of an accompaniment as form, and whose
execution effects no change in its nature through choice of key or timbre.[8]

The Indian motifs, he discovered, were perfect examples of such absolute
melody: they tenaciously retained their inherent qualities. Recorded 'by the
light of the tipi fire or under the glare of the desert sun, in adobe houses while
the women ground the corn, or in the open camp',[9] they still gave off their
particular odour lying on his writing desk in Berlin. And they submitted
stubbornly, if at all, to his attempts to organize them into a European-style
concerto. Here are the Indian melodies which Busoni used, in their original
versions and (when there are variants) in the forms in which he adopted them:

Ex. 132

'Korosta Katzina'(Hopi)

Ex. 133a

'Corn-grinding song' (Laguna)

Ex. 133b

Ex. 134a

'He-hea Katzina' (Hopi)

Ex. 134b

Adagio fantastico

accentato

pesante

ten.

non troppo

Ex. 135

'He-hea Katzina' (Hopi)

Ex. 136a

'Corn-people Yatzina' (Acoma)

Ex. 136b

Ex. 137a

'Corn-people Yatzina' (Acoma)

Ex. 137b

Ex. 138   'Blue-bird song'(Pima)

Ex. 139a   'Passamquoddy dance-song'

Ex. 139b

Ex. 140a   'He-hea Katzina'(Hopi)

Ex. 140b

Ex. 141   'Korosta Katzina'(Hopi)

Ex. 142a   'Cradle-song'(Kwakiutl)

Ex. 142b

Ex. 143a   'Hand-game song'(Cheyenne)

Ex. 143b

Ex. 143c

Particularly fruitful are the two Hopi 'Katzina' songs. (A Katzina is the Hopi word for an intermediary who takes prayers from the people to the gods.) These Katzina songs were modern, written especially for Miss Curtis. 'To seize on paper the spirit of Hopi music is a task as impossible as to put on canvas the shimmer and glare of the desert', she wrote.[10]

The other melodies are all distinguished either by harmonic or rhythmic irregularities—the falling thirds forming a major seventh in Ex. 133, for example, or the triplet of Ex. 143. 'The Blue-bird' and the Passamquoddy Dance-song could easily pass for Slavic melodies and fit best of all into a European framework. Yet none of these fragments could be described as typical of Natalie Curtis's collection; the fascination of many of the originals lies in their monotony, or in the curious vocal or rhythmic inflections with which they were sung. These, although carefully notated, are not reproduceable on the instruments of a symphony orchestra. The melodies Busoni chose are like rare wild beasts in captivity. He faced the problem of providing a congenial environment for his charges, without which they would perish. Through his attempts at solving this problem arise the fascinations—and the frustrations—of the *Indian Fantasy*.

Having completed the first section of the work by the end of the summer of 1913, he proceeded to a slower middle section based almost entirely on 'The Blue-bird'. During a visit to Paris in January 1914 he set up his portable writing-desk, improvised from suitcases and chairs, in an inadequately heated hotel room and set to work on it. In a letter to Petri he wrote: 'Five times I came to the end of the slow movement of the Red Indians, four times I had to scalp it, but I hope that I've found the solution today.'[11] From here on, the rest of the work was written at lightning speed and completed on 22 February. Less than one month later, on 12 March, came the first performance. Busoni sketched the following guide-lines for Leichtentritt to expand into a programme-note:

> . . . no story. But poetic stimulations, such as the melancholy of the race; a glimpse of the Mississipi caught in passing; an intimation of war-like proceedings; exotic colouring. . . . The third movement, uninterruptedly animated, finishes without the customary coda (heralding the end), like a vanishing phantom.[12]

Max Marschalk found the piece effective, but added, 'There is much superficial dingdong . . . in this work, and more the intellectual eloquence of a brilliant *feuilletonist* than the depth and wealth of ideas of the true poet.'[13] Most critics found few words to spare for the *Fantasy*, whose novelty was certainly overshadowed by the *Nocturne symphonique* in the concert. A few days later the second performance followed in Munich (a concert at which Rilke was present). The Bavarian critics were not impressed. One of them found the work 'liberally exotic . . . but quite tedious, an accumulation of curiosities without any apparent meaning or purpose, lacking in shape and order'.[14]

The work, nevertheless, slowly gained acceptance and was often performed during Busoni's lifetime. A particularly auspicious occasion was the American première, given in Philadelphia on 19 February 1915 with Busoni as soloist and Stokowski conducting. Natalie Curtis has left her own record of the event:

> In the empty hall we sat at the morning rehearsal, just a handful of friends, Madame Busoni on one side of me and on the other Percy Grainger, the young English [sic] composer . . . Stokowski lifted his baton, and the cellos and double basses sounded. With the first bars of the orchestral introduction . . . the walls melted away, and I was in the West, filled again with that awing sense of vastness, of solitude, of immensity. . . . The spirit of the real America (a spirit of primeval, latent power) Busoni had felt while travelling across the continent, and had tried to reproduce.[15]

Five years later, a performance in London was so successful that the whole piece had to be repeated. The critic of *The Times*, extolling the work's merits, marvelled at 'the literary tricks of antithesis and aposiopesis,* of under-statement . . . of paradox'.[16]

The opening is based on a Hopi melody that Miss Curtis did not include in her book:

Ex. 144

These flowing, overlapping melodic lines are coloured by grotesque chromatic wails and brief dissonant trills. Modern ears have grown over-accustomed to what was undoubtedly a fresh and original language. Today this opening section sounds not unlike film-music; at best an inspired cliché. The piano now enters, unaccompanied, with a lengthy Fantasia, beginning with drumming effects.† Another Hopi motif emerges:

Ex. 145

---

* Aposiopesis: 'A figure in which the speaker suddenly halts, as if unable or unwilling to proceed' (*The Shorter Oxford English Dictionary*).
† 'Strauss looked at the piano-drumming passage in the Indian score. "It's perfectly inoffensive." ' (from Busoni's diary, 12.3.1914).

Virtuoso versions of Exx. 132 and 133b follow, at all points tonally harmonized, but treated with characteristic fluidity and freedom. Ex. 134b is introduced, Adagio fantastico, each line being followed by an extravagant cadenza-flourish. Then follows Ex. 135, in which the falling semitone of the theme is answered in the harmonization:

Ex. 146

A unique and atmospheric language is created, using only the modest means of the available material: semitones and thirds. In contrast to the virtuoso glitter of its surroundings, this music suddenly rings true (yet Busoni sanctions a cut here). A brief cadenza, also based on the falling semitone figure, leads to the re-entry of the orchestra with gentle, mysterious music which gradually animates into an Allegro.

Three new themes appear, forming a section of ninety-nine bars with restless piano figuration and motivic treatment of themes which comes dangerously close to the dreaded 'Leipzig model'. A Presto cadenza leads to the second part of the work which opens with an unwarrantably dissonant harmonization of 'The Blue-bird':

Ex. 147

an aggregation of semitones and major thirds which, although clearly derived from the harmonies of Ex. 146, hardly seems appropriate to the new melody. Using this material, Busoni spins out a lengthy cadenza in parallel thirds reintroducing the same melody in pure G major, harmonized à la Dvořák. The break in style is a fatal flaw. The Canzone itself, 'four times scalped' as it was, is not without charm.

Ex. 144 serves as a bridge passage leading to the Finale. Here we find a disturbing musical paradox: a passage harmonized in a style akin to that of the *Sonatina seconda* closes with a traditional cadence in D major. The gesture, which was so telling in *An die Jugend*, seems out of place here.

The Finale opens with an expansive setting of Ex. 139a. Contrast is provided by Ex. 140b and 'The Blue-bird' returns briefly, flanked by cadenzas. The second of these leads into a fine orchestral stretta, one of the best passages in the score. Natalie Curtis has written an evocative description of this closing section:

> Though Busoni has been sparing with the drum (the pulse-beat of true Indian music), this characteristic feature enters at the last, and with perhaps the greater dynamic effect through having been withheld at first. The stirring tattoo, beginning softly, as though from afar, then drawing nearer, wakens a vivid picture of Indian life. We see a host appearing over the hill-crest, singing as they come; they pass before us, and at the end they vanish again into the distance, mysterious, causing us to ponder on the early dawn of human life on the American continent and on the passing of the primitive Red Man.[17]

Busoni reintroduces themes from the first tutti of the work (Exx. 137b, 136b and 142b). The ebullient triplet rhythm of the Korosta Katzina (Ex. 141) gives rise to a passage of Lisztian double octaves. The catchy Ex. 143 furnishes a scherzando section before the delicate music of the closing pages, based on Ex. 142b. The piano's continuing octave figuration disappears and the work closes with a stately orchestral crescendo on a plain C major chord.

Later Busoni indicated that the *Red Indian Fantasy* was an experiment 'to obtain a balance between the sound of the two elements used, in an atmosphere of weird, exotic harmonies, without losing sight of the cultivation of the subtlest soloistic virtuosity'.[18] The indecisive role of the soloist in the work hence comes as a disappointment. In comparison with the Piano Concerto, the writing is now more streamlined, textures are clearer and leaner, but the soloist too often plays the self-effacing role of musing commentator and decorator. There is too great a preoccupation with the geometrical problems of piano playing, the outcome of which is a lack of contour and character. This could have been compensated for by the contribution of the orchestra, but, compared with the *Nocturne symphonique*, this is for the most part unadventurous and earthbound. The roles of soloist and orchestra are insufficiently defined; the dramatic possibilities of the medium are underexploited.

The *Red Indian Fantasy* belongs beside such other rare birds of the European concerto repertoire as the *Egyptian Concerto* and *African Fantasy* of Saint-Saëns, the *Moorish Rhapsody* of Humperdinck or the *Scottish Fantasy* of Bruch. Despite its unevenness, the genuine intentions behind the composition are certain. In the Indians, Busoni saw the living remains of a civilization of the long-lost past. In a quotation from *The Discovery of America* by John Fiske, with which Natalie Curtis closes her book, his fascination is explained:

> Among the red men of America the social life of ages more remote than the lake villages of Switzerland is in many particulars preserved for us today, and when we study it we realize as never before the continuity of human development, its enormous duration, and the almost infinite accumulation of slow efforts by which progress has been achieved.

On 20 January 1915 Busoni arrived in New York with his wife and children, ostensibly for a tour of two or three months' duration. This time, however, instead of staying in a hotel, he rented a house in New York's Riverside area and there he remained, virtually a refugee, for nine months. Work was the only activity that prevented him becoming morose—he worked incessantly. In February he told Natalie Curtis that 'the spring may perhaps bring some leaves of the "Indian Diary." '[19] There were to be piano pieces, songs and music for chamber orchestra; on 20 June, after completing the *Rondò arlecchinesco* and the third Sonatina, he began work on a sketch (for the piece which eventually became no. 2 of the *Indian Diary*) and made a list of the qualities of the Indians which he wished to honour: 'Valour—Pride—Charm —Sorrow—Homeland —Dance—Ceremonial—Belief—Melancholy'. The sketch was completed the following day. Two days later he described his miseries to his Berlin friend, Edith Andreae: 'You can scarcely imagine how limited and limiting this country is. Every stimulus to beauty or humanity has to be created from inside oneself, which puts a facetious exasperation in my way.'[20] His only hope was to bury himself in the ideals of nobility and virtue of the Indians. Two days later he made a new, simplified setting of 'The Blue-bird', now combined with the Laguna Corn-grinding song whose potential had scarcely been tapped in the *Fantasy*. In early August followed a reworking of the best music from the beginning of the *Fantasy* (see Ex. 146) and of the hymn-like Passamquoddy Dance-song (Ex. 139b), now entitled 'The Indian National Anthem'. There was also to be a fifth piece entitled 'Tapferkeit' (Valour), using the triplet motif (Ex. 141) from the Finale of the *Fantasy*. This, however, remained unfinished. The order of the four pieces was then changed to correspond with the sequence of their appearance in the *Fantasy*, the new piece being placed second.

The *Red Indian Diary*, subtitled 'piano studies', has the same relationship to the *Red Indian Fantasy* as the first Sonatina to *An die Jugend*: the idealism of the original is tempered by experience and insight to create a more finely balanced work. Here there is nothing experimental, nothing superfluous. The individual songs, freed from the bondage of quasi-symphonic form, seem to breathe again. Each can now be simply enjoyed for what it is.

Except for a few alterations to the piano texture, the first piece is virtually identical to the parallel passage in the *Fantasy*. A new closing section, marked *recitato*, is grafted on, returning to the F sharp tonality of the opening. The music reflects the balance and simplicity of the original poem (in Natalie Curtis's translation):

Corn-blossom maidens
Here in the fields,
Patches of beans in flower,
Fields all abloom,
Water shining after rain,
Blue clouds looming above.

Now behold!
Through bright clusters of flowers
Yellow butterflies
Are chasing at play,
And through the blossoming beans
Blue butterflies
Are chasing at play.

The newly composed second piece uses a Cheyenne melody, an ancient song which accompanied the triumphal return of a war party:

Ex. 148

Here, as in the previous piece, simplicity is of the essence. Busoni limits himself to the intervals of the melody—a semitone and major and minor thirds—and their inversions throughout. The result is a tautly organized, muscular and hard-driven composition, sparing in texture but of a burning intensity. The piece mirrors the ethnic origins of the song while adhering entirely to the language of its time.

'The Blue-bird' is something of a popular favourite among the Indian tunes. In the third movement, Busoni wisely restricts himself to his simple tonal setting, placing it beside the Laguna Corn-grinding song and hence pointing to the scotch-snap rhythm which they have in common: ♪♪ Here is part of the original Laguna song (note values halved):

Ex. 149

Its rhythmic structure is altered considerably and a fluttering arpeggiando accompaniment is added—an idyllic page. Finally, 'The Blue-bird' returns in A flat major then slips deftly back to G. At the first Zurich performance of the *Indian Diary*, a Swiss critic found this movement the finest of the set, 'a poetic and sensitive piece, beside which the first two are a little overshadowed'.[21]

Although the last piece of the set was published without its original title, the fervent patriotic nature of its opening and closing sections is unmistakable. Only towards the close do the angular harmonies of the *Fantasy* momentarily recur but, due to the predominantly simple tonality of their surroundings, they no longer throw the music out of balance. The coda, surprisingly, introduces a vestige of European counterpoint, a feature which has been conspicuously absent from all the Red Indian music.

The projected songs on Indian motifs never materialized. Busoni's last essay for the *Indianisches Jahrbuch* was a composition for chamber orchestra. In this work, *Gesang vom Reigen der Geister (Song of the Spirit Dance)*, he finally achieved a true integration of his own creative personality and the chosen material. Had Busoni been endowed with a talent for publicity, the work could have become well-known; it seems, however, to have remained unperformed for several years after its completion and is even now the least familiar of his mature orchestral works. The background to this little piece is fascinating. Here is Natalie Curtis's explanation of the history of the Spirit Dance:

In about the year 1888 . . . there arose in western Nevada an Indian prophet . . . He announced that he had been with God, of God was his wisdom, and from God were the messages he brought. First, there should be no fighting; and men should love one another . . . The dead would return from the spirit-world, and all Indians would be united in deathless happiness upon a rejuvenated earth . . . As a holy rite, all people should dance a holy dance which the prophet gave to his followers.

The new religion developed into an answer to the longing of the Indian's heart. Some tribes laid aside fire-arms and everything of metal, that they might be as they were before the coming of the white man. Many were drawn to the new faith by the word that those who danced 'died' (fell into a trance).

News that the Indians were meeting and dancing spread alarm among the whites. Those who knew the Indians vainly counselled, 'This is a religious movement; do not oppose it and it will pass.' Commands to the Indians to cease dancing met with the response: 'We harm no one. The Father has bidden us to dance. We will defend our religion, if need be, with our lives.'

The agent in charge of the Dakota Indians at Pine Ridge was unable to check the dance among his people. Thoroughly frightened, he telegraphed for troops. At sight of his soldiers, the war-like Dakotas were in arms. 'We will die, but we will not give up our religion,' they cried . . . An attempt to disarm them . . . was misunderstood by the Indians, who feared massacre. An Indian fired his rifle. The shot was answered by a volley from the troops. Machine guns at close range mowed down the entire camp . . . men, women and children fell in what is now called the massacre of Wounded Knee.[22]

Busoni has used only one of the several spirit-dance songs quoted by Natalie Curtis in her book, a song of the Pawnees:

He started work on the score shortly after completion of his four Red Indian piano pieces (August 1915) and by the time he left for Europe in September it was finished. At the end of October he settled in Zurich and tried out the new composition with members of the Tonhalle Orchestra at a rehearsal on 28 October. Some revisions were necessary: the fair copy was then completed on

30 December. As Busoni explained to Leichtentritt, the work was intended as
a companion piece to the *Berceuse élégiaque* and *Nocturne symphonique*: 'It is
founded on a system which arose *out of the structure and content of the piece itself*
. . . and which, in further attempts of this kind, will always have to create its
own system anew.'[23] Later he intended to place it beside the *Sarabande*,
completed at the end of 1918. Writing to Volkmar Andreae, conductor of the
Tonhalle Orchestra, he described this second volume of the *Red Indian Diary*
as 'a sort of chorale prelude' and continued, 'these two, thoroughly *un-*
brilliant, contemplative little works represent my most personal way of
writing.'[24]

Inspired by the bare intervals and regular rhythms of his Indian cantus
firmus, Busoni devised a setting with a long theme of rising scales and falling
chromatic figures in regular quaver motion, passed from one instrument to the
next like a pipe of peace. An ostinato in the bass seems to recollect the rhythm
of Ex. 145. The quavers are taken up by the winds while the strings embark on
a second, answering line, always in thirds or tenths with the original theme. A
quasi-canonical, flowing three-part texture is gradually built up; thereafter,
the three lines of quavers run independently almost throughout, their separate
voices moving in angular intervals. However surprising the individual lines
may be, the resulting chord in each case is a regular triad, albeit often
augmented or diminished. This rapid flow of familiar chords in unrelated keys,
eight to a bar, produces a disembodied, desolate language which arises not
logically but intuitively out of the cantus firmus. Hence it is unique; we find it
in no other work of Busoni's.

Over this flow of harmonic polyphony, the spirit-dance motif is declaimed
by woodwinds in unison. After its first statement appears a new pentatonic
motif with an accompanying counter-melody which proves itself, on closer
inspection, to be a variant of the motif itself:

Ex. 151

A resulting web of counterpoint becomes ever more intricate and is gradually
fined down until the wind instruments unite on a unison B natural while the
flow of triads in the strings abates. For a few bars the tempo quickens: pizzicato
triads dance over a drum roll. Now the violins declaim a passionate theme over
tremolando lower strings, interspaced with the countersubject of Ex. 151.
There is a solemn fanfare; the dancing triads make another brief, fleeting
appearance and the piece vanishes, like the lost world it has evoked, with
fragments of the fanfare over fluttering dying figures for cellos and double
basses.

In this chapter we have charted Busoni's progress from the traditionally orientated ethnographic study of the *Red Indian Fantasy*, through the 'brightly painted boundary posts'[25] of folk-music to the closer understanding of his material, which we find in the *Red Indian Diary*. The *Song of the Spirit Dance* then advances a stage further; while maintaining and indeed strengthening the link with Indian culture, it is also a completely personal creation, one in which Busoni's powers of intuition had free play.

In the Red Indian works we find an expression of his growing concern to establish 'the Oneness of Music'—a unity that knows no frontiers between men, whatever their race or culture, no matter how widely scattered they may be on the face of the earth.

Section Five

La nuova commedia dell'arte

XII

Before *Arlecchino*

Rondò arlecchinesco [Fourth Elegy for Orchestra] op. 46. *Dedicated*: to Frederick Stock. *Composed*: April–June 1915. *First performance*: 5.3.1916. Augusteum, Rome. Orchestra of the Augusteum, conducted by Busoni. *Published*: Leipzig, 1915. PB 2449. *MS*: 59pp., 36×27cm. Deutsche Staatsbibliothek, Berlin (an earlier copy in Library of Congress, Washington). *Instrumentation*: 2(2 Picc.)–1–2–2; 3–2–3–0; Timp., Perc; Tenor solo (off-stage); Str. *Duration*: 10 minutes.

Sonatina [no. 3] **ad usum infantis** pro clavicimbalo composita. *Dedicated*: to Madeline M[anheim]. *Composed*: July 1915(?).*First performance*: 6.11.1917. Tonhalle, Zurich (?). Soloist: Busoni. *Published*: Leipzig, 1916. EB 4836. Plate number 27880. *Duration*: 7 minutes.

The histories of *Arlecchino* and *Doktor Faust* are inseparable, for the two ideas were originally one and the same. Both title figures can be traced back to the early puppet plays of Faust, in which the heretical doctor has a comic counterpart, Casperle, who takes a menial position in Faust's household, learns to summon the powers of Hell—and to tame them to his particular whim—and entertains the audience with his own variety of philosophy—the sharp-eyed observations of the simple man. Casperle was an essential part of Busoni's original Faust plan; to him, unlike Goethe, the two characters were as inseparable as Don Quixote and Sancho Panza. His original idea was hence to intersperse the serious scenes of his opera based on Faust with Casperle-intermezzi played in front of the curtain.

For a time Busoni's entire scheme tilted in favour of an Italian opera based either on Dante or Leonardo. At this stage Busoni conceived the idea of writing his Casperle-intermezzi in advance as a self-contained preparatory work, in the manner of a latter-day *Serva padrona* or *Pimpinone*. But the precise content of such an opera was problematical. In March 1909 he wrote to Gerda: 'I thought of first writing a short—one-act—Italian opera "as introduction". Perhaps an opera buffa. Subject? . . . Perhaps St. Anthony by Maeterlinck after all. Or a passionate Italian tale with women and monks.'[1] In the summer of 1909 he did indeed sketch out a few bars of a musical introduction to Maeterlinck's little-known comedy, *The Miracle of St Anthony*, but they came to nothing. The plan for an *opera buffa* remained visionary but unforgotten.

In the spring of 1912 two separate experiences in Italy gave him a new impetus. The first was an evening in the theatre in Bologna, an attempt to revive the old style of *commedia dell'arte*. He wrote to Petri:

> Yesterday evening . . . we saw a play which was acted by Italian masks. The Arlecchino cut a most impressive figure; he was personified by an actor who bestowed upon him a tinge of monumentality. Nowhere the low comedy of the Germans (into which—for example—my Thusman also lapsed). When Arlecchino entered as Captain, with an altogether false name, wearing leather knee-boots and a red cloak which stood up at the back like a cock's feathers—due to the angle of his sword—he became exactly like one of Callot's figures in Hoffmann's Prinzessin Brambilla.[2]

The second was a brief visit to Bergamo, the home-town of Arlecchino, where he was struck by the amusing contrast betweent the darkened, old buildings of the town and the bright spring sunshine. This picture became imprinted on his mind as the most effective *mise-en-scène* for his opera.

A year passed, in which the 'occult' works were written and, in the summer of 1913, he began an urgent search for a suitable libretto. He approached his friend Jakob Wassermann, who suggested an adaptation of his comedy *Hockenjos, oder die Komödie der Lüge*, written in 1898, but excused himself from collaborating on what he understood to be a mere 'musikalische Bajazzerie' (musical buffoonery) on the grounds of having too many pressing commitments.[3] Four weeks later Busoni had come no further and wrote to Petri on 9 July, discussing several alternative possibilities: *Das Geheimnis* by Villiers de l'Isle-Adam, already adapted for him by Karl Vollmoeller; Oscar Wilde's *Florentine Tragedy*, which he considered unsuited to his style of composition;* Hofmannsthal's *Die Frau am Fenster*. But then, only a few days later, inspiration suddenly arrived and in unexpected form.

On 16 October 1912, at a time when Busoni had been on tour in England, Berlin had witnessed the world première of Schoenberg's *Pierrot Lunaire*. Anxious to hear the influential new work, Busoni invited the composer to perform it privately for him before a small audience. A detailed description of this occasion is found in a letter he wrote to Egon Petri two days later:

> On 17 June, a Tuesday, I enjoyed the great privilege of receiving the *Pierrot Lunaire* ensemble in my house and of hearing a complete and well-nigh perfect performance of the cycle. A small audience was present, including Mengelberg, Schnabel, Serato [and Varèse]; Schoenberg conducted, Steuermann and Kindler were amongst the performers, also an excellent young Hungarian violinist.
>
> What a level of taste and ability these young people have attained in comparison with the youth of my younger days!—It was an ideal musical afternoon; a highly ingenious new work, a perfect musical ensemble, afterwards stimulating exchange of ideas, tea and cigarettes and charming,

---

* Wilde's play was set to music in 1916 by Zemlinsky.

intelligent women. This is the way in which art should be presented—and no other. Schoenberg's Pierrot Lunaire cycle is a work that stands alone, and one hopes it will remain so. In it one finds masterful passages and some moments of genius. As if a large musical mechanism had been assembled from crumbled ingredients, and as if some of these ingredients have been put to uses other than those for which they were originally designed. It is unforgivable that the poems have not remained in their original French, which certainly comes closer to the 'esprit' of the content.—This longing for the native hills of Bergamo doesn't 'sound' in German.

It would have to be proved geneologically that Pierrot is a native of Bergamo. He is probably a borrowed Italian masque figure (Arlecchino comes from Bergamo) who was transformed by French comedy (Molière?). Pierrot's costume is reminiscent of the Italian Bajazzo or Pagliacco (man of straw), who is however neither a masque nor theatre-character but a carnival figure.—The form of Pierrot Lunaire is very satisfactory. It is made up of three times seven poems, hence three movements. The number and sequence of these poems seems—chemin faisant—to have been first established and thought out. Everything came together during the process of composition. Although all are grotesque, one can describe the three parts respectively as lyric, tragic and humorous (according to the prevailing characteristics).—Between some of the songs, short linking passages seem to have been added *later*, struck me as 'seams'. In the second part a complete instrumental Intermezzo (without text) is inserted, a three-part paraphrase of an earlier flute monologue (which is, by the way, descended from the sad little tune in Tristan).—

The rhythmically and melodically modulated declamation often sounds affected; in certain places, however, almost like a new instrument, charming and expressive.—The heredity of this medium—often genuinely, sometimes only seemingly new—could be established. I received a similar impression when I heard Berlioz's song 'Ma belle amie est morte' (from 'Les Nuits d'Eté') for the *first* time.[4]

This extraordinary letter proves that Busoni was capable at first hearing of comprehending in intimate detail a notoriously difficult new work, of voicing his own criticisms and of formulating an objective evaluation of it. (Later he described the occasion as 'parfaite et inoubliable'.[5]) We are also afforded a unique glimpse of the hothouse world in which the arts flourished up to the outbreak of World War I, and of the stimulating intercourse between creative artists made possible by this society of salons and coffee-houses.

Besides Busoni's insights into Schoenberg's score, the letter also shows how the whole literary-historical question of the *commedia dell'arte* was at that time foremost in his thoughts. *Pierrot* appears to have been the catalyst in his own searches; within a few weeks he had sketched a first draft for his libretto of *Arlecchino* and (as one direct influence of Schoenberg) he had resolved that his protagonist was to speak rather than sing. Having so admired the disposition of the twenty-one numbers in *Pierrot*, he correspondingly divided his libretto not into scenes but movements.

At the end of September, Busoni paid another brief visit to Bergamo. The town now reminded him of the toy theatre he had played with as a boy, the loneliness of the empty piazzas recalling images of sad uninhabited cardboard sets. There he also showed the sketch of *Arlecchino* to his friend Augusto Anzoletti. In March 1914 the text was expanded and, in a sudden spate of inspiration occasioned by the outbreak of war, it was then completed between 19 and 24 October. Busoni wrote to Max Reinhardt of his new libretto, mentioning that he had conceived the title role for his star actor, Alexander Moissi (who had played the role of Kalaf in 1911), and adding, 'I can promise you a minor artistic original'.[6] A few days later he began to compose the music, finishing three pages of full score on 10 November and conceiving the idea of the quartet in the final scene on 5 December; other brief sections were also completed. However, on 22 December he bought a new sketch-block and began feverishly to write the text of the three main tableaux of *Doktor Faust*. *Arlecchino* was temporarily forgotten, and then shelved altogether. It seemed impossible to remain in Europe with war raging on all fronts and no longer any hope of the speedy settlement initially prophesied. Early in January 1915 he departed for the USA.

Busoni was cut off from his friends and transplanted into an alien milieu at a time when his only concern was to press on to the completion of his masterwork. 'I shall never overcome this criminal amputation on my life', he wrote.[7] He began to view the land of 'unlimited possibilities' as a morass of 'impossible limitations'. In particular, the narrow-mindedness of the educated Americans weighed heavily on him. One lady had the tactlessness to ask him if he was a regular church-goer: his resulting explosion of wrath must have shocked her to the core, while his account of the episode in an unpublished letter to Gerda uses unprintable language. Under the circumstances, he had no courage to proceed with *Arlecchino*, not to mention *Doktor Faust*. 'I didn't dare set to work on the opera (which shall not become an opera) for fear that a false start would destroy my last moral foothold',[8] he told Edith Andreae, and he decided to rewrite the music so far planned as an orchestral work. Should the opera materialize, this would constitute a useful study for it; should the plan fail, at least the best ideas would have been saved. First mention of the new piece came in a letter to Petri:

> An orchestral piece is under way, intended to conclude the series of '*studies*' for my new style which began with the 'Elegies'. Thus prepared, I hope for a work with the same relationship to Die Brautwahl as that of my 2nd Sonatina to my pre-elegiac piano pieces.[9]

(He was, of course, referring to *Doktor Faust*, not *Arlecchino*, as the work which should so outstrip *Die Brautwahl*.)

On 8 June the *Rondò arlecchinesco* was finished. Busoni took the manuscript back to Europe with him and on 19 November he was able to rehearse it with the Tonhalle Orchestra in Zurich. A fair copy of the score was completed at the end of that month and arrangements were made for the first performance.

Thus this brief and enigmatic scherzo has a long and complicated history. The title, as so often in Busoni's mature works, is misleading and requires explanation, for the listener will search in vain for traces of classical rondo-form in this work. Here the word *rondò* implies a life-cycle. In the few minutes' duration of the piece Arlecchino loves, betrays, mocks and disappears, just as the Red Indians, the 'vanishing race', fade into the blue horizon at the close of the *Red Indian Fantasy*. Arlecchino's dance is a witty but cynical depiction of his brief earthly sojourn.

But in Italian the word *rondò* has a further connotation: it is the term used in architecture for the lateral wings of a building. Thus, for instance, the Palazzo Pitti in Florence, designed by Brunelleschi in 1558–70, was only completed long after the architect's death by the addition in 1764–1783 of the two *rondò*, which flank and balance the original palace. In choosing the title *Rondò arlecchinesco*, Busoni implies that the work is a 'pendant to *Arlecchino*'.

The work's nearest relative is undoubtedly Strauss's *Till Eulenspiegel*, but the humour of the Bergemask is finer, more aristocratic than that of his German counterpart. Busoni's sense of the absurd makes less for a rumbustious than a disturbing atmosphere. 'If the humour in the *Rondò* manifests itself at all, it will have a heartrending effect', he wrote.[10]

Some of the most striking musical ideas in the score originate from two unfinished projects dating from the second half of 1914. The first of these, no more than a brief sketch, bears the title 'Sonatina quasi sonata' for piano; the second, dated 18 August 1914, a song for baritone and orchestra, is a fragmentary setting of Carducci's poem 'Su Monte Mario'. Three ideas were salvaged from each of these works. From the 'Sonatina quasi sonata', the following:

Ex. 152

Ex. 153

Ex. 154

while in 'Su Monte Mario'★ we find Ex. 152 again, and the original versions of Exx. 157 and 172 (the latter is the 'barbarians' theme of the opera *Arlecchino*). Ex. 152, originally marked *quasi all'italiano*, sounds cold and morose, yet in the *Rondò arlecchinesco* it is transformed into a serenade:

Ex. 155

Ex. 153, in its original guise a twelve-note theme, is transformed into a trumpet fanfare and transposed into A, the basic *Arlecchino* key. The 'Monte Mario' theme:

Ex. 156

was later transformed in a self-parodying process similar to that of Ex. 152, while Ex. 154 was held over for use in the opera.

Busoni divides the *Rondò* loosely into four sections or images:

1. The portrait of the hero in two profiles and one 'en face';
2. Arlecchino's contemplativeness and amorousness (which are fleetingly registered in the score by the gesture of the Serenade);
3. The escape, occasioned by far too risky an adventure, through which Arlecchino saves himself by flattery and argument;
4. Arlecchino, from a safe distance, allows his voice to be heard in supercilious derision of the world.[11]

The first portrait-profile opens with the trumpet fanfare (Ex. 153) and builds a brilliant fugato out of it. There follows a hushed interlude, scored for muted trumpets, clarinets and bassoons:

Ex. 157

★ Busoni noted in his diary that he started work on 'Su Monte Mario' on 25 July 1914. His original plan, 'Canti di quattro nazioni', was for a cycle of four songs in different languages, with poems by Carducci, Poe, Hugo and Heine. This project, which he devised immediately after Austria's declaration of war against Serbia, was intended as

A tambourine begins to play and a new profile emerges, lightly dancing on muted strings:

Ex. 158

A long Rossini-like crescendo builds up, in which the two profiles slowly begin to merge. At the *ff* climax, Arlecchino's twelve-note theme reappears and the music dissolves into convulsive trills, shrieked out by two piccolos and a glockenspiel. The gesture may appear Falstaffian, but there is a hard kernel which almost robs it of its mirth. An 'invocation' follows, thrice repeated, coming to rest on Arlecchino's A, which becomes an extended pedal-point. Eventually, all becomes still and desolate, save for a solitary clarinet with a new version of Ex. 158. All the wind instruments take up Ex. 157 *pianissimo*, but leave the muted trumpets and horns to finish the phrase. (At this point Busoni originally continued with a theme we later find in the fourth Sonatina—see Ex. 193.)

Now comes the serenade. It opens with a murky, unromantic version of Ex. 152 and only slowly comes to life. Even the more jovial version of the theme (Ex. 155)—for all its *leggierezza*—has a cynical effect: an over-persistent Latin lover strums disconsolately on an out-of-tune guitar. The pace quickens and suddenly the music is transformed back into the opening profile which, at its climax, introduces Arlecchino's threefold invocation once more, now in contracted form:

Ex. 159

'The flight' is a rapid, *pianissimo* fugato for the strings, reminiscent of the opening of Smetana's *Bartered Bride* overture. Out of the mêlée of semiquavers emerges a new theme (borrowed from the quartet of the opera). A brief recitative of falling thirds for lower strings and trombones, with a half-close in A major, introduces an off-stage tenor, singing a long cadenza based on Ex. 158. As he finishes, signing his name with a high A, a soft echo of the opening profile strikes up, but dissolves at once into a reminiscence of that chilling laughter we heard earlier. The distant strain of a tambourine fades into silence.

The first performance of the *Rondò arlecchinesco* took place in Rome, in the

---

an attempt to unite the hostile nations at least in an artistic gesture. As Jutta Theurich has pointed out, the intentions of Schoenberg's Four Songs op. 22 (settings of Rilke and Dowson) may well have been similar. The two composers met (evidently for the last time) on 25 September 1914.

second concert of the 1916 season at the Augusteum. Busoni was much amused that the highlight of the opening concert was Strauss's *Alpine Symphony*, a work which he heartily detested and whose epic proportions would contrast strikingly with his new 'poemetto sinfonico': 'a graceful and modest monument . . . less in the style and proportion of a public piazza than in those of a garden',[12] as he described it to Serato.

Despite some enthusiastic voices in the audience, the Romans reacted coldly to the new work of their estranged countryman. The critic of *La Tribuna*, for instance, found no ideas of worth or originality in the score, and poured scorn on the idea of incorporating an off-stage voice in a purely orchestral work. Had it been the work of an Italian composer, he commented pointedly, the public would have utterly rejected it.⋆ However, Busoni expressed his satisfaction with the *Rondò* and, having returned to the safe haven of Zurich, he reported to Petri on the eight days he had spent in Rome, speaking with evident pleasure of the première: 'The Rondò arlecchinesco had a surprising effect, positive and pliant.'[13] He had also spent an evening in the theatre at a performance of Rossini's early opera *L'occasione fa il ladro*, acted by marionettes: 'I rediscovered—cum grano [salis]—*my* theatre and *the* theatre.'[14] A performance of the *Rondò* a few days later in Zurich found a more sympathetic audience and a review of greater insight: 'Sometimes one senses that much of this motley bustle is only a mask which conceals deeper, more painful things',[15] wrote the critic of the *Neue Zürcher Zeitung*; but he too was puzzled by the coda:

> . . . one's pleasure is spoilt by the violently modern character of this music and it is also not made clear why at the end, after the thoroughly Italian carnival atmosphere, a male voice takes its leave with a 'tralala' behind the scenes.[16]

Today the tenor solo remains puzzling, an extreme instance of the composer's ability to surprise. He had even considered using a phonograph recording for the passage and had consulted Stock on the practicability of such an idea. The latter's reply was intelligent: as long as the orchestra played no louder than *pppp* and the cue for the disc could be arranged *colla parte*, there should be no problem. But this was evidently too much of an 'impossible limitation' for Busoni and he dropped the idea.

As he himself stressed, the *Rondò* is his last experimental work. The incorporation of a twelve-note melody is the least experimental facet of the piece, seeming to symbolize the all-embracing nature of the hero. The harmonic language, on the other hand, is as bold as anything of the preceding years. Busoni explained to Leichtentritt: 'The comment of a Berlin critic with regard to my *Nocturne* that my harmonic system "was only suitable for slow

---

⋆ Toscanini, who was present, evidently had no comment on the new work but criticized Busoni wittily for his cavalier treatment of the 'Eroica' Symphony in the first half of the programme. 'The only heroic element was the public', he is reported to have said.

and muted compositions" stimulated me to apply this system to an animated, noisy piece.'[17] Yet in practice he scarcely vindicated himself. Although the harmonies are not far removed from his 'occult' language, the very speed at which the music progresses blurs the picture and creates the impression of stable tonality, further emphasized by emphasis of the note A.

Busoni prefaces his score with an explanatory note, a 'philosophy' of the work, which in turn is headed by a brief motto:

In brightly speckled garments
a supple body
a bold and cunning spirit.

A is the central note which is always reconfirmed.

Arlecchino's speech is universal. Now he boldly asserts his principles through the trumpet; now he whistles at the world with the voice of the piccolo; threatens with the double basses, languishes with the cello, scampers away with violinistic agility.

The three ideas of the motto can also be apprehended in the music:
  'In brightly speckled garments'
is depicted in the form of the movements, loosely strung together;
  'a supple body'
the tempo and rhythm;
  'a bold and cunning spirit'
the content, so far as the boldness and cunning of the composer may permit it.

The *Sonatina ad usum infantis* is the only work of Busoni's in which the name of the dedicatee, although intimately linked with the composition, was deliberately concealed. However, a photograph of Madeline M*, the American girl for whom it was composed, has survived among Busoni's papers in Berlin (see plate 15). It is dated 1918 and shows a strikingly intelligent and purposeful young face; on the reverse side is pencilled what would appear to be her full name: Madeline Manheim. Judging by the picture, she must have been about eighteen. Edward Weiss, who for many years followed Busoni in his wanderings and knew him better than many, recollects that Madeline was a friend of Busoni's elder son, Benvenuto.*

In the absence of a manuscript or of any sketches it is a little difficult to date the work precisely. However, we know that it was already finished by the time Busoni began to compose the *Red Indian Diary* on 20 June 1915 (an initial sketch for that work also contains a note suggesting that the Sonatina may sound well arranged for cello or small orchestra). It also seems unlikely to have been written before the completion of the *Rondò arlecchinesco* (8 June). One

* Information supplied by Ronald Stevenson.

can therefore assume that it was written during those twelve intervening days, in June 1915.

In the third Sonatina, Busoni rounds off his decade of experimentalism and begins to turn towards Young Classicality, sheltering from the hardships of his situation by assuming the mask of a child. He confessed to Edith Andreae 'My heart . . . is in a state of adolescence again; bashful and full of longing and lacking practical impact.'[18] In the *Rondò arlecchinesco* he had looked at the world with the narrowed eyes of the cynic, had whistled and turned his back; now, in contrast, he looked again, with wide-eyed innocence, producing a composition of heartfelt simplicity and earnest tenderness—'a sonatina for a child which itself has the air of a child'.[19] A synthetic rejuvenation perhaps, but also a sincere attempt to come to terms with the world; a psychological change of perspective which gave birth to a new style.

The Sonatina is in five sections that run without a break. The first and second constitute a prelude and fughetta which are thematically linked. The opening phrase of the prelude with its etched profile:

Ex. 160

gives way to a cascading semiquaver accompaniment over which four lines of a chorale are introduced. The prelude then comes gracefully to an end. The theme of the ensuing three-part fughetta is formed from the rising figure of Ex. 160:

Ex. 161

The fughetta is broken off by a brief ostinato figure, over which the chorale returns, steering the movement to an unexpected conclusion in F major. As third movement follows a march in D major which forms itself naturally into a theme, two variations and coda. At the close, the two principal keys of the Sonatina, F major and A minor, are jumbled up into a happy confrontation of F minor and A major (Ex. 162).

Ex. 162

The fourth movement has no more than a linking function in the overall plan, but is in effect its emotional centre. A new version of Ex. 160, now in 3/4 time, is followed by this exquisite setting of the chorale:

Ex. 163

Nothing simpler could be imagined than the melody of the final Polacca. Busoni takes the little semiquaver flourish from Ex. 162, adds a pentatonic bass-line, marks the whole *un poco ceremonioso* and creates one of his most memorable moments:

Ex. 164

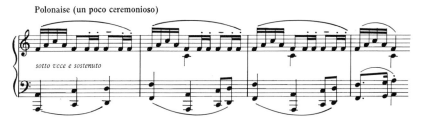

There are two trios, in B major and D major respectively, then a final appearance of the theme in inverted counterpoint, now spiced by the gentlest of dissonances, which leads through a few more troubled harmonies to a pure F major conclusion.

Judging from the title of the third Sonatina (which, like all Busoni's Sonatina titles is in Latin rather than Italian), the work is written for harpsichord, 'pro clavicimbalo composita'. Yet surely this is piano music. While no passages would be impossible on the harpsichord, the texture unambiguously demands the kind of legato playing and the range of tone colours which can only be drawn from a grand piano (as, for instance, in Ex. 163). Certainly, Busoni himself played it on the piano. And in that form it won wholehearted approval when he introduced it to the Zürich public:

> The American girl, Madeline M*, to whom this (incidentally delightful) piece is dedicated, whose themes ingeniously grow out of one another, must be a true child of the twentieth century if she has understood the Sonatina; she will have difficulty enough playing it, certainly she would be unable to bring out all its charms, as Busoni did on this occasion. Incidentally, the tiny piece demonstrates in finest cohesion the Busonian scale of feeling and character: unsentimental, almost acid expression, a tendency to constructionism, full exploitation of piano sonorities and an outlook of fantasy which modulates between the grotesque and the mystical.[20]

XIII

Arlecchino

Arlecchino, or the Windows. A theatrical capriccio in one act op. 50. *Dedicated*: to Arthur Bodanzky. *Composed*: November–December 1914 and November 1915–August 1916. *First performance*: 11.5.1917. Stadttheater, Zurich. Conductor: Busoni; producer: Hans Rogorsch; designer: Albert Isler.

Ser Matteo del Sarto, tailor-master (baritone)	Wilhelm Bockholt
Abbate Cospicuo (baritone)	Augustus Milner
Dottor Bombasto (bass)	Henrich Kuhn
Arlecchino (speaking role)	Alexander Moissi
Leandro, cavalier (tenor)	Eduard Grunert
Annunziata, Matteo's wife (silent)	Ilse Ewaldt
Colombina, Arlecchino's wife (mezzo-soprano)	Käthe Wenck
Two constables (silent)	Alfons Gorski
	Karl Hermann

Published: Leipzig, 1918. PB 1700. *Vocal score*: (Philipp Jarnach) published Leipzig, 1917. EB 6542. Plate number 28147. *MS*: 241pp., 35×27cm. Title page: Staatsbibliothek Preussischer Kulturbesitz, West Berlin; the rest of the score: Deutsche Staatsbibliothek, Berlin. *Instrumentation*: 2(2 Picc.)–2(C.A.)–2(Bel.)–2(Cfg.); 3–2–3–0; Timp., Perc.; Celesta; Str.* Stage music: 2 tpt., timp. *Translations*: Italian by Vito Levi; Portuguese by Germanade Medeiros; English by Edward Dent (all Br.u.H.).

In front of the curtain appears Arlecchino as prologue, to the sound of his brief fanfare. **First movement: Arlecchino as Rogue** The curtain rises on a street in Bergamo, shortly before evening. Ser Matteo is sitting by his front door at an improvised workbench, sewing and reading. Through a first-floor window we can see Arlecchino dallying with Annunziata, Matteo's attractive young wife. While the tailor moralizes on Dante's tale of Francesca and Paolo, Arlecchino hurriedly seeks an escape route. He jumps out of the window, landing directly in front of the astonished Matteo, whom he persuades that war has broken out and that the city is surrounded by barbarian hordes. Matteo, in his confusion, loses his coat and his house-key. Arlecchino hurries him into the house and makes off jauntily with his plunder. The Abbate and Dottore stroll past, deep in professional conversation. The Abbate's enthusiasm for God's gift of wine, women and song is hotly disputed by the Dottore. Observing that Matteo's house is shuttered and silent, they call up to him. Cautiously opening a window, he passes on the news of the siege. The Abbate fears for the safety of his ten daughters; 'Food for

---

* String strength pencilled into Busoni's MS: 8–8–6–6–6.

thought', says the Dottore. All pause for a moment—and think. Abbate and Dottore volunteer to call on the Mayor while Matteo writes his will. They set off in haste but vanish into the nearby tavern.

Second movement: Arlecchino as Warrior In true military style and accompanied by two constables, Arlecchino reappears and orders Matteo to come down: he has been called up for the army and has precisely three minutes to set his house in order. Unobtrusively Arlecchino returns the house key, of which he has meanwhile made a copy, and the bemused Matteo appears in an improvised uniform. Permission is granted him to take his Dante into battle and he trudges off sadly, accompanied by the constables.

Third movement: Arlecchino as Husband Our hero is about to enter the house when, to his considerable annoyance, his wife Colombina appears. She launches into a tirade against his infidelity, stopping only to adjust her face. While, at his behest, she is contemplating the evening star, he slips away. She knocks at the door of the house but is distracted by the approaching sounds of a serenader. Enter Leandro as troubador. Colombina immediately begins to act the abandoned woman, whereupon he draws his sword, positions himself square to the footlights and launches into an Italian vengeance aria, swearing a solemn oath of love and protection. Colombina is not convinced and, when he strikes up yet another of his vocal gems, she earnestly questions his good taste. During the *stretta* she laughingly resigns herself to the situation. Arlecchino, now in his normal costume, has been observing the two through his lorgnette. He comes forward, ushers his wife into the tavern, draws his sword and fights a brief duel. Leandro falls and Arlecchino escapes into Matteo's house.

Fourth movement: Arlecchino Victorious Colombina, the Abbate and the Dottore emerge from the inn, the two men a little uncertain of their step. By now it is quite dark. Linking arms, all three sway down the road in the direction of the Town Hall, the Dottore leading the way with a lantern. He trips over the prostrate body of Leandro. Colombina screams and falls over the corpse but soon detects signs of life in it. The Dottore heatedly challenges her diagnosis; the Abbate, however, proclaims a resurrection. All the windows around the square had opened at the sound of Colombina's scream but, as the Abbate calls on the neighbours for first aid, the inquisitive heads disappear and the windows are closed. Providence manifests itself in the form of a donkey; Leandro awakes from his faint and, after a lengthy quartet, he is hoisted into the cart and carried off to hospital.

Arlecchino appears on the roof of Matteo's house. 'Now shines my star', he exclaims, 'The world stands open! The earth is young! Love is free!' Annunziata joins him and the two disappear into the night. Matteo returns home to find a note from his wife that she is at Vespers. He reopens his Dante and begins to wait for her. The curtain falls. A procession crosses the forestage and bows: Leandro and Colombina, the Dottore and the Abbate, the donkey with his cart, the two constables and finally Arlecchino, arm in arm with Annunziata. He removes his mask, bids the public a fond farewell and dances off. As the curtain rises for a last time, we see Matteo patiently sewing, reading and—waiting.

Soon after arriving in New York in 1915, Busoni read the libretto of *Arlecchino* and put it away. Later that year, when he began to make arrangements for his return to Europe, some of his American friends urged him to stay, finish his one-acter and offer it to the director of the Metropolitan Opera, Gatti-Cassazza. In answer he wrote to Harriet Lanier (in English–French macaronic):

> J'ai relu mon libretto après 6 mois et j'étais un peu effrayé du ton plutôt philosophique et méchant de mon 'Harlequin', qui est le personnage important, 'and a grim friend of disagreeable truths'. L'action, très rapide et hors de l'ordinaire, laisse le spectateur 'at a loss'. It would represent a failure combined with astonishment . . . *La somme de mes opinions*—donnée en trois quarts d'heure dans une forme étrange et avec une musique 'éloignée', ne me semble pas l'affaire pour le *Commendatore* G–C, ni pour un public qui ne me connaît pas.[1]

Having returned to Europe he resumed work on the score towards the end of November. A double stimulus for the conclusion of the work came from his visit to Rome in March of the following year: the first performance of the *Rondò arlecchinesco* confirmed the qualities of the music so far written and his visit to the Teatro dei Piccoli to see *L'occasione fa il ladro* established clear guidelines for the rest of the score. By mid-May the opera was virtually complete and Busoni took five weeks' holiday in Pallanza (it was here that the Improvisation on 'Wie wohl ist mir' was written—see Chapter II). The opera was completed on 8 August in Zurich.

In *Arlecchino* Busoni's humour, which had always had sarcastic undertones, becomes blacker and more brutal than ever before. The manuscript classifies the work not as a 'musical capriccio', as in the printed score, but as a 'Marionetten Tragödie'. Later Busoni presented a copy of the vocal score to Dent, inscribed 'questa mia confessione giocosa'. These two aspects of the work, tragical and autobiographical, serve to outline in concise form a philosophy.

Whatever the content of the piece, its overriding quality is that blend of fantasy with humour which constitutes a caprice. E.T.A. Hoffmann influenced Busoni with his self-styled capriccio, *Prinzessin Brambilla*, showing how a world of disguise and illusion can embrace any number of philosophical strands and submerge them in stylish laughter, using humour sometimes as a weapon and sometimes as a mask. *Prinzessin Brambilla* depicts a Roman carnival, in which all the world seems to be acting out a spectacular Gozzi play. Gradually one tissue of meaning is laid upon another, magic upon myth, *commedia dell'arte* upon parodies of tragic theatre, until illusion and reality confront each other in a mirror. Out of this web of almost incomprehensible fantasy finally appears a pair of lovers:

> In that little world called the theatre, a couple had namely to be found which was not only inwardly blessed with true fantasy and humour but would also be capable of recognizing this state of mind objectively, as if in a mirror, and

to make it appear in exterior life in such a way that it should impress itself upon the wide world . . . like some powerful magic.[2]

It was this same magic mirror which Busoni invoked in writing his capriccio for marionettes. Lip service is indeed paid to Hoffmann, if only in the briefest of quotations in Arlecchino's prologue:

So spiegelt sich die kleine Welt im kleinen,
Was lebend wahr, will nachgeahmt erscheinen.

In mirrors does the little world diminish,
And living truths as metaphor do finish.

The stylistic model for the text is to be found, however, neither in the shrewd humour of Casperle, nor in Gozzi, nor in Hoffmann, but in the work of Cervantes: 'Arlecchino's speeches are just as seriously meant as those, on a monumental scale, of *Don Quixote*', wrote Busoni.[3] And he had found this same monumentality, which seemed to elevate the character out of the conventions of traditional *commedia dell'arte* situations into a new form of epic theatre, in the acting of the Arlecchino he had seen in Bologna. The most overtly Quixotic figure in the opera is Leandro. Apart from being a parody of the operatic tenor, he wears a musty odour of outmoded chivalry, while the whole episode of his duel with Arlecchino reads like one of the adventures of 'The Knight of the Sad Countenance'. Cervantes is also an influence on the pithiness of the text, and on the happy jumble of Latin, Italian and French which Busoni mixes into the German language. Here the models are Cervantes's little-known *entremeses*. Written expressly as curtain-raisers, they are notable for their lightning repartee, scurrilous—wellnigh heretical—undertones and derisive usage of epic pentameters or garbled Latin. Only two weeks after the first performance of *Arlecchino*, Busoni sketched an extension to the *entremes* 'El Teatro de los meravillos', clearly with a view to turning the piece into an opera. Had this projected work, 'Die Wunder-Bühne', ever been completed*, and had it been performed alongside *Arlecchino*, it would have been made doubly clear that the humour which came to be known as 'la gaya scienza' was the essential part of Busoni's text; that same caustic *Weltanschauung* which Nietzsche revived with the more fearsome-sounding German name, 'die fröhliche Wissenschaft'.

Busoni, however, noted on the day he completed his libretto, that *Arlecchino* is 'more than an entremes'.[4] The qualities which elevate it above the level of a harmless 'Bajazzerie' are philosophical, and can only be approached through consideration of a complex phenomenon—the reappearance of the marionette on the stage at the turn of the twentieth century. Complex because of the intersection of so many related themes and ideas—*commedia dell'arte*, the doll,

---

* Hans Werner Henze's one-act opera *Das Wundertheater* (1948, rev. 1964) is an adaptation of the same Cervantes *entremes*.

the circus and the music-hall, for example—and because the phenomenon cuts across all art forms.

The revival of *commedia dell'arte* summons up such names as Edward Gordon Craig and Max Reinhardt in the theatre, Picasso as painter and stage-designer, and such diverse composers and works as Richard Strauss (*Ariadne auf Naxos*), Stravinsky (*Petrushka, Pulcinella*), Schoenberg (*Pierrot*), Fauré (*Masques et Bergemasques*), Szymanowski (*Masques*) and Debussy (*Masques, Suite bergemasque*, Cello Sonata, subtitled 'Pierrot fâché avec la lune'). With the doll we come to Rilke, who had an almost morbid fascination for these playroom toys; we return to the nursery, hence to Mussorgsky, to Fauré and Debussy once again and to Ravel, while we touch on one of the favourite topics of the Surrealist painters. The question of circus and music hall leads to Satie, to Futurist theatre and hence to Dada, to Stravinsky in several forms, and to *les Six*, as well as dominating one of the most impressive early periods of Picasso. Perhaps an art historian will one day help to unravel the tangled renaissance of the marionette in our century, for at present it is an unwritten chapter in the history of European culture. As far as *Arlecchino* is concerned, we shall extract some of the relevant threads from the arguments that such a study would have to expound, and attempt to throw a little more light on the opera.

One initial point of fundamental importance is that for Busoni, as for Gordon Craig, *commedia dell'arte* and marionette theatre were virtually one and the same thing. By donning a motley costume and a mask, an actor dehumanizes himself, loses his individuality and, like the marionette, wears only one expression on his face. Schiller had observed how the characters in Gozzi had a marionette-like stiffness and found this the major stumbling block in his attempt to make credible human beings out of them. A century later *commedia dell'arte* came to be valued precisely because of this stiffness which, it was found, could serve to express the inhuman and hence the super-human. Gordon Craig's revolutionary concept of the actor as an 'Ueber-marionette' was the logical outcome of this process. It merged the separate traditions of masked living actors and sculpted wooden dolls into a new manifestation, *La nuova commedia dell'Arte*, as Busoni dubbed it.

One link in this chain seems illogical: that an 'inhuman' figure should be transformable into a 'super-human' one. There is a philosophical hypothesis in this transformation which has never been more succinctly expressed than by Kleist in his influential essay 'On the marionette-theatre' (1810). Marionettes, he explains, are superior to human beings in a number of ways. First, they have no affectations: 'For affectation appears . . . when the soul (vis motrix) rests in some point other than the focal point of movement.' But the soul of the marionette, he continues, is inevitably located at its centre of gravity. However, this alone cannot explain his paradoxical view that '. . . more grace can be preserved in a mechanical puppet than in the structure of the human body'. He therefore goes on to compare the state of lost innocence in which man has existed since the expulsion from the Garden of Eden with the state of grace of the marionette, a state in which only a god can rival him:

Just as the intersection of two lines on the one side of a point passes through infinity and suddenly reappears directly before us, so does it also occur that, when knowledge similarly passes through infinity, grace reappears in such manner that it is simultaneously manifested at its purest in those human anatomies which have either no consciousness or an infinity of consciousness, i.e. in a puppet or in a god.

Thus the puppet shows the way to regain Paradise—the state in which man becomes a god once again. And the two frontier posts, puppet and god, between which we stand, are in fact one and the same: '. . . the point where the two ends of the circular world interlock'.

A further attribute of the puppet which Kleist stresses is that it is 'antigrav' (weightless): 'They know nothing of the inertia of matter . . . Puppets require the ground only to glide over it, in order to reanimate the swing of their limbs through momentary hindrance.' Hence, that most wonderful attribute of music to which Busoni had drawn attention in the *New Aesthetic* is also possessed by the marionette—it floats on air, 'it touches not the ground with its feet'.

The position of man, poised between puppet and god, as outlined by Kleist, was reiterated a century later by Rilke. In his fourth Duino Elegy (conceived shortly after the outbreak of the First World War and finished in 1922) he changed only Kleist's terminology, from god to angel, from puppet to doll, when he wrote:

Engel und Puppe: dann ist endlich Schauspiel.
Dann kommt zusammen, was wir immerfort
entzweien, indem wir da sind.

Angel and doll! Then there's at last a play.
Then there unites what we continually
part by our mere existence.[5]

A question which occupied him intensively was whether the puppet possessed a soul. Certainly, Casperle had none, as he himself declares in the 'Faust' puppet-play: 'As far as a soul is concerned . . . when I came into the world there just weren't any more souls available.'[6] Rilke came to a more provocative conclusion: he spoke of the existence of a puppet-soul 'which is not made by God'.[7] He also drew a striking distinction between the doll and the marionette: 'A poet could come under the sway of a marionette, for the marionette has nothing but imagination. The doll has none and is exactly that much less than a thing than the marionette is more.'[8] And Gordon Craig saw in imagination, the divine spark, the probable soul of the marionette:

What the wires of the ueber-marionette shall be, what shall guide him, who can say? I do not believe in the mechanical . . . nor in the material. . . . The wires which stretch from Divinity to the Soul of the Poet are wires which might command him.[9]

The marionette is a little figure, but he has given birth to great ones who, if they preserve the two essentials, obedience and silence, shall preserve their race . . . Leonardo was such an Ideal. The marionette is another.[10]

We do not know to what extent Craig and Rilke exerted an influence on the libretto of *Arlecchino*. Certainly, Busoni never met Craig, although he possessed a copy of his book, *The Art of Theatre*, yet their views are strikingly similar. In the case of Rilke there is more positive evidence: his influential article on puppets, 'Zu den Wachspuppen von Lotte Pritzel', was written just one month before his first meeting with Busoni and published in the very week of that meeting in *Die Weissen Blätter*, the foremost literary journal of the German-speaking world, in March 1914. On 19 March Busoni noted in his diary: 'My fingers are itching. Dialogue about subjects, Harlequin one-acter?' Only a few days later he completed the second draft of *Arlecchino*. As with *Die Brautwahl* we come to see that thoughts of world-salvation are at the root of a comedy. The hero, Arlecchino, is the symbolic progenitor of those creatures which one day were to regain Paradise. And that, as Kleist wrote, 'is the final chapter in the history of the world'.

The oubreak of war added a further layer of meaning to the capriccio. Busoni recorded that:

The sketch of the libretto . . . was made in the spring of 1914 when there was still no war to fear . . . The butchery which meanwhile broke out resulted in the alteration of the original 'Turks' of the libretto to 'barbarians'.[11]

In fact the 'butchery' had more effect than this one slight alteration; it served to change the whole tone of the text. For Rilke, who had so enthused over puppets as living things, the war seemed to have put an end to their vitality. In 1915 he found '. . . the shattered world after Pierrot's death now only describable in beautiful fragments'.[12] *Arlecchino* ceased once and for all to have anything to do with a 'Bajazzerie', and its 'beautiful fragments' took on the gloomy undertone of Busoni's prevalent spirits. Later he was to reject the reproach that the piece was sarcastic or inhuman, and to insist that his intentions had been quite the opposite: '[It arose] out of pity for men, who make things harder for themselves than they should and can be; therefore one comes in "Arlecchino" . . . only to agonized laughter.'[13]

One cannot say that the main theme of *Arlecchino* is the search for Paradise, the lampooning of romantic opera and of the clergy, a protest against man's inhumanity to man or an attack on the concept of marital fidelity. All these ideas, and much more, are entangled in its hectic hour: its charm, just like the gaily speckled clothing of its protagonists, lies in its diversity.

Arlecchino's brief spoken prologue in front of the curtain is more enigmatic than explanatory. He beckons to the maestro d'orchestra, who starts the introduction. The music is identical to the opening of the *Rondò arlecchinesco*.

Arlecchino as Rogue Ser Matteo, Busoni explained, is 'the betrayed idealist who suspects nothing'.[14] As the curtain rises we find him reading the Fifth Canto of Dante's *Inferno*. The cor anglais plays a theme:

Ex. 165

which fits the words over which he is musing. It becomes a fugato, then a *scherzando* which, as he reads the lines over and over again with growing enthusiasm, rises to a little outburst of delight:

> Questi che mai da me non fia diviso
> la bocca mi bacciò tutto tremante.
> Galeotto fù'l libro e chi lo scrisse!

> He that may never more from me be parted
> Trembling all over, kissed my mouth. I say
> the book was Galleot, Galleot the complying
> ribald who wrote.[15]

The episode which he is so enjoying describes how Francesca da Rimini and her lover Paolo one day read the legend of Lancelot and Guinevere; how the Arthurian lovers had been united through the offices of a go-between named Galleot (or Galahad). Hence the book, and the man who wrote it, became in turn the pander to Francesca and Paolo. It is a difficult passage by any account, and Matteo, reading and rereading it, finally draws a moral from it: 'Unchastity! You are the true Galleot who finishes in Hell.' The score becomes correspondingly symbolic, introducing a phrase in a series of intervals that we shall come to recognize as Busoni's 'Faustian' language:

Ex. 166

and then a variation on Arlecchino's twelve-note theme:

Ex. 167

Indeed, while Matteo is innocently reading of 'the smile desired of lips long thwarted',[16] Arlecchino is simultaneously putting the idea into practice. The prospect of the great lovers in Hell leads Matteo to thoughts of Don Juan and the orchestra, echoing his fantasies, strikes up part of the 'Champagne' Aria but *pianissimo*. Finally, he achieves a setting of Dante's text in Mozart's tempo (using the last phrase of Ex. 165):

Ex. 168

Matteo requires only a few seconds longer for his cultural acrostic than Voswinkel did to light his cigar in *Die Brautwahl*. Busoni had originally intended to include some lines explaining the obscure Galleot quotation, but discovered that the extra text 'disturbed the shaping of the music'.[17] Had he carried out his plan of writing an opera based on Dante, for which the four movements of *Arlecchino* would have served as intermezzi, the meaning of this scene would have become clearer. We know from a letter to Gerda[18] that the episode of Paolo and Francesca would have featured in such an opera. Matteo's reading of their story some 500 years later would then have had the effect of a direct parody.

One intriguing point emerges from the sketches for this scene: Matteo's declamation of Dante was originally composed in Schoenbergian *Sprechstimme* notation. This last shred of the influence of *Pierrot Lunaire* was later replaced by conventional singing. It would anyway have represented an encroachment on Arlecchino's virtually sole right to speak over the music.

The hero seeks his escape route, and the bass falls to A, his note. He jumps down, coolly quotes the next line of Dante's Canto V:

Quel giorno più non vi leggemmo avanti.

We read no more that day.

and equally coolly informs Matteo: 'While you set Dante to music, the barbarians are marching to the gates.' Who is this creature, wonders Matteo, and where does he come from? Arlecchino answers: 'I am the Archangel Gabriel and I kill the dragon.' But the pose lasts only two seconds; he transforms himself into a barbarian—a German—a Lutheran; thoughts of Germans lead him to steer-horns and they in turn imply a warning that Matteo himself may well acquire the cuckold's horns before long. Meanwhile he snatches the tailor's scissors, hoists his coat aloft as 'the banner of religion' and thereby acquires what he actually wanted, namely the house-key. All this happens in thirty quick bars! Who, then, is Arlecchino? Gordon Craig provided this historical description of him:

> He can throw himself into any part without perpetuating it himself, just as the quicksilver, which will run into any mould, yet retains the form of none. He is always the same in essence, always different in expression. His many-faceted personality catches every ray of light, is many-coloured as the rainbow . . . the creation of sun and water, tears and smiles.[19]

Whoever he may be, his ferocious joy proves too much for Matteo, who retires bewildered and bemused into his house. Arlecchino hurls us a phrase of his credo—'The fortune of war is as changeable as the weather-cock, so when it storms, seize it by the neck!'—and vanishes. From off-stage he sings the defiant *lalalera* with which the *Rondò arlecchinesco* came to a close.

Now the Dottore and the Abbate arrive, 'honest bunglers of the body and soul' as Busoni described them.[20] We are apparently back in the world of classical *commedia dell'arte*. These two grotesques are just as mischievous as the Captain and Doctor in *Wozzeck*, just as obnoxious as their counterparts in Maeterlinck's *St. Anthony*, yet the Abbate, despite his ample girth, is almost as protean a creature as Arlecchino himself. There is a good reason for this: he represents part of the composer's own personality—he is a discarded mask. In a letter to Edith Andreae Busoni wrote:

> Do you know that in my first years of adolescence I overcame only with difficulty the desire to take holy orders? And I would certainly have made it to become a bishop. And such a bishop has a palace, a park, a library, a gallery, a cellar, a crook, a flock . . . and, I believe, many, many women.[21]

The initial dialogue of Abbate and Dottore is a series of monstrous assertions set to charming, Mozartian music. Busoni writes a series of variations on a simple idea:

Ex. 169

which follows the shuttlecock of the argument as it passes to and fro, eventually reaching a state of impasse in a confrontation of theme and inversion:

Ex. 170

The Abbate changes the subject. He would give all the Doctor's tinctures and potions for 'the content of a straw-bound flask, savoured upon a hill in Tuscany'. Suddenly the world stands still, the music takes on a shimmer of distant A major and a voice—for it is no longer the Abbate—repeats the word 'Toscana' as if it were a cry of anguish. The tonality shifts to C minor, intensifying the pain of this fleeting moment of nostalgia, then the vision vanishes and the dialogue is resumed. Only as the Abbate enthuses over 'die Frauen' does the theme of the Tuscan hills return:

Ex. 171

He suddenly realizes, however, that they are standing in front of the house of the lovely Annunziata, and the Galeotto theme (Ex. 165) returns jauntily. As they stare up at the shuttered windows a new, desolate idea sweeps in (Ex. 157) and the underlying rhythm, ♩♩ ♩ ♩♩♩ , previously so jovial, takes on a sinister form. Finally, as Matteo opens his window, a phrase of Ex. 169 returns to furnish a neat, baroque coda.

In a few words, Matteo outlines the hopeless plight of the town. The 'barbarians' theme, which Arlecchino had previously struck up, now serves as the basis for a miniature sonata Allegro—

Ex. 172

followed by an equally brief *sostenuto* and a featherweight *scherzando*. The terzet is rounded off by a coda formed from three ideas: a phrase of the *sostenuto*; a hint of the Abbate's Toscana theme (as he decides to put his love of

Chianti to a renewed test); and a musical somersault, *vivace pianissimo*, as the two figures vanish into the inn.

Arlecchino as Warrior An Allegro marziale in B flat major which bears a distinct resemblance to the march in *Fidelio* introduces Arlecchino in his latest disguise. He throws out an eight-word sermon on keys: '*Suum cuique*. For every hole there's a key' and, without pausing for breath, calls Matteo down from his room. While Matteo mumbles Dante, Arlecchino casts a professional eye on his troops—all two of them—and has them parade up and down to a theme allegedly by Donizetti.* 'What is a soldier? What is Justice? What is the Fatherland?' he asks, and answers each part of his question with biting irony, to conclude triumphantly: 'You are soldiers and are fighting for Justice and for the Fatherland.' But the three minutes are up and Matteo appears, grotesquely clad, accompanied by an equally grotesque *minore* version of the Donizetti theme, scored for bass clarinet, bassoon and contrabassoon. He asks permission to take his Dante with him and Arlecchino assents: 'Nobody shall say that culture perished in the war!' This brief exchange recalls a sad scene from Italian history. When the French captured Milan in 1499, Count Ludovico Sforza, the ruler of the city and for several years master and friend of Leonardo da Vinci, was thrown into solitary confinement. He was permitted to take just one book with him—*La divina Commedia*.

Arlecchino as Husband The theme which accompanies the entrance of Colombina is the gentle Polonaise from the third Sonatina (Ex. 164). Like many of the *Arlecchino* themes it rotates around a tonic triad and, whereas Arlecchino's own twelve-note triadic fanfare (Ex. 153) rises proudly like a cockcrow, Colombina's stays firmly in the soft stable key of F major, domestic and charming. Placed side by side, the two themes are like man and wife, a perfect illustration of Busoni's use of musical language in directly symbolic fashion.

There is, however, symbolism of another kind in this section of the opera: *Arlecchino* is a *confessione* and Busoni affirmed that 'the words of the hero himself are my own creed'.[22] He outlines a surprisingly flexible concept of marriage, an outlook in which he proves himself very much a child of our time. After the marital tiff with his wife Arlecchino tritely observes: 'Fidelity, madam, is a vice which does not become my respectability—It is a fall at the first fence . . . infidelity to oneself.' Where he usually finds little time to elaborate his ideas, here he pours out a stream of such metaphors. A further passage, not set to music, but later published in the essay, 'Arlecchinos Werdegang', also questions Colombina's fidelity: 'But do your dreams centre only on me? Are you certain? There is also a secret infidelity which leaves deep stains because it is inert, and which stinks like stagnant waters:—impotent fidelity!'

The confrontation of husband and wife takes the compact form of minuet

---

* Not even Donizetti experts have succeeded in identifying this theme. Dent asserts that it comes from *La figlia del reggimento*, but this is not the case.

and trio; the trio an energetic arietta for Colombina in alternating 3/4 and 2/4 time, and the minuet suave orchestral variants of the Polonaise theme. Arlecchino vanishes, the orchestra strikes up the serenade (Ex. 155) and Leandro appears dressed as a wandering minstrel:

Sänger ist vom Denken frei,
Ehre ist des Ritters Fleiss,
Sängesritter hält die Treue,
weil er es nicht anders weiss.

Singers are from thinking free,
honour spurs the knight along,
Singing knights must faithful be,
as they know no other song.

His pompous advances are checked by Colombina, who knows this scene only too well; she chimes in with music worthy of Donna Anna (or do we hear in the violins that same lamenting phrase with which Gluck's Orpheus mourns for his lost Eurydice?):

Ex. 173

But Leandro knows exactly what to do and, playing her Don Ottavio, he finds the fitting aria for the moment (Ex. 174).

He comes to a stormy conclusion, bows to the audience, smiling, and resumes his flirtation. Colombina is mistrustful, however, and assumes the role of Elsa, whereupon Leandro becomes her Lohengrin. The orchestra shades the scene with an appropriately Wagnerian string tremolando, interspersed with thickly spaced wind chords and fatuous fanfare rhythms. In fact, Busoni pokes fun more at the post-Wagnerians than at Wagner himself; an opera of Eugen d'Albert's, *Die toten Augen*, with a drastically Expressionist libretto by H. H. Ewers and Marc Henry, appeared in 1916. After outlining the details of the plot to Petri (it is an agonized parable of love and infidelity), Busoni

Ex. 174

explained: 'My one-acter means to scourge these things a little; it is an opera that itself turns against opera.'[23] Colombina is uncertain whether she should laugh or yawn, but her gestures seem to give the knight some cause for hope. He shows off his coloratura in a Donizetti/Bellini number:

Ex. 175

This is too much for poor Colombina, but Leandro is certain of his artistry and Busoni even writes one of those scooping portamenti into his part which some singers mistake for emotional delivery:

Ex. 176

The Stretta closes the scene. Its prototype lies somewhere in the world of Cimarosa, Mozart or Rossini but its harmonic language, with abrupt changes of key and symmetrical chromaticisms, is pure Busoni. He watches over the entire opera-parody with a glint in his eye, never involving himself so completely in a style that he cannot immediately slip out of it, never resorting to cheap pastiche and holding the diverse threads together with the finest sense of form.

Arlecchino victorious As the three figures emerge from the inn, the world of musical parody is forgotten. The last section of the opera is among the most forward-looking of Busoni's inventions: the textures remain Mozartian, the manner of delivery remains elegant yet direct. Its novelty lies in its iciness, its brightly gleaming surface and its desolate tonal harmonies. 'The scene of the windows and the inquisitive but indifferent heads is not exactly comic, and unfortunately only too true.'[24]

The opening scene of this last movement is based on an ostinato rhythm: $\frac{3}{4}$ ♪♫ | ♫ ♪ , ♪♫ | ♫ . The nervous music of Colombina is contrasted with the steadfastness of the Abbate, musically expressed by the opening out of the Arlecchino-triads into an ascending chain. As the body of Leandro is discovered, the triad assumes a new restricted form, set against a wailing, chromatic counter-subject:

Ex. 177

In the face of death, the two professionals are left speechless; neither the soothing words of the preacher nor the potions of the quack are a cure for this particular ailment. They express their helplessness in a capricious duet, which makes use of the third idea (Ex. 154) from Busoni's projected Sonatina quasi Sonata:

Ex. 178

The Abbate begins to look for help, calling first at Matteo's house. The loneliness of the scene is accentuated by the spareness of the orchestration (the theme of Ex. 177 on a solo bassoon, accompanied by a single chromatic line of pizzicato crochets) and is punctuated only by the shutting of windows. When humans fail in their duty, muses the Abbate, Providence comes to the rescue. And, sure enough, the *asinus providentialis* appears.

The donkey was the patron animal of Busoni's birthplace, Empoli. He himself once described the festival of the 'flying donkey' which was celebrated annually on Ascension Day, to commemorate the occasion when the warring inhabitants of Volterra had declared that the Empolesi could no less defeat them than they could make donkeys fly: 'A donkey was brought to the top of the *campanile* and he was lowered down on a hempen rope. To intensify the illusion, the poor beast was adorned with a pair of golden wings.'[25] Later, Busoni adopted the donkey for his mocking coat of arms, at one time with the motto 'Geduld' (patience), later crowned with a laurel wreath.

Once, in London, he caught sight of the beloved beast: '. . . in the midst of the thick motor-bus traffic he walked peacefully and innocently . . . down Shaftesbury Avenue.—All the cars had to give him a wide berth, because he moved more slowly than they did. That raised my stupid heart.'[26]

The Abbate strikes up a hymn of praise to the wonderful creature:

Ex. 179

and each of the characters joins in an ensemble, voicing their private thoughts: Leandro a little battered, but still breathing thoughts of love; the Dottore as venomous as ever, with scornful comments on love and belief; Colombina musing on the folly of menfolk. The quartet, with four contrasting emotions united in one flow of melody, brings back for a moment the spirit of opera-parody, and Busoni relieves the tension of the preceding scene with a passage strongly reminiscent of *Rigoletto*:

Ex. 180

As the sad little group moves off to the hospital, Arlecchino appears, accompanied by fanfares (Ex. 159). 'Now shines my star', he calls, and the bass-note A returns, bringing an ecstatic version of his theme:

Ex. 181

His escape with Annunziata is accompanied by the 'flight' music from the *Rondò arlecchinesco*.

Ser Matteo returns, together with the 'Donizetti' theme which has presumably accompanied him all over Bergamo and is now reduced to a drastic parody, with crisp trombone staccatos and a veiled colouring of flute and celesta. Busoni deftly combines the theme with his own Dante music (Ex. 165). As Matteo settles down to read, the mood changes to one of subdued mirth.

The final procession is accompanied by the Polonaise theme, spreading like balsam on the wounds of what has gone before. As Arlecchino makes his last triumphant entrance, the triad motif of the Colombina-music changes abruptly to his own Allegro molto and, after his biting speech of farewell, the final Presto transforms the triad into a lighthearted Mozartian gambol:

Ex. 182

'Das ist mir völlig unbegreiflich'—this is beyond my comprehension. Perhaps Matteo speaks for the audience in his parting words, for a good deal of this rapidly moving opera runs the risk of appearing 'völlig unbegreiflich'. Certainly, Busoni admitted that it was his intention to mystify: '[The opera] has a tendency to ambiguity and hyperbole in order to place the listener momentarily in a position of slight doubt; it adheres consciously to a constant play of colour between grim jest and playful seriousness.'[27]

One last curiosity is an appendix in which part of Arlecchino's closing speech is set to music (published only in the orchestral score). Although his off-stage voice was that of a tenor, our hero has now become a sonorous baritone. The score of this variant was completed on 7 May 1917—just four days before the first performance. It seems unlikely that Alexander Moissi would have sung it at such short notice (if at all) and it is indeed doubtful whether it should be sung; that Arlecchino should suddenly burst into song is one surprise too many in this already very surprising opera. The little aria itself is a compilation of diverse phrases of Mozart. One hears echoes of 'Per questa bella mano' K.612, of Guglielmo's second aria from *Così fan Tutte* and of the last finale from *Figaro*, to name but three. A producer fortunate enough to have a baritone as exponent of the title role may find it a stimulating addition to the opera.*

---

* Note for producers. Here are some extracts from letters concerning the staging of *Arlecchino* from Busoni to Franz Ludwig Hörth, chief producer of the Berlin Staats-oper. (13.3.1921): 'I am for giving Arlecchino a less authentic costume, matching the overall picture and the character of the figure.' (26.5.1921): 'I visualize the scenery of "Arlecchino" as a detailed picture of a *magnificent*, stylized Italian town. Beyond the outskirts in the foreground (to which streets and alleys lead) the city should rise high into the background with walls and towers, crowned by a church-spire, so as to raise the

Although it left a bitter taste in the mouth, *Arlecchino* was warmly received at its first performance and was soon enjoying quite a spate of productions. Stuttgart staged the first German performance, followed by Frankfurt and Cologne; there was a particularly fine production in Berlin in 1921, and in 1924 it was played in Weimar together with Stravinsky's *Petrushka* and Hindemith's *Mörder, Hoffnung der Frauen*, a production which prompted an appreciative letter from Klee, Kandinsky and Gropius, bringing a little cheer to the dying composer. *Arlecchino* has also been performed frequently in Italy (scenery and costumes for a production at La Fenice, Venice in 1942 were designed by the former Futurist, Gino Severini) and in Anglo-Saxon countries, most notably at Glyndebourne in 1954—an excellent performance which was subsequently recorded. In the 1940s Dimitri Mitropoulos introduced the opera to the United States with a cast of students.

The critics at the first performance were fairly united in their approval of the piece. Their ranks were later joined by Stefan Zweig, who wrote a lengthy report for the *Neue Freie Presse*, Vienna:

> Busoni's joy is to persist in undermining operatic pathos with little literary and musical jokes . . . Whenever the light-hearted comedy wants to sink into emotion or false theatrical depth of feeling, he holds the mood in suspense and this lightness of touch, sparkling out of the music and hovering over the lyrical passages like a butterfly, has a purity of artistic and musical taste quite seldom to be found on the operatic stage. . . .
>
> In 'Arlecchino' . . . the substance seems at first a kind of Decameron-lark . . . but the joke turns sour . . . and Arlecchino, the lively voice, finally becomes the philosophic mocker and raisonneur of the World War. The whole is a caprice, a play of moods, but of a humour which tries to conceal deathly earnest, spangled like Arlecchino's jester-costume, but nimble, brisk, light and lusty as himself.[28]

---

skyline as high as possible and in order to use the entire height of the stage. The puppet-like quality of the figures should contrast with this monumental, intricate and fascinating background in such a way that the symbolic sense of the simple action becomes more sharply etched.' (7.6.1921): 'The scene with the windows must mark more *rhythm* and the closing of the shutters should occur at intervals of approximately 8,8,4,4,2,2,2,2 bars.'

In the 1918 Zurich revival of *Arlecchino* the title role was played by the bass-baritone Alfred Jerger. Busoni authorized a transposition of Arlecchino's *lalalera* for him (in a letter to Philipp Jarnach dated 19.2.1918) as follows: at fig. 29 the singer enters a fourth lower than written on a C sharp; the orchestra part is transposed down a fourth from the third beat of the same bar until the end of the section. The singer should then also perform the aria in the appendix of the orchestral score. (Here Busoni authorized a transposition into C major for Jerger.)

XIV

Before *Turandot*

Albumleaf for Flute (or muted Violin) **and Piano**. *Dedicated*: to Albert Biolley.
Composed: Autumn (?) 1916. *Published*: Leipzig, 1917. EB 4943. Plate number 28008.
Arrangement: for viola or cello and piano (Paul Klengel) published Leipzig, 1917. EB
5023. Plate number 28077. *Orchestration*: by Otmar Nussio (1948) for 1–2(C.A.)–2–2;
3–2–1–0; Harp; Celesta; Str. MS. Wiesbaden. *Duration*: 3 minutes.

With the score of *Arlecchino* Busoni had instinctively found his way to a new
style. It was a language of wellnigh virtuosic flexibility which could withstand
the *salto mortale* from traditional tonality to free tonality better than much of
his previous work, could happily jumble up consonance and dissonance, could
glitter or melt, burn or freeze, indulge in discreet parody or unexaggeratedly
express deep emotion—without neurosis. During the coming years this style
was to be rationalized; its initial precept was simply of music as 'schönes Spiel'.
Although Busoni later found himself occasionally ignoring it (as for instance in
the *Toccata* or the song 'Schlechter Trost'), 'schönes Spiel' remained the true
foundation of Young Classicality. One could already sense this move in the
differences between the *Red Indian Fantasy* and *Red Indian Diary*; the same
material acquires a totally new *modus vivendi*, is brought out of the hothouse
and back to the meadowlands. It was a further loosening of fetters.

A small step still further along this path is marked in the Albumleaf for Flute
and Piano. Busoni composed it in the autumn of 1916, between *Arlecchino* and
Turandot, for his friend Albert Biolley, a Zurich banker. He had helped to
organize loans and (if one reads between the lines) substantial gifts for the
family in order to bridge their financial difficulties during the war. He was also
an amateur flautist, evidently of considerable ability.

The piece is short and simple. The flute plays an unbroken line of melody,
the piano accompanies with regular quaver motion and a free bass-line which
sometimes moves in imitation of the flute melody. Only in the last eight bars
does the movement of the accompaniment become a little more animated. The
elegant opening line of the theme has the same scotch-snap as 'The Blue-bird'
(cf. Ex. 138):

Ex. 183

The work, which has neither development nor coda, is remarkable above all for the variety of its harmonic rhythm, reaching its greatest density in a twice-repeated passage at its centre:

Ex. 184

By locating the second of these passages in the highest register of the piece, Busoni builds a climax without any increase in temperature. This is one of the principal features of 'schönes Spiel'. The music remains crystalline and cool; no 'human, all-too-human' emotion can ruffle its calm.

XV

Turandot

Turandot, a Chinese fable. Opera in 2 acts. Libretto by Ferruccio Busoni after Carlo Gozzi. *Dedicated*: to Arturo Toscanini. *Composed*: December 1916–March 1917. *First performance*: 11.5.1917. Stadttheater, Zurich. Conductor: Busoni; producer: Hans Rogorsch; designer: Albert Isler.

Altoum, emperor (bass)	Laurenz Saeger-Pieroth
Turandot, his daughter (soprano)	Inez Encke
Adelma, her confidante (mezzo-soprano)	Marie Smeikal
Kalaf (tenor)	August Richter
Barak, his servant (baritone)	Tristan Rawson
The queen-mother of Samarkand, a moor (soprano)	Elisabeth Rabbow
Truffaldino, chief eunuch (tenor)	Eugen Nusselt
Pantalone (bass) ⎱ ministers	Heinrich Kuhn
Tartaglia (bass) ⎰	Wilhelm Bockholt
A singer (mezzo-soprano)	Marie Smeikal
The executioner (silent)	Eduard Siding

Eight doctors; chorus of slaves, dancers, mourners, eunuchs, soldiers.

Published: Leipzig, 1917. Full score MS. *Vocal score*: (Philipp Jarnach) published Leipzig, 1918. EB 5314. Plate number 28162. *MS*: formerly Preussische Staatsbibliothek; mislaid during World War Two. *Instrumentation*: 2(Picc.)–2(C.A.)–2(Bcl.)–2(Cfg.); 4–3–3–0; Timp., Perc.; Harp; Celesta; Str. Stage music: 2 tpt., 2 tromb.; Timp., Perc. *Translations*: Italian (Oriana Previtali); English (Edward Dent). Both Br.u.H. *Duration*: 90 minutes.

Altoums Gebet, 'Konfutse, dir hab' ich geschworen' for baritone and small orchestra op. 49 no. 1: *Dedicated*: to Augustus Milner. *Composed*: as part of the opera *Turandot*. *Published*: Leipzig, 1919. PB 2481. *Duration*: 3 minutes.

Altoum appears as prologue, speaking lines from Goethe's *Festzug*.

Act I, first tableau The action is virtually identical to Gozzi's Act I (see Chapter IV), but with two variants: Busoni's cuts the part of Barak's wife and, in place of Ismael, he introduces the queen-mother of Samarkand, a negress fantastically bedecked with ostrich feathers, who is carried across the stage in a palanquin. She it is who hurls the fatal portrait of Turandot to the ground.

Second tableau Very similar to Gozzi's Act II, except for the omission of Brighella. Pantalone and Tartaglia are more stylized: the one indulges in courtly hyperbole while the other stammers grotesquely (the Italian word *tartagliare* means to stutter). Before Kalaf's entrance, Altoum sings a brief aria, praying to Confucius for an end to his troubles. Kalaf, Altoum and the two masks join in an extended quartet, after which Turandot enters. Tartaglia's reading of the decree is cut, we progress directly to the scene of the riddles. Kalaf poses the riddle of his name and the curtain falls to repeated murmurs of 'Who? who?'

Act II, third tableau The essential points of Acts III and IV in Gozzi are reduced to one unified scene which plays in Turandot's chamber. Truffaldino relates his unsuccessful attempt to establish the name of the prince, Altoum appears to inform his daughter of the secret messenger who has brought him the name; Adelma finally whispers the name to her mistress and is rewarded with elevation from slavery to her former regal state. A musical intermezzo leads directly to the

Final tableau Almost identical to Gozzi's Act V—but here, neither Kalaf nor Adelma make any attempts at suicide. The opera ends with a brilliant choral dance, at the climax of which a curtain at the back of the stage opens to reveal a gigantic golden statue of Buddha, before which Kalaf and Turandot undergo the nuptial rites.

Busoni's idea of transforming his *Turandot* music into an opera dates back to the time, in January 1913, when the Gozzi play, adapted by Vollmoeller, was staged in spectacular and tasteless fashion in London. 'What do you think of 'Turandot' as an opera—and in Italian?' he had asked Gerda.[1]

Even before *Arlecchino* was finished, he was looking to Max Reinhardt for a production of it in Berlin but, by the summer of 1916, he seems to have realized that this would not be possible as long as the war lasted. Therefore, he approached the Intendant of the Stadttheater in Zurich, Alfred Reucker, for the first performance. Many difficulties were placed in his way, especially because *Arlecchino* was clearly too short to be played on its own. The question of a suitable companion piece arose; without hesitation, Busoni proposed a new version of *Turandot*. In a letter to Egon Petri he explained:

> The important question as to which piece should be coupled with the hour-long 'Arlecchino' in order to fill an evening in the theatre . . . has led me to the hasty decision to form a 2-act opera out of the material and substance of Turandot . . . I am rewriting it closer in tone to a pantomime or stage play . . . The *mask*-figures, common to both pieces, serve to link them (though they otherwise contrast completely with each other).[2]

In exactly one month he prepared the libretto which, while following Gozzi's original play quite closely, was entirely his own work. It may seem curious that he should have written the libretto in German, for in Zurich he was by no means bound to that language. He knew, however, that the prospect of performances of his stage works in Italy at that time was virtually nil and on this occasion, instead of working from the standpoint of idealistic love for his native land, he took the more practical step of setting the opera from the outset in the language in which he knew it would be more frequently performed.

All his work on this opera reflects the practical side of his nature; this version of *Turandot* is little more than an ingenious arrangement and extension of the original incidental music. The First World War had put an end to the lavish staging of plays with orchestral backing, and the cinemas were enjoying increasing financial success, allowing them to swallow up the theatre orchestras irrevocably. If *Turandot* were to remain on the stage, it would have to be in the more viable form of an opera.

The marked contrasts between the 'Turandot' operas of Busoni and Puccini have been discussed in some detail by Mosco Carner in his book on Puccini.[3] There are, however, some further points of particular relevance to Busoni's version. Puccini's Princess is depicted as a cruel and terrifying beauty, and his librettists devised some ancient tale of bloodshed and hatred to motivate her cold-blooded acts of revenge; Busoni, following Goethe, chose to depict her as a 'höchst subtiler Geist' (highly subtle spirit), a person of considerable intellect, driven to savage extremes in the search for her equal. While Puccini depicts her father, the Emperor, as a tremulous, wellnigh senile monarch, Busoni finds in Altoum not only nobility but also humour, and creates a character (in Carner's words) 'in the image of Sarastro'.[4] Both composers retain the Masks but these are also treated in entirely different styles. Puccini's librettists adopted Schiller's suggestion of giving them Oriental-sounding names (Ping, Pang and Pong) and their participation in the action is divided for the most part between playful buffoonery and a cloying sentimentality; Busoni's Masks are more cold-blooded creatures, blessed with a humour akin to that of Arlecchino which constantly serves to disturb the action, to make it unreal and consciously 'theatrical'. Both composers make considerable use of the chorus, the *vox populi*. Here, it must be granted, Puccini is Busoni's superior. But where the former had the lavish forces of La Scala, Milan, in mind for his opera, the latter had to consider the limited scope of the Zurich Stadttheater in war time.

Busoni's most striking innovations in *Turandot* come in the opening and closing moments of the opera. His Kalaf is a fiery idealist with a truly Faustian urge. 'I wish for the exceptional' is his call—and he achieves it. At the close comes Busoni's *coup de théâtre*, the revelation of the Godhead in all its splendour—an affirmation of life and of the possibility, at least in fairy tales, of attaining the Unattainable. In this sense, *Turandot* redresses the balance of scorn, doubt and mistrust in the world which we find in *Arlecchino*. But this jubilant tone only rings out in the fantasy world of the mythical Orient. As Stefan Zweig wrote: 'Each figure, the facetious eunuch, the gloomy Princess, the executioner, the wise King, has a feeling of existing in this world of the Exceptional, yet only as a guest, as the phantom of a light, sounding dream.'[5]

Act I The first tableau draws almost entirely on the first movement of the *Turandot Suite*. Barak's narration is a new addition and an arioso, in which Kalaf contemplates the picture of Turandot, is salvaged from the score of the incidental music. For this haunting little piece, Busoni had drawn on a rhythmical figure cited by Ambros in Vol. I of his *Geschichte der Musik* (p. 15) as an ancient Nubian chant. By dividing the gamelan-like figure into two voices and adding a B flat pedal, a delicately perfumed Oriental atmosphere is evoked:

Ex. 185

The Second Tableau opens with Truffaldino's march, now transformed into a brilliant buffo aria. Altoum's march follows immediately, the opening fanfare now being used for the entrance of the eight doctors. The following number, Altoum's aria, is Busoni's most substantial new addition. Written in a freely flowing E major, it is based on a brief motif that seems to depict the dignity and sorrow of the Emperor:

Ex. 186

This soft-edged solemnity is further stressed by repeated use of sixth-chords. Busoni himself was sufficiently proud of this aria, written in the spirit of 'In diesen heil'gen Hallen', to publish it separately as 'Altoums Gebet' op. 49 no. 1, in which form it is coupled with the 'Lied des Mephistopheles' (see Chapter XVII).

The ensuing quartet is cast simply and concisely around a group of four notes:

Ex. 187

which form ostinatos of steadily increasing animation. 'Turandot's March' (No. 4 of the Suite) follows without a break. It has been almost completely recomposed for its new purpose. The riddle music, based on a scheme of parallel triads, is taken verbatim from the incidental music, but with much

new material added to form a through-composed setting. Kalaf sings his riddle
(Finale I) to the noble Indian melody from 'Verzweiflung und Ergebung'.

Act II opens with 'Greensleeves', now in a somewhat modified version (closer
in fact to the fourth Elegy, 'Turandots Frauengemach'), and is followed by the
'Tanz und Gesang' (no. 6 of the Suite), in unaltered form.★ The scene seems to
irritate the Princess and she calls a halt: 'My mind is set on other matters!' Her
ensuing recitative and aria are adapted from the 'Nächtlicher Walzer' (no. 7 of
the Suite), interpolating a resolute version of her main theme in 4/4 time,
before closing dramatically with music from the waltz, to the words, 'Let
Turandot die, but untainted!' Truffaldino's scene and aria, respecting his
European origins, are Mozartian in tone; a delightful new invention coming
closer in style to the music of *Arlecchino* than the rest of the score. Now comes
Altoum. His arioso is a setting of the Albumleaf for Flute and Piano,
occasionally interrupted by the mocking comments of his two ministers. As
they withdraw, their placatory mission unaccomplished, Turandot turns to
Adelma, her last ally, in tones of sad innocence. Had we ever been led to
believe the Princess to be a monster, this music proves us mistaken:

Ex. 188

Adelma's ensuing arioso, *tranquillo e grazioso*, is fully attuned to the ideas of
Young Classicality: a jaunty, wide-ranging flow of melody accompanies a

---

★ The reduced orchestration of 'Tanz und Gesang' was carried out by Philipp Jarnach.

Note for producers. For the Berlin production of 1921 Busoni solved the problem
of staging this lengthy musical interlude in ingenious fashion—as a shadow-play:

'I imagine the scene running as follows: the set depicts a hall with an opening to the
back leading to the river and a background which depicts the city.—Boats appear with
women who sing the song. They disembark. A curtain closes off the scene, behind
which a shadow-play is enacted.'[6a]

'For the . . . shadow-play . . . I would suggest the choice of a humorous and
fantastical depiction of the *Turandot story* itself, so that the spectator is made aware of
the reverse side of the action and so that it can make Turandot nervous . . . Turandot as
a dragon with a woman's head, guards and the executioner, Truffaldino as a clown,
Altoum decrepit and supported by his Ministers.'[6b]

'At the word "genug" the shadow-play vanishes, the curtain rises again and the
background lighting gradually merges into a sunset. This indicates that between the
close of this scene and the beginning of the next one night passes.'[6a]

despicable act of betrayal. Adelma whispers in Turandot's ear and the orchestra mysteriously sounds the Kalaf theme, canonically in descending registers, over an ominous timpani roll.

There follows an Intermezzo, taken literally from the 'Nächtlicher Walzer' and closing with the trumpet fanfare from 'Verzweiflung und Ergebung'. The curtain rises at once on the Final Tableau, which opens with the 'In modo di marcia funebre' from the Suite, now accompanied by wailing women. The ensuing crucial scene, in which Turandot reveals Kalaf's name and origin, was originally conceived as spoken dialogue and is printed in the vocal score in that form. However, it turned out to be unsatisfactory and, for the revival of the Berlin production in the 1921–2 season, Busoni wrote a new musical number which begins with Turandot's words, 'Diese Zeichen von Trauer' and leads straight into the Finale. (This new passage is not included in the published vocal score.)

The Finale itself is a cleverly constructed apotheosis of the principal themes of the opera, culminating in the bright rococo dance with which the Suite also ends. Despite the 'light and unreal tone'[7] in which the score is written, one is left with the impression that Busoni was pressing on to the end as fast as possible; an impression confirmed by his comments in a letter to Petri written shortly after completing the opera. *Doktor Faust* was now beginning to take shape in his mind and the first notes of the full score were written down just three months later: 'I have already had to think about my next work, which will take longer than my "100 day" Turandot. For it shall contain nothing which does not reflect the *best* of my abilities.'[8]

The opera *Turandot*, while not revealing the master in more than a handful of moments, is designed to entertain and amuse. Since 1925 it has been over-shadowed—justifiably—by Puccini's opera, a work which occupies a place in his oeuvre comparable to that of *Doktor Faust* in Busoni's, that of a grand and final synthesis of ideas and techniques. It seems a curious quirk of fate that these two Tuscan composers, who died within four months of each other, should both have been obliged to leave their intended masterpieces unfinished.

As *Turandot* is neither dramatically nor musically on a par with *Arlecchino*, there have been many attempts to find new companion pieces for the latter. Possibilities range from Hindemith's *Nusch-Nuschi* to Stravinsky's ballets *Pulcinella* or *Petrushka*, from de Falla's *El Retablo de Maese Pedro* to Henze's *Das Wundertheater* or Weill's *Die Sieben Todsünden*. One could also couple it with a classical one-act opera: here Rossini's *L'occasione fa il ladro* or Pergolesis's *La Serva padrona* would be obvious choices. An interesting contrast could be afforded by Satie's ballet *Parade*, whose world première took place only seven days after that of *Arlecchino*.

XVI

Arlecchino Part II

During the summer of 1918 Busoni wrote the text for a sequel to *Arlecchino* entitled 'The Harlequiniad, Part II or The Geese of the Capitol', which he completed on 25 July. For a time he seriously contemplated setting it to music which in turn would have presented him with the delightful task of finding a new lightweight companion piece for *Turandot* (he even had hopes of collaborating with Bernard Shaw on such a venture). Yet the idea of composing an 'Arlecchino II' was eventually abandoned and the libretto remains unpublished. It is arguably too personal a document for publication: Busoni explores his own family background with an accuracy and cynicism that amounts to virtual cruelty, and gives unrestrained vent to his personal likes and dislikes. On the other hand, the Nietzschean grand finale, related in manner and style to the 'Classical Walpurgis-night' in Goethe's *Faust* Part II and entitled 'The Parnassus of Masks and Beasts', reveals in unique manner the innermost workings of his mind and presents the missing link between his published dramas and his dreams. We are presented with clear confirmation of the identicality of his three great heroes, Leonhard Thurnheiser, Leonardo da Vinci and Faust; but it is also made clear that the creature represented by this trinity is mythical, not real.

This forgotten libretto presents the key to the unity of Busoni's stage works. The following resumé is intended to give some idea of the content of this extraordinary piece.

Scene I Arlecchino has been imprisoned for 'murder, abduction and one or two other matters' but has planned an escape with the aid of three accomplices. The warder appears; Arlecchino knocks him unconscious, then removes his uniform, wig and beard. Under the uniform, the warder wears a Harlequin costume. A quick change of garments and Arlecchino can now pass as the warder and vice versa. The prison director appears and Arlecchino shows him the escape route he has 'discovered'. The prisoner seems to have gone mad, he remarks—he keeps insisting that he is the warder. While the director is puzzling all this out, Arlecchino escapes.

Scene II Arlecchino's parents at home—a modest middle-class dwelling in nineteenth-century Italian style. His father has 'a flowing beard and long hair, a Turkish fez on his head, a long pipe in his mouth; close beside him a flask of wine, behind him, on a perch, three cockatoos'. His mother, 'snow-white and wearing a crown with a halo' is playing a

Field nocturne on the square piano. Enter Arlecchino, bringing cigars and champagne for his father. The old man seems unable to speak in coherent phrases. Annunziata rings the doorbell; Arlecchino hides under the table. She enters in mourning and gives way to a dreadful outburst of self-pity: she is no longer the youngest, she has to find herself a job now, and so on. Receiving little sympathy from her father-in-law, she makes for the door. Arlecchino jumps out in front of her and she faints. He runs off. As the father wearily makes his way to bed, the mother calls up to him in hectoring tones, 'Mind you don't fall on the stairs now!'

Intermezzo The poet, lying in bed for want of warmth or decent clothing, is entertained with a male-voice chorus sung by four cats. Arlecchino forces his father to make out his will in favour of Annunziata, after which the old man dies of shock. Now Arlecchino forces Annunziata to change the will in his favour. Finally, he himself changes it again, this time in favour of the poet. He presents it to him 'with respect and joy'. [The scene is written in the style of Gozzi's comic scenes. There is no prescribed text, merely an outline from which the actors improvise or mime.]

Scene III The Parnassus of Masks and Beasts. Arlecchino is seated upon a throne. He shows us his kingdom. We can see, for instance, the Pyramids, the temples of Benares, the Pantheon, Strasbourg Cathedral, the Guillotine and the Eiffel Tower. Invisible to us, he tells us, are the bomb factories and the gypsy bands. In the far distance we can just make out 'the new Middle Ages, rejuvenated with the aid of daily baths and whitewashed morals' [the U.S.A.]. He points out the newspaper offices—lie factories— and the police with their rubber stamps and bayonets. Behold the Guillotine, 'symbol of enlightenment!' And there, the banking houses, the abode of the new alchemists, where landscape is converted into pieces of paper. We can see soldiers too, '*enemies* from the front, *cowards* from behind'. But, in complete contrast, there are also his Masks and his Beasts, 'the True Ones, the Dependable Ones'. For them he has prepared the Feast of the Millennium—and here they come!

The first guest to arrive is the Abbate, riding on a donkey, followed by Pantalone, then by the sad Pierrot who speaks French and is 'trop peu spirituel pour aider à la bonne farce'. Now comes Giotto Bernardone [Busoni's beloved dog] barking at the four cats, who are still singing. They strike up a glee and Giotto vomits. The next guest is a gate-crasher, the dragon from Wagner's *Siegfried*. Arlecchino shows him the door, commenting, 'of all your Master's boring creations you are probably the most tedious'.

Others follow: the ape from the puppet-play in *Don Quixote*, disguised as a concert-agent; the white elephant; the cock; the sheep; the geese of the Capitol; the cockatoos and 'the very latest', led by Herr Sauberwasser, their great Master. In his school, he boasts, every pupil can learn to be an instant Expressionist: 'I spit, and lo!, 'tis greatest art, a symphony needs just a fart.' The Carabinieri lead him away.

The next arrivals are a flea-theatre and a troupe of ants; Pegasus flies by. Enter Leandro on a wooden horse, Don Quixote on Rosinante (he is led to a place of honour) and Sancho Panza on his donkey. Hanswurst follows [Casperle by another name]. Arlecchino welcomes him warmly and embraces him, 'the greatest German brainwave, harmless and humorous'.

A man in black approaches but does not speak. He seems to be Leonhard Thurnheiser from *Die Brautwahl*, and the frogs from the Froschteich are close behind him. But who is he? Pantalone recognizes him as his fellow countryman, Leonardo da Vinci; Hanswurst greets him as his old master, Doktor Faust: 'I thought he was in Hell;

but there now, there he stands, fit as a fiddle!' But, whoever he is, Arlecchino explains, this is 'the one who is able to reach out in a trice beyond the frontiers of Mankind'. All bow before him. Enter the author in the mask of a piano virtuoso.

A horde of people rushes forward, diplomats, soldiers, merchants, industrialists, munitions manufacturers, journalists and 'other rabble'. 'We are the Masks, we are the Beasts', they cry. 'Wait', calls Arlecchino, 'that was not what I meant . . . You *were* the Masks . . . But now you are *unmasked*!'. He beckons to Faust, who conjures up a wall of flowers reaching to the sky, shutting out the rabble. Arlecchino's father strikes up an 'elevatedly jovial' tune on his clarinet; his mother appears in a niche and blesses him. 'And now', he calls, 'pour out the champagne!'

Section Six

Zurich and Berlin
(1917–24)

XVII

Faust Unfolds

Sonatina [no. 4] **in diem nativitatis Christi MCMXVII** [for piano]. *Dedicated*: to Benvenuto Busoni. *Composed*: December 1917. *First performance*: 24.1.1920. Tonhalle, Zurich (?). Soloist: Busoni. *Published*: Leipzig, 1918. EB 5071. Plate number 27744. *MS*: 8 pp., 33.5×25cm., Breitkopf & Härtel, Wiesbaden. *Duration*: 8 minutes.

Concertino for Clarinet and small Orchestra op. 48. *Dedicated*: to Edmondo Allegra. *Composed*: March–April 1918. *First performance*: 9.12.1918. Tonhalle, Zurich. Edmondo Allegra, Tonhalle Orchestra, conducted by Volkmar Andreae. *Published*: Leipzig, 1918. PB 2480. *Arrangement*: for clarinet and piano (Otto Taubmann) published Leipzig, 1918. EB 5140. Plate numbers 28303, 28535. *Instrumentation*: 0–2–0–2; 2–0–0–0; Perc.; Str. *Duration*: 10 minutes.

Lied des Brander (from Goethe's *Faust*): 'Es war eine Ratte im Kellernest' [for voice and piano]. *Composed*: March 1918 (?). *Published*: Wiesbaden, 1964 as no. 1 of Fünf Goethelieder. EB 6461. *MS*: (incomplete) Deutsche Staatsbibliothek, Berlin. *Orchestration*: by Philipp Jarnach (1938) published Wiesbaden, 1964. MS. *Instrumentation*: 2–2–2–2; 2–2–3–0; Timp.; Str. *Duration*: 2 minutes.

Lied des Mephistopheles (from Goethe's *Faust*): 'Es war einmal ein König' [for voice and orchestra or piano] op. 49 no. 2. *Dedicated*: to Augustus Milner. *Composed*: (both versions) March 1918. *First performance*: 6.10.1920. Tonhalle, kleine Saal, Zurich. Augustus Milner (baritone) and Philipp Jarnach (piano). *Published*: Leipzig, 1918. PB 2482. Version for voice and piano publ. Leipzig, 1919. DLV 3529. Later republished Wiesbaden, 1964 as no. 2 of Fünf Goethelieder. EB 6461. *MS*: (orchestral version) 6pp., 34×25cm. Deutsche Staatsbibliothek, Berlin. *Instrumentation*: 0–2–2–0; 0–1–0–0; Timp.; Str. *Duration*: 2 minutes.

Lied des Unmuts (from Goethe's *West-östlicher Divan*): 'Keinen Reimer wird man finden' [for voice and orchestra or piano]. *Dedicated*: to Augustus Milner. *Composed*: March (?) 1918. *Orchestrated*: February 1924. *First performance*: 6.10.1920. Tonhalle, kleine Saal, Zurich, with 'Lied des Mephistopheles'. *Published*: (version for voice and piano) Leipzig, 1919. DLV 3528. Republished Wiesbaden, 1964 as no. 3 of Fünf Goethelieder. EB 6461. Orchestral version published Wiesbaden, 1964. MS. *MS*: (orchestral version) 13pp., 33×27cm., Deutsche Staatsbibliothek, Berlin. *Instrumentation*: 2–2–2–2; 2–0–0–0; Timp.; Str. *Duration*: 3 minutes.

Sarabande and Cortège op. 51 (Two studies for *Doktor Faust*) [Fifth and Sixth Elegies for Orchestra]. *Dedicated*: to Volkmar Andreae. *Composed*: December 1918–January

1919. *First performance*: 31.3.1919. Tonhalle, Zürich. Tonhalle Orchestra, conducted by Volkmar Andreae. *Published*: Leipzig, 1922. PB 2606. *MS*: last known owner Leo Blech. *Instrumentation*: 3(Picc.)–3(2 C.A.)–3(Bcl.)–3(Cfg,); 4–3–3–1; Timp., Perc.; 2 Harps; Celesta; Str. *Duration*: 19 minutes.

Elegy for Clarinet and Piano. *Dedicated*: to Edmondo Allegra. *Composed*: September 1919 and January 1920. *Published*: Leipzig, 1921. EB 5188. Plate number 28672. *Duration*: 3 minutes.

Divertimento for Flute [and small Orchestra] op. 52. *Dedicated*: to Philippe Gaubert. *Composed*: May 1920. *First performance*: 13.1.1921. Philharmonie, Berlin. Henrik de Vries, Berlin Philharmonic Orchestra, conducted by Busoni. *Published*: Leipzig, 1922. PB 2607. *MS*: 37pp., 35×27cm. Deutsche Staatsbibliothek, Berlin. *Arrangement*: for flute and piano (Kurt Weill) published Leipzig, 1922. EB 5205. Plate number 28730. *Instrumentation*: 0–2–2–2; 2–2–0–0; Timp., Perc.; Str. *Duration*: 9 minutes.

Busoni constructed his masterpiece, *Doktor Faust*, in truly Leonardo-like manner: he assembled the work slowly and painstakingly from a large number of sketches. Many of these are perfectly shaped, complete entities and have a life and colour of their own. Dent tells us that Busoni rarely talked about the score of *Doktor Faust*; in fact, this was scarcely necessary, for he was regularly hearing performances of these studies (let us call them 'satellite' works) and was thus able to test the strength and sonority of his great edifice at all stages. In most cases the completion of a satellite work and its incorporation in the score of the opera were consecutive occurrences. Occasionally the process was reversed: the *Sarabande* and *Cortège*, for example, were evidently assembled from a large number of fragments of the opera score.

By this time Busoni's composition technique was so fluent that he scarcely needed to polish and improve. An idea would be hastily jotted down, sometimes without so much as a harmonization; then the fair copy would be written out in ink, fully orchestrated. The intermediate stages were carried out entirely in the composer's head, sometimes during long walks and occasionally, as Philipp Jarnach has recounted, while entertaining visitors. Busoni had been endowed with this amazing facility since his childhood. Gradually, he had learned to communicate, even at high speed, thoughts of greater significance; his uninhibited creative urge was now tempered by the expression of ideas slowly matured. Furthermore, his Zurich years, which also saw the celebration of his fiftieth birthday, brought the final integration of those elements which we crudely divided into Italianate and Nordic in the personality of the young composer.

There are altogether twenty-three published satellite works for *Doktor Faust*. First came the short passage from the *versio minore* of the *Fantasia Contrappuntistica*, followed by the *Sonatina seconda* and *Nocturne symphonique*, all dating from 1912–13, before completion of the libretto of the opera.* The

---

* The initial draft of the *Faust* libretto dates as far back as 1910 (see Section Seven).

fifth Sonatina, of which only a brief passage is quoted in the opera, is discussed in Chapter XVIII. Two études which Busoni composed in 1923–4 for the second edition of the *Klavierübung* and were intended for the missing final scene of the opera are discussed in Chapter XXI. One single phrase of the *Prélude en arpèges* (also discussed in Chapter XXI) found its way into the opera, likewise one chord progression from the *Song of the Spirit Dance* (Chapter XI). Two of the Five short pieces for the cultivation of part-playing (Chapter XXI) were also intended for the final scene.

The remaining fifteen works are divided between Chapters XVII and XX, separating the *Faust* compositions into those dating from Busoni's Zurich years (up to the end of August 1920) and those from his final years in Berlin. There also exists one brief unpublished satellite work, a Nocturne for piano, dated 20 May 1918, which is discussed in Section Seven.

The first of the Zurich satellite works, the fourth Sonatina, is a perfect example of Young Classicality: it strictly avoids any outward show of emotion while in fact reflecting strong feeling. In it one senses something of the hopes and sorrows of Busoni's situation at Christmas 1917, the turning point in the war. Then there is a Faustian element in the work: Busoni's drama ends in the snow-covered town square of Wittenberg. Christmas bells ring out as the curtain falls (that, at least, was the intention). Thus, some of the music for the fourth Sonatina was undoubtedly intended for the closing moments of the opera. Finally, there are the emotions Busoni felt at the end of each year: a ritual sense of new beginning, expressed through childlike naïvety, a blend of apprehension and joy at the prospect of being reborn. These diverse components are welded into a work of the greatest pianistic and textural simplicity. Like the *Berceuse élégiaque*, this is a profound miniature. Only the final appearance of the principal theme, marked *quasi trasfigurato*, gives some inkling of the inner upheaval concealed beneath the mask of serenity.

The opening phrases set a mood of intimacy and sweetness which is never disturbed. A gently dissonant tonal language (based on A major) permits an easy flow from one key centre to another. The finely-spun lines of the opening three-part invention initially move in contrary motion, then curve gently round to parallel motion:

Ex. 189

A more earnest motif rings out, based on the fall of an octave (Ex. 190). In its fateful contour it looks back to a phrase from the *Pezzo serioso* of the Piano Concerto of which it is in fact the inversion (cf. Ex. 33).

Ex. 190

An angular theme in fourths, *un poco vivace*, introduces a new section. The sharp outlines of the theme are filled in by flowing triplet scales:

Ex. 191

A brief crescendo leads to a weighty F major chord, repeated three times, after which the opening theme returns as a pliant codetta.

At this point Busoni originally continued with a passage of aggressive, stamping chords, some thirty-four bars long. As they interrupted the idyllic atmosphere too rudely and added nothing of great thematic interest, he deleted them; an object lesson in the art of musical proportion. The following section, *Calmo*, brings a series of rising phrases, at whose peak the opening theme returns in augmentation before ushering in the gentle modulations of the first page once again. As final gesture, a single strand of melody climbs from the lower regions to a high, isolated fermata, like some benevolent echo of the first bar of the *Sonatina seconda* (cf. Ex. 118):

Ex. 192

The second section opens with a hushed, unsettling chorale:

Ex. 193

This is a theme originally intended for the *Rondò arlecchinesco* and hence, probably, for the opera *Arlecchino*. It followed immediately after the solemn brass chorale at fig. 20 of the *Rondò*, the music also used to depict Matteo's house, deserted and shuttered up, in the first scene of the opera. In contrast to Busoni's earlier chorale themes, this is a static block of harmony, looking back to the homophony of Palestrina rather than to Bach; yet his insistently dissonant harmonization makes for a typically twentieth-century sound. The chorale with which Britten closes his *War Requiem*—significantly with the words 'Dona nobis pacem'—is very similar.

The chorale is then split up over a low descending ostinato, while the harmonies are confused by the sustaining pedal: the result is a lugubrious tolling of bells, marked in the sketches 'Campane di Natale', and is probably the music originally visualized for the end of *Doktor Faust*. On the piano these bell sounds come close in timbre to those of Liszt in one of his lesser-known and more remarkable operatic fantasies—the *Paraphrase on the Grail March from 'Parsifal'*. Busoni's bell-music, a disturbing and visionary interlude, comes to rest on a combination of D flat major and D minor chords.

The mood changes to rustic joviality: the angular theme of Ex. 191 is now transformed into a *pifferata*, a rough-hewn mediaeval dance, reminiscent of 'Nuit de Noël'. The bell-music returns and then disintegrates, heralding the closing section of the work. Here the opening theme is subjected to a brief four-part fugal exposition, dissolves into murmuring triplet patterns and is finally and solemnly stated in augmentation.

Slender its proportions may be, but the fourth Sonatina shows Busoni's art at its most distinguished and refined. In its gentleness and its ability to say much with few notes it speaks the same language as *L'Enfance du Christ* of Berlioz and the *Weihnachtsbaum* of Liszt. As Busoni remarked a few days after its completion (it took him only four days to compose it), it is 'bien autre chose que la "Nuit de Noël" d'autrefois'.[1] The critic of the *Neue Zürcher Zeitung*, probably well aware of the composer's personal misfortunes, heard in the work 'ringing of bells and Christmas atmosphere seen with the eyes and felt with the heart of an artist shaken by the griefs of the world'.[2]

Three months later, in March 1918, Busoni composed the Concertino for Clarinet and dedicated it to Edmondo Allegra, the principal clarinettist of the Tonhalle Orchestra in Zurich. In April of the same year he asked his friend Volkmar Andreae for some rehearsal time to try the new work; the trial took place on 10 May and the piece, which won universal admiration, was scheduled for performance the following season. Since then it has enjoyed an undemonstrative place in the repertoire, still occasionally aired by clarinettists looking for alternatives to their somewhat limited choices of Mozart, Rossini, Weber and Spohr. It is a gentle and amiable work with none of the soul-searching to be detected under the surface of the fourth Sonatina, rather an elegant air of optimism.

The first movement is a relaxed Allegretto sostenuto. The galanteries of the language are not far removed from the parodistic classicism of Strauss's

Ariadne auf Naxos, while the opening theme is cut of the same cloth as one of the last works of Strauss, the Oboe Concerto. A more spirited middle section brings a spiky dialogue between soloist and first violins, after which there is a brief recapitulation.

The second movement, an Andantino, originates in a discarded sketch for a song. In March 1918 Busoni made several settings of texts from Goethe's *Faust*, intended no doubt as studies for his own Faustian language. Of these settings, only two were actually completed and only one of these, the 'Lied des Mephistopheles', was published during the composer's lifetime. However, fragments of several others have survived, including a few bars of Gretchen's song, 'Es war ein König in Thule':

Ex. 194

Es war ein Kö - nig in Thu - le gar treu bis an das Grab, ___

Like Berlioz's 'Le Roi de Thulé' in *La Damnation de Faust*, this too would have been a *chanson gothique*. Busoni must soon have realized that he had borrowed the accompanying rhythmical figure from Berlioz and would have been forced to admit that it was difficult to compete with that masterpiece. His own idea was incorporated into the Clarinet Concertino and spun out (without any further adherence to the rhythm of Goethe's text) into a lengthy cantilena. The spareness of these opening bars sets the tone for the whole movement, whose idiosyncratic harmonic language later hovers around E minor.

A brief, mildly dramatic recitative leads back to the B flat major of the first movement for a leisurely quasi-development. In the finale, a fanciful minuet, the *orchestrino* (as Busoni describes his ensemble) is augmented by a triangle. The main theme is closely related to the pompous music to which Baron Ochs first enters in *Der Rosenkavalier* (and that in turn, curiously enough, is borrowed from the 'Fire and Water' music of *Die Zauberflöte*). The marionette-like grandeur of Busoni's minuet later provided exactly the right atmosphere for the entrance of the Duke and Duchess of Parma in *Doktor Faust*:

Ex. 195

Tempo di Minuetto, sostenuto e pomposo

Busoni develops the theme briefly and brilliantly, concluding with an expostulation from the soloist and three gentle chords.

Although its exact date of composition is uncertain, the 'Lied des Brander' was probably also written in March 1918. Neither Gretchen nor Brander play any part in Busoni's Faust-drama and his interest in their songs was therefore more or less academic. As he left it, the 'Lied des Brander' is indeed more of a sketch than a finished composition: a setting of the first verse, marked at the end *da capo*. Had Busoni himself published this song, he would certainly have written new accompaniments for the second and third verses; it was quite contrary to his nature to repeat the same idea three times, especially in this case where the texture is so bare, with much reliance on repeated chordal sequences. The version for voice and piano, as first published in 1964, can hardly represent Busoni's intentions. However, Philipp Jarnach made a free orchestral arrangement of it in 1938, adding a number of new instrumental details to the second and third verses, fully in accordance with Busoni's own style. In this form the song is more effective and can stand comparison with Busoni's other Goethe settings.

The 'Lied des Mephistopheles', dated 30 March 1918, is more successful. At that time Busoni was also working on the scene in the opera where Faust first invokes the servants of Lucifer. This text, therefore, had greater relevance to his search for a vocal characterization of Mephisto. The outline of his setting of Goethe's 'Song of the Flea' is similar to that of 'Lied des Brander', with a motoric ostinato, a spare texture and simple strophic construction. By the simplest means, Busoni achieves a striking intensification from verse to verse. Starting with a simple semiquaver accompaniment:

Ex. 196

he progresses to dotted rhythms, then running triplets and, as the fleas begin to itch the whole court, buzzing chromatic runs in demisemiquavers.

Busoni was so delighted with his 'Song of the Flea' that he promptly orchestrated it. Using a small ensemble (five wind instruments, timpani and strings) he added deft piquant touches to the piano version, entrusting the original accompaniment entirely to the strings. In this form, using his own text and transposed into the tenor range, it later became Mephisto's ballad in the Second Tableau of *Doktor Faust*.★

★ Note for performers. In Busoni's own printed copy of the orchestral score he has indicated that the last three words, 'Wenn einer sticht', should be sung unaccompanied, before the final chord.

Also dating from 1918 (possibly a little later in the year) is another Goethe song, the 'Lied des Unmuts', which has no direct bearing on the score of *Doktor Faust*. Instead, it is a brief paroxysm of rage, curbed only by the classicality of Busoni's language. Goethe himself explains:

> *Unmut* (ill-temper) is always self-centred. It arises out of demands which cannot be conceded; it is arrogant, repellent and pleases nobody, not even he who is possessed of such feeling. Yet, in spite of this, one cannot always restrain oneself from such explosions.[3]

Dent speaks of Busoni's oppressive loneliness at this time, and of his tendency to brief outbursts of bad temper. 'More than once, Busoni had to do what he could to soothe an irritation which some hasty outspoken words of his had caused,' he writes, 'for everybody in all countries was suffering from a mental fever which inevitably led to misunderstanding.'[4] And we have seen such an explosion, on the grandest scale, in *Arlecchino* Part II, written a few months later. The 'Lied des Unmuts' has the same icy humour as the music of *Arlecchino*; in contrast to the two *Faust* songs of 1918, it is 'masked'.

If the 'Lied des Unmuts' is the most angular and declamatory of these three Goethe songs, all of them are far removed from the traditional concept of an art-song. Certainly, Busoni had never had much time for the 'voice beautiful': effusions such as the love-scene in Act I part 1 of *Die Brautwahl* are rare in his vocal music and, by the time of *Arlecchino*, singers' joy at the emission of golden tones had become a subject for ridicule. Busoni's own vocal writing is now concentrated on just declamation, on the clarity of the text and on expression through a strongly characterized but uncomplicated vocal line. His ideal was that the voice part should be performable on its own, without any accompaniment—a theory he had tested on the best classical German Lieder and found to hold true. The piano, or orchestra, is used only to accompany and never permitted equal partnership. Hence this is a complete break with the style of Wolf or even Schoeck,★ in whose songs the piano often interprets, or comments upon, the text; it is a return to the simpler song style of Haydn and Mozart. In this minor revolution, Busoni achieves a directness of utterance which can be almost embarrassing in effect.

Shortly before he died, Busoni prepared a version of the 'Lied des Unmuts' for small orchestra. He was planning a cycle of songs with instrumental accompaniment, consisting of the 'Grausige Geschichte vom Münzjuden Lippold' and four Goethe songs. (A few days later, on 24 February 1924, he composed the song 'Schlechter Trost'—see Chapter XX.) After his death, Jarnach prepared the Goethe songs for publication, adding his own instrumentation of the 'Lied des Brander' to replace the allegedly anti-Semitic 'Grausige Geschichte'. In this form the five Goethe songs make an excellent concert item, though singers performing them with piano would be well advised to omit the

---

★ Schoeck also composed a setting of Goethe's 'Lied des Unmuts'; it dates from 1915 (op. 19b no. 5).

'Lied des Brander'. The spare angular manner of these songs demands relatively little voice but great artistry.

The autumn of 1918 brought an astonishing surge of creativity. Large portions of the score of *Doktor Faust* were completed, including Faust's last entrance, the beginning of which was finished in fair copy. Busoni's thoughts now turned to the great closing scene, in which Faust transfers his soul to another body. With this scene of magic in mind—the triumph over the devil and its implied destruction of all previous values of good and evil—the *Sarabande* was composed. He told Volkmar Andreae: 'I have the habit of rounding off the year with a small composition so as to put my signature to it, as it were. (A somewhat superstitious habit.)—This time I am working on a Sarabande for orchestra.'[5]

The choice of a sarabande for Faust's conjuration is by no means arbitrary. Busoni uses the form in the way we know it since Bach and Handel—as a slow dance. Yet he was aware that it was originally a rapid measure which was generally considered blasphemous and ungodly; he was well acquainted with Cervantes's witty condemnation of sarabandes in his *entremes*, 'The Caves of Salamanca':

Pancracio: Tell me señor: where were all those dances devised, the Zarabande, the Zambapalo and even the accursed famous new Escarramàn?
Barber: Where? In Hell.

Busoni heads his score with a special device:

He has left us no explanation of this symbol. Van Dieren surmised it to be 'the statement of the basic rhythm . . . in antique square notes'.[6] But one could search in vain in old musical treatises for this figure: although its appearance is antiquated, it is in fact Busoni's own invention. A notebook of his has survived in which several pages are devoted to working out this 'sphinx'. As to its meaning—one can only hazard a guess.

The vertical notes to the left and right can be seen to symbolize the extremes of our dualistic world: black and white, hot and cold, good and evil. As such, they are immovable. Or seemingly immovable, for they are here expressed as the accepted way of notating music, upwards or downwards. But, assuming these outer notes represent good and evil, then firstly, they are bounded by the stave—they are visibly limited in range. Secondly, the one is no more than an inversion of the other—they are interchangeable, the magic mirror of the theatre, for instance, will reverse their roles. Certainly, from the standpoint of the immoralist (Nietzsche's word for the man untouched by Christian morality), whose place in this acrostic is outside the stave, they are invertible. The two notes in the middle, placed on their side, seem to respect this standpoint. They are the first two paces which bound the gap between good and evil in one stride, and it seems it would be a simple matter to extend their path in either direction, above or below the stave. Like that silent figure, dressed in black, who appears at the end of *Arlecchino* Part II, they are 'able to reach out in a trice beyond the frontiers of Mankind'. The diagram points the way, while not taking that decisive step.

But, all such speculation aside—and there are certainly other ways of interpreting the 'sphinx'—the *Sarabande* is one of Busoni's most sublime compositions. Like the *Berceuse élégiaque*, it is a meditation on death and rebirth. The traditional rhythm of the Sarabande, two slow beats and one fast—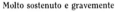—marches relentlessly through the piece at a stately tempo, leaving no doubt in the listener's mind—whatever the inner symbolism of the score—that a profound and solemn moment is being unfolded.

At the beginning there is a motto theme, a chain of descending thirds at the root of the harmony (Ex. 197), luminously orchestrated with pizzicato strings and two harps. The third beat is marked in every bar by a soft trombone triad.

Ex. 197

The falling-third motif is employed frequently in the score of the opera and is an important element in the symbolic, self-styled 'Faustian' language which Busoni developed in his last years. (This language is further discussed in Section Seven, pp. 341–4.)

The very first sketch for the music of the *Sarabande* consists of a fan-shaped chromatic progression:

Ex. 198

over which is superimposed a freely flowing melody:

Ex. 199

This idea is extended over twenty-eight bars, passing through the four principal registers of the orchestra: first the alto range (violins and violas), then tenor (cor anglais and cello), bass (contrabassoon, cello and bass) and finally soprano (flute, then violins)—an almost ritualistic procedure. A third theme, taken from the scene where Faust momentarily abandons his hellish invocation (Vorspiel II) and steps out of the magic circle, brings a ray of light to the score. The motif in the third bar, similar to that in bar three of Ex. 199, is often associated with Mephistopheles:

Ex. 200

In the middle section of the *Sarabande* the three beats to a bar are reduced to two, and this Mephisto motif, in augmentation, becomes an ostinato over which is unfolded a ruminative contrapuntal invention. Its melodic leaps become ever wider, until the leading voices rise and fall in intervals of sevenths, ninths and augmented octaves, with an unearthly sense of rapture. The theme of Ex. 199 returns like a sad cry and the solemn round-dance of the sarabande is resumed, this time by three solo string instruments, softening the inflexible rhythm of the opening into sighing phrases. The motto theme of falling thirds is now inverted, turned into the major and declaimed by the woodwind as a chorale:

Ex. 201

This sinks slowly away and gives place to a new, passionate violin melody (reminiscent of a phrase in the penultimate section of the *Song of the Spirit Dance*). The motto theme sounds once more on unison trombones, this time bare and fatal, the rhythm punctuated by soft tamtam strokes. Finally, the music dies away in a long trill, at the end of which the little Mephisto motif curls questioningly like a snake.

In the *Sarabande* Busoni uses his new, undynamic language to penetrate that same world of darkness and mystery to which he had pointed in the *Sonatina seconda* and *Nocturne symphonique*, but without for a moment resorting to any extremes of dissonance or rhythmic freedom. Nor is his use of the orchestra as complex as in the *Nocturne symphonique*. The *Sarabande* is a miracle of orchestration, its sonorities governed by its restrictions. At one end of the sound-spectrum are three flutes, at the other three trombones; a rich and melancholy middle register is provided by one oboe and two cors anglais; apart from a contrabassoon, there are no other wind instruments. The uppermost registers of the woodwind are scarcely used, while the trombones play either in closely spaced chords or in unison, reminiscent of Equali, the old funeral compositions; two harps and a celesta discretely add further gleams of colour at the higher limits of the spectrum, while the sarabande rhythm is often punctuated by a unison of bass drum and tamtam (sometimes also with timpani)—a remote and menacing effect. Busoni exercises a masterly control over those few sources of chiaroscuro, directing the ebb and flow of tension by precise division of the ensemble into registers. Climaxes are formed through a play of tessitura. There are no sensuous crescendi and there is scarcely any *forte*. The lesson of the new style, briefly learned in the Albumleaf for Flute, is applied on a grand scale. To borrow a scientific term, the music is adiabatic —impervious to external changes of temperature, an enclosed system. Even if the sound of the music is unfamiliar, Busoni explained, this must be the characteristic sonority of his *Faust* score: 'My sounds must of necessity appear abstract, "inevitable" . . . but not "spasmodic": thus generally reflective and reserved.'[7]

An inspired criticism of the *Sarabande* came from Bernard Shaw, who heard it in London in 1919:

> Its not quite so sarabandy a sarabande as 'lascia ch'io pianga', but its striking as an example of what used to be called melodrama. Despite all its beauties and the intricate workings, it gave the impression of a very interesting piece from which the vocal line has been removed: it needs drama and the atmosphere of the stage to round it off.[8]

Having completed the *Sarabande* to his satisfaction, Busoni looked for a work to accompany it. He first thought of coupling it with the *Song of the Spirit Dance*, which was still unperformed. However, during the month of January 1919 he assembled a number of passages from the score of *Doktor Faust* into a *Cortège* and could soon announce, with characteristic whimsy, 'the engagement of his daughter Sarabande to Mr. Cortège'.[9] The two Faust studies were performed a few weeks later to mark the composer's fifty-third birthday.

In the *Cortège* a full orchestra is used. It opens with the Polonaise which in the opera introduces the festive scenes at Parma. An unaccustomed strangeness results from the alternation of 3/4 and 2/4 time:

Ex. 202

Poco vivace e misurato (in carattere d'una polacca)

Almost every phrase encompasses a menacing crescendo, but again a *forte* is rarely demanded; the orchestration, though generous in doublings, has a light and unearthly effect. Several metamorphoses of the chains of thirds from the

Sarabande (Ex. 197) appear, as in the following examples:

Ex. 203

Ex. 204

The lengthy Polonaise, in which Busoni permits himself the unaccustomed luxury of a literal repeat, is followed by a hymn-like trio in two sections. In the first, a solemnly striding wind chorale is accompanied by restless triplet figures; in the second, a greater sense of repose is achieved and one of Busoni's long themes winds its way through thirty-four bars. The trio closes with a falling chordal sequence which has a dual air of ceremony and malice:

Ex. 205

In the bass-line is concealed a chain of thirds, linking these chords with Ex. 197; but their prototype is to be found in another of Busoni's abandoned settings of Goethe from 1918, a fragment of the poem 'Freudvoll und leidvoll':

Ex. 206

Some earlier settings of this poem have differentiated between 'Freude' and 'Leid' (joy and sorrow) by a simple alternation of major and minor. To Busoni this would have seemed an inadequate contrast, for a constant oscillation between major and minor was a long-established element of his harmonic language. He therefore chose to seek harmonies which themselves are ambiguous, whose content can be sensed as a mixture of joy and sorrow. Although the song itself was never finished, he seems in principle to have succeeded: during the whole *Cortège*, by maintaining a careful control of the harmony (as well as the orchestration), he breathes a sense of uneasiness into the outwardly festive character of the music.

After the trio Busoni dispenses with a reprise of the Polonaise, passing directly to the coda. Here the Polonaise theme is recast into a fleeting Allegro and the motto theme of the *Sarabande* is mocked in gleeful Mephistophelian *tempo doppio*:

Ex. 207

a passage strongly reminiscent of Arlecchino in flight. The work closes with an earnestness equal to that of the *Sarabande*, the Mephisto-call (Ex. 200) ringing out in C minor.

Busoni considered the *Sarabande and Cortège* to represent his greatest success as a composer. The *Sarabande* was, of course, crucial to the opera, its nerve-centre, and he must have been delighted when a critic wrote, 'I can only imagine this piece as the climax of this "Faust" tragedy'.[10] However, the reception accorded the two Faust-studies over the ensuing years was sometimes cool or apathetic. For instance, the reaction of a London music critic: 'It does not strike one as being great or inspired music, but it is extremely clever and quite out of the common.'[11] In 1923 a section of the public in Berlin actually hissed the work at a Furtwängler concert. Those who had looked to Busoni before the war as a leader of the avant-garde were disappointed by the conservatism of his new language; few could understand the missionary zeal with which he was attempting to rebuild—not even his old friend, Frederick Delius. Two days after the first London performance of the work in 1919, the two composers, friends since their student days, met for dinner. As they were parting, Delius turned round once more: 'as if he had forgotten a point of etiquette:—"I liked the Sarabande" (he said in consoling tones) "best of all—"; I turned my back on him and—in the taxi I let myself go: I had to cry.'[12]

At last, in 1919, after four years of complete isolation in Switzerland, Busoni began to enjoy a certain freedom of movement again, spending the whole of the autumn in London.

In his last years Busoni occasionally honoured special friends with musical messages of greeting. There exists, for example, a 'Reminiscenza Rossiniana' written for Dent in March 1923, in which the composer begs for some of the works of Wilkie Collins.[13] Jarnach once received a three-part chorus of eight bars in answer to his request for information about a composer by the name of Platti.[14] When he began to write a 'Ricordo di Londra' for clarinet and piano in 1919, Busoni no doubt had such an occasional piece in mind, perhaps for Edmondo Allegra, the dedicatee of the Clarinet Concertino. Here is the opening of the sketch:

Ex. 208

The fragment breaks off after thirteen bars. Busoni, no doubt realizing that the idea was too valuable for a mere greeting, noted down the possibility of using it in the Second Tableau of *Doktor Faust*. He took the sketch back to Zurich where it was completed early the following year with the title Elegy for Clarinet and Piano.

A flowing cantilena with the simplest of accompaniments, the Elegy is a counterpart to the Albumleaf for Flute. It shares with the earlier work the ability to surprise and the desire to remain serene, while we also sense in it that fine-nerved melancholy which is common to all the elegiac compositions. A Faustian touch is found in the third phrase of the long theme, which leaps in intervals of sevenths:

Ex. 209

In this piece Busoni's idiosyncratic use of major–minor harmony reaches an extreme point: scarcely a bar is without such a turning. In Mahler, the use of major–minor antithesis is a musical shorthand, expressing in an instant what classical composers expressed in larger forms—for instance, the sudden ray of sunshine with which Mozart illumines the finales of his D minor and C minor Piano Concertos K.466 and 491, by introducing the *Maggiore*; or the sudden gloom into which Beethoven casts many of his sets of variations through introducing the *Minore*. By his final period, Beethoven had developed this antithesis into a self-sufficient closed system. Hence the Piano Sonatas op. 90 and 111 are cast into a two-movement form which is all-embracing; in both works, the tragedy of the minor-key first movement is balanced by the serenity of the major in the second. When Mahler introduces a major–minor shift he presupposes an instinctive understanding of the pessimism of his gesture. Busoni presumes infinitely more. The difference between the two spheres of major and minor is undeniable, he would argue, but a small step in the infinity of the sounding universe. It is in such problematical aspects of his music that we can understand Paul Bekker's comment, 'he flew, and did not want to grasp that others had to walk or ride', and it is his elusiveness in the handling of traditional materials that makes many a tonal composition of Busoni's far harder to comprehend than some of the stridently dissonant works of his friends and contemporaries. A short piece like this Elegy seems to have been conceived for the diversion of a public on Parnassus. One thinks of the 'elevatedly jovial' tune which Arlecchino's father was to strike up on the clarinet at the close of *Arlecchino* Part II—perhaps Busoni had this music in mind for that scene.

In August 1919 he wrote to Albert Biolley with news of some progress on a Flute Concertino: 'Hier encore j'ai ebauché un Tutti et un début . . . la thème de l'Andante a suivi naturellement. Mais en ce moment je ne sais pas où mettre la tête.'[15] What became of these sketches is uncertain; it could be that they were incorporated in the score of *Doktor Faust*. Yet, at this time the opera was stagnating while Busoni practised the piano for his English tour. Nevertheless, towards the end of the 1919–20 concert season he set to work and composed the Divertimento for flute 'as easily as writing a letter'.[16] The date at the end of the score is 24 May 1920. On that day he also wrote to Biolley:

> Je viens de terminer le *Divertissement* pour *Flûte et Orchestre* (manquent encore trois notes à la 2de trompette) et je me sens content.—C'est un 'pendant' au Concertino de Clarinette; plus fantastique peut-être, peut-être aussi plus viril. Et une idée plus court (probablement par 'l'idée' qui m'a manquée).

The Divertimento opens with a generously proportioned tutti. Although the language is unmistakably Mozartian, especially in rhythmical matters, Busoni's use of tonality is as paradoxical as ever. The firm ground of B flat major, which he establishes in the opening phrases, is slowly eliminated and, after a few bars, the work floats from one key-centre to another as if defying the laws of gravity, with only the briefest references to the tonic. At the end of the tutti a D major fanfare is passed down the line from first trumpet (*naturale*) to second trumpet (*con sordino*) and eventually to the solo flute, which makes its first entry disguised, as it were, as a third trumpet—a delightful touch of Busonian humour. The flute then demonstrates its superiority over the trumpets by running the fanfare over the full range of the instrument and from now on dominates at all points. Its varied statement of the opening theme is a good example of the major–minor dialectic (Ex. 210).

Ex. 210

A second theme of a more plaintive nature appears, and the material is handled much in the manner of classical sonata form. Yet Busoni runs the same danger in this music as he had experienced as librettist in *Arlecchino*—that of over-compression. His tendency to conciseness is taken so far in the Divertimento that a logical unfolding of the material is no longer apparent, except perhaps to a musician with an abnormally rapid mind. In the *Cortège* the reprise of the Polonaise was omitted on the grounds that such repetitions were obvious, therefore unnecessary. And a catchphrase which passed between Busoni and Jarnach at that time was 'encore deux pages de la même façon'. Any music that seemed to outstay its welcome would be dismissed with these words (even Stravinsky's 'Tombeau pour Debussy', the piano piece which was later expanded into the *Symphonies of Wind Instruments*). To Busoni such repetitions were tedious. Faust chooses Mephistopheles as his servant because he is 'as swift as human thought'. Yet Faust's own speed of thought is superhuman. Busoni's musical mind was becoming as swift as Leonardo's optical percep-tion. The one could capture and note down stages in the flight of birds with an accuracy that could only be corroborated by slow-motion photography 500 years later; the other could foresee the turnings a composition was to take so far in advance that he seemed to have heard the music before it had even sounded. Hence his delight in those composers who systematically avoided the obvious, notably Berlioz, and his growing discontent with Mozart, whom he was eventually to rebuke for repeating too often that which he preferred.

In the Divertimento, this speed of thought makes the listener's task dizzy but stimulating, yet the classical landscape of the piece is sufficiently familiar to prevent him losing his bearings altogether. The sonata Allegro with which the work opens is followed by an Andante sostenuto, a literal rearrangement of the Elegy for Clarinet (without its coda), lightly scored for pizzicato strings and occasionally giving the orchestral clarinet the lead, as if to remind the listener of the music's rightful owner. At the end of the long theme Busoni introduces a reminiscence of the second subject of the opening Allegro, effecting a transition to the closing section. This begins as a literal recapitulation, but after eight bars the main theme is thrown away in favour of a fleeting chromatic tarantella. The flute increases the pace with a long and dazzling run, punctuated by a syncopated figure in the orchestra:

Ex. 211

In the First Tableau of *Doktor Faust* Busoni uses this phrase just once, to depict laughter. He was probably influenced by the Act I finale of *Così fan Tutte*, an opera with which he had only recently become acquainted:

Ex. 212

On 21 August 1920, Busoni's staunchest friends in Zurich, including Volkmar Andreae, Philipp Jarnach, Albert Biolley and the members of the Tonhalle Orchestra, were present at a small and unceremonious farewell—a trial rehearsal of the Divertimento. On 9 September Busoni left Zurich for ever and returned to Berlin, 'the city of darkness' as Dent so aptly described it. He took with him 1,000 new books which he had acquired during the war, the first half of the full score of *Doktor Faust* and the sketches for his next work, the *Toccata* for piano. He left his wife and children temporarily in Zurich; to his beloved Giotto and many Zurich friends he bade a final farewell. He wrote:

> In Berlin I shall find discord and deprivation, but also satisfaction and diversity of interests . . . I would in any case have departed from Zurich, which has returned to a state of stupor; the people of Switzerland will have to find their miracles among their own ranks.[17]

XVIII

In Signo Joannis Sebastiani Magni

Sonatina brevis [Sonatina no. 5 for piano]. In Signo Joannis Sebastiani Magni. Freely paraphrased from Bach's Little Fantasy and Fugue in D minor [BWV 905]. *Dedicated*: to Philipp Jarnach. *Composed*: August 1918. *Published*: Leipzig 1919. EB 5093. Plate number 28396. Republished in the Bach–Busoni Edition, Vol. VII. *MS*: 4pp., 34×25cm. Staatsbibliothek Preussischer Kulturbesitz, West Berlin. *Duration*: 4 minutes.

Shortly before the First World War, Breitkopf und Härtel had decided to reissue all Busoni's Bach transcriptions and arrangements in a de luxe edition; the plan was at last completed on 20 July 1918. It was a monumental undertaking, spreading over seven volumes (and an eighth was added in 1925, the second edition of Busoni's *Klavierübung*).

Volumes I and II are devoted to arrangements (*Bearbeitungen*). Those which Busoni considered suitable only for study purposes are grouped together in Volume I. All these were made expressly for the new edition, while he was teaching at Bologna in 1914. They are the eighteen short Preludes and a Fughetta BWV 924–42, the two- and three-part Inventions (a revised version of his edition of 1892), four Duets BWV 802–5 and the Prelude, Fugue and Allegro in E flat major BWV 998 (originally for lute).

Volume II is devoted to those arrangements intended for concert use. There are just three works: the Chromatic Fantasia and Fugue, the Concerto for Piano and Strings in D minor and the Goldberg Variations. It should be explained that the word *Bearbeitung* has many shades of meaning in these two volumes. Sometimes it implies minor alterations of notes or rhythms, intended to improve the effect of a passage on the piano or to clarify the part-writing; sometimes it implies an analytical study (as with the Prelude, Fugue and Allegro); in the case of the Goldberg Variations it signifies a far-reaching adaptation of the original text to render it playable on one keyboard, as well as detailed suggestions for phrasing and interpretation, even for possible cuts.

The earliest of Busoni's Bach transcriptions—virtuoso re-workings of major organ works—appear in Volume III. These are the Prelude and Fugue in D major BWV 532 and Prelude and Fugue in E flat major (St Anne) BWV 552; the Toccatas and Fugues in D minor and C major BWV 565 and 564; ten Chorale Preludes. Also in this volume we find Busoni's transcription of the

Chaconne for solo violin, made in Boston in 1892. The first two works in the volume represent his oldest and most directly impressive style—transcriptions made in Leipzig during the 1880s, when he first became acquainted with the true sound of Bach's organ music. The multiple blind octave technique which he developed for these transcriptions, an extension of Brahmsian and Lisztian textures, draws an organ-like richness from the piano. The technique is carried to its logical conclusion in the two Toccatas and Fugues, transcriptions which date from around 1900. The Chorale Preludes, much simpler in style, are divided into two groups, the first originating from the same period as the Second Violin Sonata (1897–8), the second contemporary with the Fantasia after J. S. Bach (1909).

A rather strange group of original compositions and *Nachdichtungen* forms Volume IV. First the Fantasia after J. S. Bach, then the 'Preludio, Fuga e Fuga figurata' from *An die Jugend*; the *Capriccio on the Departure of a beloved Brother* BWV 992, in which the editorial work would today be described as a realization, dates from 1914 and is dedicated to Artur Schnabel. There follows a Fantasia, Adagio and Fugue, two movements transcribed from originals for solo violin, preceded by an introduction; finally the *Versio minore* and *Versio definitivo* of the *Fantasia Contrappuntistica*.

Volume V is devoted to Book I of *The well-tempered Clavier*, an edition which Busoni originally published in 1894.

Volume VI, Book II of *The well-tempered Clavier*, is the most complex and visionary of all Busoni's Bach editions. The accumulation of wisdom in these pages is astonishing—the threefold insight of a virtuoso of the highest rank, of a brilliant contrapuntist and of a great humanist. On 20 September 1912, Busoni noted: 'Bach's "well-tempered", Part I for pianists, Part 2 for composers: my testament.'[1]

Volume VII, which was not assembled until 1920, contains supplements to all the preceding volumes. The first of these is an edition of three Toccatas (in E minor, G minor and G major, BWV 914–16), then comes an analytical edition of the Fantasia and Fugue in A minor BWV 904, written for Hugo Leichtentritt in gratitude for his Busoni biography, and published in 1916. There follow two rarities. The first is a synthetic grouping of three miscellaneous pieces, Fantasia and Fugue BWV 905, Andante BWV 969 and Scherzo BWV 844; the second a transcription for cello and piano of the Chromatic Fantasia and Fugue, made in 1917 for the cellist-conductor, Hans Kindler, who was a member of the original *Pierrot Lunaire* ensemble and also Bernard van Dieren's brother-in-law. The volume continues with the Improvisation for two Pianos on 'Wie wohl ist mir' which was completed too late for inclusion in Volume IV. In the afterglow of creativity with which 'Wie wohl ist mir' was completed, Busoni had made new realizations of the puzzle-canons from the *Musical Offering*. These take the penultimate place in the volume. Finally, setting the seal on the whole enterprise, comes the Sonatina *in Signo Joannis Sebastiani Magni*, a free *Nachdichtung* of the little Fantasy and Fugue, BWV 905, the original of which we find earlier in the same volume. There is also an appendix—a reprint of Busoni's 'Attempt at an organic piano-notation'. He devised this curious and short-lived scheme in 1909, with the intention of abolishing accidentals in piano notation, thus facilitating sight-reading and transposition of more complex harmonies. As first fruit of his experiment he published the Chromatic Fantasia, transcribed into the new notation. Eventually, new systems of notation arose, and we can see that Busoni did not 'grueble' in vain. But most methods fulfil Schoenberg's hope that 'our future notations will be—how should I say—"wirelesser" '.[2]

Like all Busoni's major projects, the Bach–Busoni Edition is Janus-faced, neither a museum catalogue nor a school book, but a living document looking into the future and, through parallels drawn between contrapuntal art and Gothic architecture, further into the past. Even those who adhere to *Urtext* editions and authentic instruments will find much brilliant and controversial material, as well as practical advice, in its pages.

For the opening of Volume I, Busoni had composed a brief dedication in which he ingeniously combined the BACH theme with that of the first fugue from Book I of the '48'. For the end of Volume VII he created something on a larger scale: the fifth Sonatina was envisaged as a musical signature to the whole enterprise; in its monogram of notes the souls of Bach and Busoni are intertwined. One of Busoni's personal musical symbols is declaimed in the opening bars, that pattern of falling sevenths which we recognize as the *Merlin* motif (see Ex. 119, last four notes). Here the sevenths are diminished:

Ex. 213

although they also appear later in the work as major sevenths. They point to a device not uncommon in Bach, a melodic line derived from a series of diminished-seventh chords. An extreme case is to be found in the finale of Mozart's G minor Symphony K.550:

Ex. 214

And Busoni later uses them—with diabolic insinuations—for the appearance of Megaeros, the fifth spirit of Hell, in *Doktor Faust* (see Ex. 272).

In bars 4–5 of the Sonatina one of Bach's monograms, D, E flat, C sharp, appears; a transposition of the first three notes of the Kyrie II in the B minor

Mass.* Busoni superimposes upon it a variant of the Megaeros motif:

Ex. 215

The rest of the piece is an extremely free arrangement of the original Fantasy and Fugue, in the strict sense of the word a ricercare, calling for close attention and analysis. In this spirit, a small offering for the connoisseur of twentieth-century polyphony and its possibilities, Busoni dedicated it to his friend Philipp Jarnach. Nowhere more than in this work does one think of Busoni's comment on *Pierrot Lunaire*: 'As if a large musical mechanism had been assembled from crumbled ingredients, and as if some of these ingredients have been put to uses other than those for which they were originally intended.'[3]

After the introductory measures of Ex. 213, the Fantasy runs its course, but the upper voices are inverted and the plain lines of the original are filled in with chromatic passing notes. The last five bars are repeated an octave lower and lead to a further intertwining of motifs (as in Ex. 215). Without any break a Fughetta follows, in which only the theme of the original remains intact; Busoni takes it as the basis for a completely new speculative counterpoint. The following extract, which shows the third entry of the subject and the beginning of a sequential episode, gives some idea of the style:

Ex. 216

[Poco più mosso, ma tranquillo]

The Megaeros motif returns, then a combination of the theme of the Andante and of the Fughetta. After an extensive working out, the Megaeros motif is inverted, seeming to symbolize a reversal of its fateful quality: now it leads 'upwards' and introduces a new version of Bach's theme from the Fantasy, in augmentation, opened out into D major, a passage reminiscent of the *quasi trasfigurato* close of the fourth Sonatina and anticipating the purified closing bars of Vorspiel II of *Doktor Faust* (cf. Exx. 268 and 279). A serene conclusion seems to be in sight, but an interrupted cadence inverts the Megaeros motif once more and with its gloomy falling intervals the work comes to an end:

* According to Schmieder, the authenticity of this Little Fantasy and Fugue is dubious.

Ex. 217

XIX

Light Relief

Sonatina [no. 6] **super Carmen**. Chamber fantasy [for piano] on Bizet's *Carmen*. *Dedicated*: to Leonhard Tauber. *Composed*: March 1920. *First performance*: 22.6.1920. Wigmore Hall, London. Soloist: Busoni. *Published*: Leipzig, 1921. EB 5186. Plate number 28666. *MS*: 12pp., 35×27cm. Deutsche Staatsbibliothek, Berlin. *Duration*: 8 minutes.

Die Bekehrte for soprano and piano, 'Bei dem Glanze der Abendröte' (Goethe). *Dedicated*: to Lola Artôt de Padilla. *Composed*: September 1921. *Published*: Leipzig, 1937. DLV 4791. *MS*: 5pp., 34×26.5cm. Library of Congress, Washington. *Duration*: 4 minutes.

Not all of Busoni's later compositions belong to the canon of satellite works to *Doktor Faust*. There are also his regular contributions to the *Klavierübung* (some of these also Faustian, however) and just two independent compositions, both modestly proportioned gentle diversions from the serious task of composing a major work. The first of these, the so-called *'Carmen' Fantasy*, was written during a visit to Paris, a city which Busoni seems to have enjoyed with a mixture of abandon and critical detachment. Here he could move in society quite different from that in Berlin or Zurich and there was, of course, every possible opportunity for gastronomic excursions. As in London or New York there was also an interesting circle of friends: before the war d'Annunzio, Rilke and Widor, later the Hungarian pianist Isidor Philipp, the composer Maurice Emmanuel and many others. Unfortunately, the Busoni–Rilke correspondence has disappeared, but for one rapid exchange of notes and telegrams dating from March 1914: they deal with the choice of restaurant for a meeting. Perhaps it was this very occasion which Magda von Hattingberg has evoked so vividly:

> Rainer explained minutely and ceremoniously how one prepares apple-tea, Busoni enthused about scartozzetti and scampi. The poet and the musician inspired each other to gastronomical hymns, that is, Rainer's hymns were more ascetic in tone while Busoni's had a truly Gallic fervour.[1]

Post-war Paris afforded a striking contrast to Zurich. Busoni wrote to Jarnach:

> It is like a homecoming for me . . . to find life on the grand scale again . . . Here one is not assessed according to one's age or how much one spends,

whether one is seen in the company of a lady or climbing into an automobile.[2]

What strange folk they are . . . While it is difficult to keep them interested, armed as they are with a disdainful indifference, the moment one has gained their attention they are capable of the greatest achievements and are quick of understanding. . . . The golden light of these spring days has had an irresistible magic. The South vibrates in the air. And yet the indifferent faces of everybody one meets contrast unpleasantly with these palmy days. Truly: one could scarcely find less agreeable people anywhere.[3]

An old family friend was Leonhard Tauber. As proprietor of an inn at Klagenfurt during the 1870s, he had often heard the young Ferruccio play the piano. Now he was a wealthy hotelier, the owner of the Hotel Foyôt where Busoni usually stayed when visiting Paris. However, after being accommodated there for only a few days during the 1920 visit, Busoni and his wife moved into Tauber's newly acquired home in the Rue Ville-Juste. Apart from the pleasant surroundings of the Bois de Boulogne, there was a fine collection of rare books and pictures to be admired. A copy by Fantin-Latour of Veronese's 'Wedding at Cana' was just one example of the riches.

Here Busoni could momentarily relax from his Faust project and between concerts and rehearsals he rapidly composed a fantasy on themes from *Carmen*. No detailed planning was necessary, for the work had in fact been conceived three years earlier. In 1917 Busoni had prepared a new 'critical-instructive' edition of Liszt's Fantasy on themes from *Don Giovanni*. In a lengthy foreword he had analysed the work's tripartite construction which, based on a simple principle of contrast, serves to accentuate the demonic aspects of Mozart's score. As an example of the universal applicability of Liszt's principle, Busoni indicated how one could construct a *Carmen* fantasy in the same manner:

Following Liszt's example, one would begin with the auspicious market-scene from the fourth act and interpolate the fatal Carmen theme, based on the gypsy scale, as a contrast in the introduction. The 'Habanera' would form the central movement (with an ensuing variation), the 'Arena-music' would then form the Finale.[4]

While the eventual outline of the '*Carmen*' *Fantasy* is a little more complex than this original plan, the basic structure of the work is just as delineated here. José's 'Flower Song' was interpolated before the Habanera, and Busoni also conceived a sombre coda as contrast to the flamboyance of the rest of the piece.

Thus, in characteristically unconventional fashion, the set of six Sonatinas was completed. Busoni declared that 'Bach is the Alpha of piano composition and Liszt the Omega'; hence, where the fifth Sonatina is a tribute to Bach, the sixth is a homage to Liszt. Furthermore, while the fifth represents almost exclusively the Nordic part of Busoni's personality, the sixth expresses in compact form his many un-German qualities. The choice of Carmen as the focal point of such a work is revealing, for she too is an outsider, a free spirit—

sensuous, humorous, fatalistic and elusive, the demonic rebel in the midst of
an orderly world. Through Nietzsche, intellectuals have been led to find in
Carmen the archetypal antidote to Wagner, and Bizet's score became a symbol
of defiance. For Nietzsche, this opera was the ideal answer to his aphorism, 'Il
faut méditerraniser la musique'.[5] In later years he moderated his standpoint,
yet he still maintained that 'it has a strong effect as an *ironic* antithesis to
Wagner'.[6] It is this irony that Busoni tacitly expresses in his sixth Sonatina.
Because of this, the work received a cold greeting in some circles. Bernard van
Dieren has wittily catalogued the work's alleged vices:

> A cause for displeasure was [Busoni's] advocacy of Bizet. When it moved
> him to the composition of a 'Sonatina super Carmen' he perpetrated three
> branding sins simultaneously. He had resumed the despised Lisztian
> tradition of the Piano Fantasia on operatic fragments, he had chosen a
> composer whose name, in connection with chamber music, jarred on
> Teutonically critical ears, and by his reference to sonata form he intensified
> the general sinfulness of the proceedings.[7]

Outwardly, this little work is nonchalant, almost a cliché. Yet on the closing
page comes music cut from altogether different cloth. Just as isolated sentences
or scenes in *Arlecchino* stand out as reminders of grim truths, so do the closing
bars of the *'Carmen' Fantasy* seem to raise a warning finger against the light-
heartedness of the rest of the piece. This does not make for a unified
composition; it does, however, elevate an otherwise insubstantial work to the
level of a miniature psycho-drama. (The Introduction to the *Tanzwalzer*,
composed in the autumn of the same year, fulfils a similar function.)

The opening chorus of Bizet's Act III part 2 serves as the material for the
first section of the Fantasy, flitting brilliantly from key to key. Then follows
the 'Flower Song', decked out with ornamentation of ever-increasing complexity. It is a superfical and sentimental arrangement that intentionally
sidesteps the pathos of the original aria. Busoni invents a free extension to
Bizet's melody and then introduces, as originally planned, the Carmen theme:

Ex. 218

A surprising modulation that leads nowhere (that is, back to the D flat major
with which it set out) dreamily introduces Carmen's Habanera, not in the
intense, minor-key version of the song itself, but in the taunting, flirting

manner in which Bizet reintroduces it at the end of Act I. There is a sly contrapuntal joke:

Ex. 219

and this tongue-in-cheek humour is carried through in a startling jump into D minor. A dazzling variation ensues, then the chromatic-scale figure of the Habanera melody is expanded into a running semiquaver bass and a transition passage, *tempestoso*, leads to a brilliant and vulgar setting of the 'Arena' music from the last scene. The picture fades out with brooding arpeggiated chords, alternating between G major and G sharp minor.

The closing page uses only two elements from Bizet's score: the Carmen theme, with its sinister drum taps, and the descending chromatic scales of the Habanera. With these simplest of means Busoni has fashioned an Andante visionario, a contemplative and disembodied dream-vision. The Carmen theme is forcibly pulled down by the chromatic scales from F sharp major to A minor. An ingenious yet simple piece of necromancy: out of a few fragments by another composer, Busoni has formed a lament in his personal, elegiac idiom. More than just a postlude to the drama, it is a concentration of the dark forces lurking beneath the brightly smiling music of Bizet's score. In the progression of keys embraced by the passage lies a symbol: Busoni takes the F sharp major tonality of Bizet's closing bars and carries on to an A minor conclusion, one small step removed from the A major with which the opera opens. Thus he closes the circle implied by the drama.

The *'Carmen' Fantasy* is a joke with a bitter sting in its tail; a composition inspired by the bonhomie of the composer's Parisian surroundings turns unexpectedly into an ironical, even caustic gesture. Characteristic was the way in which Busoni wrote to Petri of the first performance in London: 'Peut-être ça t'amusera d'apprendre que j'ai *risqué* en public une Sonatine mienne sur des motifs de *Carmen*.'[8]

It was Leo Kestenberg who was instrumental in arranging Busoni's return to Berlin in 1920. Kestenberg, who had risen to an influential position in the Prussian Ministry of Education, was responsible for the appointment of the professors of music at the State Academy of Arts and Sciences. For the composition classes he secured the strongly contrasting offices of Schreker, Pfitzner and Busoni. One has visions of the three professors glowering at each

other from opposite corners of some conservatoire common-room,*—in fact
the pupils visited Busoni at his home, generally in the afternoon, twice a
week.† The circle of actual pupils was small (six to begin with), but there was
often open house for all manner of people. These occasions were evidently
somewhat grotesque. Ernst Křenek was for a while a member of the Busoni
circle, and has left the following impressions of one such gathering:

> The composer sat between a fortune-telling mystic and, for good luck, like
> Verdi's Prince of Mantua, a hunchback. . . . This strange trinity was
> separated from the guests by a row of chairs. Busoni did all the talking and
> was never less than brilliant. . . . Coffee was served regularly, but once we
> were given *Sekt*, which had not been paid for; even as we were drinking it the
> merchant pounded on the door asking for his money.[9]

This report is not as eccentric as it sounds. The identity of the 'mystic' is
uncertain, but the hunchback was simply Busoni's secretary, Rita Boetticher.
The wine merchant only had to climb the stairs to Busoni's appartment, for the
ground floor of Victorie-Luise Platz No. 11 was occupied by Wein-Restaurant
Emil Adloff—and the proprietor would certainly have called for his money, for
those were the days of galloping inflation when the Mark was losing value
sometimes at the rate of fifty per cent per day. That the Busoni circle was not
without its curiosities is however confirmed by Artur Schnabel:

> He was nearly always surrounded by a group of people who were a bit too
> expensive—I would say—for me to take into the bargain. He had a great
> affection for freakish people. . . . Every day after lunch he had this group for
> two to three hours—a strange collection, not very gifted either. . . . With a
> kind of devilish glee he would tell them the most absurd things about music
> which he simply invented. . . . There was this somewhat impish trait in his
> make-up.[10]

The inner circle of composition pupils in those years included Kurt Weill,
Erwin Bodky, Vladimir Vogel, Luc Balmer, Walter Geiser and Robert Blum.
The students were initiated into the concept of Young Classicality. Orchestration was taught through the study of Mozart; a lean, sharp-edged polyphonic
style of writing was encouraged. Expressionism, Impressionism or any such
tendencies were anathema.

Certainly, the hours devoted to the encouragement and enlightenment of the
younger generation were a pleasant diversion to Busoni. Yet there was little
direct profit from them; there was no one stunning talent among the pupils,
and this teaching was more an idealistic than a practical task. He must have felt
it was his duty towards the musical world.

---

* Busoni disliked Schreker as heartily as Pfitzner, describing his most famous opera,
Der ferner Klang (the far-off sound) as *Der ferner Schreck* (the distant fright).
† From 1921 on, Pfitzner's pupils did not even live in Berlin, but followed their master
to the Bavarian village of Schondorf, which he had chosen as his post-war domicile.

On 1 July 1921 the composition class officially opened. Busoni wrote: 'That means appearing in armour before a dozen critical youngsters, withstanding each cut and thrust, parrying objections and contradictions, playing the "Master".'[11] In September he set the class a specific task, the composition of a fugue on a given theme or a song for voice and piano, choosing as text Goethe's poem 'Die Bekehrte'. Of the several efforts, the best in his opinion was the Goethe setting of Vladimir Vogel. It was therefore published in the November 1921 issue of a short-lived journal, *Faust*, of which Busoni was the music editor. The issue was entitled 'The struggle for the New Style'. Introducing Vogel's song (the composer was at that time twenty-five years old), Busoni wrote: 'The so-called "new ways" are today no longer new. The epoch of experiments and of the overrating of means of expression at the expense of content and artistic durability is rapidly drawing to a close.'[12]

Busoni modestly made no mention in his article of the fact that he himself had also written a setting of the same poem. (He had also begun a setting of Goethe's 'Die Spröde' as companion piece, but this was left unfinished.) 'Die Bekehrte' was composed on 22 September; Vogel recalls that Busoni showed it to his class, comparing it with their own attempts. However, he never troubled to publish it nor is there any record of a public performance of it during his lifetime. The song bears a dedication to Lola Artôt de Padilla, who had sung the title role in the recent highly successful Berlin production of the opera *Turandot* (see Plate 19).

The song itself is something of a collector's item. It has a style of its own, with perhaps the purest melodic inspiration of Busoni's last period. The vocal writing, unlike that of his other Goethe-songs, has a flowing, cantabile line and there is even a number of modest melismas. Like the poem, the song is constructed strophically; for the last verse, where the text demands an intensification, the simple, swaying accompaniment of the first two verses gives way to movement in semiquavers. The poem speaks of Damon's flute-playing and of its seductive powers—a brief Dionysian scene whose sensuousness is communicated with the aid of Busoni's beloved major–minor oscillations:

Ex. 220

Goethe's erotic song seems scarcely the sober stuff with which young pupils were to be instructed in the art of Young Classicality. But precisely because of this it presented a challenge, namely to create the voluptuous atmosphere demanded by the text without spilling over into any grand Expressionist gestures. An ambitious young composer, inspired by such models as Ravel's *Daphnis et Chloë* for Damon's flute-playing, or Schoenberg's *Erwartung* for the anxieties of the seduced listener, may well have produced an extravagant, well-nigh orgiastic setting. The teacher would then, perhaps, patiently remind him that he was dealing with a classical poet, explaining: 'Uncommon things—says Schopenhauer—should be expressed with common words and not the reverse. Hence: Mozart and Goethe.'[13]

This was the essence of Busoni's teaching. His own setting of 'Die Bekehrte' is an object lesson in the New Style.

XX

Faust Progresses

Toccata (Preludio, Fantasia, Ciaconna) [for piano]. *Dedicated*: to Isidor Philipp. *Composed*: July–September 1920. *First performance*: 18.11.1920. Philharmonie, Berlin. Soloist: Busoni. *Published*: Vienna, 1921 as supplement to *Musikblätter des Anbruch*, Jan. 1921 (Busoni number). M.A.21. Republished Leipzig, 1922. EB 5187. Plate number 28667. *MS*: property of Mr Daniell Revenaugh; penultimate draft in Bibliothèque Nationale, Paris. *Duration*: 10 minutes.

Tanzwalzer op. 53 [for orchestra]. *Dedicated*: to the memory of Johann Strauss. *Composed*: September–October 1920. *First performance*: 13.1.1921. Philharmonie, Berlin. Berlin Philharmonic Orchestra, conducted by Busoni. *Published*: Leipzig, 1922. PB 2605. *MS*: 43pp., 35×27cm. Deutsche Staatsbibliothek, Berlin. *Arrangements*: 1) for piano (Michael von Zadora) published Leipzig, 1921. EB 5197. Plate number 28725; 2) for 2 pianos (Heinz Munkel, 1958) published Wiesbaden, 1959. MS. *Instrumentation*: 2(Picc.)–2–2–2; 4–2–3–0; Timp., Perc.; Str. *Duration*: 12 minutes.

Three Albumleaves for Piano. *Dedicated*: 1) to Albert Biolley; 2) to Francesco Ticciati; 3) to Felice Boghen. *Composed*: 1) August 1917; 2) April 1921; 3) May 1921. *First performance*: 4.2.1922. Wigmore Hall, London. Soloist: Busoni. *Published*: (No. 1 only) Leipzig, 1918. EB 5056. Plate number 28172; (all three) Leipzig, 1921. EB 5193. Plate number 28698. *MSS*: 2) 1p., 24×33cm; 3) 3pp., 35×27cm. Both Deutsche Staatsbibliothek, Berlin. *Durations*: 1) 3 minutes; 2) 1 minute; 3) 4 minutes. (For other versions of Albumleaf no. 1 see Altoums Warnung [Ch. IV] and Albumleaf for Flute [Ch. XIV].)

Romanza e Scherzoso op. 54 for piano and orchestra. (When preceded by the *Konzertstück* op. 31a [see Ch. I] entitled Concertino for Piano and Orchestra.) *Dedicated*: to Alfredo Casella. *Composed*: June 1921. *First performance*: 10.12.1921. Casino, Basle. Egon Petri, Basle Symphony Orchestra, conducted by Heinrich Suter. *Published*: Leipzig, 1922. PB 2639. *MS*: 44pp., 35×27cm. Deutsche Staatsbibliothek, Berlin. *Instrumentation*: 2(Picc.)–2–2–2; 4–2–3–0; Timp., Perc. (ad lib).); Str. *Duration*: 8 minutes.

Zigeunerlied op. 55 no. 2. 'Im Nebelgeriesel, im tiefen Schnee' (Goethe) [for baritone and orchestra or piano]. *Composed*: March 1923. *First performance*: 27.4.1923. Philharmonie, Berlin. Wilhelm Guttmann (baritone), Berlin Philharmonic Orchestra, conducted by Werner Wolff. *Published*: (orchestral version) Leipzig, undated. PB 2826; (piano version) Berlin, 1923 as supplement to *Die Musik*, May 1923. Republished Leipzig, undated, DLV 4788. Later republished as no. 5 of Fünf Goethelieder,

Wiesbaden, 1964. EB 6461. *MS*: (orchestral version) 12pp., 33×26cm. Deutsche Staatsbibliothek, Berlin. *Instrumentation*: 2–2–2–2; 2–0–0–0; Perc.; Str. *Duration*: 2 minutes.

Schlechter Trost, 'Mitternachts weint und schluchzt ich' (Goethe) [for baritone and orchestra or piano]. *Composed*: February 1924. *First performance*: (?)16.4.1967. Liederhalle, Stuttgart. Dietrich Fischer-Dieskau (baritone), Württemberg State Orchestra, conducted by Ferdinand Leitner. *Published*: (orchestral version) Wiesbaden, 1960, MS; (piano version) Leipzig, 1924 in *Navigare Necesse est*, Festschrift for Anton Kippenberg, Insel Verlag. Republished Wiesbaden, 1960. Wb. 417; and as no. 4 of Fünf Goethelieder, Wiesbaden, 1964. EB 6461. *MS*: (orchestral version) 4pp., 33×26cm. Deutsche Staatsbibliothek, Berlin. *Instrumentation*: 1–0–1–1; 0–0–0–0; Str. (Vla., Vc., Cb.) *Duration*: 3 minutes.

Busoni's last major piano composition, the *Toccata*, is a mirror of the unsettling emotions underlying his return to Berlin. At the age of fifty-four he bade farewell to his restricted but settled existence in Switzerland, arriving back home in Berlin on 11 September 1920. The *Toccata* was already virtually complete; he had set it aside in August, 'presque complète déjà, et nullement parfaite encore',[1] at a time when his spirits had been at their lowest ebb and when, apart from some pages of studies for the *Klavierübung*, he had written nothing. 'Il m'est impossible de terminer la Toccata en les conditions dans lesquelles je me trouve', he had told Isidor Philipp.[2] In Berlin he set to work and rapidly wrote a fair copy. It was finished on 16 September, signed and dated. Five days later, however, he still felt the need to improve it and several alterations were made, including the addition of a new variation to the concluding Ciaconna. Despite being an unusually intractable project which took a long time to form itself, the *Toccata* turns out to be one of his most powerful works.

   The opening three pages (Preludio) are a virtuoso fantasy on 'The Ballad of Lippold the Jew-Coiner' from *Die Brautwahl*. The original key of A flat minor is retained and the glittering figuration, originally depicting the flames licking round the stake, burns fiercely. Only the first phrases of the Ballad are used (see Ex. 65); for the most part it appears in its original form, but two new figures are also evolved from it. The second of these:

Ex. 221

is transformed into an ostinato:

Ex. 222

This is virtually identical to the figure which accompanies the first heralding of Mephistopheles in *Doktor Faust* (see Ex. 273). Thus we have an implied musical link between Manasse and Mephisto (the music of that part of Vorspiel II in *Doktor Faust* had already been completed in 1919). Busoni indicated the link between Leonhard and Faust in *Arlecchino* Part II; in the Toccata he extends this imagery to the evil forces in the two operas.

The central movement of the *Toccata*, the Fantasia, is the most complex, divided into seven sections of varying length. All the material can be related to three themes, the first of which appears as a motto at the beginning of the Fantasia:

Ex. 223

There follows a recitative-like two-part invention in which a motivic cell:

Ex. 224

is expanded in a manner derived from Ziehn's techniques of symmetry:

Ex. 225

Over the ostinato figure (Ex. 224), now stabilized into B flat major, appears a second theme, more lyrical than anything heretofore but, like Ex. 223, ending in a pathetic falling minor second:

Ex. 226

The third theme is introduced in the brief second section of the Fantasia:

Ex. 227

This motif is taken up twice, begins to expand, but is interrupted by new versions of Ex. 223 (Exx. 228 and 229).

Again there is a link with the Manasse music from the opening of the Preludio: the motto theme in its original form (Ex. 223) is closely related in rhythm to the main theme of the Ballad— ♩. ♩ ♩ | ♩. ♪♩ ‿ | —and the harmonic

Ex. 228

Ex. 229

progression of Ex. 229 has a similar shape to this version of the Ballad theme:

Ex. 230

Ex. 229 is in fact the prototype of a Mephisto motif in *Doktor Faust*; thus we are presented with a further musical link between Manasse and Mephistopheles.

The third section of the Fantasia introduces yet another version of the motto theme:

Ex. 231

and begins to build a polyphonic movement in combination with Ex. 227 (the notes with crosses in Ex. 231 indicate the actual melodic outline and demonstrate its relationship to Ex. 223 more clearly—it is a typically Busonian transformation). This quasi-fugato is abruptly broken off after eighteen bars. The ensuing fourth section, fifteen bars long, is improvisatory, unrelated to its surroundings—a rising scale motif is combined with a figure based on falling thirds. The fifth section combines the chordal outline of Ex. 229 (tonic–dominant minor) with Ex. 227, then develops into a brief canon, also based on Ex. 227. Sections three, four and five give the impression of one continuous movement, but their varied thematic contents separate them more clearly to the ear than to the eye.

Section six begins with a restatement of Ex. 229. Then the expressive Ex. 226 returns softly under a euphonious broken-chord figure. The last section of the Fantasia is a bridge-passage in faster tempo. As in the first section, a small motif is extended by symmetrical means into a longer figure (Ex. 232).

Ex. 232

Meanwhile a rising-octave figure is introduced in the left hand, the first leap of the impending Ciaconna.

The Ciaconna theme, with the same sarabande rhythm as Bach's Chaconne for violin, is four bars long:

Ex. 233

while an extension of the theme uses exactly the same pattern of falling thirds and rising sixths as we find at the opening of Brahms' Fourth Symphony. This is an unrelenting, uncompromising movement, adventurously exploiting many of the possibilities of the theme. There is, for example, a fugato opening, then a three-part variation repeated in transposition, a chordal variation with a free, thundering bass and a variation which could be marked *quaerendo invenietis*, as Bach marked his most abstruse puzzle-canon in *A Musical Offering*; a seemingly unrelated two-part invention poses a riddle but is then combined with the Chaconne theme, which offers the solution. The final variations (Busoni's inspired afterthought) are based on Lisztian broken-chord figures. The coda, *un poco stretto*, introduces Ex. 227 in new guise, then a virtuosic octave passage, *più stretto*, introduces fragments of the lyric theme of the Fantasia (the continuation of Ex. 226). In its new form it strongly resembles one of the Mephisto motifs (cf. Ex. 274), indeed the word 'Mephistopheles' could be sung to it:

Ex. 234

The work ends with two statements of the other Mephisto motif, Ex. 229, brilliantly in D major, then brutally, reduced to its naked rhythm, in A flat minor.

The Fantasia is fan-shaped (ABCDCBA) even if this design is obscured by a wealth of small motifs whose relationships are not immediately obvious. The flanking movements of the *Toccata*, the Preludio and Ciaconna, also have striking similarities of proportion and texture: they are both monolithic constructions, while the Preludio, based on a progression of three chords, is also a form of Chaconne. Hence the fan shape is extended to the whole structure. After the violent Preludio, the Fantasia represents a repeated series of attempts to strike a more lyrical vein; each is negated by Mephistophelean gestures. Yet these contrasting forces are eventually cancelled out, bringing about the thematically unrelated central section which forms the focal point of the whole work. In the onslaught of the Ciaconna we return to completely Mephistophelean domains.

This is one of Busoni's most one-sided, obsessive compositions, about which he himself admitted, 'Il est très sévère et pas trop agréable'.[3] He was well aware that the nervous tension under which it was written remained readily detectable. To Jarnach he spoke of the work 'arising out of anguish and unstable emotions'.[4]

Within a few weeks of resettling in Berlin, Busoni gave two piano recitals in the Philharmonie. Previously he had always performed in the smaller Beethovensaal, but after his absence of six years these recitals were something of a sensation in the city. Dent, who was present, recounts that the hall, with its capacity of 3,000 seats, was full to bursting point. The first evening was devoted to Chopin, Beethoven and Liszt. In the second, Busoni played his *Toccata* for the first time. The young critic Hans Stuckenschmidt was quick to comprehend the essence of the new work: '. . . a tough and substantial piece, formed out of his unique polyphony which is nourished by Bach but points the way to impressions of the spirits of our own age, more nervous and multifarious.'[5] A modern interpretor of the *Toccata*, Alfred Brendel, confirms this impression: 'The erosion of time has not smoothed out the uncongenial contours. No patina of familiarity softens [its] sharpness.'[6]

Busoni has headed the score of his *Toccata* with a quotation from Frescobaldi, 'Non è senza difficoltà che si arriva al fine'. He was quoting from memory, for the original of this cryptic comment—'Non senza fatica si giunge al fine'—is to be found at the head of Frescobaldi's *Toccata Nona* from the second book of Toccatas and Canzonas, published in 1637. (Busoni probably knew the piece from a collection of keyboard works by various old Italian masters which his friend Felice Boghen had published in Milan in 1918.) The slight alteration, from 'fatiga' to 'difficoltà', can be understood at three different levels. It refers, first, to the sheer physical difficulty of the *Toccata* for the performer; secondly, it suggests the emotional difficulties encountered in completing the work (and the opera, of which it forms a substantial part); finally, simply by dint of quoting Frescobaldi, Busoni identifies his ideals of form and style with those of the remote past, indicating in a new way the unbroken line which he sensed through musical history, the line which future generations, 'not without difficulty', were to stretch into a completed circle.

Although he had edited and published some of Bach's Toccatas in 1917, the form of Busoni's work is influenced neither by Bach nor by Frescobaldi. As we have so often observed in his music, the frequent references to older, traditional forms never imply 'new wine in old bottles'.

Recognition of Busoni's return to Berlin came in several ways: the Staatsoper staged *Turandot* and *Arlecchino* and the talented young Eduard Erdmann played his Piano Concerto.★ The journal *Anbruch* honoured the master in two ways: the series of orchestral concerts which it promoted in January 1921 presented a retrospective of Busoni's major works over thirty years, while the musical wing of the magazine, the *Musikblätter des Anbruch*, devoted an entire issue to him in the same month. As well as a collection of minor writings by Busoni himself, the issue contained major articles by Chantavoine, Leichtentritt, Dent and Jarnach as well as tributes from the pianist James Simon and two other friends, Gisella Selden-Goth and H. W. Draber. Further came stage designs for scenes from *Die Brautwahl*, *Arlecchino* and *Doktor Faust* and, as musical appendix, the first publication of the *Toccata*.

An antidote to the unrelenting blackness of the *Toccata* was quick to follow. Even while Busoni was working·on the fair copy of that work he was formulating something lighter and on 19 September 1920 he wrote down 'for fun'[7] the entire sketch for a *Tanzwalzer*. He orchestrated it immediately and signed the final double-bar on 1 October. In the evening of the same day he added an introduction (originally marked *ad libitum*) which he aptly described as 'demi-pathétique, demi-farceuse'.[8] The first performance followed soon after, in the second of the *Anbruch* concerts.

Busoni provided a brief note for the programme:

> The 'Tanzwalzer' was originally written in jest (and as a personal test of my own lighter talents), inspired by strains of a waltz issuing from inside a coffee-house, heard while walking in the street. . . . The work is dedicated to the memory of Johann Strauss, whom the composer sincerely admires.

In his homage Busoni has carefully followed the formal outline of the typical Strauss waltz, for once deliberately going against his customary avoidance·of 'new wine in old bottles'. The slow introduction is followed by four numbered, contrasting sections and a coda in which the various themes are developed and juxtaposed, leading to a jubilant close. The orchestra employed is also exactly that of Johann Strauss, but the uses Busoni makes of it are more complex; the harmonic language, although not exactly Straussian, is almost consistently diatonic.

The *Tanzwalzer* represents the end of a line of lighter compositions extending from the *Comedy Overture* and the *Scènes de Ballet* for piano to the 'Carmen' Fantasy. Those who are drawn primarily to the sublime and serious in Busoni are often perplexed by these pieces—none of which really aspire to the ranks of great music. It is disturbing that they have been performed more frequently than his more ambitious compositions. (The Italian composer Roman Vlad describes this as downright 'harmful'.[9]) Yet it is clear that Busoni needed to write these pieces in order to maintain an inner equilibrium.

★ Erdmann was not nineteen years old, as stated by Dent (p. 254 of *Ferruccio Busoni, a biography*); he was in fact twenty-four.

The *Tanzwalzer* would seem, then, to belong to a small group of works which could classify Busoni as a popular composer. Yet, like the *'Carmen' Fantasy*, it also has its disquieting side. This is particularly obvious in the short Introduction, but the clouded mood of the third waltz and the savage glee of its second theme:

Ex. 235

reinforce this sensation. This is light music for a public which, knowing Busoni, can penetrate to the bitter core of the idiom. Coming directly after the *Toccata* in Busoni's *oeuvre*, its effect is comparable to that of the Scherzo-waltz which follows the life-and-death drama of the first movement of Mahler's Ninth Symphony; earnest light music—a twentieth-century paradox. The composer stands as an outsider, observing the hollow merriment of others, sometimes scornfully, sometimes wittily.

At least the Berlin public in 1921 was sufficiently familiar with its hero to comprehend the paradox in his latest work. Adolf Weissmann, one of Berlin's most dreaded critics, heartily acclaimed the *Tanzwalzer*, which had been introduced almost apologetically in the programme note:

> Esteemed Maestro, no apology necessary. It was a charming finale. . . . The 'Tanzwalzer', with its French opening and Viennese continuation, demonstrates, apart from rhythmical variegation, so much genuine Busonian incident, satirical and melancholy, that, despite its amiability and obviousness, it is truly not unworthy of the musician.[10]

The three Albumleaves for Piano, published in 1921, are a diverse group. Their one common feature is the key of E minor, but their harmonic language is kaleidoscopic and firm tonality is rarely established.

The first Albumleaf is an arrangement of the Albumleaf for Flute and Piano, dating from 1917. It therefore belongs to the world of *Turandot*.

A mere twenty-four bars long, the second Albumleaf is a new composition. Busoni pencilled the word 'Salome?' on the manuscript, and in fact he later used it for the vision of Salome and John the Baptist in the First Tableau of *Doktor Faust*. The piece is a brief fugato on a seemingly dry subject:

Ex. 236

The origin of this idea can be traced to Mozart's *Idomeneo* Overture. After
eight bars of pure D major it appears there as a disquieting contrast, perhaps to
suggest the supernatural elements in the drama which undermine and threaten
the people of Crete:

Ex. 237   Mozart : 'Idomeneo'

Busoni had only become acquainted with the opera in 1918 and was fascinated
by it. A comparison between *Idomeneo* and *Figaro* was an object lesson in the
art of music-theatre, while the libretto of *Idomeneo* had a striking similarity to
the biblical story of Jephtha. In August 1918 Busoni arranged a concert suite
from *Idomeneo* which was published the following year, dedicated to Othmar
Schoeck.

Bereft of its surrounding cushion of orchestral sound, Mozart's 'sea-
monster' motif attains an intensified air of foreboding which is sustained
throughout the short Albumleaf. After a three-part fugal exposition, the group
of four descending semitones, from the second phrase of the theme, falls in
parallel triads over an ostinato bass. The theme makes another forlorn
appearance, now accompanied by rising semitones, but the free semiquaver
bass-line begins to fall and the whole edifice crumbles with it. An abstract and
mystifying page.

Most substantial of the group is the third Albumleaf (in the style of a Chorale
Prelude). The chorale theme is dark and brooding, Bach's harmonization of
'Christ lag in Todesbanden' transposed down an octave (the original is to be
found in the Kirnberger chorale collection BWV 278):

Ex. 238

Twice the theme is interrupted by exclamations in a higher register which give
the impression of sudden flashes of light. There follow four variations. In the
first and third, the tenor part, now in the major, is brought out as an
independent melody (Ex. 239).

Ex. 239

In the first variation it appears in a free broken-chord harmonization, then in three-part counterpoint, *amoroso*, decidedly profane, and not unlike a theme in Rachmaninov's Second Piano Concerto:

Ex. 240

Yet at its first appearance this sensuous theme was concealed within the solemnity of the chorale. In this thematic metamorphosis Busoni expresses in an indirect way the *idée fixe* of his *Faust* and *Leonardo* years: the swiftness with which good can be changed into evil.

Straightforward and charming music is to be found in the Concertino for Piano and Orchestra op. 54. The work arose out of a plan by Frida Kwast-Hodapp to revive the early *Konzertstück* op. 31a. She asked Busoni if he would consider extending the piece into a full-length concerto, no doubt hoping for something in the massive style of the earlier work (Kwast-Hodapp was a celebrated Reger interpretor). At first Busoni considered the idea unworkable. Then he suggested a Romanza and short finale which, while not avoiding a stylistic discrepancy, might form a satisfactory lighter pendant to his early work. He put this suggestion to her in a letter on 7 June 1921. A few days later he set to work and finished the *Romanza e Scherzoso* in less than two weeks. He recorded: 'I am unable to surmount the stylistic discrepancy, but the new piece could effectively round off [the Konzertstück] and give it greater significance.'[11]

While the *Romanza*, an Italianate cantabile, has only slight thematic links with the *Scherzoso*, there are no links at all between the earlier and later works. The opening bar of the *Romanza*, added as an afterthought, states a small motto which suggests the D major of the *Scherzoso* as well as the prevailing F minor:

Ex. 241

This also anticipates one of the themes of the *Scherzoso*:

Ex. 242

The piano's first entry introduces a theme (Ex. 243) related to the 'Freudvoll und leidvoll' motif of the *Cortège* (cf. Ex. 205).

Ex. 243

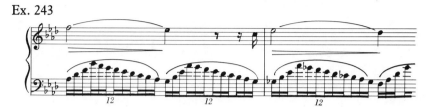

The *Romanza* is a mere forty-eight bars long, interspersing its gently plaintive tone with *scherzando* passages for woodwind and piano. The *Scherzoso* in turn introduces, by way of middle section, music of a more elegiac mood, gracefully interrupting the sparkling *moto perpetuo* of the outer sections. When Frida Kwast-Hodapp played the first performance of the whole Concertino in Berlin under Busoni's direction, she described the *Scherzoso* to Dent as being 'like a soap-bubble'. This brilliant study in thirds—a fleeting *perpetuum mobile* with the lightest of orchestration—closes with a chromatic ascent into the unclouded skies which shine over the whole work. It is the only truly optimistic music of Busoni's last years yet, paradoxically, music from the *Scherzoso* was later used in association with Mephistopheles.

The last two Goethe songs are among Busoni's most persuasive compositions. In March 1923, after a long bout of severe illness, he wrote the 'Zigeunerlied' op. 55 no. 2. There are two versions of the song: one with piano and one with small orchestra.

Goethe's poem (the last of his *Gesellige Lieder*) is a laconically narrated ghost-story. On a cold, stormy winter's night seven werewolves appear through the mist; the poet recognizes them as women from the village and calls after them by name. They rush off with blood-curdling howls.

The lack of humour or sarcasm in Busoni's setting is perhaps surprising. Instead he invokes once more the black mood of the *Toccata*, creating an uninterruptedly savage and menacing atmosphere. Particularly important, at a technical level, is his renewed preoccupation with harmonic symmetry. Motoric movement is built out of symmetrical rotations around a central note. The right-hand figure which opens the song presents a first and simple instance:

Ex. 244   Vivace, con impeto

The accompaniment of the last verse is more complex. Here, the right-hand chords open and close in semitone steps, while the left-hand ostinato rotates accordingly around the note A:

Ex. 245

The vocal line is for the most part declamatory, sharply rhythmical and stark in outline; it consists almost entirely of rising semitone steps, drawn from the violent left-hand figure of Ex. 244. Sometimes the interval is inverted into the Faustian melodic leap of a falling major seventh. Busoni's setting of Goethe's owl-cry illustrates this well:

Ex. 246

wi - to - hu   wi - to - hu ____   hu hu hu hu hu hu hu   hu! ____

and also indicates the taxing vocal and dramatic demands made upon the singer.

Towards the end of 1923 Busoni received a letter from Katherina Kippenberg. Her husband Anton, head of Insel Verlag, was approaching his fiftieth birthday and, to mark the occasion, she was secretly contacting Insel authors and inviting them to contribute to a Festschrift in his honour. Busoni eventually sent her the song 'Schlechter Trost' which he composed in February 1924. The Festschrift, entitled *Navigare necesse est*, a tribute to the man who had so long steered the Insel ship on its course, appeared in May of the same year. The song is Busoni's last composition.

Nothing less suited to a Festschrift could be imagined! One might have expected some gratulatory ode of little permanent value but Busoni, idealist to the last, did his one-time publisher the greater honour of sending him one of his finest short works.

The poem of 'Schlechter Trost' originates, like the 'Lied des Unmuts', in Goethe's *West-östlicher Divan*, where it is to be found in the *Buch der Liebe*. No doubt it was the biographical similarity of Goethe's situation to his own that led Busoni back to this anthology. (Four days earlier he had orchestrated the 'Lied des Unmuts'.) Ill-health forced Goethe temporarily to abandon his struggle to complete the second part of *Faust*, a project which had occupied him for forty-eight years. Thus in the summer of 1818, while convalescing in Karlsbad, he wrote this last collection of poems. There was something almost superstitious in Busoni's choice of text, the hope that the spirit of his beloved Goethe may watch over his own *Faust* and steer it successfully to the close.

The song itself tells us a different story. This is burnt-out music, speaking of measureless sadness and death. The 'Zigeunerlied' was vituperative and energetic, the fierce stand of an outsider against the howling wolves which turn out to be his neighbours. In 'Schlechter Trost', the poet is visited by other ghosts. This time he addresses them in apologetic tones:

Schluchzend und weinend
Findet ihr mich, dem ihr sonst
Schlafendem vorüberzogt.
Grosse Güter vermiss' ich,
Denkt nicht schlimmer von mir,
Den ihr sonst weise nanntet;
Grosses Übel betrifft ihn!—

Sobbing and weeping you find me, the sleeper whom you otherwise passed by. My greatest treasure is lost, do not think evil of the one whom you once called wise; a great misfortune has befallen him!—

and the ghosts go their way, unheeding. Isolation is no longer matched by defiance; instead we find an intense pessimism. The music is little more than a single, bare line; the vocal part is no more than a series of plaintive fragments:

Ex. 247

Ten days after composing 'Schlechter Trost' Busoni wrote to his lifelong friend, Baroness Jella Oppenheimer. It was one of his last letters; in it he puts into words the agony expressed in the song, the agony of a living soul in a dying body: '. . . d'Annunzio once said to me Leonardo was a skeleton that carried a blazing torch in place of a skull. I think . . . that the head of even a dead body can still glow.'[12]

XXI

The *Klavierübung*

Perpetuum mobile [for piano] (after the second movement of the Concertino op. 54). *Dedicated*: to Cella Delavrancea. *Composed*: February 1922. *Published*: Leipzig, 1922. EB 5231. Plate number 28765. Also incorporated in the *Klavierübung*, Book 5 (1st edition) and Vol. 9 (2nd edition). *Duration*: 3 minutes.

Ten Variations on a Prelude of Chopin [for piano. Revised version of the Variations and Fugue in free form on Fr. Chopin's C minor Prelude (op. 28 no. 20) op. 22, composed in 1884]. *Dedicated*: to Gino Tagliapietra. *Composed*: April 1922. *First performance*: May 1923, Hochschule für Musik, Berlin. Soloist: Gunnar Johansen. *Published*: Leipzig, 1922. EB 5230. Plate number 28765. Also incorporated in the Klavierübung, Book 5 (1st edition) and (abbreviated) Vol. 8 (2nd edition). *MS*: 20pp., 34×26cm. Property of Mr Ronald Stevenson. *Duration*: 11 minutes.

Prélude et étude (en arpèges) pour piano. *Composed*: January–February 1923. *First performance*: 18.8.1923. Deutsches Nationaltheater, Weimar. Soloist: Egon Petri. *Published*: Paris, 1923. Heugel H 28,336 [Rare]. *MS*: Galston–Busoni archive, University of Tennessee, Knoxville. A further MS of Prélude at Stiftung Rychenberg, Winterthur. *Duration*: 7 minutes.

Five short pieces for the cultivation of part-playing on the pianoforte. *Dedicated*: to Edwin Fischer. *Composed*: March–July 1923. *First performance*: (nos. 1–3 only) 18.8.1923. Deutsches Nationaltheater, Weimar. Soloist: Egon Petri. *Published*: Leipzig, 1923. EB 5240. Plate number 29025. Also incorporated in the *Klavierübung*, Vol. 9 (2nd edition). Republished with Preludietto from Book 1 of the *Klavierübung*, 1st edition, as Six short pieces for the cultivation of part-playing, Wiesbaden, 1954. EB 6205. *MS*: Property of Mr Daniell Revenaugh. A further MS of the 2nd piece only in the Galston–Busoni collection, University of Tennessee, Knoxville. *Duration*: 16 minutes.

Klavierübung:
1. **First Edition** in five books. *Dedicated*: to the Musikschule and the Conservatoire, Basle. **Book 1**: Six Piano Studies and Preludes. *Composed*: September–October 1917. *Published*: Leipzig, 1918. EB 5066. Plate number 28210. **Book 2**: Three Piano Studies and Preludes. *Composed*: November 1917 and June 1918. *Published*: Leipzig, 1919. EB 5067. Plate number 28321. **Book 3**: Lo Staccato. *Composed*: June 1919–March 1921. *Published*: Leipzig, 1921. EB 5068. Plate number 28665. **Book 4**: Eight Etudes after Cramer. *Dedicated*: to Carl Lütschg. *Transcribed*: ca. 1896. *Published*: Berlin, 1897, Schlesinger. S.8772. Re-published for the *Klavierübung*, Leipzig, 1922. EB 5224. Plate

number 28809. **Book 5**: Variations—Perpetuum mobile—Scales. *Dedicated*: to Gino Tagliapietra. *Composed*: April–May 1922. *Published*: Leipzig, 1922. EB 5225. Plate number 28765. *MS*: Deutsche Staatsbibliothek, Berlin.

2. Second Edition in ten volumes. **Vol. 1**: Scales; **Vol. 2**: Forms derived from Scales; **Vol. 3**: Chord playing; **Vol. 4**: 'À trois mains'; **Vol. 5**: Trills; **Vol. 6**: Lo Staccato; **Vol. 7**: Eight Etudes after Cramer; **Vol. 8**: Variations and Variants on Chopin; **Vol. 9**: Seven short pieces for the cultivation of part-playing. **Vol. 10**: Studies after Paganini–Liszt. *Compiled and composed*: December 1923–January 1924. *Published*: Leipzig, 1925. F. B. VIII (as Vol. VIII of the Bach–Busoni Edition) [Rare]. Books 1–5 republished by State Publishing House, Moscow, 1968, ed. J. Milstein. Plate number 4135. *MS*: Deutsche Staatsbibliothek, Berlin. Further MS material in the Galston–Busoni archive, University of Tennessee, Knoxville and in the Staatsbibliothek Preussischer Kulturbesitz, West Berlin.

3. The New Busoni. Exercises and Studies for the Piano. Compiled and with an introduction by Franzpeter Goebels (1966). **Part I**: Exercises; **Part II**: Exercises and Studies after Bach, Mozart, Beethoven, Chopin and Cramer. *Published*: Wiesbaden, 1968. EB 6532a–b.

The *Klavierübung* was a project on which Busoni worked sporadically during the last seven years of his life, intended to pass on in concise form the fruits of his lifelong occupation with keyboard technique. Its five books (and the ten volumes of the revised edition) present a diverse assortment of short pieces, studies and exercises, and include transcriptions of well known and less familiar classics, elaborated versions of piano études by other composers and full-scale original compositions.

The first original piece of any significance to be written for the collection was the *Perpetuum mobile*, a shortened version of the *Scherzoso* from the Concertino for Piano. It lays particular emphasis on passages in thirds but also demands firm staccato and octave-technique, thus combining several of the specific centres of interest in the *Klavierübung* in one piece. The *Scherzoso* is shortened to omit the middle section, for which a new sequential passage is substituted. While certainly effective and brilliant, it would be wrong to claim too high a place for it among Busoni's piano works.

Of his earlier compositions, one of the most substantial was a set of variations and a fugue on the C minor Prelude of Chopin. He wrote it in 1884, while studying in Graz with Mayer-Rémy, and it was published the following year. The piano writing is weighty and the harmonic language largely traditional, yet it is an altogether remarkable achievement for a boy of eighteen. Nevertheless, when Busoni looked through the variations in 1912, he exclaimed 'They are not worth saving!'[1] Ten years later, the indefatigable Frida Kwast-Hodapp wrote to ask if he would consider revising them. Now his opinion of his youthful *chef d'oeuvre* was milder; he decided to rewrite the work for incorporation in the *Klavierübung*. Three letters he wrote to Frau Kwast-Hodapp give a lively picture of the process of reconstruction upon which he embarked, and occasion other acute observations. Here are some extracts:

20.4.1922
Today I looked through my Chopin variations, nearly 40 years old. There isn't much to 'patch up' in them. Each work corresponds to the moment at which it came into being; provided that it corresponds to that moment at all! —I would preface the theme (right at the beginning) with the following 'Faustian' introduction:

[Ex. 248]

Omit: the variations on p. 7
           and the two last, pp 22 and 23.
I am conditionally in agreement with the fugue. I wanted to develop the first part (today!) in tarantella-rhythm, with the theme:

[Ex. 249]

For an 18-year-old, which I was when I composed it, the piece is presentable.
           On the whole it should remain so!—
22.4.1922 [Busoni had now begun to write his new score]
I was tormented by the formal deficiencies of my youthful work. The term *Variations and Fugue* is completely satisfying to the 'musicologists' and they don't look any further. However: an alternation of fast and slow, minor and major, is not yet 'form' and even less a plan, an idea.—
25.4.1922
I sense that they [the variations] are strongly Germanic (i.e. remote from that lineage which, in the completion of my circle, I am steadily approaching) and more prosaic than romantic.—In general I have noticed that one takes prosaic music in Germany for romantic, and romantic music for prosaic; an example of the former would be: *Schumann*, of the latter: *Berlioz*.

On 28 April he signed and dated the final double bar of the new work and wrote once more to Frau Kwast-Hodapp: '[The remodelled work] . . . is—or so I hope—freed from heaviness and more rounded in form . . . (you will see that I end with a scherzo). . . . Scarcely a trace of "depth" or "meaningfulness". But hopefully fun to play and entertaining.'

In the 'Faustian' introductory measures (Ex. 248), we find a classic example of the symmetrical harmony which Busoni had been developing over the past twelve years. He attached much significance to these bars—so much so that he later requested that they should even be played in performances of the original variations of 1884.

Comparing the earlier and later versions, the following points stand out:

1. Not all variations remain in C minor. The wider range of keys is complemented by a more fluid form, uninterrupted by double bars.

2. The third variation is completely transformed and becomes a carillon:

Ex. 250

Ex. 251

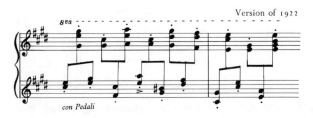

3. The finale now contains only a suggestion of a fugue; this is followed by a waltz ('aus weiter Ferne'—from a great distance—as Busoni described it to Kwast-Hodapp), written as 'Hommage à Chopin'. It opens with a figure reminiscent of the 'Minute' Waltz and continues as a direct parody of Chopin's style. This is even carried into pianistic realms. In later years Busoni largely avoided the so-called 'thumb under' style of fingering so essential to Chopinesque technique, but here there are passages which clearly call for it.

4. Since composing the first version, Busoni had come to consider Chopin over-popularized. He regarded the Etudes, Préludes and Ballades highly and performed them in a unique, monumental style, but was appalled by the salon idol that had been made of the composer, a 'typical Balzac novel-figure of the 1830s: the pale, interesting, mysterious, elegant stranger in Paris'.[2]

5. Comparison of the two versions demonstrates, above all, what a metamorphosis Busoni had undergone in the intervening thirty-eight years. The formalism of the apprentice has been replaced by the functional economy

of the master; the earnestness expected of the serious composer in the 1880s
has largely given way to playfulness, yet this in turn is a cover for a new
earnestness. The new Chopin Variations wear that 'smile of the wise man' of
which Busoni sometimes spoke.*

During these years the American pedagogue Alberto Jonàs and Busoni's friend
Isidor Philipp were also preparing major study-works for piano. Exercises
devised to further the various technicalities of piano playing were to be
amplified by short compositions exploiting these various problems. Jonàs
assembled a large and impressive work, the *Master School of Modern Piano
Playing and Virtuosity*, in seven volumes, published by Carl Fisher, New York
in 1922–9. Several pianist-composers of the day contributed short pieces: Josef
Lhévinne, Arthur Friedheim and Isidor Philipp himself, to name but three;
and Busoni also contributed a few exercises, none of any musical value. The
most interesting is a study in which chord sequences are played with terraced
dynamics. In the last phase of the exercise each chord is marked with a separate
dynamic, resulting in a visual impression similar to more recent, totally
serialized pieces.
   Philipp approached a large number of composers for contributions to his
study-books. His volume devoted to octave playing, for instance, includes
pieces by Fauré, Widor, Pugno and several others. In October 1922 he asked
Busoni to write an original composition for a projected arpeggio volume; the
reply was positive. Busoni's thoughts must have revolved around the pleasant
gourmet days he had spent in Paris with Philipp and other friends, so strongly
contrasting with the scarcities in Berlin brought about by galloping inflation.
In one of the most light-hearted letters of his last years he playfully confuses the
word for arpeggios (*arpèges*) with that for asparagus (*asperges*):

Voulez-vous des Etudes ou des Exercises? Chameau ou Dromedaire?
. . . Maintenant j'attends
L'INSPIRATION
pour les asperges, sauce-Pédale.[3]

Illness slowed down inspiration, but by February of 1923 a Prélude and an

---

* Note for performers. In the second edition of the *Klavierübung*, Busoni cuts the
lengthy Fantasia; this was presumably his definitive version of the work. The new
transition from the preceding variation to the Scherzo–Finale runs as follows:

Etude were completed. It was a typically generous gesture; for his friend's
potentially rival venture he produced a composition that ranks amongst the
finest of his late works and which transcends the pedagogic purpose for which
it was written. (Philipp's arpeggio-school, however, never appeared and
Busoni's piece was published on its own.)

The Prélude takes the form of an arioso, marked *volante ma tranquillo*.
Bitonal arpeggio figures decorate fragments of melody in the first sixteen bars,
after which a melancholy single line, in *tempo plastico*, devoid of all ornament,
introduces various forms of a rising scale figure. These phrases are answered by
a longer passage based on a falling figure, music which was subsequently
adapted for Mephisto's invocation of Helena in the Second Tableau of *Doktor
Faust*:

Ex. 252

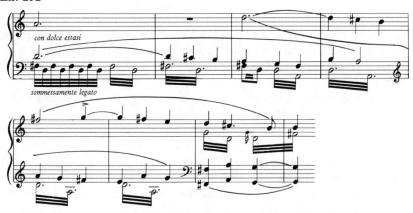

There follows a free reprise of the opening section. The coda, *un poco vivace*, is
based on a staccato semiquaver motif not unlike that of the *Toccata* (Ex. 232),
accompanied by regular quavers in the left hand. Imbued with a remote,
mystic air, the Prélude comes close in spirit to the Fantasia of the *Toccata*. 'De
cette pièce je réponds avec meilleure conscience' wrote Busoni on the manuscript of the first draft.

The Etude is more of a show-piece, extrovert and muscular, corresponding
to the outer sections of the *Toccata*. Over a sustained bass-line a pattern of
rising and falling arpeggio figures (*violinisticamente articolato*) sets the pianistic
problem of playing broken-chord sequences without recourse to 'thumb
under' fingering. Busoni places the tails respectively under and over the notes
in order to indicate the two positions of the hand (Ex. 253).

The last section begins *sotto voce, occultamente, velato*, then builds to a
vehement climax. The skies clear to introduce C major, in which key this
brilliant, monolithic movement comes to an end.

Ex. 253

Functional economy is carried a stage further in the 'Five short pieces for the cultivation of part-playing',★ written later in 1923. Three of them, consecutively nos. 3, 1 and 5, date from March of that year and were originally entitled 'Three pieces for the promotion of part-playing' (*zum Beitrag des polyphonen Spiels*); this was soon changed to 'for the study' (*Studium*), and only later to the title 'for the cultivation' (*Pflege*). Two more pieces followed, no. 2 in May 1923 and no. 4 in July. Like all Busoni's studies, they presuppose a basic pianistic ability of a high level and are intended to further that ability—they are not intended for beginners!

The first piece is an elegant chromatic invention. Its opening, built up of motivic strands in symmetrical array, is reminiscent of the introduction to the Chopin Variations:

Ex. 254

This chromatic language is intensified in the second piece. It has two components of equal importance, a two-part canonical invention and a smoothly flowing accompaniment in triplets. The only intervals used in this accompaniment are thirds and sixths (both major and minor), but these are continuously changing and rotating. The many figures can all be traced back to one motif:

Ex. 255

and this is turned and twisted through countless diminutions, augmentations

★ Original title: *Fünf kurze Stücke zur Pflege des polyphonen Spiels.*

and inversions, all based on the symmetrical principle. The manifold possibilities of this technique are demonstrated in the closing bars:

Ex. 256

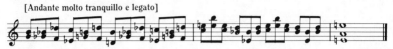

The canonical invention restricts itself correspondingly to seconds, fifths and their inversions. Not since the second movement of the *Red Indian Diary* had Busoni composed so rigorously economical a study, nor had he ever before written any music so abstract as this.

Following without a break, the third piece takes a chorale as cantus firmus:

Ex. 257

and builds up a three-part texture through canonic imitation of the theme against an uninterrupted flow of triplets. The notable feature of the chorale is a reappearance of the 'Death motif', the threefold reiteration of one note, which had appeared long before in the Second Violin Sonata and the Fantasia after J. S. Bach. Busoni's last sketch for *Doktor Faust* shows us that this piece was indeed visualized for the closing section of the opera, just before the death of Faust.

The last two pieces form a Prelude and Fugue, the latter being an arrangement of the music of the Two Armed Men from *Die Zauberflöte*, lovingly transcribed and furnished with a coda. The Prelude is a free invention in Bachian style in which the chorale of the Armed Men, 'Ach Gott vom Himmel sieh' darein', appears briefly towards the close.

In August 1923 three of these short pieces (nos. 1–3) and the *Prélude et étude en arpèges* received their first performance at Weimar. The concert, which also included the world première of Hindemith's song-cycle *Das Marienleben*, formed part of a Bauhaus week, a series of concerts organized by Hermann Scherchen. During Busoni's two-day visit to Weimar for this concert he met Stravinsky and heard *The Soldier's Tale*, performed the following morning; he met leading members of the Bauhaus group, including Klee, Kandinsky and Gropius; and, by making this brief journey to the city of Goethe and Liszt, now blossoming with a new and highly significant artistic movement, he pointed to the similarity of purpose linking his Young Classicality with the Bauhaus ideals.

Book 1 of the *Klavierübung* was written in three days—10–12 September 1917—with the exception of the sixth section which was added one month later. Each section is organically built up from studies to short pieces. Thus section one begins with traditional scales (though the prescribed fingerings are untraditional) and these lead to two fragments which demand particular power and velocity in scale playing; the first from Liszt's *Totentanz*, the second taking a bar from Busoni's own 'Turandots Frauengemach'. Then follow two new original compositions, a Tempo di Valse of sixteen bars and a Preludio of thirty-three bars. Both of these are studies in soft, legato scales at a moderate speed. Finally, an example is cited of a major piece for further study of scale playing, the first of Alkan's Studies in all the major keys.

This pattern—challenging, helpful and unconventional—sets the style for all of Book 1. The second section examines the problems of chords based on scale patterns; the third presents some examples of the technique of sliding the fingers from black to white keys. Repeated notes are the subject of the fourth part, arpeggios and broken chords of the fifth. Part six, entitled 'à trois mains', explores the various forms of the so-called three-handed effect. The examples Busoni uses are curiously assorted: 1) a study taken from his own 'All' Italia!'; 2) the Barcarolle from Offenbach's *Tales of Hoffmann*; 3) the Scherzo from Beethoven's Quartet in C sharp minor op. 131.

Book 2 is devoted to the many problems of trills and tremolandi, starting from first principles. In a prelude, Busoni examines the problems in slow motion, then uses passages from the Goldberg Variations and the 'Hammerklavier' Sonata, as well as a transcription of the vision of Gretchen from the first act of Gounod's *Faust*, to illustrate more specifically the difficulties of extended trill passages. Broken chord studies are taken from Beethoven's Sonata op. 26, Busoni's Improvisation on 'Wie wohl ist mir' and his Fourth *Scène de Ballet*. A final group of studies is devoted to further examination of the three-handed effect, in which Busoni's Bach study from *An die Jugend* is followed by part of the Liszt–Schubert *Erlkönig* (marked *visionario*). Finally, a passage from the *Pezzo giocoso* of Busoni's Piano Concerto illustrates a combination of trills with three-handed effect, summing up much of the material in the first two books.

The opening Prelude of Book 2 was written on 7 November 1917. The rest of the book followed during 4–10 June of the following year. After that, work on the *Klavierübung* was set aside in favour of *Doktor Faust* and its satellite works. Book 3, devoted entirely to staccato playing, took much longer to be completed. Two studies were written in June and December 1919; then, as it seemed uncertain if any more would be added, Busoni wrote a foreword addressed to the dedicatees of the *Klavierübung*, the music students of Basle. In effect, the work is dedicated to all students of the piano everywhere, yet Busoni's piano classes in Helsinki, Moscow, Boston, Weimar and Vienna were eclipsed in his memory by the particularly receptive youngsters in Basle, by the kind attention of their director, Hans Huber, and by some particularly important personal memories of the city, dating back to 1910: the first performances of the *Fantasia Contrappuntistica* and the first Sonatina, a fine rendering of the Piano Concerto, with Egon Petri as soloist, and the completion of the first half of the libretto of *Doktor Faust* at nearby Schloss Bottmingen.

The tone of Busoni's foreword is unusually aggressive and he makes several important points: first, those pedagogues of the piano who set their students physically unperformable tasks are attacked as 'cheap and irresponsible' and Busoni insists that his own studies should never be considered daunting; second, he defends his use of lighter music for piano études—primarily because each piece he has chosen throws up certain problems of technique, but also 'as a protest against an age which sets store by boredom and cultivates ugliness'; third, he demands that the new generations of pianists should 'maintain an awareness . . . that Art is something pleasing'.

Book 3, 'Lo Staccato', after an introductory chordal study, includes two Mozart studies: the first a transcription of Don Giovanni's serenade, the second the Giga from *An die Jugend*. Then follows the opening section of Busoni's *Toccata* (a copy which he made just before leaving Zurich, on 22 August 1920), a transcription of Mendelssohn's fairy-music for *A Midsummer-Night's Dream* and the opening of the *'Carmen' Fantasy*. The final part of the book is devoted entirely to Liszt: first with a Galop based on the first Mephisto Waltz and then with variants on two of the Paganini Etudes. Almost as an afterthought, a passage from the coda of the first movement of Beethoven's 'Emperor' Concerto is transformed into a sevenfold study in chording. The book was completed in March 1921.

In a footnote to his foreword, Busoni had announced a 'Chromaticon' as Book 4, but this never materialized. The actual fourth and fifth volumes were hastily assembled from already extant material. For Book 4 Busoni republished his transcriptions of Eight Etudes after Cramer, which he had made in the later 1890s. The first four are devoted to legato playing (the third, 'en Carillon', is yet another example of Busoni's love of bell effects; the fourth, 'Allegro di Bravura', is a taxing study in thirds), and the other four to staccato playing. Thus they represent a consolidation of what the pupil will have learned from Books 1 to 3; furthermore, Cramer's unpretentious music certainly furnishes the player with 'something pleasing'.

Book 5 consists of the Chopin Variations and the *Perpetuum mobile*, together with six studies based on Chopin Etudes and Preludes (of extreme difficulty) and six further scale studies. Particularly novel are some bitonal combinations of scales which Busoni rounds off with a 'Faustian' cadence:

Ex. 258

This brief description of the *Klavierübung* gives some idea of the large scale on which it was conceived and of the haphazard manner in which it was in fact completed. Had Busoni lived longer, he would doubtless have added much more material—we have no precise idea, for instance, of his theories of pedalling. However, he did find time to organize a second edition of the *Klavierübung* in which the illogicalities of grouping of the first edition are ironed out and a certain amount of new material is added. The new edition, amounting to 284 pages, was published posthumously in 1925 as Volume VIII of the Bach–Busoni Edition. Unfortunately only a very small number of copies was printed and the second edition is a major rarity today. However, it contains all Busoni's last piano compositions, two of which are not to be found elsewhere, and these alone make the collection particularly significant, for both pieces were intended for the missing final scene of *Doktor Faust*.

Volumes 1 and 2 reorganize all the diverse exercises using scales and forms derived from scales, which were previously scattered over several books. Volume 3 deals with broken chords, adding a new arpeggio study (dated 13 December 1923) which is a considerably shortened version of the *Etude en arpèges*, written earlier that year. Volume 4 retains the first edition's sequence of 'à trois mains'. Volume 5 is devoted to trills. As well as the original material from Book 2 of the first edition, the 'Emperor' Concerto studies from Book 3 have been incorporated. The final piece of the volume is a new Trills Study, written 1–3 January 1924, and hence Busoni's last piano piece. In this study rotational symmetry is carried several stages further than in the 'Zigeunerlied', bringing Busoni's harmonic language to a point of organized atonality. There are two kinds of rotation in the opening bars: quaver movement around a central B natural and semiquavers around a G sharp:

Ex. 259

Both centres of rotation then move irregularly in semitone steps, giving rise to extraordinary harmonies: a striking example of Busoni's 'Serapiontic' ability to combine free fantasy with logical control. The idea is then taken over by the left hand alone and a new theme is superimposed upon it, distinguished by its angular leaps around the axis of the note A:

Ex. 260

A glittering 'feux follets' texture dominates this astonishing piece.

Volume 6 features the original 'Lo Staccato', but without the Paganini-Liszt studies. Volume 7 reintroduces the Eight Studies after Cramer without any alterations. Volume 8 is devoted entirely to Chopin (the shortened version of the Chopin Variations and the six studies from Book 5 of the first edition). Volume 9 consists of 'Seven short pieces for the cultivation of part-playing '. No. 1 is the brief Preludietto from Book 1 of the first edition, nos. 2–6 are the original 'Five short pieces . . .' while no. 7 is another important late work, a study for the Steinway piano with a third pedal, written on four staves which are divided into *Hauptstimme* and *liegende Töne* (principal part and held notes). Busoni completed it on 13 November 1923 during his last visit to Paris and dedicated it to his host, Leonhard Tauber. It is a gentle, reflective invention in F major, visualized for the moment of Faust's death. The 'death motif' makes its last appearance in Busoni's *oeuvre*:

Ex. 261

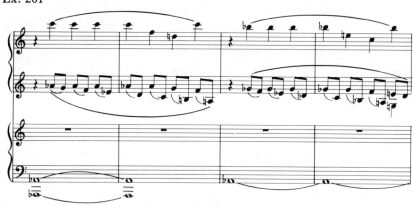

Volume 9 closes with the *Perpetuum mobile*. Volume 10 consists of Busoni's edition of the six Paganini–Liszt studies, originally published in 1916–17. The sixth (variations) study has a new coda in chromatic style, of formidable difficulty. As a pendant to the set Busoni includes his own 'Paganinesco' from *An die Jugend*. Thus, at the close, we find 'La Campanella' and 'La Chasse' (amongst others), pieces through which we still know Busoni as a pianist. He made excellent piano-roll recordings of these works which have been transferred in recent years to long-playing record—a slender living reminder of a great artist.

Just how little of Busoni's achievement as a pianist has in fact been handed down is made clear by the various contradictory reports of his playing. In this field, as with his teaching of composition, free imagination on the part of certain pupils and well-wishers has served more to confuse than enlighten. Busoni's playing certainly produced a highly subjective reaction from his audience; some accounts of his recitals read more like descriptions of seances.

To write about the physical problems of playing an instrument is no easy matter. A technical point which a good teacher can demonstrate in a few moments becomes inordinately cumbersome when expressed in words or diagrams. Therefore in the *Klavierübung* Busoni wisely avoided any attempt at verbal elucidations of his technique and let his fingerings say virtually all. Throughout his teaching one points stands out: technique was of secondary importance, the duty of the teacher lay in the overall musical education of his pupils, indeed in the extension of such considerations to all the arts. The *Klavierübung* takes a standard piano technique, developed to a virtuoso level, as a *sine qua non*; Busoni then points out refinements and short cuts. How exactly he tensed his forearms or angled his wrists he does not tell us, for the good reason that every player is built differently and must adjust his technique to his personal abilities. It is an established fact that any slavish attempt to imitate the style of a great player is doomed to failure.

A profitable application of Busoni's technical ideas has been made by the pianist Franzpeter Goebels. In 1968 he published a study work with the title *The new Busoni*. In producing this abbreviated and annotated edition of the *Klavierübung* he has achieved a useful consensus of practical advice. Some valuable comments on octave playing from Busoni's edition of Book I of the '48' have been included in Volume I of his study, which is devoted entirely to matters of geometry on the keyboard. Volume II is a collection of Busoni's adaptations of Bach, Mozart, Beethoven, Chopin and Cramer. Here Goebels has not been entirely successful in his choices: some of the Bach variants he has included represent Busoni's earlier, massive style of playing and contradict his later principles of economy of movement; a composition study has been included which could scarcely be of value in this strictly pianistic publication; the omission of all the Liszt studies and such light-hearted transcriptions as those of Offenbach, Gounod and others presents a one-sided picture of the composer and verges too far towards un-Busonian earnestness. However, the inclusion of the 'Practice rules for pianists' (taken from a letter to Gerda dated 20.7.1898) and of other quotations concerning the art of piano playing helps to redress the balance.

Section Seven

Doktor Faust

Doktor Faust

Doktor Faust, poem for music. *Libretto dedicated*: to the Faculty of Philosophy, University of Zurich. *Composed*: September 1916 to May 1923; left unfinished. *First performance*: 21.5.1925. Sächsisches Staatstheater, Dresden. Conductor: Fritz Busch; producer: Alfred Reucker; designer: Karl Dannemann.

Doktor Faust (baritone)		Robert Burg
Wagner, his famulus, later Rector magnificus (bass)		Willy Bader
A voice		
A man dressed in black		
A monk		
A herald	Mephistopheles (tenor)	Theo Strack
Court chaplain		
Courier		
Night-watchman		
The Duke of Parma (tenor or baritone)		Josef Correck
The Duchess of Parma (soprano)		Meta Seinemeyer
Master of Ceremonies (bass)		Adolph Schoepflin
The girl's brother (tenor or baritone)		Rudolf Schmalnauer
A lieutenant (tenor)		Ludwig Eybisch
	(tenor)	E. Meyerolbersleben
Three students from Cracow	(tenor)	Paul Schöffler
	(bass)	Wilhelm Moy
Theologian (baritone)		Robert Büssel
Law student (baritone)		Wilhelm Moy
Natural scientist (baritone)		Heinrich Hermanns
	(tenor)	Heinrich Tessmer
Students from Wittenberg	(tenor)	E. Meyerolbersleben
	(tenor)	Ludwig Eybisch
	(baritone)	Paul Schöffler
Gravis (bass)		Heinrich Hermanns
Levis (bass)		Robert Büssel
Asmodus (baritone)	Spirit voices	Paul Schöffler
Beelzebuth (tenor)		Heinrich Kuppinger
Megaeros (tenor)		Lugwig Eybisch
	(soprano)	Erna Berger
	(soprano)	Irmgard Quitzow
	(alto)	Adelma von Tinty
	(alto)	Elfriede Haberkorn
Voices from on high	(tenor)	Ludwig Eybisch
	(tenor)	E. Meyerolbersleben
	(bass)	Paul Schöffler
	(bass)	Heinrich Hermanns

Prologue (speaker)   Erich Ponto

Choruses (Chorus master: Ernst Hintze)
Churchgoers, spirit voices, soldiers, courtiers, Catholic and Lutheran students,
huntsmen, peasants.
Ballet (Choreography: Ellen von Cleve-Petz)
Fencing pages.
Visions
Solomon and the Queen of Sheba; Samson and Dalilah; Salome, John the Baptist,
Executioner. A beggar woman. The girl's brother. Helena. A naked youth.
Published: Leipzig, 1925. Completed and edited by Philipp Jarnach. Full score MS;
Wiesbaden, 1984. Newly completed according to Busoni's last sketches by Antony
Beaumont (1982): Full score MS; vocal score publ. Wiesbaden, 1984, Wb. 1799. *Vocal
score*: (Egon Petri and Michael von Zadora) published Leipzig, 1926. EB 5289. Plate
number: 29212. *MS*: 370pp. 48×33cm. Destroyed by fire during Second World War. 2
photocopies exist (11 pages missing) in Deutsche Staatsbibliothek, Berlin and Library
of Norddeutscher Rundfunk, Hamburg.★ *Instrumentation*: 3 (2 Picc.)–3 (2 C.A.)–3
(Bcl.)–3 (Cfg.); 5–3–3–1; Timp., Perc.; 2 Harps; Celesta; Organ; Str. Stage music: 3
tpt., 2 trmb.; Bells; Timp., Str. (1–0–1–1–0). *Translations*: Italian (Oriana Previtali);
English (Edward Dent); Swedish (Axel Strindberg)—all Br.u.H.

Symphonia—Easter vespers and augurs of spring Busoni's musical introduction to
the opera begins with bell imitations, at first for orchestra alone, later with the chorus,
which intones the single word 'Pax'.

The Poet addresses the audience in front of the curtain, to describe how he set aside
earlier ideas of Merlin and Don Juan as subject material in favour of Faust; further to
emphasize the play's puppet origins.

Vorspiel I Faust's study in Wittenberg. Morning. Wagner announces the arrival of
three students. Faust's annoyance at being disturbed in his work changes rapidly to
great excitement when he hears that they have brought him a book, *Clavis Astartis
Magica*. Left alone, he rejoices over the power soon to be in his hands. The three
students from Cracow present him with the book, a key and a deed of possession, then
disappear.

Vorspiel II The same scene at midnight. Faust draws a magic circle on the ground with
his belt and steps inside it, holding the key in his hand. He summons the servants of
Lucifer: spirit voices answer him. Suddenly all is dark; six tongues of flame hang
suspended in the air. Faust questions them one by one: 'How swift are you?' The
answers of the first five do not satisfy him but, to his relief, they obey him. Faust steps
out of the circle, disappointed. The sixth flame calls to him, 'Faust, I am swift as the
thoughts of man'. A few moments later Mephistopheles, dressed in black, stands before
him. During the ensuing drawing up of the pact, off-stage voices intone the Credo as
day begins to break on Easter morning. Faust signs the contract with his own blood,
then falls unconscious. The voices of churchgoers fade away as bells ring out joyfully.

★ The conductor of the world première, Fritz Busch, used the original MS as
performing score. The Busoni family therefore had these two facsimiles made as a
precautionary measure.

Scenic intermezzo In an ancient Romanesque chapel. Faust and Mephistopheles silently observe the girl's brother, clad in armour, praying for vengeance on his sister's honour. 'Kill him', orders Faust. Mephistopheles, disguised as a monk, kneels at the soldier's side: perhaps he would like to confess? His end is at hand. Soldiers are heard approaching. A brief skirmish, and the victim falls dead. For sacrilege and murder Faust must be held responsible, reflects Mephisto gleefully.

Hauptspiel
First tableau The festivities at the court of Parma to celebrate the wedding of the Duke. In the palace gardens the assembled crowd admires a procession of huntsmen, a fencing display by pages, and later the magic arts of the celebrated Dr Faust. The Duke is more suspicious than impressed, but the young Duchess is spellbound by Faust. In a sequence of visions from antiquity, he conjures up Solomon and the Queen of Sheba, Samson and Dalilah, Salome and John the Baptist—in each case their faces resemble those of the Duchess and Faust. He bids her follow him. The Duke abruptly terminates the display and invites Faust to dine with him. Mephistopheles advises him to flee—the food is poisoned. As in a dream, the Duchess reappears, drawn to Faust 'as if by a thousand arms'. Mephistopheles, as court chaplain, advises the Duke to forget her, rather to marry the sister of the Duke of Ferrara. 'Heaven has inspired you', says the Duke. Mephisto raises his claw-like right hand in blessing.

Symphonic intermezzo The Sarabande.

Second tableau A tavern in Wittenberg. Lively and humorous argument between Catholic and Protestant students, with Faust leading the discussion, erupts into a lighthearted brawl between the two groups. When the tumult has died down, Faust is prompted to reminisce on his past loves. He speaks of the Duchess. Mephisto appears as dust-spattered courier to announce her death. At Faust's feet he throws the body of her new-born child, which he transforms into a bundle of straw. He sets it alight and out of the flames conjures up a vision of Helen of Troy. The students depart in horror; Mephisto also slinks away. Helena now stands before Faust in all her beauty. As he tries to take hold of her, she vanishes. 'Mankind is not yet ready for perfection', he muses. The three students from Cracow reappear to demand the return of the book, the key and the letter. 'Too late,' says Faust, 'I have destroyed them.' At midnight, they tell him, he shall die. Faust, elated, welcomes his last hour.

Final tableau A snow-covered street in Wittenberg, showing an entrance to the Minster and a crucifix. The night-watchman calls—it is ten o'clock. Students appear with Wagner who, in Faust's mysterious absence, has himself been appointed Rector. The students sing a lively serenade, but flee as the sinister night-watchman reappears. Faust now enters, looking scornfully up at the light burning in Wagner's house, that was once his own. He stoops to give alms to a poor beggar-woman, but as she turns he recognizes the Duchess. She hands him her dead child with the words, 'There is still time: finish the work before midnight.' Faust turns to the church, but his way is barred by a vision of the girl's brother, menacingly stretching out his sword. Faust kneels before the crucifix but cannot find the words to pray. The night-watchman returns and raises his lantern: as Faust looks up to the figure on the Cross, Christ's face is transformed into that of Helena. 'Is there no mercy?' he asks. He lays the dead child on the snow and draws a magic circle around it, into which he steps. With a last supreme effort, he transfers his life-force to the child. As the night-watchman calls the midnight hour and Faust falls dead, a naked youth rises from the ground with a blossoming branch in his right hand and steps forth through the snow into the night. The night-watchman, now revealed as Mephistopheles, throws Faust's body over his shoulder. 'Has this man met with an accident?' he asks. [He trudges off; distant voices repeat Faust's last words and bells resound from all directions.]

Dent has traced the origins of Busoni's Faust project back to 1892, when he was planning an opera on the legend of Ahasuerus, the Wandering Jew. In fact we can trace it at least ten years further back, to the *Racconti Fantastici*, written at the age of sixteen. The third piece of the set, inspired by Wilhelm Hauff's story 'The Cave of Steenfoll', depicts the tale of a fisherman who sells his soul to the devil in exchange for the recovery of a sunken treasure trove. Thereafter, throughout Busoni's formative years, the Faustian idea seems to have obsessed him, expressing itself variously in *Sigune, Der mächtige Zauberer* and *Die Brautwahl*. There were elements of Merlin and Don Juan in Busoni's vision, but also of contemporary figures. At one stage, during his 'occult' period, a source of inspiration was Villiers de l'Isle-Adams's Faustian novel about Edison, *L'Ève future*. During his later years, Balzac's *La peau de chagrin* was a constant influence.

In 1907 Busoni formulated the idea of a figure embodying three legends in one:

> A highly gifted man signs his soul away to the devil, on condition that he lives *three* lives. He makes use of each one—consecutively—to be a great artist, an irresistible womaniser and a financial tycoon. The devil loses his rights, because the man has in each occupation *given of the highest*.[1]

The plan was soon discarded, but its essence, the defeat of the devil, remained the crucial feature of his idea.

Busoni often contemplated two Italian alternatives to the figure of Faust: Dante and Leonardo. The latter seemed to offer the greater possibilities and in 1908 Busoni re-read Vasari's biography of that artist as well as the newly published *Romance of Leonardo da Vinci* by the Russian novelist Mereshkovsky. Here, in the author's description of the artist as 'a man who awoke too early in the dark, while all the others were still sleeping'[2] and in his *idée fixe* of the interchangeability of good and evil, Busoni found affinities with the mythical figure of his own vision and an expression of the duality which we find in the music of such works as the *Sarabande* and the third Albumleaf.

A few months after reading Mereshkovsky, Busoni sketched out the text for two scenes of a drama entitled *Leonardo da Vinci*. The first of these is strikingly similar in outline to the church-vision of *Die Brautwahl*. Leonardo is discovered alone in the Refectory of Santa Maria delle Grazie in Milan before a bare wall against which a scaffolding has been erected. His commission is to paint a representation of the Last Supper. 'Futile struggle!' he cries. 'No sooner do I think the idea at last securely grasped than it slips through my fingers once more; my labours begin anew! Too mighty is the task!' Suddenly darkness falls and the wall begins to glow with light. Before his very eyes Leonardo sees Christ and his disciples perform the entire ceremony of the Sacrament. The vision fades and vanishes. As the curtain falls, the painter, in a state of feverish excitement, dips his brush into a pot of red paint and sets to work.

The figure Busoni visualized was to experience the failure of one scheme after another (as Leonardo actually did): 'He . . . progressively more lonely and isolated, gains an even higher and freer vantage point until—with his death—the highest wisdom is attained and is proclaimed in a prophecy.'[3] In this tragic, prophetical figure we can already recognize the closing scene of the Faust opera.

One year later, in 1910, Busoni returned to the idea of a true Faust drama, taking the puppet play of the sixteenth century as his source material. Between master-classes and recitals at Basle during September of that year he wrote almost half of the *Faust* libretto as we now know it. At the beginning, as in the puppet play and as in Goethe, Faust is given a lengthy monologue. Then Mephisto appears as theatre manager and introduces the play. The serious action was to be interspersed with Casperle scenes, with little or possibly no music, played in front of a painted curtain. The 'unreal' or magical scenes, which were to have a complete musical score, were to make use of the full stage area. Otherwise the 1910 sketch differs only in small details from the final version; but at the end of the Scenic Intermezzo it breaks off. Plagued by doubts, Busoni noted in his diary at the end of that year: 'F? From a literary point of view too difficult, owing to comparison with Goethe. Or it would have to be something quite new.'[4] After the première of *Die Brautwahl* he mentioned his Faust plans to Dent but added despairingly, 'the subject is too mighty, I shall have to develop still further'.[5] A few weeks later, by way of encouragement, Dent sent him a copy of the plays of Marlowe. Thanking him, Busoni wrote: 'They will spur me to occupy myself with the problem of Faust (and perhaps to bring it to its conclusion).'[6]

From then on, Faust was never far from his thoughts, yet his immediate aim was still an Italian opera. With this in mind, he visited the poet d'Annunzio in Paris in August 1912, in the hope of engaging his collaboration on such a project; little definite came of the meeting. In London, in January 1913, Busoni saw a poster advertising a film, *Dante's Hell*, which prompted him to renewed contemplation: 'In consideration of my age and the level of my development, I believe I should no longer hesitate to start on a major and monumental work, for which all previous achievements are intended.'[7] A month later he had again changed his mind about the subject: 'I am resolved to write to d'Annunzio, and almost believe that the Leonardo project is more appealing to me than Dante.'[8]

In June 1913 he visited d'Annunzio for a second time. The poet was none too enthusiastic about putting Leonardo on the stage, describing him as 'a brain borne by a skeleton, like the flame of a torch'. Busoni noted: 'However, as I spoke of the concept of an "Italian Faust", as catch phrase, he began to see the possibilities. "No *historical* Leonardo, but a symbolic one". "The supervention of the mystical". "A series of scenes without dramatic connections".'[9]

'Lionardo: italienischer Faust'[10]: Busoni noted his catch phrase again some twelve months later. His equation of the two figures may seem provocative, even fanciful, but there are some factual links between them which may help to explain the idea. Firstly, the grandiose canalization and land-reclamation schemes which Leonardo often planned and sometimes even attempted to execute—they were the dreams of a visionary, for there was scarcely a chance of carrying them to a successful conclusion without machines which were only invented centuries later. Yet it was precisely such a scheme with which Goethe's Faust intended to make a creative end to his career on earth. (Goethe is thought to have implied this link because Leonardo and the historical Dr Faustus were almost exact contemporaries.) Busoni himself found a further affinity in the lavish pageants and entertainments which Leonardo organized for the ruling house of Sforza in Milan. Descriptions of the magical machines which he built, found in Vasari and elsewhere, are a reminder of the displays of conjuring with which the mythical Faust is said to have enchanted the Duke and Duchess of Parma.

One December evening in 1914, while looking for his Leonardo sketches, Busoni's Faust plan suddenly crystallized. He noted in his diary:

> Everything came together like a vision. Five movements. Monologue about studies falls out. Assumed that Gretchen episode is all over. During the pact Easter bells ring! Garden festival at the court of Parma, the Duchess betrays her love, in a vision appear Herod (Salome) and John with resemblance: Duke, Faust. Three students from Cracow, beginning. Night-watchman —end. Query, Casperle-*Intermezzi* in front of curtain, without music, or not?[11]

Almost as if in a dream, he began to write. Before the year was out, the text was finished and he recorded: 'On the third day of Christmas [1914] I completed the text of Dr F. . . . I have taken possession of the stage and broken with the traditions of opera. If the work evolves as it should, it will offer as much to the layman as to the connoisseur.'[12] In the evening of that same day, 26 December, he read the entire libretto through to his family as they sadly celebrated the first Christmas of the war together.

'Das Wetter ist umgeschlagen', he wrote. 'Tristesse de l'âme.'* A few days later he and his family sailed for New York on the SS *Rotterdam*. He took the new libretto with him, together with that of *Arlecchino* but, apart from his plans for the edition of Book II of the '48', he did not take a single sheet of manuscript paper. In a letter to Petri he wrote: 'My art seems to be becoming ever harder for me, and the Ideal (perhaps fortunately) quite unattainable.'[13]

---

* 'The weather has turned' (a quotation from the closing page of the libretto), 'Sadness of the soul'.

During his nine unendurable months in America, Busoni made only one addition to his Faust text—the spoken prologue, which he finished in June 1915. When he finally settled in Switzerland, he at last felt able to devote himself again to *Faust*. During his visit to Pallanza, as guest of the Marchese di Casanova, he noted down his first musical plans for the work: 'F.—Espressione concentrata—forma concisa—masse (terrazze)—instrumentazione a gruppi—polifonia—risultati degli studi di contrapp., d'armonia, d'orchestrazione—illustrazione immateriale.'* After careful revision of the libretto, including a complete reconstruction of the final scene, he published it in the autumn 1918 issue of *Die weissen Blätter*.

Busoni describes his libretto neither as an opera nor as a music drama, but as a *Dichtung für Musik*—a poem for music. Thus he wished to indicate that the text should not be evaluated on its own, whatever its actual literary qualities, but together with the music, as a complete entity. As he explained in his essay, 'The Score of *Doktor Faust*':

> There are intentional gaps in the libretto and it is apparently fragmentary. In this way space is left free to be filled out by the music. . . . My principal task was to mould musically independent forms which at one and the same time would match the words and scenic events and also have a separate and meaningful existence detached from word and situation.[14]

His intention was to reconcile his principle of 'absolute music' with the conception he had outlined of the theatre as 'universal domain'—as the richest and most advanced means of purely musical expression. In Wagner, a magic fire, a storm or even a gesture is simultaneously visible on stage and audible in the orchestra; Busoni's theatre, on the other hand, uses music to complete a sphere implied by the stage, literally to add a further dimension to the action:

> In the score, I have made the first attempt (not completely carried through) to create an horizon of sound, an acoustical perspective, in which I frequently make use of what is sung and acted behind the scenes, so that what is not seen is revealed through hearing.[15]

Just as Mozart had no need for literal representations of fire or water in *Die Zauberflöte*, so is Busoni content to let the eyes and ears of the spectator fulfil their separate functions.† Kurt Weill singled out the most striking example of this independent use of words and music: 'When Mephisto kills the creditors outside the door [Vorspiel II], the music leaves the bare bones of the action to

---

* 'Concentrated expression—concise form—blocks (terraces)—use of instrumental groups—polyphony—fruits of contrapuntal, harmonic and orchestral studies—abstract illustrations.'
† Busoni wrote to Jarnach (2.12.1919): 'Wagner—like the two later composers

the listener's imagination, contenting itself with a gentle gesture of release and freedom.'[16]

In the formal construction of the libretto Busoni departs most radically from the conventions of opera. Despite their nomenclature, the various introductory sections (Symphonia, Prologue, Vorspiel I, Vorspiel II) and the twin Intermezzi are central to the drama. The introduction, from the opening of the Symphonia to the end of Vorspiel II, is one closed form with sectional divisions, equivalent to the first act of a conventional opera. Here the traditional part of the Faust legend is expounded. Thereafter, Busoni's interpretation of the Faustian idea becomes freely autobiographical, the overall structure of the *Hauptspiel* is only loosely strung together like the stages of a dream, while the Serapiontic principle is often applied to free the action from its strict chronology—most notably in the several vision scenes.

The Intermezzos have the function of turning points in the drama. The first depicts in scenic terms Faust's irreversible commitment to the powers of Evil; the second, expressing itself in the language of 'absolute music', anticipates the conclusion of the work and gives an inkling of a realm 'beyond Good and Evil'.

Having excised the Casperle scenes from the original version of the libretto and transformed them into the independent work *Arlecchino*, Busoni redressed the balance of the *Hauptspiel* by dividing each tableau into contrasting sections of serious action and theatrical *Spass* (the element of funfair which Brecht considered essential to modern epic theatre). In the First Tableau we have the festivities at Parma, with fencing pages, huntsmen and peasants, in the Second, the students' good-natured brawling (a satirical depiction of Germany's 'lesser Martin Luthers') and, in the Third, their scurrilous serenade and hasty flight.

There are substantial differences between the first edition of 1918 and the final version of the libretto. Of these, the most important are:

1. the reduction of the seven spirit voices in Vorspiel II to six
2. the alteration of 'Gretchen's brother', as he is called in the original version, to the later 'the girl's brother'
3. the presence of Helena amongst the *dramatis personae*, rather than in the list of visions
4. an important passage in the final scene which was not set to music by Jarnach when he completed the score. (This passage, and the reasons for its omission, are discussed below on page 325.)

[Debussy and Strauss]—would not have resisted the "Trial by Fire and Water" in Die Zauberflöte. The waterfall in the Alpine Symphony is the companion piece to the magic fire [in *Die Walküre*]. Mozart alone does what is necessary.—That is the difference between Zauberflöte and Idomeneo.—Idomeneo could be described as almost Wagnerian: *the idea alone is not yet sufficient*—it is externally embellished.'

Busoni modelled his text for the scene of the spirit voices on Lessing's 'Faust' fragment of circa 1759. In Lessing there are seven spirit voices who must answer Faust's question, 'How swift are you?'. By altering the number to six, Busoni indicates a parallel with the final scene of Goethe's *Faust* Part II. In an unfinished critical essay on Goethe's closing scene, Busoni pointed out how the action progresses 'with its gaze directed upwards'.* In his own Vorspiel II the spirit voices rise from the lowest to the highest regions of the male compass as their swiftness—and hence their power—ascends. Thus one can draw a parallel between Goethe's six heavenly spirits and Busoni's six *voces diabolorum*:

Goethe—	Busoni—
Pater Profundus	Gravis
Pater Ecstaticus	Levis
Pater Seraphicus	Asmodus
Magna Peccatrix	Beelzebuth
Mulier Samaritana	Megaeros
Maria Aegyptiaca	Mephistopheles

Busoni first envisaged the seven flames distributed around a hexagram, the six lesser spirits at the circumference, Mephisto at the centre:

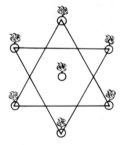

This arrangement assigns Mephisto the dominant role. Busoni later simplified the arrangement to that of a Pythagorean triangle in which Mephisto appears as *primus inter pares*:

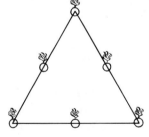

* Busoni's criticism of Mahler's setting of this scene in the Eighth Symphony: 'Dans Goethe, toute la direction est *verticale* et tend au sommet; dans Mahler elle se présente plutôt *horizontalement*, moins superposée qu'accostée en une série d'épisodes.' (Letter to Harriet Lanier, 9.5.1916.)

At this point it must have become clear that one spirit voice would have to be removed; the role of Astaroth, originally the fourth voice, was cut.

As to 'Gretchen's brother', the German reader, confronted with a new Faust drama, would automatically make direct comparisons with Goethe. Busoni removed Gretchen's name from his text partly in an attempt to prevent such comparisons (for Gretchen was Goethe's own original addition to the saga), and partly in tacit observance of Nietzsche's criticism of Goethe—that so lofty an intellectual would scarcely stoop to seducing a mere seamstress. Busoni, while implying in the Scenic Intermezzo that the Gretchen episode had already occurred, returns to the more elevated love affair with the Duchess of Parma, the origins of which are in the puppet play.

On 20 May 1920 the celebrated actor Heinrich Devrient gave a public reading of Busoni's libretto in the Goethe House at Weimar. One of the critics wrote: 'Goethe casts his shadow, against which no will to oblivion can be of any help.'[17] It was at this point that Busoni, his worst suspicions confirmed, struck out the name of Gretchen throughout his libretto, replacing it with the anonymous 'das Mädchen'. When the text was published for a second time later that year by Gustav Kiepenheuer, Potsdam, this alteration was incorporated.

As for the third difference, Helena belongs amongst the *dramatis personae* because her role was actually conceived for a solo dancer. All Busoni's sketches, and indeed the versions of the libretto published during his lifetime, are unambiguous on this point. He probably envisaged the kind of interpretative dance in which his two distinguished friends—Isadora Duncan and Maud Allan—both excelled. In Jarnach's edition of the vocal score, the important stage direction (p. 267), 'Sie führt einen gemessenen Tanz aus', is omitted. Jarnach's music for this scene is anyway so brief that a choreographic realization would scarcely be possible.

Writing to Gisella Selden-Goth, who had arranged the Weimar reading of the libretto, Busoni explained why he had decided to publish it so far in advance of the completion of the score: 'Because I predict that a performance in the theatre will demand so much of *eyes* and *ears* that no room could be left for the comprehension of the text.'[18] Clearly, the bad experiences with *Die Brautwahl* played a considerable part in this decision.

On 10 March 1921, the writer Paul Alfred Merbach introduced Lessing's 'Faust' fragment and Busoni's libretto, which were then read by the actor Julius Schmock in the Lessing Museum, Berlin. This time the reception was more enthusiastic than in Weimar but the critics again found imitations of Goethe in Busoni's work and remarked upon the abruptness of the style.

Busoni's desire to measure his libretto against the German classics is an indication of the enormous ambitiousness of his project. His libretto is well constructed and convincing as a drama; but if it has any affinity with Goethe's *Faust*, then this lies primarily in the fact that Busoni uses the figure of Faust as a mouthpiece for his own beliefs and for his personal *Weltanschauung*.

The scenes of *Doktor Faust* are linked not so much by a continuous story line as by the development and inter-relationships of the three principal characters: Mephisto, the Duchess of Parma and Faust himself.

'Meph. = Bosheit und Grösse' ('Meph. = Malice and grandeur') noted Busoni in a sketch for the scene of the pact. Three times we see Mephisto in attitudes of fearsome triumph: in his cry of 'Gefangen!' ('My captive!') as he stands over the unconscious Faust after the signing of the pact; in his secret rejoicing over the murder on holy ground in the Scenic Intermezzo; as he raises his claw in 'benediction' of the totally outwitted Duke of Parma. Subsequently, as Faust begins to comprehend the true nature of his mission, Mephisto dominates no longer; by the final scene, as Busoni wrote, 'the devil as night watchman is very far from evil and comes close to common human beings'[19]. Musically his malice is characterized through the use of the highest, most inhuman tessitura of the tenor voice, an inspired deviation from the dark-timbred baritone usually associated with the role. We are most aware of his greatness or awesomeness at his first appearance, where Faust is visibly terrified of him. 'It is in fact no easy thing to give orders to the Devil', wrote Busoni.[20] Yet his intellect is by no means equal to that of Faust. The other five demons are dull, sluggish things and Mephisto himself can only claim to be 'as swift as the thoughts of *man*', while Faust, satisfied at least to have found Lucifer's most able servant, says with relief: 'Could I have hoped for so much? What more do I wish for?' This Mephisto should not be overestimated then. He is, above all, a German devil, that creature of whom E. T. A. Hoffmann wrote (auspiciously enough, in his preamble to *Die Brautwahl*):

> He is actually a thoroughly honest man, for he abides by the written contract precisely and punctually, and so it happens quite often that he is outwitted and truly appears as a poor devil. . . . But even more, the character of the German Satan includes a wonderful tinge of burlesque through which his truly perplexing horror and dismay, which crush the soul, are released and dissolved.[21]

Among human beings, Faust finds his spiritual equal: in the Duchess of Parma. 'You proudest of women shall be my prize,' he murmurs when he first sets eyes on her, and Mephisto, not realizing that the combined wills of the two can destroy him, helps to unite them. The Duchess is the ideal companion and, as in *Die Brautwahl*, the only woman in the action. Yet she has an unearthly rival in Helena, whose function in the drama is more complex. Mephisto conjures her up, as Hoffmann would say, for contractual reasons: during Faust's remaining twenty-four years of life he must be permitted to savour physical beauty in its highest form. Helena is Mephisto's trump card. Faust understands her differently, as the Ideal which has so long eluded him. Hence his terror at her apparition in the Second Tableau: he is unwilling to be confronted in tangible form with that which he knows must remain beyond his grasp. In the final scene, where the ultimate outrage is committed of superimposing Helena's features on the figure of the Crucified (again, a direct quotation from the puppet play), Mephisto is little more than a passive witness. It is the 'Übermächte' (to use Hofmannsthal's word from *Die Frau ohne Schatten*) who are pitted against each other here.

The twin figures of the Duchess of Parma and Helena have already appeared in other forms in Busoni's earlier dramas. The Attainable was Lenore in *Sigune*, Adelma in *Turandot* or Albertine in *Die Brautwahl*; the Unattainable was Sigune herself, Turandot, until her capitulation, and the great altarpiece of *Die Brautwahl*. The Unattainable can only be pursued through self-sacrifice: Diethart dies in order to be united with Sigune; Kalaf stakes his life for Turandot; Lehsen deserts Albertine for his art. In *Doktor Faust* this sacrifice is carried one stage further: that the Work may be finished, the Duchess also lays down her life.

According to Vladimir Vogel: 'Faust is a man, not a hero, neither on stilts (Wagner) nor on his knees (Dostoievsky) . . . the embodiment of Busoni's realistic idealism which even today has forfeited nothing of its timeliness.'[22] Yet Faust has, at the outset, already exhausted the potential of the society in which he lives. When, as in the puppet play, Busoni's Faust resorts to magic, he merely sees this as the best method of avenging himself on his enemies. The clergy suspect him of dealings with the devil and the girl's brother is after his blood. From the beginning he is an outcast hounded by his neighbours (to use the imagery of the 'Zigeunerlied'), a role in which the composer also often saw himself. Thus it is not difficult for Mephisto to win Faust over and he seals the bargain by slaying, with a mere gesture, the churchmen knocking at the door.

Faust demands freedom of him, above all:

Procure for me for the rest of my life
the unconditional fulfilment of every wish,
Let me embrace the world,
the East and the South which call me.
Let me comprehend the deeds of Man
and extend them in ways undreamed of;
give me genius and give me too its suffering,
until I may rejoice like no other . . .
Make me free!

It takes Faust a long time to understand the true purpose of his strangely won freedom. As Busoni pointed out, the scenes of magic at the court of Parma are in fact 'time-wasting'* and we can read into Faust's exaggeratedly sensational entrance and his cheap fairground tricks an elaborate allegory on the unhappy,

---

* In his notebook, October 1913, Busoni compared his activities as Director of the Liceo Musicale in Bologna to those of Faust at Parma (cf. Dent, p. 294).

empty life of a travelling virtuoso. But not until the final scene where, by destroying the book, Faust has already abandoned his magic, does he realize that his freedom can bring him beyond the power of God or the Devil.

It is in the Wittenberg tavern, surrounded by admiring youngsters, that Faust begins to assume more overtly Busonian characteristics. In the contrast between the hilarity of the students and his morose, introspective mood one sees perhaps a 'reincarnation' of Hoffmann in Lutter's cellar, while Faust's words—'Only he is happy who looks to the future'—became the dauntingly optimistic catch phrase of Busoni's later years.

As the tavern fades away into an antique landscape, Helena stands before him. Only three weeks before his death, Busoni came to describe the Ideal for which she stands as 'the Essence of music':

> In the pursuit of my observations, I have gradually been forced to the opinion that our conception of the essence of music is still fragmentary and dim; that only very few are able to perceive it and fewer still to grasp it, and they are quite unable to define it.[23]

To compose music which expresses music's very essence: the problem is insoluble.

Faust realizes that he must look to a coming generation for the attainment of his Ideal: 'I look far into the distance; I see new terrain, as yet uncultivated hillsides which swell out, leading to new ascents. Life smiles as if in promise.' Thus he can now rapturously greet the inevitability of his death.

The closing scene underwent considerable revision before attaining its final form. Doubts about the original version were already voiced in a letter to Gerda dated 31 March 1915, only three months after it was written:

> As for the end of my piece, I have first of all two ostensible reasons.
> 1. *I follow the tradition of the puppet play,*
> 2. *It makes for a strong picture.*
> But this close is inevitable if one obeys inner logic. This man is sufficiently wise to be able to have his own laws; but he has made use of his wisdom in vain: he is guilty of several murders and is actually undeserving of a good deed.
>
> Moreover, the Devil as night-watchman is very far from evil and comes close to common human beings, thus the situation is scarcely symbolic any more.
>
> Finally, Faust himself says:
>   'Ist das Leben nur ein Wahn,
>   Was kann der Tod mehr sein?'*
>
>   ['If life is but delusion,
>   What more can death be?']

* These lines, strongly influenced by Lenau, do not in fact appear in the final version of the libretto.

What does the last act have to do with the devil any more?—A man, sick, disappointed and stricken by conscience, dies of a heart attack and is discovered by the night-watchman.—The last word is also: '*ein Verunglück-ter*' [a casualty] (and not for instance: '*Verdammt*' [damned] or the like.)

Two years later Busoni was still dissatisfied with the scene, which lacked a clear sense of direction. He discussed his problem with the little-known Expressionist writer Ludwig Rubiner★ and it was, strangely enough, thanks to his comments that Busoni was able to reach a satisfactory conclusion. Nothing of their discussion appears to have been recorded, but his advice to Busoni may well be reflected in these lines from the preface to his own last play, *Die Gewaltlosen* (1919): 'The characters of this drama are the exponents of ideas. A work of ideas helps an era to reach its goal by transcending that era to expound the ultimate goal itself as a reality.'[24] On the last page of Busoni's manuscript libretto, which bears the date 4 October 1917, any lingering indecisiveness as to the message of the drama is finally removed in the threefold alteration of Faust's last words: 'an eternal concept'—'an eternal spirit'—'an eternal will' (see Facsimile 41).

This closing scene has several layers of meaning. There is, first of all, the new beginning, symbolized by the Art Nouveau gesture of the naked youth striding boldly into the night. Then there is the lonely, abandoned figure lying in the snow (reminiscent of the wounded Leandro in *Arlecchino*) left to die in a suddenly inhospitable town square—a true picture of our century. And the night-watchman's indifferent comment, 'Has this man met with an accident?', emphasizes the wartime background of the drama, of an age in which so many people met with 'accidents'. There is also the uplifting role of the *Ewigweibliche*:

> From instinct Faust aspires to union with the Duchess, not yet being conscious of the final aim himself. A reminder of the final aim is the transmission of the dead child, with Mephistopheles as courier. . . In the last tableau the vision of the Duchess makes it forcibly clear to Faust what the child signifies to him.[25]

Faust's death then comes neither as a 'dreadful and terrifying end', as in the

---

★ Rubiner (1881–1920) had been a friend of Busoni's since about 1910, when he published an enthusiastic review of the *New Aesthetic* in Franz Pfemfert's magazine *Der Demokrat 2* (No. 28). In April 1916 he published an equally warm-hearted, indeed hyperbolic, appreciation of Busoni in *Die Weissen Blätter* (entitled 'Tröster'). Like Busoni, he spent the war years in Zurich, subsequently returning to Berlin, where he joined the German Communist Party and was employed by Gustav Kiepenheuer as drama editor. His play *Die Gewaltlosen* was published by Kiepenheuer as one of a series which bore the general title *Der dramatische Wille*. It was no doubt through Rubiner's offices that Kiepenheuer also published Busoni's libretto; indeed the alteration of Faust's last words to 'Ich, Faust, ein ewiger Wille' was quite possibly due to Rubiner's influence.

puppet play, nor is it the beginning of his salvation, as in Goethe. It would be over-simplifying the issue to view it as the tragedy of one man. Dent, in an article entitled 'The Return of Busoni',[26] drew attention to a passage from the closing scene which seemed to him to be the kernel of the whole drama. Professor Dent was an atheist and these lines will certainly have struck a note of concord in him. For here Faust addresses himself directly to Heaven and Hell, snuffing out God and the Devil as derisively as he had earlier extinguished the flames of the lesser spirit voices. In Jarnach's completion of the score, and hence in all later re-publications of the libretto, these lines are missing:

> [So let the Work be finished,]
> in defiance of you,
> of you all,
> who hold yourselves for good,
> whom we call evil,
> who,
> for the sake of old quarrels
> take Mankind as a pretext
> and pile upon him
> the consequence of your discord.
> Upon this highest insight of my wisdom
> is your malice now broken to pieces
> and in my self-won freedom
> expire both God and Devil at once.

When asked who could, or should, write music for his *Faust*, Goethe replied, 'the repulsive, unpleasant and terrifying qualities that it would in some places require are out of tune with our age'.[27] In the *Sonatina seconda* and *Nocturne symphonique* of 1912–13 Busoni had established a basic vocabulary of musical terror, expressly intended for his own *Faust*, and he wrote: 'These . . . studies were absorbed motivically and stylistically into the score [of the opera], where they fulfilled their preparatory nature in terms of stimulation, scale and atmosphere.'[28] How the other elements of the score were assembled is indicated here in the form of a diary:

1916 At San Remigio, Pallanza, the first ideas were jotted down. The work was to be encircled by bells: at the beginning an orchestral imitation, then a choral imitation, later chorus with organ and real bells and, at the very end, Christmas bells (but without chorus). Furthermore the organ was to play a chorale prelude during the Second Tableau (sic) and Helena's music was to feature the glass harmonica. Back in Zurich, Busoni wrote to his Polish musicologist friend, Alicja Simon:

> I would like to ask you—as a connoisseur of Polish music—if you could tell me of any ancient, solemn melody connected with *Cracow*. Something that might symbolize the city, an old chorale, ceremonial song or the like—but would not on that account need to be well known.[29]

She sent him several possible melodies but, in actual fact, nothing came of this, and the 'Cracow' music was later drawn from the *Sonatina seconda*. A few days later, the opening of the Symphonia was sketched out. In the meantime, the full score of *Arlecchino* had been completed, and the composition of *Turandot*, followed by preparations for the premières of these two operas, prevented any further work on *Doktor Faust*.

1917 11 May: the premières of *Turandot* and *Arlecchino*. On Friday 13 July Busoni wrote down the opening bars of the full score of *Doktor Faust*. He then worked steadily through the summer and autumn, completing both Vorspiel I and the Scenic Intermezzo before Christmas. As final offering for the year came the *Sonatina in diem nativitatis Christi MCMXVII*, and a sketch for Faust's conjuring up of the demons.

1918 Apart from the Clarinet Concertino and the various Goethe songs, the first half of the year brought only a few sketches for Vorspiel II; the setting of the 'Lied des Mephistopheles' sparked off renewed activity during the summer. In late September the libretto went to the press, while on 18 September Busoni could count 1,500 bars of completed full score: 'This means about half of the whole work. The way I write, however, this makes no guarantee for the second half, as I don't use leitmotivs and have always to stand anew before closed doors, which only inspiration can open.'[30] Subsequently came a Polonaise (later to become the *Cortège*), the music for Faust's last entrance and, as New Year's offering, the *Sarabande*.

1919 January saw the completion of the *Sarabande and Cortège* as separate 'Faust studies', and on 31 March they were given their first performance. Encouraged by their success, Busoni proposed a concert performance of the portions of the score already completed. 'Thank God, we don't need a primadonna', he wrote.[31] A performance of the *Sarabande and Cortège* in London in November brought a very cool response.

1920 The year brought forth a number of satellite works: the Elegy for Clarinet, Divertimento for Flute, the *Toccata* and the *Tanzwalzer*. All these pieces found their way into the First Tableau of the *Hauptspiel*, which made steady progress. The year also saw the second publication of the *Faust* libretto and, in mid-September, Busoni's return to Berlin.

1921 The spring brought the second and third Albumleaves and further work on the First Tableau. Later came the Concertino for Piano, the two-piano version of the *Fantasia Contrappuntistica* as well as other smaller projects. In this fruitful summer the students' scene of the Second Tableau was also completed. The autumn brought the first realization of serious illness.

1922 In March, Werner Wolff conducted the *Sarabande and Cortège* in Hamburg. 'The pieces pleased me again', wrote Ferruccio to Gerda. 'This gave me further courage to complete the work.'[32] In the summer he worked on the final scene (up to the point where the score breaks off), as well as the essay, 'The Score of *Doktor Faust*'. The completion of the opera was in sight but, at the end of the year, another bout of illness made him an invalid for four months. With this came a drop in spirits; he finally decided against performing extracts from *Faust* in concert form. 'I am not sufficiently accredited as a composer to let myself in for games of chance', he wrote.[33]

1923 The *Sarabande and Cortège* were conducted by Furtwängler in Berlin in February, meeting with a cold and hostile response. In March the 'Zigeunerlied' was composed. (These facts could well be related.) Despite severe illness, the exquisite 'Traum der Jugend' monologue, which precedes the appearance of Helena, was completed on 13 April and on 9 May followed the closing scene of the Second Tableau. Only the Helena scene itself and the conclusion of the Final Tableau were now missing. In mid-August Busoni visited the Bauhaus exhibition in Weimar. Entranced by Stravinsky's *Soldier's Tale*—itself a miniature Faust drama—Busoni exclaimed, 'He has succeeded in writing an opera—without voices!'[34]. In November he travelled to Paris where he composed the Study for the third pedal and where Man Ray made a portrait photograph of the ailing composer.

1924 Busoni was now too ill to do more than jot down a few short pieces, including the Trills Study and the song, 'Schlechter Trost'. To his friend Jella Oppenheimer he wrote: 'Temporarily the remainder of the work is "within the soul of its creator"—assuming that he still possesses a soul.'[35] The heart and kidney inflammation from which he had been suffering for some years became acute. On 1 April, his fifty-eighth birthday, he drew up a detailed plan for the missing final scene, but was no longer able to execute it. He died early in the morning of 27 July.

Symphonia Busoni's orchestral carillon is an ingenious sustaining-pedal effect, achieved by superimposing open-fifth chords in diverse rhythms, chiming in and out of phase with each other.★ The dynamic rises gradually to *piano*, then sinks back to the opening *ppp*, leaving a single octave-strand in the strings. Woodwinds answer a third lower and a theme in canon emerges, often to be associated with Faust himself:

Ex. 262

★ This music could also have served as the opening of Busoni's planned Leonardo drama: 'On a hill in the distance, the silhouette of the St Florentine church near Amboise. We see a procession of masked men, carrying a coffin and sixty candles, climb the hill and enter the church. Silence. The bells still ring.'

It is the opening of the *Nocturne symphonique*, carrying us into the dark realms inhabited by that work. The atmosphere clears and a bucolic canon theme sings out in the woodwind, followed by a plainchant melody in the horns, again in canon. But the peace and joy of this Easter music do not last. The music of the *Nocturne symphonique* returns, interrupted for a moment by an echo of the chorale. Out of the ensuing cauldron of sound we hear distant voices. It is the chorus, behind the curtain, chiming out the word 'Pax' like bells:

Ex. 263

The Symphonia, as Busoni himself pointed out, was completed towards the end of 1917. It is his personal plea for peace, in the same subdued but fervent vein as the fourth Sonatina.

The poet addresses the audience The prologue, spoken or sung, was something of a passing phase in the history of opera at the beginning of the twentieth century. It had little in common, however, with the highly involved allegorical prologues to the earliest operas of the Baroque. Bartók calls for a spoken introduction to *Duke Bluebeard's Castle*; Vaughan Williams frames his entire *Pilgrim's Progress* with a sung prologue and epilogue (as later also Britten in *Billy Budd*); Berg brings an animal trainer onto the stage to introduce the cast of *Lulu*: Busoni, like Janáček in *Mr Brouček's Excursion into the Fifteenth Century*, has an *apologia* spoken by the poet himself. The function of Busoni's prologue is to remind the spectator that he is in the theatre, that he should not expect to see real life mirrored on the stage, but rather the magic of the unreal.

Perhaps this prologue, or at least its essence, belongs today in the programme book. At any rate, the content of the verses is not essential to the unfolding of the drama.★

Vorspiel I The main curtain now rises. We see Faust in his study, bent in concentration over a chemical experiment. The music is nervous and tense: it takes as its basis the opening section of the *Sonatina seconda*, adding one new motif:

Ex. 264

We also hear the *Merlin* motif from the *Sonatina seconda* with its characteristic sparks of fire, coming to rest as Wagner enters:

Ex. 265

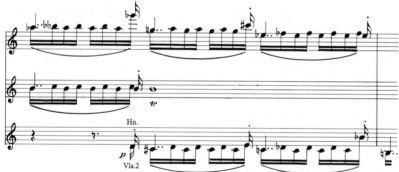

The *Merlin* motif appears too in the 'remarkable title' of the book:

Ex. 266

★ In the Frankfurt production (1980) an abbreviated version of Baudelaire's 'Le Voyage' (from *Les fleurs du mal*) was read in place of Busoni's poem—a creative experiment not without logic and effectiveness.

As Wagner leaves to admit the students, Faust sings an arioso of furious intensity. At its climax the main theme of the *Nocturne symphonique* rings out terrifyingly; Faust's unholy joy gives way to doubt (a more subdued passage from the *Nocturne symphonique*). The three students from Cracow enter to the march theme from the *Sonatina seconda*, lugubriously orchestrated with four-part pizzicato chords for double-basses. As Faust bids them welcome, we hear the opening phrase of the same work, as also when he offers them hospitality:

Ex. 267

With solemn intonations the students hand over their gifts; the chorale theme from the trio of the *Cortège* accompanies them. Faust asks if he can repay them. 'Later!' is their ominous reply, whereupon they take their leave. Wagner re-enters; he has seen nobody leave the room. 'Ah, now I know WHO they were!' cries Faust. At the same moment the experiment boils over, crackling and hissing; Wagner rushes to attend to it. As the curtain falls, the closing phrase of the *Sonatina seconda* thunders out in C minor.

The scene is composed in simple ternary form, the outer wings relating to Faust's experiment, the central part to the scene with the students. An ingenious reworking of the earliest Faust studies, it is a compact and telling piece of theatrical craftsmanship.

Vorspiel II This is built in quasi-symphonic form:

1) Introduction—in modo d'un Adagio
2) Invocation—ternary Allegro
3) Questioning of the spirits—orchestral variations
4) Appearance of Mephistopheles—Sarabande
5) Aria of Mephistopheles—Scherzo
6) The pact (Credo)—choral variations
7) Postlude—quasi Adagio

Introduction: an elegiac orchestral movement, opening in an ambiguous C sharp minor. Its principal features: a long theme in two sections, the first in smaller intervals (mostly thirds and circles bounded by thirds), the second in chains of descending sevenths; later a rocking motif in faster rhythmic units. Here are the opening phrases (Ex. 268):

Ex. 268

There are two interpolations from the *Nocturne symphonique*, the first just before the curtain rises, the second at Faust's words, 'I can begin'.⋆

Invocation: the opening is forthright and determined. An ostinato figure: ♪♪ ♪ ♪♪♪ ♪ ♪♪♪ ♪ ♪♪ | ♪♪ supports a dramatic canon, reminiscent of the climax of the Piano Concerto's *Pezzo serioso*:

Ex. 269

Faust calls upon Lucifer; the key, which he holds in his right hand, begins to glow. In a hectic *tempo doppio*, recalling the music which opened Vorspiel I, we recognize the opening phrase of the Adagio (Ex. 268) in diminution and stretto:

Ex. 270

An off-stage chorus questions Faust: he repeats his command. Suddenly darkness falls, the music is reduced to a trill, that same trill which Leonhard conjured up in the first act of *Die Brautwahl* in setting the scene for the *Erscheinung*. 'What have I done?' gasps Faust. The tempo of the opening returns, but the formerly active rhythmic figure is reduced to a passive,

⋆ Originally at this point an invisible chorus of good spirits was to let out a gentle sigh (accompanied by the final chord of the *Nocturne symphonique*).

nervous pulsation:  The chorus calls on Faust to question the flames which are seen hanging suspended in the room.

Questioning of the spirits: each spirit answers Faust in increasing tempo and rising vocal tessitura. At the time of composition, Busoni wrote to Gerda: 'I have made a small, self-contained piece out of the scene of the 6 spirits, like a set of variations.'[36] All five sections do indeed bear the contrasts of rhythm and texture expected of variations, while one can trace shreds of thematic material in each which seem to be related to the opening Adagio of the scene. Yet attempts to analyse these variations (as made, for instance, by Stuckenschmidt) will always be confounded. As in the scene of the caskets in *Die Brautwahl*, these are 'variations in the fantastic sense': one can search in vain for any larger melodic or harmonic links between them.

At the appearance of Beelzebuth (Variation 4), the chorus joins the ensemble; for Megaeros (Variation 5) the chorus 'breaks out in a kind of scorn, to intimidate Faust'.[37] The play of falling sevenths becomes of ever greater thematic importance (taking its cue from the second part of the Adagio theme). As Faust dismisses Beelzebuth he sings:

Ex. 271

and the followers of Megaeros sing:

Ex. 272

the sequence of sevenths which opened the fifth Sonatina. As Megaeros, the 'agile storm', is snuffed out, the theme of the Adagio returns in its original form and Faust steps out of the circle. The experiment is finished, evidently without success; the music also returns to its point of departure. Faust turns back to his work, the 'healing wave'. We hear a theme from the *Sarabande* in which one of the Mephisto motifs is embedded. Indeed, his flame, unnoticed by Faust, still hangs flickering in the air. The spirit calls to him. 'How brightly gleams the light', exclaims Faust. The music has now reached the tempo of Faust's own restless personality, as we first observed him in Vorspiel I, a tempo which none of the other spirits could achieve. But the thematic content of this music is now entirely that of Mephisto (Ex. 273).

Ex. 273

The voice calls, 'I am swift as the thoughts of man' and rises to a ringing high C, sustained over a sequence of chords which originally appears in the *Song of the Spirit Dance*. As Mephistopheles proudly calls his name, the invisible chorus takes up the chant. The chain of thirds, descending to span a major seventh, is an important motif:

Ex. 274

'Then show yourself in tangible form', orders Faust, again to the sevenths motif:

Ex. 275

Appearance of Mephistopheles: with further chains of thirds, sarabande rhythm, widely spaced *ff* chords, suddenly he is there—a man dressed in a close-fitting black garment, standing before Faust 'in servile attitude'. Struggling to suppress a feeling of repulsion, Faust outlines his wishes—and afterwards? 'Afterwards you must serve me for ever', replies Mephisto. Faust refuses, he tries to rid himself of the demon. But, by stepping out of the magic circle at the crucial moment, he has placed himself in his power. The music of this confrontation is an extended paraphrase of *Sarabande* material.

Aria of Mephistopheles: a brilliant scherzo in 3/4 time, whose first theme is repeated frequently and insistently as Mephisto outlines Faust's predicament. The falling seventh is again strongly evident (Ex. 276)—

Ex. 276

while, for the Devil's gleeful laughter, we hear the motif of thirds with which
he had first announced himself (Ex. 274):

Ex. 277

Here Busoni introduces that most 'diabolic' of percussion instruments, the
xylophone; Exx. 276 and 277 are developed, inverted and superimposed in
devilishly clever counterpoint. As middle section a passage taken from the
Nocturne symphonique is wildly accelerated. The final gesture, the coda of the
aria, is another of Mephisto's principal motifs, originating in the *Toccata* and
also to be found, in a different guise, at the opening of the *Tanzwalzer* (cf. Ex.
286):

Ex. 278

The Pact: the scene is interrupted by knocking at the door (in sarabande
rhythm). The clergy's paid thugs are outside. In a moment of chilling
simplicity, Mephisto liquidates them.* Faust's horror is reflected in a further
variant of his 'Invocation' rhythm: ♪♪ 𝄽 ♪♪ 𝄽 ♪♪ 𝄽 ♪│♪♪ This rhythm
is a universal musical heartbeat: we find it in Antonia's raging pulse in
Offenbach's *Les Contes d'Hoffmann*, in the ebbing life-blood of the two
'suicides' in *Così fan tutte*, in Lehsen's surging spirits as he first meets Albertine
in *Die Brautwahl*.

'But leave me now', says Faust, 'I cannot endure you.' 'You must learn to',
retorts Mephisto. Off-stage voices, distant at first, later coming steadily closer,

---

* In the first version of the libretto he also mutters to himself, 'The first murder.'

begin to intone the Credo to music from the middle section of the fourth Sonatina. A second Credo, for three solo voices and three stringed instruments, emulates Palestrina in its gentle euphony and smoothness of rhythm.★

The choral variations bring back the Easter music of the Symphonia to the words 'Et resurrexit'. 'Easter Day!' reflects Faust, 'Day of my chilhood.' The comment is autobiographical, for 1 April 1866, the day of Busoni's birth, was an Easter Sunday. In the ensuing 'Et iterum', an Allegro fiero in D minor, the separate spheres of action on and off stage move simultaneously towards their respective climaxes:

Stage	*Off-stage*
Faust laments, 'You are but a dead man.'	'Et iterum venturus est cum gloria judicare vivos et mortuos.' A vigorous *stretta* in which the chorus is joined by trumpets, horns, timpani and organ.
'Your signature', insists Mephistopheles.	Bells ring out as the chorus fervently repeats the word 'Credo'.
Faust signs the pact. The chords of the opening Credo rise ominously in the orchestra.	
Faust collapses	'Gloria in excelsis Deo'. The bells ring more wildly, brass fanfares.
Mephisto tears the parchment from Faust's hand with a shout of triumph and disappears. Thunder; fragments of sarabande rhythm.	The rejoicing comes to an abrupt halt. With a soft E major chord, the chorus repeats the word 'Pax'.

Postlude: the Adagio theme of the introduction returns, rising slowly with gentle discords, now softened into C major:

Ex. 279

★ Among the sketches for this scene are copies Busoni made of two motets by Palestrina.

The chorus, gradually disappearing into the distance, intones a plainsong 'Allelujah'. Sunlight begins to fill Faust's study, illuminating his prostrate body.'

Vorspiel II is divided into two equal parts, each reaching its climax through a set of ascending variations. The Adagio theme, which appears three times, is the symmetrical axis of the whole, flanking the scene and reappearing at its central point.

Scenic Intermezzo The movement opens with a long organ solo, which Busoni wished to resound through the entire theatre. The leading melodic strand—here in its most complete form:

Ex. 280

is spun into an elaborate polyphonic fantasia of considerable bravura. As the girl's brother begins to pray, the music becomes more static and is eventually reduced to block chords. In the bass-line of these chords appear the descending thirds of the *Sarabande*, while a new theme has (in common with the main theme of the *Sarabande*) a fanlike progression in the inner parts (cf. Ex. 199):

Ex. 281

Faust and Mephisto appear, occasioning a sudden *stretta*. In the ensuing hushed dialogue between the soldier and the devil-monk the orchestra begins to play a more prominent part (taking up the chorale Ex. 280). From off-stage we hear a roll of drums and, a few seconds later, a trumpet fanfare. This military music originates in the *versio minore* of the *Fantasia Contrappuntistica*, and hence from the chorale 'Allein Gott sei in der Höh':

Ex. 282

The fight which Mephisto conjures up between the soldiers and the girl's brother is accompanied by a brutal *stretta*. Later, as the Devil blesses the murderers, his characteristic thirds are blared out by the low brass, while his closing words are set to the most extreme version of the falling-seventh motif:

Ex. 283

Der wei – se Faust la – dets auf sein Ge – wis – sen: Drei

Rat – ten in ei – ner Fal – le.

The scene ends, as it began, with full organ alone as the soldier lies dead, illuminated by a pale ray of moonlight.

According to Busoni, the Scenic Intermezzo is constructed in the form of a rondo. Yet, as with the *Rondò arlecchinesco*, the structure is scarcely traditional. Its stream-of-consciousness style is reminiscent of the Elegies for piano; the whole scene has a meditative, dreamlike quality which vividly off-sets the brutality of the actual happenings on stage.

While all the other scenes of the opera are centred around C major or minor, the two Intermezzi are linked by their foreign keys: the Scenic Intermezzo is in D minor, the Symphonic Intermezzo in B minor.

Hauptspiel

First Tableau The Parma scene begins with a dance suite which draws its material from diverse sources.

1. *Polonaise*. The opening music of the *Cortège* op. 51, with some cuts and a few instrumental retouchings. At the close, the curtain rises.

2. *Pastorale*. A lively 6/8 ryhthm with bagpipe effects and wordless chorus in mixolydian F major. The thematic material comes largely from the *pifferata* of the fourth Sonatina.

3. *Galop*. Huntsmen with horns blow a blithely dissonant D major fanfare also based on the *pifferata*, against an ostinato counter-rhythm in the orchestra. The chorus takes up the fanfare.

4. *Waltz*. Pages play games of fencing. The music is taken directly from the *Tanzwalzer*, but with lightened orchestration. The E major opening is contrasted with a gentle C major middle section, a dance for girls with garlands of flowers. As coda, a distant chorus intones the opening *Pastorale* melisma over a drone fifth in the orchestra.

5. *Minuetto*. A roll of drums in the portentous rhythm of the last section of the Clarinet Concertino, ♩. ♪♫♫ ♫♫♫♫ ♪♫♫ ♫♫♫♫ | ♩. ♪♯ , heralds the approach of the Duke and his bride. As the pair rides ceremoniously onto the stage, we hear music drawn from the *Cortège*.

6. *da Capo*. To a brief, recitative-like phrase, the Master of Ceremonies steps forward and introduces the 'amazing Dr Faust', while absolving himself

of any responsibility for his actions. The Suite is rounded off by music from the *Polonaise*.

Now Mephisto suddenly appears, dressed as a herald, to a fanfare theme built in thirds:*

Ex. 284

Faust makes a grotesquely pompous entrance with apes as train-bearers. His approach is accompanied by a march in A minor, underpinned by an assymetrical rhythmic figure of three beats: ♪ ♩ ♩ ♫ ♪ ♩ ♩ ♫ ♪ ♩ ♩ ♫ ♪ The middle section of the march, in which the chorus, later joined by the Duke and Duchess, stare in amazement at the famous magician, draws its material from the 'Freudvoll und leidvoll' music of the *Cortège*. As Faust contemplates the Duchess, the sinister undertones of the outwardly festive atmosphere are further exaggerated by a reminiscence of the *Nocturne symphonique*:

Ex. 285

He raises his hand and a swarm of little devils rushes out of the bushes, shocking the ladies and amusing the gentlemen. Then he turns night into day, for 'day is not propitious for miracles'. The display of magic now begins with the summoning up of visions from antiquity. The music is formed into a second dance suite, opening with the introduction to the *Tanzwalzer*:

Ex. 286

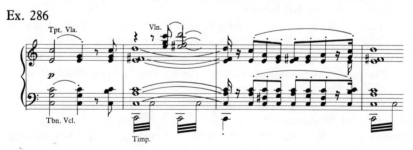

* Kurt Weill appropriated this fanfare in his little-known music for Strindberg's *Gustav III*, written in 1927.

The first vision—Solomon and the Queen of Sheba—also uses music from the *Tanzwalzer*. In this innocent and beguiling music one detects once again the sarabande rhythm and falling sevenths of Busoni's Faustian language:

Ex. 287

Solomon begins to play the harp, and we hear Mephisto's fanfare (Ex. 284), delicately scored for an ensemble of oboes, trombones, harps, celesta and percussion. 'A new vision', calls the Duchess, entranced, and the introductory music of Ex. 286 is varied to stress a yearning phrase which we shall often associate with her:

Ex. 288

Samson and Delilah, 'in love's embrace', appear to lilting, pastoral music but, as Delilah raises her shears over the sleeping Samson, the mood becomes frenetic and the Duchess calls for a new vision, asking Faust to choose the subject himself. He conjures up Salome, John the Baptist and the executioner; the music is from the second Albumleaf but now marked Allegro concitato. 'At a sign from Salome', says Faust, 'his head falls'. 'He may not die!' cries the Duchess. 'So you love me!' he replies, 'come, follow me!' Faust's passionate theme, one of the rare moments in the opera (indeed in all Busoni's music) which is truly sensuous, is taken from the third Albumleaf. And there it was extrapolated from a Bach chorale! (cf. Exx. 238 and 239).

The Duke breaks the spell abruptly: 'Make an end to the play!' 'The play', replies Mephisto mockingly, 'is as good as ended.' In a second *da capo*, which binds the two dance suites of the Tableau into a unity, the *Polonaise* music returns to accompany the exit of the bridal pair. As Mephisto also vanishes, we hear the scampering parody of the *Sarabande* theme (Ex. 207) from the coda of the *Cortège*. Here it is extended with a passage of whirling string scales, reminiscent of the music in *La Damnation de Faust* with which Berlioz often links his scenes: 'Serapiontic' music, which serves to put time and place out of focus.

The sound of a distant violin, echoed by sombre chords in the lower brass, now conjures up an elegiac world far removed from the foregoing festivities. The Duchess reappears, as if in a dream. Most of the music for her scene is drawn from the Fantasia section of the *Toccata* and from the Elegy for Clarinet. In reworking and orchestrating this material, Busoni creates an extended dramatic scena; not exactly 'in the grand operatic tradition'[38], as Stuckenschmidt would have it, for the element of display is lacking, but nevertheless more conventional than any of Faust's own monologues.

The first phrase, a variant of the opening of the Clarinet Elegy (cf. Ex. 208):

Ex. 289

has two distinguished forebears:*

Ex. 290

Ex. 291

* The similarity of these two passages is noted by Deryck Cooke in his book, *The Language of Music*, London, New York, 1959.

A later phrase, drawn from the closing bars of the Clarinet Elegy, echoes an
amorous passage from Herod's music in *Salome*:

Ex. 292

Ex. 293

Suddenly day breaks. Mephistopheles, dressed as court chaplain, is in
conversation with the Duke. Their dialogue is accompanied by the restlessly
brilliant music from the closing Ciaconna of the *Toccata*, interwoven with
elements from Mephisto's aria in Vorspiel II. One of his utterances unambiguously explains the meaning of the falling seventh:

Ex. 294

Once again, and for the last time, he triumphs. The turning point in the drama
is represented by the meditative
Symphonic Intermezzo a slightly abbreviated version of the *Sarabande* op.
51. The beauty of this music conceals a wealth of symbols, both musical and
extra-musical.

In the era of Bach and Händel, the sarabande was considered to be a dance
measure of dignity and solemnity; during the course of the ensuing centuries it
often came to stand for the enigmatic or mystical. Thus one finds sarabande
rhythm in the opening bars of Beethoven's 'Egmont' Overture and in the 'Ihr
stürzt nieder' of the Ninth Symphony, in the finale of Brahms's Fourth

Symphony and in Tristan's first confrontation with Isolde. The triple rhythm of the sarabande, which occurs so frequently in the score of *Doktor Faust*, can also be traced to various sources intimately associated with Busoni: in the speech rhythm of Oehlenschlaeger's *Hymn to Allah* and of the *Chorus mysticus* in Goethe's *Faust* Part II; in the Commendatore's words, 'Ribaldo, audace! lascia a'morti la pace!' from the graveyard scene of *Don Giovanni* and as the *grandioso* fourth theme of Liszt's Piano Sonata.

In *Doktor Faust* the number three often dictates rhythmical or melodic contours and even influences matters of harmony and orchestration. In the foregoing musical examples there have been many examples of melodies based on thirds; in many passages the harmony is rich in seventh and ninth chords; in the *Sarabande* itself the groups of flutes, oboe and cors anglais, trombones and even harps and celesta conform to this rule of three, while a trio of solo stringed instruments plays a leading role in the score. Busoni himself admitted having had 'mystical reasons' for introducing three students from Cracow instead of the two of the puppet play.

J. E. Cirlot, the Spanish disciple of Jung, has outlined the numerologists' interpretation of the number three:

> Three symbolizes spiritual synthesis, and is the formula for the creation of each of the worlds. It represents the solution of the conflict posed by dualism. The reconciling function of the third element represents the magic or miraculous solution desired and sought after; but this third element may . . . also be negative.[39]

In the 'sphinx' at the head of the *Sarabande* score we detect precisely such a 'solution of the conflict posed by dualism' (see pp. 259–60).

In music, the third is often forged into an endless chain or magic circle of notes, which hence becomes a symbol of power. In Brahms, a preoccupation with chains of falling thirds can be followed from his earliest to very last works, reaching its most striking application in the third of the *Four Serious Songs* op. 121 ('O Tod, wie bitter bist du'). Those leitmotifs in Wagner's *Ring* which express power are also based on chains of thirds. Here are just two examples:

Ex. 295

Wagner : 'Ring' Motif

Ex. 296

Wagner : 'Valhalla' Motif

Many musicologists have noted that Liszt's *Faust Symphony* opens with a twelve-note row; but few, if any, have commented on the deeper significance of this chain of thirds as a Faustian magic circle:

Ex. 297

All these, and many more, are striking examples of what Schoenberg once described (in a letter to Busoni, dated 24.8.1909) as 'the cabbalistic mathematics' of tonal harmony. These properties of our musical language are natural phenomena, recognized by the Ancient Greeks and rationalized by the Pythagoreans; phenomena which speak straight to our inner selves.

There is a paradox which intensifies the symbolism of Busoni's Faustian language still further: in music, three times three makes seven:

Ex. 298

And with seven we come to Mephistopheles. Until the advent of serialism, the falling major seventh had been a comparatively rare interval in Western music, generally to be found in a context of death or evil. Hence the unison command, 'Morrà' (he shall die), in the sextet of *Don Giovanni*, the falling seventh of Pamina's attempted suicide in *Die Zauberflöte*, in Pizzaro's ominous word 'Morden' in his duet with Rocco from *Fidelio*, even in Hagen's exclamation, 'Siegfried's Tod!' *Götterdämmerung* Act II). These and other verbal examples in turn help to throw some light on occurrences of the interval in instrumental music. Here are three specifically Faustian examples of the fateful falling seventh:

Ex. 299

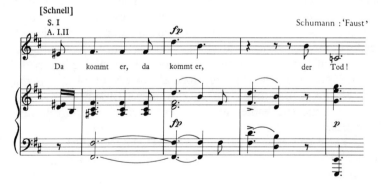

Ex. 300

Ex. 301

In numerology, the number seven is a symbol of perfect order, of the completion of a cycle. Thus, one could take a falling seventh to represent its antithesis—chaos, destruction, negation: the falling major seventh occupies the same position in diatonic music as did the tritone in earlier polyphonic music: 'diabolus in musica'.

It should be stressed that these observations are marginalia, an analysis of the partly subconscious workings of the composer's mind. Yet, in the score of *Doktor Faust*, such symbolic language plays a unifying role akin to that of tonality in a classical symphony or of the note-row in a serial composition.

Second Tableau The scene opens with a rustic minuet in C minor, not unlike a Mahler scherzo. As the curtain rises on the Wittenberg tavern, we see students expounding a mock-Platonic dialogue. The score accordingly breaks into an ingenious parody of 'learned' counterpoint. The students chatter amiable nonsense, but there are serious undertones in what they have to say, especially in the prophetic words of the natural scientist: 'Everything decays, but forms itself anew, transforms itself perpetually, evolving in varied shapes and sorts.' He refers perhaps to Goethe's theory of plants, perhaps to Nietzsche's theory of eternal recurrence; whatever Busoni's actual intention, we can read into the banter of this scene a concise historical survey of philosophies.

Faust, older and gloomier than before, is asked to add his voice to the discussion. He finds only negative words; with them returns his old motto theme (Ex. 302):

Ex. 302

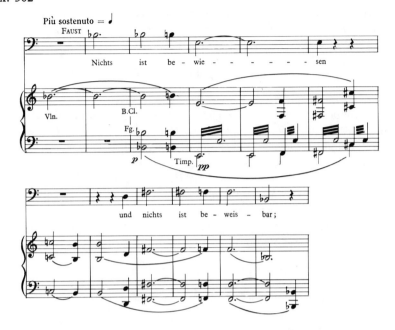

But he still radiates something of his former charm and even love of life. He quotes Luther in praise of wine, women and song. 'Long live Doctor Martin', shout some of the Protestant students. Suddenly there is uproar: the Catholics group together and bawl out a 'Te Deum' while the Lutherans try to out-sing them with snatches of 'Ein fester Burg ist unser Gott'. Some righteously indignant Protestants leave the stage in goose-march; the remaining students embrace one another and empty their glasses.

Busoni composed this entire scene at lightning speed in the summer of 1921. From the scantest of sketches he progressed directly to the fair copy of the full score, all within a period of about ten days, in a scene calling for double chorus and large orchestra, deployed in complex polyphony—testament indeed to his remarkable command and facility as a composer. To Gerda he described the scene as 'technically, probably my most accomplished piece in an opera'.[40]

Silence returns, and Faust reminisces. Clouds of gloom are portrayed almost pictorially (undulating muted string chords set against rising and falling woodwind scales). 'He looks unhappy', murmur some of the students. 'Only he is happy who looks to the future', he replies. As he speaks of the Duchess, the *Polonaise* music from Parma returns, but the reminiscence breaks off uncertainly. 'Does she still think of me?' muses Faust. Now Mephisto rushes in—dressed as a courier, the Duchess's dead child in his arms—to the animated music of the *Scherzoso* from the Piano Concertino of 1921. Mephisto tells his story in Ballad form: the Duchess, dying, had entrusted her new-born child to his care and he flew to Faust with the babe in his arms; but somehow, on the way, it died. Busoni's Ballad has the same scansion as Goethe's 'Song of the Flea', is indeed a transposition of his 'Lied des Mephistopheles' of 1918. True to form, the accompaniment also features a falling seventh:

Ex. 303

while, in adapting the song for the opera, Busoni has also worked the Mephisto motif (Ex. 273) into the accompaniment. The derisive tone of the Ballad is brilliantly caught in the new orchestration, an exemplary piece of legerdemain, recalling in its use of two piccolos certain passages from *Arlecchino*.

The 'child', now revealed as a bundle of straw, is set alight. The *Merlin* motif returns, surrounded by a rising-flame figure in the orchestra (one of the few moments in the score where Busoni indulges in a pictorial effect). Mephisto invokes Helena in a passage evolved from the *Prélude en arpèges* of 1923, based on long, overlapping scale figures:

Ex. 304

In a brief reprise of the *Scherzoso* theme, now in slower tempo, the students leave the room, muttering 'Sacrilege!'. 'Three's a crowd', observes Mephisto sardonically, and vanishes.

The passage which follows is one of the last sections of the score that Busoni lived to complete. Faust calls upon Helena, the 'Dream of Youth'; out of the columns of smoke rising from Mephisto's fire her form slowly emerges, the Ideal incarnate. The wine-cellar disappears and the scene is transformed into the 'visionary picture of a classical landscape'. The music has a simplicity and beauty without equal in the score; it bears out Busoni's remark in a letter to Jarnach written later in 1923: '. . . the greatest continue to develop until their death and leave behind unfulfilled expectations'.[41] Never before in his long career as a composer had Busoni attained such nobility or intangibility.

As Helena's form becomes clearly distinguishable, music from the *Nocturne symphonique* (Ex. 128) is blended into the score and an invisible chorus joins Faust in exhorting her: 'Unattained, Unrecognized, Unfulfilled, step forth!' It was Busoni's belief that it was, under certain circumstances, possible to see and communicate with figures from the past. Shortly before composing the *Nocturne symphonique*, he wrote to Petri of his theory:

Assuming the omnipresence of Time (which is harder to disprove than to postulate), it should be possible for a particularly qualified person, at a particularly clairvoyant moment, to perceive an individual from 'other' times; naturally not as a ghost, but in whichever way the moment affects the individual.[42]

In his 'Traum der Jugend' we find Busoni's musical realization of this 'particularly clairvoyant moment'.

The following scene, in which Helena dances, evades Faust's attempts to grasp her and eventually vanishes, was never composed. We know that the score would have included a glass harmonica, quite possibly the same music for that instrument intended for the *Nocturne symphonique* but never written. Since 1913, Busoni had actually acquired his own glass harmonica, probably in Zurich; a magnificent instrument as he described it, with a compass of four octaves. 'Mais je n'ai pas encore appris à la manière (not as easy as playing the piano)', he wrote to Albert Biolley.[43] Although he never managed to pluck these sounds out of the air and write them down, he had expressed something of their nature some years before, in his essay 'The Realm of Music': 'Listen, every star has its rhythm and every world its measure. And on each of the stars and each of the worlds, the heart of every separate living being is beating in its own individual way. And all the beats agree and are separate yet are a whole.' These words seem to hark back to Ancient Greece, once again, and to the theories of the Pythagoreans. Lucian, for example, once wrote: 'The chorus of the stars, the relationships of the planets to the fixed stars, the eurhythmics of their community and their ordered harmony were the model for the first dance.'[44] It would seem that it was such a 'music of the spheres' which Busoni sought; music to match this prophetical confrontation of the present day with the world of antiquity.

Jarnach has provided an abbreviated, stop-gap solution to the problem of the missing Helena scene, taking a passage from the *Nocturne symphonique*, then adding twenty-five bars in his own flamboyant style. Busoni's own score resumes at the words, 'Mankind is not yet ready for perfection'. Once the vision has vanished, the wine-cellar becomes visible again. Faust, who remains in his state of heightened perception, can now see as far into the future as into the past. He sings a long monologue of indescribable eloquence and beauty.

Solemn fanfares shatter the mood abruptly, and the three students from Cracow appear. Music drawn from the *Sarabande* accompanies their brief scene with Faust and, after their departure, it is with further music from the *Sarabande, con calore*, that the Tableau comes to an end.

Apart from the opening scene with the students and Mephisto's Ballad, there are no closed forms in the Second Tableau. As Faust becomes freer and more deeply perceptive, the musical argument becomes correspondingly more refined, less graspable, cast in a free form independent of harmonic conventions or motivic links.

Final Tableau The first half of this scene, the students' serenade and Faust's last entrance, dates from the summer and autumn of 1918: the sketch for the orchestral introduction and the night-watchman's call are both dated 18–19 July, while the scene with Wagner was hastily written down on 4–5 September of that year. The full score of the opening scene was then completed on 18 September, while Faust's soliloquy, up to the point where voices are heard from inside the Minster, was completed on 10 October. The chorale ('Christ lag in Todesbanden'), and hence the continuation of the scene, was copied out on 1 April 1921, headed 'To myself on my birthday', and later used for the third Albumleaf. The scene of the visions was then continued in the autumn of 1922 and the full score officially breaks off at Faust's words, 'O beten, wo die Worte finden? Sie tanzen durchs Gehirn wie Zauber . . . [formeln]' (bar 491, vocal score p. 310). A further eleven bars of full score exist, crossed out by Busoni in red pencil; of these, the first four are to be found on the last page of the manuscript, while the page containing the other seven has been used as wrapping material for other *Faust* sketches in the Berlin archive. These bars, reproduced in short score, break off at precisely the moment where Helena's music would have to return. They appear here in print for the first time:

Ex. 305

The Final Tableau opens with a solemn Andante in C, originally conceived as the opening tutti of a flute concerto, the slow movement of which was to be the Albumleaf for Flute in an expanded orchestral version. Busoni wrote of his plan to Albert Biolley: 'J'ai dû m'apercevoir que en realité j'avais travaillé à la musique pour Faust, et (contre mon intention) le Tutti s'est transformé sous ma plume en une introduction au dernier tableau.'[45]

The curtain rises and, in the distance, we hear the night-watchman's horn, followed by his call. The bareness of the snow-covered street is mirrored in the music, spun out of long, sinking canonic phrases in the strings, based on the Mephisto motif (Ex. 273). Students appear, and a jovial note is struck at once. The material for their entrance originates in a projected set of Nocturnes for piano, of which Busoni only completed the first, a Prologo (dated 20 May 1918), a mere twenty-three bars long. This is the only unpublished satellite work for the opera, light, delicate and extremely simple to play, in Busoni's Mozartian manner (see Facsimile 42).

Soon the pompous old professor takes his leave, whereupon the students tune their instruments and sing a lusty serenade, framed by a vigorous ritornello in 6/8 time. At its second appearance, the night-watchman calls again while, during its third reprise, the students flee at his approach; their song disappears into the distance.

Faust enters, physically a broken man. An unfinished fragment of a second Nocturne, entitled 'Il Sagramento', written in October 1918, furnishes the thematic material for his soliloquy. It was from this short minor-key contrapuntal study that the whole middle section of the *Sarabande* was also later built. Voices are heard from inside the Minster, singing the chorale from the third Albumleaf (to Busoni's own text, 'Der Tag des Gerichts. . .'). Faust stoops to succour the beggar woman crouched on a doorstep with a child in her arms (music from the Fantasia of the *Toccata*). The ghost of the Duchess hands him their child 'for the third time'; the music of her vision scene, now more dramatic and urgent, underlies her words, 'Finish the work before midnight'. She vanishes.

The air is full of noises, whirling woodwind scales, an eery orchestration of a passage from the organ music of the Scenic Intermezzo. 'My evil spirits are playing their tricks', observes Faust. As he steps towards the church door, the ghost of the murdered soldier, the girl's brother, bars his way, and a male voice chorus, echoed by trombones, thunders out his prayer of vengeance. It is with a restatement of further music from the Scenic Intermezzo that Busoni's score here breaks off.

We know that Philipp Jarnach undertook the completion of the score of *Doktor Faust* with considerable reluctance. And understandably so, for the task facing him was immense. Although he based his completion to a large extent on themes from earlier passages in the opera, he also incorporated a good deal of his own material. Here a certain bombastic element appears, a tendency to passionate outbursts, which contradicts the powerful restraint shown by Busoni throughout the score. This may seem strange in a composer who professed such reverence for Busoni's maxims of Young Classicality, but one only needs to read through the score of Jarnach's *Sinfonia brevis*, also composed in 1925, to ascertain that his style had developed along very different paths to those of his master and that his dense handling of the orchestra had nothing more in common with the transparency of Busoni's Faustian textures. A degree of stylistic discrepancy was certainly inevitable; more disturbing is the fact that Jarnach has overlooked some crucial points in relation to the drama as a whole. Apart from the question of the cut in the libretto, discussed above, there is, first, his setting of Mephisto's last line, 'Has this man met with an accident?' Jarnach notates it in a kind of *Sprechstimme*, out of keeping with the entire role and implying a certain alienating superiority in Mephisto at this point—like that of Arlecchino—which reverses Busoni's intentions. We have also noted that all the major scenes of the opera, indeed all Busoni's major works, are based in C major. Yet, for no good reason at all, Jarnach has chosen to conclude in an almost Wagnerian E flat minor. Of the intended Christmas bells at the close there is no trace.*

In his defence, it must be stated that there were several pressures on Jarnach while he was preparing the score of the closing scene: from the Busoni family, who evidently spurred him to the task much against his will, from the opera house in Dresden, naturally eager to have a complete score at the earliest opportunity and, one can safely assume, from his own conscience. To an intelligent musician, and one who had known Busoni extremely closely, the very performance of such a task must have appeared almost sacrilegious. Thanks to his efforts, the opera was rendered performable. One must be grateful for that. But honest opinion is bound to find his contribution less than ideal.

Two alternative ways of concluding the opera can be considered. The first returns to Busoni's original conception whereby, as he told Dent, the *Sarabande* should immediately precede Faust's death. One would accordingly cut the Symphonic Intermezzo from the opera and use the unabbreviated score of the *Sarabande* to accompany Faust's last monologue. Only a vocal line would have to be devised. Then, just before the close, as Faust dies, Mephisto's midnight call would interrupt the flow, after which the piece would run its course, leading directly into the 'Campane di Natale' music from the fourth Sonatina, with which the opera would end. Bearing in mind that G. B. Shaw found the *Sarabande* 'a very interesting piece from which the vocal line has been removed', this reconstruction could perhaps be artistically viable.

Alternatively one would carry out the plan which Busoni drew up on his last birthday.†

The music with which the score breaks off is extended with material from the second of the Five short pieces for the cultivation of part-playing, written

---

* An orchestral sketch dated 27.8.1919, headed 'Debole Imitazione di Campane' for brass, glockenspiel, four tamtams and organ, may have been intended for the final scene. Its material is similar to the opening of the Symphonia.

† Author's note. Between 1976 and 1982 I worked sporadically on a reconstruction of Busoni's final plan. In 1984 the orchestral and vocal scores of my version were published by Breitkopf und Härtel, Wiesbaden. The Helena scene uses music from the

in 1923. The text 'So sei das Werk vollendet' takes the theme of the Trills Study (Ex. 260), accompanied by the semiquaver figure of the 'Zigeunerlied' (Ex. 244). This is followed by the middle section of the *Sarabande*, more powerfully orchestrated (which Jarnach actually does give us in his completion). 'Hilf Sehnsucht', the text to which Faust draws his magic circle in the snow, uses material from the earlier magic circle ceremony in Vorspiel II (Ex. 268), but now in the major key. The soul transference itself ('Blut meines Blutes. . .') uses the music of the third of the Five short pieces, polyphonically enriched, in one uninterrupted flow. Faust's death is accompanied by music from the Study for the third pedal (Ex. 261), giving way to the night-watchman's call, now accompanied by bells. As Mephisto drags the body away, the music of the song 'Schlechter Trost' appears (Ex. 247), after which a drop curtain falls. The closing music is drawn from the Study for the third pedal, now joined by off-stage chorus.

The sheet of manuscript paper on which Busoni drew up this detailed plan was for fifty years the property of Philipp Jarnach. Evidently it was not made available to him until several years after the world première of the opera.

In both of the versions suggested here, the music for the transformation of the face of Christ into that of Helena is missing. This link is provided (in very sketchy form, however) by a passage of eleven bars which draws on motifs from the Trills Study. In a shaky hand Busoni has added the text of the passage in question: 'Damnation! Is there no mercy? Is there no atonement?' This is probably the last music the composer ever lived to write down.

Doktor Faust is an opera that can only be adequately performed in the largest and best equipped theatres. For the roles of Faust and Mephistopheles truly exceptional singers are required, not only in terms of stamina (Faust scarcely leaves the stage; Mephisto has to battle with his extremely high tessitura) but also in terms of acting ability of the first order and total commitment to the roles. The demands made upon the chorus, both on and off the stage, also put the work beyond the reach of any but the largest houses. These factors have tended to scare conductors and producers away from the piece and it can be safely said that there has never yet been a production which has done full justice to it. A fair number of concert performances of the opera have done much to keep interest in the work alive, however, and have helped to establish it as one of the great and rare masterpieces of twentieth-century opera.

At the first performance of *Doktor Faust* in Dresden, conditions were far from ideal. The score had been delivered in isolated fragments, as and when they were ready, so that little idea could be gleaned of the overall shape until shortly before the dress rehearsal. The casting was not entirely successful: the

---

Sonatina seconda and the 1924 Trills study (see Chapter XXI). The final scene, which is 155 bars longer than Jarnach's version, closely follows the outline drawn up by Busoni on 1 April 1924 (Staatsbibliothek Preussischer Kulturbesitz, N. Mus. MS. 11,3).

role of Mephistopheles proved too high for the tenor, Theo Strack, while Robert Burg, in the title role, seems to have sung well, but not identified himself any too closely with his part. There was universal acclaim for Meta Seinemeyer's Duchess, but she had sustained an injury in one of the final rehearsals and sang the première under duress. The painter Karl Dannemann (a pupil of Max Slevogt) had sketched the sets for this production several years earlier in Zurich, and they had won Busoni's wholehearted approval. Whether the production, by the theatre's Intendant, Alfred Reucker, came up to Busoni's expectations seems doubtful, however; certainly, considering the restricted rehearsal time, this seems unlikely. Universal praise was expressed for Fritz Busch, the conductor, while many critics singled out Jarnach's contribution to the score for special acclaim. It was, at least, an auspicious première attended by a select and sophisticated public, many of whom had journeyed down from the I.S.C.M. Festival, which had just closed in Prague.

Unfortunately, as with *Die Brautwahl*, the publishers were unable to prepare the vocal score in time for the first performance (it only appeared several months later) while, although the Kiepenheuer edition of the libretto had been available for five years, very few of the critics seem to have read it. Therefore it was hardly surprising that most of them failed to come to terms with the meaning of the work. H. Platzbecker, writing for the *Neue Musik-Zeitung*, was one of many who missed the point of the final scene. According to him, Faust 'collapses at the foot of the Cross, with a vision of spiritual reincarnation'.[46] Eugen Schmitz, in *Die Musik*, misinterpreted Busoni's description of the work as a puppet play, finding an absence of 'naïvety, which is anyway . . . thoroughly foreign to Busoni'.[47] Paul Stefan, writing for the *Musikblätter des Anbruch*, was virtually alone in grasping the message of this new version of the Faust legend, of 'the will for knowledge and for impact, which vanquishes death and the Devil'. Many of his colleagues, even if left in the dark, agreed with him in his description of the opera as 'a drama of thrilling greatness'.[48] Paul Schwers (*Allgemeine Musik-Zeitschrift*) wrote, '*Busoni has written nothing of greater worth*' and ascribed the only moderate success of the première to the fact that 'this is an art not attuned to our present tastes'.[49] Hermann Gurtler (*La Revue Musicale*) was more honest, if also more non-committal: 'Les dix années pendant lesquelles Busoni a écrit sa partition furent des années de transition. Il est encore impossible aujourd'hui de juger à son prix la valeur de l'oeuvre.'[50] Those who knew Busoni well were a little disappointed at the conservativeness of the idiom in the score. According to Bernard van Dieren:

> Some of Busoni's admirers would have been happier to see a new departure. . . . As it happened, with his early death, it was better that the work should have been a final autosynthesis. This . . . increased the chances for the understanding of his last work, and thereby of the previous ones.[51]

In the first fifty years of its existence, *Doktor Faust* was staged over twenty times and there have also been several notable concert performances. It was taken up before the Second World War by most of the larger theatres in the German-speaking world, where its complexity and its lofty aspirations often gave it the renommée of a latter-day *Parsifal*. Adrian Boult was the first to prove the effectiveness of the work in the concert hall, introducing it to British listeners at a BBC concert in 1934 (using Edward Dent's translation). In the Berlin production of 1954, Dietrich Fischer-Dieskau proved himself the finest living interpretor of the title role and his performance was later preserved on record. The opera remains a rarity, a fact which has served to surround it with an aura of mystery.

This was indeed Busoni's intention. As he wrote in his essay, 'The Score of *Doktor Faust*': 'Taking its cue from the old Mystery plays, opera should be cast in the form of a ceremony, unconventional, half-religious, uplifting but also stimulating and entertaining.'[52] Through the experiences of *Die Brautwahl* and *La nuova commedia dell'arte* he had learned to transfer his entire world of the spirit, his hopes and fears, his loneliness and his laughter to the world of the theatre. Through the over-leisurely pace of his first stage work and the breakneck speed of *Arlecchino* he had learned to erect an edifice of monumental proportions which nevertheless maintains an uninterrupted span of dramatic tension.

Where *Doktor Faust* differs most radically from Busoni's earlier stage works is the strong polyphonic element in the score. Nowhere do we find the severely disciplined counterpoint of the *Fantasia Contrappuntistica*; rather a flexible and organic polyphonic language which appears to evolve naturally out of the melodic invention. As Kurt Weill wrote:

> Polyphony is not an end in itself in Busoni's Faust-opera, it is the only possible musical means of expressing the Faustian material, as much the milieu of this opera as the Turkish colouring in 'Entführung' or the Spanish rhythms of 'Carmen', and its single function is that of accompanying the work's central figure through all stages of the turning of perception into sound.[53]

Some of the most telling passages of the score, on the other hand, are the plainest: the distant din of bells which opens the work, the stark, Gothic chords of the organ prelude, the home-spun pastoral music of the peasants at Parma, the serene music of the 'Traum der Jugend' soliloquy in the Second Tableau. Busoni's Gothic harmonies, which we first found in the church-vision scene from *Die Brautwahl* and in the music of the third and fourth Sonatinas, are here brought to perfection and played off with the greatest effect against the free tonality of the rest of the score. Yet, even in the most 'advanced' passages of the opera, many an idea seems to recall the musical language of distant times and near-forgotten composers. Busoni himself was aware of this mysterious ancestry: Leichtentritt once sent him his edition of Monteverdi madrigals, which drew the following—revealing—response:

Although I scarcely knew this old Italian music, I identify myself very closely with it: a tinge of atavism, which must be lying dormant in me, draws me towards it.—You will come upon a few phrases in Faust which betray a heredity for which I can find no other explanation.[54]

The Faustian language of Busoni's score, whether contrapuntal or homophonic, whether looking to the past or to the future, whether eclectic or popular in tone, proves itself to be capable of the widest range of expression, never failing in its role of faithful companion to the highly involved psychological and philosophical idea inherent in the Faustian journey which was his life's work.

A brief spoken epilogue to *Doktor Faust* serves to indicate the meaning of this journey:

> Still unexhausted all the symbols wait
> That in this work are hidden and concealed;
> Their seeds a later school shall procreate
> Whose fruits to those unborn shall be revealed.
> Let each take what he finds appropriate;
> The seed is sown, others may reap the field.
> So, rising on the shoulders of the past. . . .
> Mankind will close the circle at the last.[55]

Yet the significance of the opera, symbolically at least, lies in the very fact of its incompleteness.

We come to the end of Busoni's journey, of his search for Aladdin's Cave, without having quite attained it. The 'Realm of Music', the vast subterranean space of his imagination, dominated by the organ pipes of the voice of Nature, proves itself to be nothing more than a dream. Strindberg, indeed, evoked this same image in his *Dream-Play* (he called it 'Fingal's Cave') and compared its conch shape to the interior of the human ear. His implication—which Busoni knew and endorsed—would seem to be that the search for the music of the 'World-Organ' is a journey into one's own soul, a dream-journey. And many have come to share Busoni's love of dreaming, have found dreams more convincing than reality, have found a freedom in dreaming that is not granted to us in reality.

Appendix A
Chronological catalogue of Busoni's works

Reference has been made to five principal sources:

1) the Busoni catalogue published by Breitkopf & Härtel in 1924
2) Edward Dent's catalogue, published as appendix to his biography of Busoni
3) Friedrich Schnapp's catalogue of MSS in the Busoni Archive. The contents of the archive are divided between the Staatsbibliothek Preussischer Kulturbesitz, Music Department, in West Berlin (SPK) and the Deutsche Staatsbibliothek, Music Department, in Berlin GDR (DSB)
4) Ulrich Prinz's chronological survey of Busoni's piano compositions, published in his thesis of 1970 (see Bibliography)
5) Jürgen Kindermann's *Thematisch-chronologisches Verzeichnis der Werke von Ferruccio Busoni*, published in 1980 (see Bibliography).

Those works of Busoni's which are purely transcriptions or cadenzas are listed in Appendix B. Some MSS of earlier works are untraceable and a number of unpublished works are undated, making the task of strict chronology virtually impossible. Kindermann's catalogue, the first serious attempt at organizing Busoni's extensive oeuvre, lists the works chronologically, but incorporates the published items according to date of publication rather than of composition. This accounts for some of the discrepancies between his catalogue and the one below. A number of errors and omissions in Kindermann have been corrected here, mostly thanks to the availability of material from lesser-known or private collections.

Busoni's use of opus numbers is misleading. Although his numbering bears no relation to the actual date of composition it is retained here in the following manner: the opus number of a published work is placed before the title, that of an unpublished work after the title (sometimes there are two of these). Titles printed in bold type are works discussed in this book, those in square brackets are unfinished, those in italics are lost or untraceable. The titles of works are given in their original languages, but as follows: not Berceuse pour le piano (as is printed on the title page of that work) but Berceuse, for piano. Key signatures are only given where the composer himself has included them in the title of a particular work. Unless otherwise indicated, the date of composition given is that of completion.

Canzone op. 1, for piano. Comp. June 1873. MS: SPK.

'Berceuse' op. 2, for piano. Comp. June 1873. MS: SPK.

Introduzione, Tempo di Walzer e Finale op. 3, for piano. Comp. Aug. 1873. MS: SPK.

Cadenza-Esercizio op. 4, for piano. Comp. Sept. 1873. MS: SPK.

Studio op. 5, for piano. Comp. Oct. 1873. MS: SPK.

Tema con Variazioni op. 6, for piano. Comp. Oct. 1873. MS: SPK.

Menuetto op. 17, for piano. Comp. 5.10.1873. MS: SPK (also a second copy dated 15.10.1873).

Preghiera alla Madonna, 'Vergin santa benedetta Madre' (Ferdinando Busoni) op. 7, for voice and piano. Comp. 15.10.1873. MS: SPK.

Marcia funebre op. 8, for piano. Comp. 22.2.1874. MS: SPK.

Romanza senza parole op. 9, for piano. Comp. 24.5.1874. MS: SPK.

Canzone popolare op. 13, for piano. Comp. 17.9.1874. MS: SPK.

La Canzone del Cacciatore op. 10, for piano. Comp. 20.9.1874. MS: SPK.

Preludio op. 11, for piano. Comp. Oct. 1874. MS: SPK. The same, transcr. for clarinet and piano. Comp. 12.7.1875. MS: SPK.

Scherzo op. 14, for piano. Comp. Oct. 1874. MS: SPK.

Inno-Variato op. 12, for piano. Comp. Nov. 1874. MS: SPK.

Polka op. 16, for piano. Comp. Jan. 1875. MS: SPK.

Scherzo in B flat major op. 15, for piano. Comp. Feb. 1875. MS: SPK.

Preludio op. 18, for clarinet and piano. Comp. 26.2.1875, rev. 14.7.1875. MS: SPK.

Preludio op. 19, for piano. Comp. March 1875. MS: SPK.

Preludio op. 20, for piano. Comp. March 1875. MS: SPK.

Sonata in D major, for piano. Comp. 20.8.1875. MS: SPK.

Fuga a 2 voci in stile libero, for piano. Comp. 23.8.1875. MS: SPK.

Studio in C major, for piano. Comp. 29.8.1875. MS: SPK.

Fuga a 3 voci, for piano. Comp. 2.9.1875. MS: SPK.

Gavotta, for piano. Comp. 26.9.1875. MS: SPK.

Inno, for piano. Comp. 28.9.1875. MS: SPK.

Studio contrappuntato, for piano. Comp. 14.10.1875. MS: SPK.

Capriccio in C minor, for piano. Comp. 1.11.1875, rev. 1.12.1875. MS: SPK.

Presto in C minor, for piano. Comp. 25.11.1875. MS: SPK.

Invenzione a due voci, for piano. Comp. 2.12.1875. MS: SPK.

Inno, for piano. Comp. 5.12.1875. MS: SPK.

Mandolinata, for piano. Comp. 25.12.1875. MS: SPK.

Waltzer da Concerto. Momento Musicale, for piano. Comp. 25–7.12.1875. MS: SPK.

Fuga a tre voci, for harmonium or organ. Comp. 5.1.1876. MS: SPK.

'Du bist wie eine Blume' (Heine), for voice and piano. Comp. 24.1.1876. MS: SPK.

Scherzo in C minor, for piano. Comp. 11.2.1876. MS: SPK.

String quartet no. 1. Comp. 20–3.2.1876, rev. 6.12.1877. MS: SPK.

'Die Abendglocke schallet', for voice and piano. Comp. 3.3.1876. MS: SPK.

Marcia funebre, for piano. Comp. 15.3.1876. MS: SPK.

Sonata in C major, for violin and piano. Comp. 19.3.1876. MS: SPK.

String quartet no. 2. Comp. 28.4.1876 (1st movement). MS: SPK.

Fantasie-Impromptu, for piano. Comp. 6.6.1876. MS: SPK.

Wiegenlied: 'Schlafe süß in Gottes Schoß', for voice and piano. Comp. 15.6.1876. MS: SPK.

Il Dolore. Romanza senza parole, for piano. Comp. 21.6.1876. MS: SPK.

Menuetto, for piano. Comp. 3.7.1876. MS: SPK.

Fughetta, for piano. Comp. 9.9.1876. MS: SPK.

[Ouverture, for orchestra. Also for piano duet (MS lost). Comp. 1876. MS: SPK.]

Gavottina op. 3 no. 3, for piano. Comp. 11.11.1876. MS: SPK. (Evidently intended for Cinq Pièces, op. 3.).

op. 3. Cinq Pièces, for piano: Preludio, Minuetto, Gavotta, Etude, Gigue. Publ. Cranz, Leipzig, (?) 1877.

Meditazione, for piano. Comp. 10.12.1876. MS: SPK.

Invention, for piano. Comp. 31.12.1876. MS: SPK.

Studio, for piano. Comp. 1.1.1877. MS: SPK.

Allegretto, for piano. Comp. 8.1.1877. MS: SPK.

Fuga in G major, for piano. Comp. 23.1.1877. MS: SPK.

Waise und Rose, 'Wie bin ich armes Kind allein', for mezzo-soprano and piano. Comp. 7.3.1877. MS: SPK.

['Deh si guarda benedetta', for SATB. Comp. 11.5.1877. MS: SPK.]

[2 pieces op. 6, for piano. Comp. (?) May 1877. MS: SPK.]

Sonata no. 1 in C major op. 7, for piano. Comp. 20.5.1877. MS: SPK.

Invenzione, for piano. Comp. 20.6.1877. MS: SPK.

Menuetto, for string quartet. Comp. 24.6.1877. MS: SPK.

Sonata no. 2 in D major op. 8, for piano. Comp. 5.7.1877. MS: SPK. Scherzo publ. Lucca, Milan, (?) 1882. MS: Ricordi, Milan.

Antiphon, 'Salve decus patriarcharum', for soprano, mezzo-soprano, baritone and harmonium. Comp. 19.8.1877. MS: SPK.

Preludio 'Du bist wie eine Blume', for piano. Comp. 4.9.1877. MS: SPK.

[Sonata no. 3 in E major op. 9, for piano. Comp. 14.9.1877. MS: SPK.]

Allegro fugato, for piano. Comp. 30.9.1877. MS: SPK.

op. 1. 'Ave Maria', for voice and piano or string orchestra. Comp. (?) 1.10.1877, transcr. 20.6.1878. Version with piano publ. Spina, Vienna, (?) 1878. MS (string version): SPK.

'Salve Regina' op. 2 (op. 4), for mezzo-soprano and piano or string orchestra. Comp. 9.10.1877. MS (both versions): SPK.

'Pater noster', for mezzo-soprano, three-part male-voice choir and piano or harmonium. Comp. 23.12.1877. MS: SPK.

L'Invalido op. 31, 'Ho quarant' anni per la patria' (Michele Buono), Ballata, for tenor and piano. Comp. 31.12.1877. MS: SPK.

Suite op. 10, for clarinet and piano. Comp. 1877. MS: SPK. (Only one movement ·exists, also numbered op. 11.)

Menuetto op. 4, for piano. Comp. 1.2.1878. MS: SPK.

Toccata op. 4, for piano. Comp. 17.2.1878. MS: SPK.

Studio in C minor op. 12, for piano. Comp. Feb. 1878. MS: SPK.

Andante ed Allegro vivace op. 13, for string quartet. Comp. 23.2.1878. MS: SPK.

op. 14. Menuetto, for piano. Comp. 26.2.1878. Publ. Lucca, Milan, (?) 1882. MS: Ricordi, Milan. Republ. Ricordi, Milan, 1927 (ed. Gino Tagliapietra), together with Gavotta op. 25.

Preludio e Fuga in C major op. 15, for piano left hand. Comp. 27.2.1878. MS: SPK.

Fuga in stile libero op. 16, for piano. Comp. 5.3.1878. MS: SPK.

Concerto op. 17, for piano and string quartet (obbligato). Comp. 21.3.1878. MS: SPK.

op. 18. Suite campestre, 5 pezzi caratteristici, for piano. Canzone Villereccia del Mattino (op. 5). Comp. 3.4.1878; La Caccia (op. 6). Comp. 2.4.1878; L'Orgia (op. 7). Comp. 4.4.1878; Il Ritorno (op. 9). Comp. 5.4.1878; Preghiera della Sera (op. 10). Comp. 1.4.1878. Publ. Breitkopf & Härtel, Wiesbaden, 1981 (ed. Franzpeter Goebels). MS: SPK.

'Pater noster' a tre voci op. 20. Comp. 6.4.1878. MS: SPK.

[Piano piece, untitled. Comp. 6.4.1878. MS: SPK.]

Preludio in F minor op. 19, for piano. Comp. 5.5.1878. MS: SPK.

op. 21. Preludio e Fuga in C minor, for piano. Comp. 13.5.1878. Publ. Lucca, Milan, (?) 1880. MS: Ricordi, Milan and SPK (fugue only). Republ. Ricordi, Milan, (?) 1926, (ed. Gino Tagliapietra), together with Preludio e Fuga op. 36.

Tristezza, 'Dimmi perchè si pallido' (Heine, trans. Vincenzo Baffi) op. 22, for mezzo-soprano and piano. Comp. 18.5.1878. MS: SPK.

Antiphon, 'Tota pulchra es Maria' op. 23, for SATB. Comp. 13.6.1878. MS: SPK.

Suite op. 10, for clarinet and piano. Comp. May–June 1878. MS: SPK.

[Andante maestoso, for orchestra (undated). MS: DSB.]

[Preghiera alla Madonna, 'Vergin santa benedetta' for SATBB (undated). MS: DSB.]

Andante, for piano (undated).

[*Moderato, for piano (undated).*]

Andante con moto (dietro l'antico stile), for piano (undated).

Piano piece in B minor (untitled, undated).

Piano piece in D minor (untitled, undated). MS: DSB.

op. 25. Gavotta, for piano. Comp. 11.7.1878. Publ. Lucca, Milan, (?) 1880. MS: Ricordi, Milan. Republ. Ricordi, Milan, 1927 (ed. Gino Tagliapietra), together with Menuetto op. 14.

Minuetto op. 12 (op. 26), for piano. Comp. 22.7.1878. (Later publ. as no. 1 of Danze antiche op. 11.) MS: Ricordi, Milan.

Graduale delle Messe comuni della Madonna, 'Benedicta et venerabilis es' op. 27 (op. 15), for mezzo-soprano, SATB and organ or piano. Comp. 30.7.1878. MS: SPK.

op. 2. 'Ave Maria', for voice and piano. Comp. (?) Aug. 1878. Publ. Spina, Vienna, (?) 1879.

[Rhapsodie hongroise op. 28, for piano. Comp. 4–22.9.1878. MS: SPK.]

'Salve Regina' op. 29, for contralto and piano. Comp. 30.9.1878. MS: SPK.

op. 38. Lied der Klage, 'Die Luft ist trübe' (Otto von Kapff), for alto voice and piano. Comp. 14.10.1878. Publ. Cranz, Hamburg, (?) 1879. MS: SPK.

op. 39. Des Sängers Fluch, 'Es stand in alten Zeiten' (Uhland), ballad for alto voice and piano or orchestra. Comp. (?) Nov. 1878, orch. 13.4.1879. Version with piano publ. Cranz, Leipzig, (?) 1879. MS (orchestral version): SPK.

'Ave Maria' in the style of Palestrina op. 11, for SATB. Comp. 20.10.1878. MS: SPK.

Piece for violin and piano op. 70 (untitled). Comp. Nov. 1878.

Rondo brillant, for piano. Comp. Nov. 1878.

Preludio e Fuga op. 32, for 2 pianos. Comp. 5.12.1878. MS: SPK.

Solo dramatique op. 13 (op. 33), for clarinet and piano. Comp. 2.2.1879. MS: SPK.

Missa I. op. 34, for SATB. Comp. 12.2.1879. MS: SPK.

Menuetto op. 15 (op. 25), for string quartet. Comp. 12.2.1879. MS: SPK.

Capriccio op. 36, for 2 pianos. Comp. 21.2.1879. MS: SPK.

'Benedicta et venerabilis es' op. 16, for SAB. Comp. 1.4.1879. MS: SPK.

Scherzo op. 17, for piano. Comp. May 1879.

Andantino op. 41 (op. 18), for clarinet and piano. Comp. 4.5.1879.

Serenade no. 2 op. 42 (op. 19), for clarinet and piano. Comp. 4–31.5.1879.

Piece for piano duet op. 43 (untitled). Comp. (?) May 1879.

[Concerto for piano and orchestra op. 46, in one movement. Comp. (?) May 1879.]

Scherzo op. 47 (op. 20), for string quartet. Comp. 31.5.1879.

Variationen über ein Minnesängerlied aus dem XIII. Jahrhundert op. 48 (op. 22), for piano and violin. Comp. 23.6.1879.

Sternenlied, 'Es glänzt am Himmel Stern an Stern' (Oskar von Redwitz) op. 49 (op. 23), for alto voice and piano. Comp. 26.6.1879.

Präludium und Fuge in D minor op. 51 (op. 26), for piano. Comp. 23.7.1879.

Novelette op. 52 (op. 27), for clarinet and piano. Comp. 2.8.1879.

Scherzo op. 53 (op. 28), for piano. Comp. 14.8.1879.

Scherzo in A minor op. 54 (op. 29), for piano. Comp. 20.8.1879.

'Stabat Mater' op. 55, for SSATBB and strings. Comp. Aug. 1879.

Tragische Geschichte, 'Es war einer dem's zu Herzen ging' (Chamisso) op. 56 (op. 30), for low voice and piano. Comp. Oct. 1879.
The same for TTBB (undated). MS: DSB.

'Lieb Liebchen, leg's Händchen aufs Herze mein' (Heine) op. 57 (op. 31), for soprano and piano. Comp. (?) 2.10.1879.

'Es fiel ein Reif in der Frühlingsnacht' (trad. Rheinland) op. 59 (op. 33), for mezzo-soprano and piano. Comp. 13.10.1879

Märchen op. 60 (op. 34), for cello (or clarinet) and piano. Comp. Oct. 1879.

op. 61. Menuetto capriccioso in C major, for piano. Comp. Oct. 1879. Publ. Spina, Vienna, 1880 (together with Gavotte op. 70).

Introduzione e Capriccio, for 2 pianos. Comp. (?) Nov. 1879.

op. 11. Danze antiche, for piano. Minuetto op. 26 (op. 12). Comp. 22.6.1878; Gavotta op. 62 (op. 35). Comp. 13.12.1879; Gigue op. 63 (op. 36). Comp. 22.12.1879; Bourée (undated). Publ. Lucca, Milan, (?) 1882. MS: Ricordi, Milan. Republ. Ricordi, Milan, (?) 1926 (ed. Gino Tagliapietra).

'Kyrie' op. 64, for SATB. Comp. 30.12.1879.

Andante e Tarantella, for piano (undated). MS: DSB.

String Quartet no. 3 [in F minor] (undated). MS: DSB.

Allegretto, for string quartet (undated). MS: DSB.

[Andante Sostenuto–Allegro Vivace, for string quartet (undated). MS: DSB.]

Sonata in D major, for piano and clarinet (undated). MS: DSB.

Novellett, for clarinet and piano (undated). MS: DSB.

[Piece for clarinet and piano (untitled, undated). MS: DSB.]

['Non torna più', for voice and piano (undated). MS: DSB.]

'Mein Herz gleicht dem Meere' (Heine), for voice and piano (undated). MS: DSB.

'Espère enfant demain' (Victor Hugo), for voice and piano. Comp. (?) 1880. MS: DSB.

['Gloria', for SATB. Comp. 1.1.1880. MS: DSB.]

[Das Erkennen op. 65, for voice and piano. Comp. 20.1.1880. MS: DSB.]

['Ave Maria' op. 67, for voice and strings (undated). MS: DSB.]

Praeludium [und] Fuge in D major a 3 voci, for piano. Comp. 30.2.1880. MS: DSB.

Marsch op. 41, for piano. Comp. 5.4.1880.

op. 70. Gavotte in F minor, for piano. Comp. 11.4.1880. Publ. Spina, Vienna, 1880. MS: DSB.

Invention, for piano. Comp. 14.5.1880. MS: DSB.

Der Tanz: (Walzer), for piano (undated). MS: DSB.

Fugue in F major on a theme of W. A. Remy, for piano (undated). MS: DSB.

Duo op. 73 (op. 43), for 2 flutes and piano. Comp. (?) June 1880. MS: DSB.

op. 10. Tre Pezzi nello stile antico, for piano. Menuett op. 40. Comp. 2.4.1880;

Sonatine op. 46. Comp. July 1880; Gigue op. 75 (op. 44). Comp. June 1880. Publ. Lucca, Milan, (?) 1882. MS: Ricordi, Milan. Republ. Ricordi, Milan, 1927 (ed. Gino Tagliapietra).

Praeludio [und] Fuge op. 75, for piano. Comp. May 1880. MS: DSB.

op. 7. Praeludium (Basso ostinato) und Fuge (Doppelfuge zum Choral), for organ (op. 76). Comp. 23.1.1880 and 30.6.1880. Publ. Cranz, Hamburg, 1881. MS: DSB. Republ. Cranz, London, 1973.

Frühlingslied, 'Ich grüße euch liebe Vögelein' (Otto von Kapff) op. 44, for TTBB. Comp. (?) June 1880. MS: DSB.

Rondo op. 77 (op. 45). for piano. Comp. July 1880. MS: DSB.

Scherzo op. 47, for piano. Comp. Aug. 1880.

[Impromptu op. 48, for clarinet and piano. Comp. Aug. 1880. MS: DSB.]

[Piece for clarinet and piano (untitled, undated). MS: DSB.]

Phantasiestück op. 49, for piano. Comp. Aug. 1880.

Sonate [in F minor] op. 49 (op. 50), for piano. Comp. 1.9.1880. MS: DSB.

Praeludium & Fuge in D major op. 73, for piano. Comp. Oct. 1880.

Praeludium [und] Fuge in G minor op. 74, for piano. Comp. Oct. 1880. MS: DSB. Rev. and transposed (?) 1885. MS: DSB.

op. 31. Zwei Lieder. 'Wer hat das erste Lied erdacht' (Victor Blüthgen), for mezzo-soprano or tenor and piano; 'Bin ein fahrender Gesell' (Rudolf Baumbach) (op. 77), for bass or baritone and piano. Comp. 12.10. 1880. Publ. Vicentini, Trieste, (?) 1884. MS: DSB and Museo del Teatro Verdi, Trieste. Republ. Breitkopf & Härtel, Leipzig, 1919.

Missa in honorem Beatae Mariae Virginis op. 51, for double chorus. Comp. (?) Nov. 1880. MS: DSB.

Scherzo op. 52, for violin, cello and piano. Comp. Nov. 1880.

Der Wirtin Töchterlein, 'Es zogen drei Burschen' (Uhland) op. 45 (op. 53), for TTBB. Comp. Nov. 1880. MS: DSB.

'Guten Abend, gute Nacht' (Des Knaben Wunderhorn), for TTBB. Comp. (?) Nov. 1880. MS: DSB.

Motet, 'Gott erbarme sich unser' op. 55, for SATB and piano or orchestra. Comp. 15.11.1880, orch. 23.12.1880. MSS: DSB.

Six short piano pieces (untitled, undated). MS: DSB.

Studio in A minor, for piano. Comp. (?) 1880. MS: DSB.

Suite, for clarinet and string quartet. Comp. (?) 1880. MS: DSB.

[Introduzione e Fuga sopra un Corale di G. S. Bach, for orchestra. Comp. (?) 1881. MS: DSB.]

Andante mit Variationen op. 18, for violin, cello and piano. Comp. 1881. MS: DSB.

String quartet no. 2 in C major op. 56. Comp. Jan–Feb. 1881 and Dec. 1881–Jan. 1882. MS: DSB.

Praeludium [und] Fuge, for piano. Comp. 1.4.1881. MS: DSB.

op. 36. Preludio e Fuga, for piano. Comp. 10.4.1881. Publ. Lucca, Milan, 1882. MS: Ricordi, Milan. Republ. Ricordi, Milan, 1926 (together with op. 21) and 1934 (ed. Gino Tagliapietra).

op. 37. 24 Préludes, for piano. Comp. May 1881. Publ. Lucca, Milan, 1881. MS: Ricordi, Milan. Republ. Ricordi, Milan, 1927 (ed. Gino Tagliapietra).

Requiem (Missa funebre), for soli, chorus and orchestra. Comp. May–July 1881. MS: DSB.

Fuge in C op. 72, for piano. Comp. 1881.

op. 9. Una Festa di Villaggio, 6 pezzi caratteristici, for piano. Comp. Dec. 1881. Publ. Lucca, Milan, (?) 1882. MS: Ricordi, Milan. Republ. Ricordi, Milan, 1926 (ed. Gino Tagliapietra). 5th movt. (Danza) publ. in *Album of piano music by Italian composers*, Boston, 1915 (ed. G. V. Palladino).

Notturno, for clarinet and piano (undated).

Fuga op. 57, per l'esame di Bologna. Comp. 27.3.1882. MSS: DSB and Liceo Musicale, Bologna.

op. 12. Racconti Fantastici. 3 Pezzi caratteristici, for piano. Comp. (?) 1882. Publ. Trebbi, Bologna, 1882. Republ. Breitkopf & Härtel, Wiesbaden, 1981 (ed. Franzpeter Goebels).

op. 13. Danza Notturna, for piano. Comp. 16.6.1882. Publ. Trebbi, Bologna, 1882.

op. 35. 'Ave Maria', for baritone and orchestra or piano. Comp. 22–23.6.1882. Publ. Lucca, Milan, (?) 1882. MS: Nino Bezzi.

op. 40. Le quattro stagioni (Francesco dell'Ongaro), for male voice soli and chorus, with orchestra or piano. Comp. July 1882. Publ. Lucca, Milan, 1882. MS: Ricordi, Milan. 1st movt. (La Primavera) also exists in a version for TTBB a capella (in German). MS: DSB.

Il Sabato del Villaggio (Giacomo Leopardi), poema campestre, for soli, chorus and orchestra. Comp. 5.8.1882. MS (orch. and vocal scores): SPK.

Introduction et Scherzo, for piano and orchestra. Comp. Oct. 1882, rev. Aug. 1884. MS: DSB.

op. 32. Marcia di Paesani e Contadine (Una Festa di Villaggio), for piano. Comp. 4.8.1883. Publ. Vicentini, Trieste, 1883. MS: Museo del Teatro Verdi, Trieste. (Intended as replacement for 2nd movt. of Una Festa di Villaggio.)

op. 33. Macchiette medioevali, for piano. Comp. 1882–3. Publ. Trebbi, Bologna, 1883. Republ. Breitkopf & Härtel, Wiesbaden, 1982 (ed. Franzpeter Goebels).

op. 34. Serenata, for cello and piano. Comp. 1.1.1883. Publ. Lucca, Milan, (?) 1883. MS: Ricordi, Milan.

op. 16. Six études, for piano. Comp. 1883. Publ. Gutmann, Vienna, 1884.

Etude en forme d'Adagio d'une Sonate (no. 15). Comp. 1883. MS: DSB.

Etude no. 16 (Nocturne), for piano. Comp. 1883. MS. DSB.

Etude no. 18 in F minor, for piano. Comp. 14.2.1883. MS: DSB.

op. 17. Etude en forme de variations, for piano. Comp. (?) 1883. Publ. Gutmann, Vienna, 1884.

op. 25. Symphonische Suite, for orchestra. Comp. Aug. 1883. Publ. Kahnt, Leipzig. 1888. MS (4th movt. only): DSB. 2nd movt. (Gavotte), arr. for piano, publ. Breitkopf & Härtel, Leipzig, 1888 (dubious).

op. 4, 5 and 6. Trois morceaux, for piano. Scherzo, Prélude et Fugue, Scène de Ballet. Comp. (?) 1883. Publ. Wetzler, Vienna, 1884. Republ. Doblinger, Vienna–Munich, 1976.

Sonata in F minor op. 20, for piano. Comp. Christmas 1883. Publ. Breitkopf & Härtel, Leipzig, 1983 (ed. Jutta Theurich). MS: DSB.

op. 18. Zwei altdeutsche Lieder, 'Wohlauf! Der kühle Winter ist vergangen' (Neidhard von Reuenthal) and 'Unter den Linden' (Walter von der Vogelweide), for voice and piano. Comp. (?) 1884. Publ. Kistner, Leipzig, 1884. No. 2 orch. 1893, MS: DSB.

'So lang man jung' (Alice Worms) op. 16, for male voice chorus and orchestra. Comp. Jan. 1884. MS: DSB.

op. 30. Album vocale, for voice and piano: Il fiore del Pensiero (Ferdinando Busoni); L'ultimo sonno (Michele Buono); Un organetto suona per la via (Lorenzo Stecchetti); Ballatella, 'Luna fedel ti chiamo' (Arrigo Boito). Comp. 10.2.1884. (No. 2:3.7.1879) Publ. Vicentini, Trieste, (?) 1884. MS: Museo del Teatro Verdi, Trieste.

op. 15. Zwei Lieder, 'Ich sah die Träne' and 'An Babylons Wassern' (Byron). Comp. March 1884 (no. 1 rev. 1901). Publ. Gutmann, Vienna, 1884.

Eine alte Geschichte in neue Reime gebracht, 'Es hat Mirza Jussuf ein Lied geschrieben' (Bodenstedt), melodrama for voice and piano (undated). MS: DSB.

Gesang aus Mirza Schaffy, 'Auf dem Dache stand sie, als ich schied' (Bodenstedt), for voice and piano. Comp. 1884. MS: Collection Walter Labhart.

op. 19. String quartet in C. Comp. (?) 1884. Publ. Kistner, Leipzig, 1886.

op. 20. Zweite Balletszene, for piano. Comp. 1884. Publ. Breitkopf & Härtel, Leipzig, 1885.

op. 22. Variationen und Fuge in freier Form über Fr. Chopin's C-moll-Präludium (op. 28 no. 20), for piano. Comp. 1884. Publ. Breitkopf & Härtel, Leipzig, 1885.

['Es blüht ein Blümlein', for TTBB. Comp. 17.1.1885. MS: DSB.]

Invenzione, for piano. Comp. 28.7.1885. MS (facsimile): DSB.

Tempo di minuetto, for orchestra. Comp. (?) 1885. MS: DSB.

op. 24. Zwei Lieder. Lied des Monmouth, 'Es zieht sich eine blut'ge Spur' (Fontane); 'Es ist bestimmt in Gottes Rat' (E. von Feuchtersleben). Comp. 21.8.1885 and March 1884. Publ. Kahnt, Leipzig, 1886. MS: Kahnt, Lindau. Republ. Breitkopf & Härtel, Leipzig, 1919.

op. 23. Kleine Suite, for cello and piano. Comp. 1886. Publ. Kahnt, Leipzig and Breitkopf & Härtel, Leipzig, 1886.

Anhang zu Siegfried Ochs 'Kommt a Vogerl g'flogen', [five variations] for piano. Comp. (?) 1886. MS: DSB.

Fughette, for violin and piano. Comp. (?) 1886.

Fantasie über Motive aus 'Der Barbier von Bagdad', komische Oper von Peter Cornelius, for piano. Comp. Dec. 1886. Publ. Kahnt, Leipzig, 1887.

Kanon. Huldigung der Töne FBB, dargebracht den Tönen aRemi. Comp. March 1887.

Transcrizione di Concerto sopra motivi dell'opera 'Merlin' del Maestro Carl Goldmark, for piano. Comp. May 1887. Publ. Lucca, Milan, 1888. MS: Ricordi, Milan.

op. 26. String quartet no. 2 in D minor. Comp. June 1887. Publ. Breitkopf & Härtel, Leipzig, 1889.

op. 27. Finnländische Volksweisen, for piano duet. Comp. 1888. Publ. Peters, Leipzig, 1889. MS: Centro Studi Musicali Ferruccio Busoni, Empoli.

Piece for piano (untitled, undated). MS: DSB.

op. 28. Bagatellen, for violin and piano. Comp. (?) 1888. Publ. Peters, Leipzig, 1888. MS: Daniell Revenaugh.

Fuge über das Volkslied 'O, du mein lieber Augustin', for piano duet. Comp. June 1888. MS: DSB. Publ. Breitkopf & Härtel, Wiesbaden, 1985 (ed. Franzpeter Goebels).

[Ouvertüre zu einem gedachten Singspiele nach der Tradition des 'Lieben Augustins', for orchestra (undated). MS: DSB.]

[Marche Funèbre, for orchestra (undated). MS: DSB.]

[Sonata I, for piano (two unfinished movts., undated). MS: DSB.]

[Sigune, oder das stille Dorf. Opera in 2 acts and a prelude. From a tale by Rudolf Baumbach, adapted by L. and Fr. Soyaux. Comp. 1.2.1885–June 1889. Libretto publ. privately, Leipzig, (?) 1887. Complete short score, orchestral score of prelude: DSB.]

Concert-Fantasie op. 29, for piano and orchestra. Comp. Dec. 1888–89. MS: DSB. (Later rev. as Symphonisches Tongedicht.)

Kultaselle. Zehn kurze Variationen über ein finnisches Volkslied, for piano and cello. Comp. (?) May 1889. Publ. Rudolf Dietrich, Leipzig and Breitkopf & Härtel, Leipzig, 1891.

op. 29. Sonata [no. 1] for violin and piano. Comp. 1889. Publ. Rahter, Hamburg, 1891.

op. 30a. Zwei Klavierstücke. Contrapunctisches Tanzstück, Kleine (III) Ballet-Scene. Comp. 1889. Publ. Rahter, Hamburg, 1891. Rev. 1914 as Waffentanz and Friedens-tanz, publ. Breitkopf & Härtel, Leipzig, 1914.

op. 31a. Konzertstück (Introduction und Allegro), for piano and orchestra. Comp. 1889–June 1890. Publ. Breitkopf & Härtel, Leipzig, 1892. MS: DSB.

Chorlied der Deutschen in Amerika, 'Nicht festgebannt an Deutschlands mächt'ge Eichen', for TTBB. Comp. (?) 1892. MS: DSB.

op 32a. Symphonisches Tongedicht. Comp. 1.3.1893. Publ. Breitkopf & Härtel, Leipzig, 1894. MS: DSB.

Ballade, for piano (undated). MS: DSB.

[Introduktion, Marsch, Walzer, for orchestra. Comp. (?) 1894. MS: DSB.]

op. 33a. Vierte Balletszene in Form eines Concert–Walzers, for piano. Comp. June 1894. Publ. Breitkopf & Härtel, Leipzig, 1894. Rev. 16.2.1913, publ. Breitkopf & Härtel, Leipzig, 1913. MS (rev. version): DSB.

[5ᵉ Scène de Ballet, for piano (undated). MS: DSB.]

op. 33b. Stücke, for piano. Comp. 1895. Publ. Peters, Leipzig, 1896. MS sketches for no. 5 (Finnische Ballade): DSB.

op. 34a. Geharnischte Suite, for orchestra. Comp. 1894–5. Rev. 1903. Publ. Breitkopf & Härtel, Leipzig, 1905.

op. 35a. **Concerto in D major, for violin and orchestra.** Comp. 1896–March 1897. Publ. Breitkopf & Härtel, Leipzig, 1899.

op. 36a. **Sonata no. 2, for violin and piano.** Comp. May 1898 and Aug. 1900. Publ. Breitkopf & Härtel, Leipzig, 1901. MS: SPK.

op. 38. **Eine Lustspielouvertüre,** for orchestra. Comp. July 1897. Rev. 1904. Publ. Breitkopf & Härtel, Leipzig, 1904.

op. XXXIX. **Concerto per un Pianoforte principale e diversi strumenti ad arco a fiato ed a percussione.** Aggiuntovi un coro finale per voci d'uomini a sei parti. Le parole alemanne del poeta Oehlenschlaeger danese. Comp. 1901–13.8.1904. Publ. Breitkopf & Härtel, Leipzig, 1906. Cadenza rev. 1909, publ. 1909. Version without chorus arr. 1908 (MS: Daniell Revenaugh).

Music for Gozzi's 'Turandot', for orchestra and female voices. Comp. June 1905.

op. 41. **Suite aus der Musik zu Gozzi's Märchendrama Turandot,** for orchestra and female voices. Arr. (?) August 1905. Publ. Breitkopf & Härtel, Leipzig, 1906.

Elegien. 6 neue Klavierstücke. Comp. Sept. 1907–1.1.1908. Publ. Breitkopf & Härtel, Leipzig, 1908. MS (mostly sketches): DSB.

Nuit de Noël. Esquisse, for piano. Comp. Dec. 1908. Publ. Durand et Fils, Paris, 1909.

Berceuse, for piano. Comp. 5.6.1909. Publ. Breitkopf & Härtel, Leipzig, 1909. MS: Staatsarchiv, Leipzig.

Fantasia nach Johann Sebastian Bach, for piano. Comp. 8.6.1909. Publ. Breitkopf & Härtel, Leipzig, 1909. MS: DSB.

An die Jugend. Eine Folge von Klavierstücken. Comp. June–Aug. 1909. Publ. Jul. Heinr. Zimmermann, Leipzig, 1909. MS (only sketches): DSB.

op. 42. **Berceuse élégiaque.** Des Mannes Wiegenlied am Sarge seiner Mutter. Poesie, for small orchestra. Comp. 27.10.1909. Publ. Breitkopf & Härtel, Leipzig, 1910. MS: DSB.

Grosse Fuge. Kontrapunktische Fantasie über Joh. Seb. Bach's letztes unvollendetes Werk, for piano. Comp. Jan.–1.3.1910. Publ. Schirmer, New York, 1910 (limited edition). MS: DSB.

Fantasia Contrappuntistica. Preludio al Corale 'Gloria al Signore nei Cieli' e Fuga a quattro soggetti obbligati sopra un frammento di Bach. **Edizione definitiva,** for piano. Comp. June 1910. Publ. Breitkopf & Härtel, Leipzig, 1910.

Sonatina, for piano. Comp. 4.8.1910. Publ. Jul. Heinr. Zimmermann, Leipzig, 1910. MS: DSB.

Die Brautwahl. Musikalisch-fantastische Komödie nach E. T. A. Hoffmann. Text by Ferruccio Busoni. Comp. 2.2.1906–8.10.1911. Publ. Harmonie Verlag, Berlin, 1912 (full score 1914). MS: DSB. (Also MS libretto).

Verzweiflung und Ergebung, from the music for Gozzi's drama 'Turandot' op. 41. Comp. 1911. Publ. Breitkopf & Härtel, Leipzig, 1911.

Sonatina seconda, for piano. Comp. May–6.7.1912. Publ. Breitkopf & Härtel, Leipzig, 1912. MS: DSB.

[Operetten Musik, for Wedekind's 'Franziska'. Comp. July 1912. MS: DSB.]

Choral-Vorspiel und Fuge über ein Bachsches Fragment (Der 'Fantasia contrappuntistica' kleine Ausgabe), for piano. Comp. 20.7.1912. Publ. Breitkopf & Härtel, Leipzig, 1912. MS: DSB.

op. 45. Die Brautwahl Suite for orchestra. Arr. Aug. 1912. Publ. Breitkopf & Härtel, Leipzig, 1917.

op. 43. Nocturne symphonique, for orchestra. Comp. Oct. 1912–6.7.1913. Publ. Breitkopf & Härtel, Leipzig, 1914. MS: Breitkopf & Härtel, Wiesbaden.

op. 44. Indianische Fantasie, for piano and orchestra. Comp. April 1913–22.2.1914. Publ. Breitkopf & Härtel, Leipzig, 1915. MS: Staatsarchiv, Leipzig.

[Su monte Mario, 'Solenni in vetta a Monte Mario' (Carducci), for baritone and orchestra. Comp. 18.8.1914. MS: SPK.]

'Floh-Sprung'—Canon mit oblig. Bass. Comp. 21.8.1914. Publ. (facsimile of MS) in *Zeitschrift für Musik*, 1932, p. 1095.

op. 46. Rondò arlecchinesco, for orchestra and tenor solo. Comp. 8.6.1915. Publ. Breitkopf & Härtel, Leipzig, 1917. MSS: Library of Congress, Washington and DSB.

Sonatina ad usum infantis Madeline M★ Americanae, for piano. (Pro clavicimbalo composita). Comp. (?) July 1915. Publ. Breitkopf & Härtel, Leipzig, 1916.

Indianisches Tagebuch. Erstes Buch. Vier Klavierstudien über Motive der Rothäute Amerikas, for piano. Comp. June–8.8.1915. Publ. Breitkopf & Härtel, Leipzig, 1916. MS (sketches): DSB.

op. 47. Gesang vom Reigen der Geister. Indianisches Tagebuch. Zweites Buch, for small orchestra. Comp. Aug.–30.12.1915. Publ. Breitkopf & Härtel, Leipzig, 1916. MS: DSB.

op. 50. Arlecchino. Ein theatralisches Capriccio, in one act. Text by Ferruccio Busoni. Comp. Nov.–Dec. 1914, Nov. 1915–8.8.1916. Publ. Breitkopf & Härtel, Leipzig, 1917 (full score 1918). MS: DSB.

Improvisation über das Bachsche Chorallied 'Wie wohl ist mir, o Freund der Seele', for 2 pianos. Comp. June–26.8.1916. Publ. Breitkopf & Härtel, Leipzig, 1917. MS: DSB.

Albumblatt, for flute (or muted violin) and piano. Comp. 1916. Publ. Breitkopf & Härtel, Leipzig, 1917. Arr. for piano solo, publ. Breitkopf & Härtel, Leipzig, 1918.

Turandot. Eine chinesische Fabel nach Gozzi in zwei Akten. Text by Ferruccio Busoni. Comp. Dec. 1916–March 1917. Publ. Breitkopf & Härtel, Leipzig, 1918 (vocal score only).

Altoums Warnung. Zweiter Anhang zur Turandot-Suite op. 41. Comp. (?) 1917. Publ. Breitkopf & Härtel, Leipzig, 1918.

Sechs Klavierübungen und Präludien. (Der Klavierübung erster Teil). Comp. 10.9.–10.10.1917. Publ. Breitkopf & Härtel, Leipzig, 1918. MS: DSB.

Sonatina in diem nativitatis Christi MCMXVII, for piano. Comp. 22.12.1917. Publ. Breitkopf & Härtel, Leipzig, 1918. MS: Breitkopf & Härtel, Wiesbaden.

op. 48. Concertino, for clarinet and small orchestra. Comp. March–April 1918. Publ. Breitkopf & Härtel, Leipzig, 1918.

[**Lied des Brander,** 'Es war eine Ratt' im Kellernest' (Goethe), for baritone and piano. Comp. (?) March 1918. Publ. Breitkopf & Härtel, Wiesbaden, 1964. MS: DSB.]

op. 49. Zwei Gesänge. Altoums Gebet, 'Konfutse, dir hab' ich geschworen' (Busoni); Lied des Mephistopheles, 'Es war einmal ein König' (Goethe), for male voice and small orchestra. Comp. 1917 and 30.3.1918. Lied des Mephistopheles also for male voice and piano. Publ. Breitkopf & Härtel, Leipzig, 1919. MS (Lied des Mephistopheles only, both versions): DSB.

Lied des Unmuts, 'Keinen Reimer wird man finden' (Goethe), for baritone and orchestra or piano. Comp. (?) May 1918, orch. 20.2.1924. Publ. Breitkopf & Härtel, Leipzig, 1919 (orch. version: 1964.) MS (orch. version): DSB.

['Es war ein König in Thule' (Goethe), for voice and piano. Comp. 1918. MS: DSB.]

['Wie an dem Tag, der dich der Welt verliehen' (Goethe), for voice and piano. Comp. 1918. MS: DSB.]

['Freudvoll und leidvoll' (Goethe), for voice and piano. Comp. 1918. MS: DSB.]

Notturni. Prologo, for piano. Comp. 20.5.1918. MS: DSB.

Drei Klavierübungen und Präludien (der Klavierübung zweiter Teil). Comp. 7.11.1917–7.6.1918. Publ. Breitkopf & Härtel, Leipzig, 1919. MS: DSB.

Sonatina brevis. In Signo Joannis Sebastiani Magni, for piano. Comp. 19.8.1918. Publ. Breitkopf & Härtel, Leipzig, 1919. MS: SPK.

op. 51. Sarabande und Cortège. Zwei Studien zu 'Doktor Faust', for orchestra. Comp. Dec. 1918–Jan. 1919. Publ. Breitkopf & Härtel, Leipzig, 1920.

[Eldorado. 'Gladly bedight a gallant knight' (Poe), for voice and piano. Comp. 10.6.1919. MS: DSB.]

Elegie, for clarinet and piano. Comp. Sept. 1919 and Jan. 1920. Publ. Breitkopf & Härtel, Leipzig, 1921. MS sketch: DSB.

Kammer-Fantasie über Carmen, for piano. Comp. 20.3.1920. Publ. Breitkopf & Härtel, Leipzig, 1920. MS: DSB.

op. 52. Divertimento, for flute and small orchestra. Comp. 24.5.1920. Publ. Breitkopf & Härtel, Leipzig, 1922. MS: DSB.

Toccata. Preludio—Fantasia—Ciaconna, for piano. Comp. July–21.9.1920. Publ. in *Musikblätter des Anbruch*, Vienna, Jan. 1921. Republ. Breitkopf & Härtel, Leipzig, 1922. MSS: Daniell Revenaugh and Bibliothèque Nationale, Paris.

op. 53. Tanzwalzer, for orchestra. Comp. 2.10.1920. Publ. Breitkopf & Härtel, Leipzig, 1922. MS: DSB.

Lo Staccato. (Der Klavierübung dritter Teil). Comp. 31.12.1919–10.3.1921. Publ. Breitkopf & Härtel, Leipzig, 1921. MS: DSB.

Drei Albumblätter, for piano. Comp. 1917, April 1921, 25.5.1921. Publ. (no. 1 only) Breitkopf & Härtel, Leipzig, 1918. (All three) Breitkopf & Härtel, Leipzig, 1921. MS (no. 2): DSB; (no. 3): SPK.

op. 54. Concertino. Romanza e Scherzoso, for piano and orchestra. Comp. 21.6.1921. Publ. Breitkopf & Härtel, Leipzig, 1922. MS: DSB.

Nachtrag zu Turandot, 'Diese Zeichen von Trauer'. Comp. 22.6.1921. MS: (sketch) DSB; (copy) Breitkopf & Härtel, Wiesbaden.

Fantasia Contrappuntistica. Choral-Variationen über 'Ehre sei Gott in der Höhe' gefolgt von einer Quadrupel-Fuge über ein Bachsches Fragment, **for 2 pianos.** Comp. 3.7.1921. Publ. Breitkopf & Härtel, Leipzig, 1922.

Die Bekehrte, 'Bei dem Glanze der Abendröte' (Goethe), for female voice and piano. Comp. 22.9.1921. Publ. Breitkopf & Härtel, Leipzig, 1937. MS: Library of Congress, Washington.

[Die Spröde, 'An dem reinsten Frühlingsmorgen' (Goethe), for voice and piano. Comp. Sept. 1921. MS: University of Tennessee, Knoxville.]

Perpetuum mobile (nach des Concertino II. Satz op. 54), for piano. Comp. Feb. 1922. Publ. Breitkopf & Härtel, Leipzig, 1922.

Zehn Variationen über ein Präludium von Chopin, for piano. Comp. 28.4.1922. Publ. Breitkopf & Härtel, Leipzig, 1922. MS: Ronald Stevenson.

Variationen. Perpetuum mobile. Tonleitern. (Der Klavierübung fünfter Teil). Comp. 8.5.1922. Publ. Breitkopf & Härtel, Leipzig, 1922. MS: DSB.

Prélude et Etude en Arpèges, for piano. Comp. 29.1.1923 and 12.2.1923. Publ. Heugel, Paris, 1923. MS: University of Tennessee, Knoxville and Stiftung Rychenberg, Winterthur.

Grausige Geschichte vom Münzjuden Lippold aus der Oper 'Die Brautwahl', for voice and orchestra. Comp. 16.2.1923–2.3.1923. MS: DSB (also of vocal score).

Reminiscenza Rossiniana, 'Caro Dent due paroline in confidenza' (Busoni), for voice and piano. Comp. 3.3.1923. Publ. (facscimile of MS) in Edward J. Dent: *Ferruccio Busoni, a biography*. Clarendon Press, Oxford, 1933, pp. 278–9.

op. 55 no. 2. Zigeunerlied, 'Im Nebelgeriesel, im tiefen Schnee' (Goethe), for baritone and orchestra or piano. Comp. 27.3.1923. Publ. Breitkopf & Härtel, Leipzig, 1923. Piano version first publ. in *Die Musik*, Jg. XV, 8 May 1923. Publ. Breitkopf & Härtel, Leipzig, (?) 1923. MS (orch. version only): DSB.

Lied der Schieber am Kurfürstendamm, 'Wir schieben, wir schieben' (Busoni), for unison choir and piano. Comp. 20.4.1923. MS: SPK.

Fünf kurze Stücke zur Pflege des polyphonen Spiels auf dem Pianoforte. Comp. March–May 1923 (compl. 19.5.1923). Publ. Breitkopf & Härtel, Leipzig, (?) 1925. MS: Daniell Revenaugh.

Klavierübung in zehn Büchern. Zweite umgearbeitete und bereicherte Ausgabe. Comp. Dec. 1923–Jan. 1924. Publ. Breitkopf & Härtel, Leipzig, 1925. MS: DSB, SPK and University of Tennessee, Knoxville.

'Ich hab' gesucht und nichts gefunden' (Busoni), for SSA. Comp. 14.1.1924. Publ. (facsimile of MS) in Ferruccio Busoni: *Wesen und Einheit der Musik*, Max Hesses Verlag, Berlin–Halensee, 1955, p. IX.

Schlechter Trost, 'Mitternachts weint und schluchzt ich' (Goethe), for baritone and orchestra or piano. Comp. 24.2.1924. Publ. (piano version only) in: *Navigare necesse* *est*. Eine Festgabe für Anton Kippenberg zum zweiundzwanzigsten Mai 1924, Inselverlag, Leipzig, 1924, after p. 168. Republ. Breitkopf & Härtel, Wiesbaden, 1960. MS (orch. version only): DSB.

[**Doktor Faust,** Dichtung für Musik. Text by Ferruccio Busoni. Music edited and completed by Philipp Jarnach; newly completed according to Busoni's last sketches by Antony Beaumont (1982). Comp. begun 13.6.1917. Libretto publ. (1) in *Die Weissen Blätter*, Oct.–Dec. 1918, pp. 11–29; (2) Gustav Kiepenheuer, Potsdam, 1920; (3) Breitkopf & Härtel, Leipzig, 1925. Vocal score publ. Breitkopf & Härtel, Leipzig, 1926. MS (photocopies): DSB and Norddeutscher Rundfunk, Hamburg.]

Appendix B

Catalogue of Busoni's transcriptions and cadenzas

As well as the various categories of transcription and arrangement, all Busoni's critical editions or revisions of works by other composers are listed here. The catalogue is based on that of Edward Dent (pp. 346–52 in *Ferruccio Busoni, a biography*), which in turn is derived from the official catalogue published by Breitkopf & Härtel in 1924. Some additional material, particularly with regard to unpublished items, is to be found here.

J. S. BACH

Bach–Busoni Edition

Vol. I: Arrangements I. Study works.
Dedication — 18 little Preludes and a Fughetta — 15 two-part inventions—15 three-part inventions — 4 Duets — Prelude, Fugue and Allegro in E flat major.

Vol. II: Arrangements II. Master works.
Chromatic Fantasy and Fugue — Piano Concerto in D minor — Aria with 30 Variations (Goldberg Variations).

Vol. III: Transcriptions.
Prelude and Fugue in D major for organ — Prelude and Fugue in E flat major for organ — Toccata in D minor for organ — Toccata in C major for organ — 10 Chorale Preludes — Chaconne for violin.

Vol. IV: Compositions and free transcriptions.
Fantasia after J. S. Bach (alla memoria di mio padre Ferdinando Busoni † il 12 Maggio 1909) — Preludio, Fuga e Fuga figurata — Capriccio on the departure of a beloved brother — Fantasia, Adagio e Fuga — Chorale Prelude and Fugue on a fragment by Bach (Versio minore of the Fantasia Contrappuntistica) — Fantasia Contrappuntistica, edizione definitiva.

Vol. V: *The Well-tempered Clavier* (Book I).
Arranged and explained with examples and directions for the study of modern pianoforte technique in connection with it, together with an appendix on the transcription of Bach's organ works for the pianoforte.

Vol VI: *The Well-tempered Clavier* (Book II).
With notes and studies.

Vol. VII: Supplements to Vols. I–IV.
a) Arrangements: Three Toccatas, in E minor, G minor and G major —
Fantasy and Fugue in A minor — Fantasy, Fugue, Andante and Scherzo — b)
Transcriptions: Chromatic Fantasy and Fugue for cello and piano — c)
Compositions and free transcriptions: Improvisation on Bach's chorale-song
'Wie wohl ist mir, o Freund der Seele' for two pianos — Canonical variations
and canonical fugue on the theme by Frederick the Great, from 'A musical
offering' — Sonatina brevis in Signo Joannis Sebastiani Magni — d)
Appendix: Attempt at an organic piano notation.

Included in the first edition of *The Well-tempered Clavier* (Book I): Prelude and Fugue in
E minor for organ.
Bach transcriptions not included in the Bach–Busoni Edition: Sarabande con Partite in
C major; Aria variata alla maniera italiana in A minor.

LUDWIG van BEETHOVEN

Benedictus from the *Missa Solemnis*, transcribed for violin and orchestra (oboe, viola
and cello as obligato voices).
Ecossaises, arranged for concert performance.
Three cadenzas for the Violin Concerto op. 61, for solo violin, strings and timpani.
Beethoven's cadenzas to the Piano Concertos in C major, C minor and G major, edited
by Busoni.
Two cadenzas for the fourth Piano Concerto in G major.
Included in the first edition of Bach's *Well-tempered Clavier* (Book I): Analysis of the
fugue from the Piano Sonata op. 106.

JOHANNES BRAHMS

Six chorale preludes from op. 122 transcribed for piano.
Cadenza, for the Violin Concerto op. 77, for violin and timpani.

FREDERICK CHOPIN

Polonaise in A flat major op. 53, edited by Busoni.
Variations and Variants (in Vol. V of the *Klavierübung*, first edition).

J. B. CRAMER

Eight Etudes (Book I: Legato, Book II: Staccato) (Vol. IV of the *Klavierübung*, first
edition and Book 7 of the second edition).

NIELS W. GADE

Novelletten op. 29, arranged for two pianos, four hands.

CARL GOLDMARK

Merlin. Vocal score.

FRANZ LISZT

(a) FOR PIANO SOLO:

Compositions published by the Franz-Liszt-Stiftung.

II: Piano works: Complete Etudes.

Vol. I. 1. Etüden in zwölf Übungen. 2. Zwölf grosse Etüden. 3. Mazeppa. Vol. II. 4. Etudes d'exécution transcendante. 5. Grosse Bravour-Fantasie über das Glöckchen von Paganini. Vol. III. 6. Bravour-Studien nach Paganinis Capricen. 7. Grandes Etudes d'après Paganini. 8. Salonstück. Etüde zur Vervollkommnung aus der 'Schule der Schulen'. 9. Ab-Irato. 10. Drei Konzert-Etüden. 11. Gnomenreigen. 12. Waldesrauschen.

Other Busoni editions published by the Franz-Liszt-Stiftung: Harmonies du Soir. La Campanella. Gnomenreigen. Concert study no. 3 in D flat major. Waldesrauschen.

Six Paganini Etudes. Revised by Busoni: 1. G minor — 2. E flat major — 3. La Campanella — 4. E major — 5. E major — 6. A minor.

Arrangements for study and concert use. Transcription studies: 1. Tremolo, G minor. 2. Andantino capriccioso, E flat major. 3. La Campanella. 4. Arpeggio, E major. 5. La Chasse, E major. 6. Tema e variazioni, A minor.

Three Fantasies: 1. Fantasy and Fugue on the chorale 'Ad nos, ad salutarem undam' from Meyerbeer's *Le Prophète*, freely transcribed for piano. — 2. Fantasy on two motifs from Mozart's opera *Le Nozze di Figaro*. Completed from the partly unfinished original. — 3. Réminiscences de Don Juan. Concert Fantasy on themes from Mozart's *Don Giovanni*. Critical-instructive edition.

Heroischer Marsch im ungarischen Stil.

Hungarian Rhapsody no. 19. Freely arranged for concert use.

Hungarian Rhapsody no. 20. (Unpubl. MS: SPK.)

Scherzo in G minor.

Mephisto-Waltz (Der Tanz in der Dorfschenke). Newly transcribed from the orchestral score.

Polonaise in E major, with final cadenza.

Coeli enarrant (Psalm 18), arranged for 2 pianos (unfinished. MS: DSB.)

(b) WITH ORCHESTRA:

Spanish Rhapsody, arranged as a concert-piece for piano and orchestra.

Totentanz. Fantasy for piano and orchestra. 'Completed on 21st October 1849'. — First edition based on definitive autographs (the manuscripts in the possession of the Marquis Casanova in Pallanza).

Sonetto 104 di Petrarca ('Pace non trovo'). Transcription for voice and orchestra.

(c) INSTRUMENTAL MUSIC:

Valse oubliée, transcribed for cello and piano.

FELIX MENDELSSOHN-BARTHOLDY

Symphony no. 1 in C minor op. 11, arranged for 2 pianos, 8 hands.

W. A. MOZART

(a) FOR PIANO SOLO:

Cadenzas for piano concertos:
1. E flat major K. 271. — 2. G major K. 453. — 3. F major K. 459. — 4. D minor K. 466. Two versions. — 5. C major K. 467. — 6. E flat major K. 482 — 7. A major K. 488. — 8. C minor K. 491 — 9. C major K. 503.
Three symphonies: D major K. 202; G major K. 318; G major K. 444. Arrangements for piano solo.
Andantino from the Piano Concerto no. 9 in E flat major K. 271, freely transcribed for piano solo, with a cadenza.
Fugue for String Quartet in C minor K. 546, arranged for piano (unfinished. MS: DSB.)

(b) FOR TWO PIANOS:

Duettino Concertante, based on the finale of the Piano Concerto in F major K. 459.
Fantasia for a mechanical organ K. 608. Introduction, Fugue, Andante, Fugue.
Overture to *Die Zauberflöte* K. 620.
Sonata in D major K. 448, for two pianos. Arranged with a cadenza (unpubl. MS: lost, except for cadenza, MS: DSB).

(c) FOR AND WITH ORCHESTRA:

Overture to *Die Entführung aus dem Serail* with a concert ending.
Overture to *Don Giovanni* with a concert ending.
Concert Suite from the opera *Idomeneo*: Overture, Sacrificial Scene, Festal March.
Rondo Concertante, based on the finale of the Piano Concerto in E flat major K. 482, newly arranged for piano and orchestra.
Adagio from the Clarinet Concerto K. 622, edited with a cadenza, for clarinet and orchestra.
Cadenza Strumentata for the slow movement of the Flute Concerto in G major K. 313 (unpubl. MS copy: SPK).
Cadenza Strumentata for the slow movement of the Flute Concerto in D major K. 314 (unpubl. MS copy: SPK).

(d) FOR PIANOLA:

Overture to *Die Zauberflöte* (unpubl. MS: Daniell Revenaugh).

OTTOKAR NOVÁČEK

Scherzo from the First String Quartet, transcribed for piano.

ARNOLD SCHOENBERG

Piano Piece op. 11 no. 2. Concertante transcription (Konzertmässige Interpretation).

FRANZ SCHUBERT

Five German Dances with Coda and seven Trios D. 90. Arranged for piano.
Five Minuets with six Trios and Minuet D. 89. Arranged for piano.
Overture in B flat major D. 470. Arranged for piano.
Overture in D major D. 26. Arranged for piano.
Overture in D major D. 556. Arranged for piano.
Overture in D major (in the Italian style) D. 590. Arranged for piano.
Overture in C major (in the Italian style) D. 591. Arranged for piano.
Overture in E minor D. 648. Arranged for piano.
Overture to the musical comedy *Der Teufel als Hydraulicus* D. 4. Arranged for piano.

ROBERT SCHUMANN

Concert Allegro with Introduction in D minor op. 134. Arranged for two pianos, 4 hands.
Abendlied op. 107 no. 6. Arranged for clarinet and string quartet. (unpubl. MS: DSB).
3 Romances for oboe op. 94. Arranged for clarinet. (Unpubl. MS: DSB).

LOUIS SPOHR

Introduction and Elegy by H. W. Ernst. Arranged for clarinet and string quartet. (Unpubl. MS: DSB).

RICHARD WAGNER

Funeral March for the death of Siegfried from *Die Götterdämmerung*. Piano transcription.

CARL MARIA von WEBER

Clarinet Concerto no. 1 in F minor. Newly arranged with cadenzas. (Unpubl. MS: DSB).

KURT WEILL

Frauentanz op. 10 no. 3, 'Ach wär' mein Lieb ein Brünnlein kalt' (Anon). Arranged for voice and piano.

Select Bibliography

1) PUBLISHED WRITINGS OF BUSONI

Von der Einheit der Musik. Verstreute Aufzeichnungen, Max Hesses Verlag, Berlin, 1922. Revised edition with contributions by Philipp Jarnach, Vladimir Vogel and Joachim Herrmann: *Wesen und Einheit der Musik,* Max Hesses Verlag, Berlin, 1956. English trans.: *The Essence of Music and other papers,* trans. Rosamond Ley. Rockliff, London, 1957 (slightly shortened version of *Wesen und Einheit der Musik*). Republ. Dover Books, New York, 1965.

Sketch (Outline) of a new aesthetic of music. English trans. by Theodore Baker. Publ. Schirmer, New York, 1911. Republ. in: *Three Classics in the Aesthetic of Music,* Dover Publications Inc., New York, 1962.

Lo sguardo lieto: tutti gli scritti sulla musica e le arti, ed. by Fedele d'Amico. Publ. Milan, 1977. (To date the most complete edition of Busoni's writings.)

'Scritti giovanile di Ferruccio Busoni', ed. Piero Rattalino in *Musica d'oggi,* Milan, Anno 2, no. 3–4 (March–April 1959), pp. 105–11.

'Ungedrucktes aus dem Nachlass: Aphorismen; "Das Geheimnis", ein Opernentwurf', in *Blätter der Staatsoper,* Berlin, November 1924, pp. 1–10.

'Music, a look backward and a look forward'. An unpublished article trans. and introduced by Edward J. Dent in *Monthly Musical Record,* June 1932, pp. 99–100.

'Über Melodie. Nachgelassene Skizzen', herausgegeben von Friedrich Schnapp, *Zeitschrift für Musik,* 97. Jg., Feb. 1930, pp. 95–101.

Über die Möglichkeiten der Oper und über die Partitur des 'Doktor Faust'. Publ. Breitkopf & Härtel, Leipzig, 1926. Also included in later editions of *The Essence of Music and other papers.* Republ. Breitkopf & Härtel, Wiesbaden, 1966.

'Ce que doit être un grand pianiste', *La Vie Musicale,* Lausanne, 1909, no. 15.

'Franz Liszts Vorrede zur ersten Kollektivausgabe von Fields Nocturnes', *Die Musik,* Jg. 16, Feb. 1924, pp. 309–16.

.

2) LETTERS

To Edith Andreae. Ed. and foreword by Andres Briner. *Neujahrsblatt der Allgemeinen Musikgesellschaft,* Zürich, 1976.

To and from Béla Bartók. Ed. Denis Dille in *Dokumenta Bartókiana,* Budapest, n.d., pp. 62–71.

To Gerda Busoni (selected letters). In Busoni: *Briefe an seine Frau*, ed. Friedrich Schnapp, foreword Willi Schuh, Zurich/Leipzig, 1935. English edition:*Letters to his wife*, trans. Rosamond Ley. Edward Arnold & Co., London, 1935. Republ. Da Capo Press, New York, 1975.

To the Marchese Silvio della Valle di Casanova. In *Musica Università*, Rome, no. 23, Dec. 1966, pp. 16–25.

To Alfredo Casella and Guido M. Gatti. In Fiamma Nicolodi: *Gusti e tendenze del Novecento musicale in Italia*, Florence, 1982, pp. 245–61.

To Hans Huber. In Edgar Refardt: *Hans Huber*, Zurich, 1939. Also publ. as *Neujahrsblatt der Allgemeinen Musikgesellschaft*, Zürich, 1939.

To Margarete Klinckerfuss. In Klinckerfuss: *Aufklänge aus versunkener Zeit*, Urach, 1947.

To Baroness Jella Oppenheimer (selected letters). In *Neue Zürcher Zeitung*, 21.–22.6.1931.

To Henri and Kathi Petri (selected letters). In *Neue Rundschau*, Berlin, July 1934, pp. 71–84. Ed. and introduction by Friedrich Schnapp.

To Melanie Prelinger. In 'Erinnerungen und Briefe aus Ferruccio Busonis Jugendzeit', *Neue Musik-Zeitung*, 48. Jg., 1927, pp. 6–10, 37–40, 57–61.

To Hans Reinhart (selected letters). In *Die Individualität*, Buch 3, Oct. 1926, pp. 49–53.

To Marcel Rémy. Letter in *Zeitschrift für Musik*, 99. Jg., 1932, p. 1058 (German trans. by Friedrich Schnapp).

To and from Arnold Schoenberg. In *Beiträge zur Musikwissenschaft*, 19. Jg., 1977, Heft 3, pp. 163–211. Ed. by Jutta Theurich.

To Othmar Schoeck. 'Briefe und Widmungen', *Schweizerische Musikzeitung*, March 1966, pp. 132–5.

To Gisella Selden-Goth. *Fünfundzwanzig Busonibriefe*, Vienna–Leipzig–Zurich, 1937.

To Arrigo Serato. In Andrea della Corte: *Arrigo Serato*, Siena, 1950.

'Zwei unbekannte Briefe Busonis' (to an anonymous benefactor; to Raffaello Busoni). Ed. by Willi Reich in *Der Auftakt*, Jg. 16. Prague, 1936, pp. 180–3.

Ferruccio Busoni: Selected Letters. Trans., ed. and foreword by Antony Beaumont. Faber & Faber, London. In preparation. (Chronological edition of 352 letters and the complete Schoenberg–Busoni correspondence.)

3) SPECIAL BUSONI NUMBERS

Musikblätter des Anbruch, Jan. 1921.
Chantavoine, J. P.: 'Ferruccio Busoni'.
Leichtentritt, Hugo: 'Busoni und Bach'.
Jarnach, Philipp: 'Das Stilproblem der neuen Klassizität im Werke Busonis'.
Busoni, Ferruccio: 'Aufzeichnungen und Tagebuchblätter'.
Dent, Edward J.: 'Busoni und das Klavier'. 'Busoni als Komponist'.
Simon, James: 'Der musikalische Stil'.

Selden-Goth, Gisella: 'Das Goethesche in Busoni'.

Draber, H. W.: 'Busoni in Weimar'.

Musical supplement: Toccata, for piano.

Blätter der Staatsoper, Berlin, Heft 7, 13. May 1921 (ed. Julius Kapp).

Zweig, Stefan: 'Busoni'.

Kapp, Julius: 'Schlaglichter auf Leben und Werk'.

Pfohl, Ferdinand: *'Die Brautwahl'*.

Busoni, Ferruccio: *'Arlecchino.* Sein Werdegang'. *'Arlecchino.* Zu seiner Deutung'.

Kapp, Julius: *'Turandot.* Die Dichtung im Wandel der Zeiten'.

Busoni, Ferruccio: 'Zur *Turandot*-Musik'. *'Die Götterbraut.* Heroisch-heiteres Sagenspiel in drei Bildern (Textbuch)'.

Il Pianoforte, Turin, 15 June 1921.

Leichtentritt, Hugo: 'Busoni e Bach'.

Casella, Alfredo: 'Busoni pianista'.

Dent, Edward J.: 'Busoni a Berlino e il *Dottor Faust*'.

Brugnoli, Attilio: 'La cerebralita e il paradossale nell' arte di Ferruccio Busoni'.

Busoni, Ferruccio: 'Pensieri sull'Arte e sulla Musica'.

La Rassegna Musicale, Jan. 1940.

Bontempelli, M.: 'Busoni teorico'.

Casella, A.: 'Busoni pianista'.

Tagliapietra, G.: 'Ferruccio Busoni transcritore e revisore'.

Corti, M: 'Ricordi di Ferruccio Busoni'.

Pannain, G.: 'Il *Dottor Faust*'.

Gui, V.: *'Arlecchino'*.

Previtali, F.: *'Turandot'*.

Dallapiccola, L.: 'Pensieri su Busoni'.

Guerrini, G.: 'Ferruccio Busoni maestro'.

Jarnach, P.: 'In memoria di Ferruccio Busoni'.

Schnapp, F.: 'Ferruccio Busoni e Anton Rubinstein'.

Sulzberger, M. H. S.: 'Ferruccio Busoni nel ricordo di un discepolo'.

L'Approdo Musicale, Turin, 1966, No. 22.

Pinzauti, L.: 'Ferruccio Busoni problema aperto'.

Vlad, R.: 'Busoni'.

Ugolini, G.: *'La sposa sorteggiata*—nascito di uno stile'.

Leibowitz, R.: 'L'arte dell' interpretazione musicale secondo F. B. Busoni'.

Martinotti, S.: 'I Lieder—Primi dati per la vocalità busoniana'.

Malipiero, G. F.: 'I miei incontri con Ferruccio Busoni'.

Vogel, W.: 'Ricordi personali'.

Selden-Goth, G.: 'L'amico dei giovani'.

Piano Quarterly, New York, 28th year, Winter 1979–80, No. 108.

Agostini, Franco: Introduction.

Sitsky, Larry: 'A short survey of the piano music'.

Armstrong, Peter: 'Why play and teach Busoni?'

Beaumont, Antony: 'Busoni and Schoenberg'.

Raessler, Daniel M.: 'Ferruccio Busoni as experimental keyboard composer'.

Johansen, Gunnar: 'Busoni the pianist—in perspective'.

Hsu, Dolores M.: 'The paradox of Busoni'.

Kirby, F. E.: 'New recordings: the six Sonatinas'.

Agosti, Guido: 'The Busoni pupil (interview with Daniel M. Raessler)'.

4) GENERAL BIBLIOGRAPHY

Bekker, Paul: *Kritische Zeitbilder*, Berlin, 1921.
Neue Musik, Berlin, 1919.

Brendel, Alfred: *Musical thoughts and afterthoughts*, London, 1976.

Busoni, Gerda: *Erinnerungen an Ferruccio Busoni*, Berlin, 1958.

Debusmann, Emil: *Ferruccio Busoni*, Wiesbaden, 1949.

Dent, Edward J.: *Ferruccio Busoni, a biography*, Oxford, 1933.

van Dieren, Bernard: *Down among the Dead Men*, London, 1935.

Giazotto, Remo: *Busoni, la vita nell'opera*, Milan, 1947.

Gray, Cecil: *A survey of contemporary music*, Oxford, 1927.

Guerrini, Guido: *Ferruccio Busoni—La vita, la figura, l'opera*, Florence, 1944.

Hilmar, Ernst: *Eine stilkritische Untersuchung der Werke Ferruccio Busonis aus den Jahren 1880–1890*, Diss. Graz, 1962.

Jelmoli, Hans: *Ferruccio Busonis Züricherjahre*, Neujahrsblatt der Allgemeinen Musikgesellschaft, Zurich, 1929.

Kestenberg, Leo: *Bewegte Zeiten*, Wolfenbüttel, 1961.

Kindermann, Jürgen: *Thematisch-chronologisches Verzeichnis der Werke von Ferruccio Busoni*, Regensburg, 1980.

Klinckerfuss, Margerete: *Aufklänge aus versunkener Zeit*, Urach, 1947.

Kogan, Grigori: *Ferruccio Busoni*, Moscow, 1964.

Kolb, Annette: *Kleine Fanfare*, Berlin, 1930.

Krellmann, Hanspeter: *Studien zu den Bearbeitungen Ferruccio Busonis*, Diss., Regensburg, 1966.

Leichtentritt, Hugo: *Ferruccio Busoni*, Leipzig, 1916.

Meyer, Hans: *Die Klaviermusik Ferruccio Busonis, eine musikkritische Untersuchung*, Diss., Zurich, 1969.

Nadel, Siegfried F.: *Ferruccio Busoni*, Leipzig, 1931.

Pfitzner, Hans: *Futuristengefahr—bei Gelegenheit von Busonis Aesthetik*, Stuttgart, 1917.

Ponnelle, Lazare: *À Munich*, Paris, 1939.

Prinz, Ulrich: *Ferruccio Busoni als Klavierkomponist*, Diss., Heidelberg, 1970.

Sablich, Sergio: *Busoni*, Turin, 1982.

Samson, Jim: *Music in transition: a study of tonal expansion and tonality, 1900–1920*, London, 1977.

Santelli, Adolfo: *Ferruccio Busoni*, Rome, 1939.

Selden-Goth, Gisella: *Ferruccio Busoni—Versuch eines Porträts*, Leipzig–

Zurich–Vienna, 1922.

Sorabji, Khaikosru: *Around Music*, London, 1932.

Mi contra Fa, London, 1947.

Stuckenschmidt, H. H.: *Ferruccio Busoni, Chronicle of a European*, trans. Sandra Morris, London, 1970.

Theurich, Jutta: *Der Briefwechsel zwischen Arnold Schönberg und Ferruccio Busoni 1903–1919 (1927)*. Edition, Kommentierung und Untersuchung unter besonderer Berücksichtigung der im Busoni-Nachlass der Deutschen Staatsbibliothek enthaltenen Quellen, Diss., Berlin, 1979.

Varèse, Louise: *A looking-glass diary*, New York, 1972.

Vogel, Wladimir: *Schriften und Aufzeichnungen über Musik*, herausgegeben von Walter Labhart, Zurich, 1977.

Wassermann, Jakob: *In memoriam Ferruccio Busoni*, Berlin, 1925. *Lebensdienst*, Leipzig–Zurich, 1928.

Selbstbetrachtungen, Berlin, 1933.

Weill, Kurt: *Ausgewählte Schriften*, herausgegeben von David Drew, Frankfurt am Main, 1975.

5) IMPORTANT ARTICLES IN PERIODICALS

Bekker, Paul: 'Busoni', *Musikblätter des Anbruch*, Aug. 1924, pp. 347–51.

Bonavia, F.: 'Giacomo Puccini and Ferruccio Busoni', *Music and Letters*, Vol. 6, 1925, pp. 99–109.

Busoni, Benvenuto: 'Um das Erbe Busonis', *Die Musik*, 1935, p. 187.

Dent, Edward J.: 'The return of Busoni', *The Athenaeum*, 17.12.1920.

'Busoni's *Doktor Faust*', *Music and Letters*, July 1926, pp. 224–35.

'The Italian Busoni', *Monthly Musical Record*, Jan. 1930, pp. 257–60.

'Busoni's pianoforte music', *The Listener*, 25.11.1936.

'Busoni's *Arlecchino*', *The Listener*, 26.1.1939.

'Busoni and his operas', *Opera*, July 1954, pp. 391–7.

Flodin, Karl: 'Ferruccio Busoni', *Atheneum*, Helsinki, Nov. 15, 1898, pp. 422–5.

Gervais, Terence White: 'Busoni's possible influence', *The Chesterian*, London, July 1953, pp. 1–5.

Goebels, Franzpeter: 'Busonis Klavierübung—eine Revision', *Musik und Unterricht*, 1966, Band 10, pp. 317–25.

Halm, August: 'Busonis Bachausgabe', *Melos*, 2. Jg., 1921, p. 207.

Krenek, Ernst: 'Busoni—then and now', *Modern Music*, New York, 1942, Vol. 19, pp. 88–91.

Leichtentritt, Hugo: 'Ferruccio Busoni', *Music Review*, Nov. 1945, pp. 205–19.

Maine, Basil: 'Some Busoni recollections', *Musical Opinion*, 1960–61, p. 586.

Mellers, Wilfrid: 'The problem of Busoni', *Music and Letters*, 1937, pp. 240–7.

Mersmann, Hans: 'Pfitzner und Busoni', *Allgemeine Musik-Zeitung*, 1917, pp. 447–8.

Proctor-Gregg, Humphrey: 'Busoni, Pianist and Composer', *The Sackbut*, July, 1920, pp. 101–4.

Searle, Humphrey: 'Busoni's *Doktor Faust*', *Monthly Musical Record*, March–April 1937, pp. 54–6.

Stevenson, Ronald: 'Busoni—the legend of a prodigal', *The Score*, March, 1956, pp. 15–30.

'Busoni's *Arlecchino*', *Musical Times*, June 1954, pp. 307–8.

'Busoni and Mozart', *The Score*, Sept. 1955, pp. 25–38.

Vlad, Roman: 'Busoni's destiny', *The Score*, Dec. 1952, pp. 3–10.

Vogel, Wladimir: 'Über Busoni's *Doktor Faust*', *Schweizerische Musikzeitung*, 1966, no. 2, pp. 66–7.

'Impressions of Ferruccio Busoni', *Perspectives of New Music*, spring–summer 1968, p. 167.

Wis, Robert: 'Ferruccio Busoni and Finland', *Acta Musicologica*, Vol. II, 1977, pp. 250–69.

Notes

Sources of the quotations on page 17

Stefan Zweig: 'Busoni', *Blätter des Deutschen Theaters*, 1. Jg., 1911, Nr. 6, pp. 92–4. Republ. in *Begegnungen mit Menschen, Büchern, Städten*, Vienna–Leipzig–Zurich, 1937.

Sacheverell Sitwell: *Liszt*, London, 1934.

Peter Tchaikovsky: 'Diary of my tour in 1888', trans. Rosa Newmarch in *Tchaikovsky*, London, 1908.

Louise Varèse: *A looking-glass diary*, New York, 1972.

Alfred Einstein: 'Busoni als Briefschreiber' (ca. 1934). In *Von Schütz bis Hindemith*, Zurich–Stuttgart, 1957.

Willi Schuh: 'Zu den Briefen', foreword to *Busoni, Briefe an seine Frau*, ed. Friedrich Schnapp, Zurich/Leipzig, 1935.

FOREWORD

1. Erich Heller: *Nirgends wird Welt sein als innen*. Frankfurt am Main, 1975. The essay 'Rilke und Nietzsche' first appeared in *Enterbte Geist*, Frankfurt am Main, 1954.

Section One: The Composer

1. Letter to H. W. Draber, 9.4.1919.
2. Letter to Paul Bekker, Jan. 1920. Publ. in *Frankfurter Zeitung*, 7.2.1920. Republ. in *The Essence of Music and other papers* (see Bibliography).
3. Letter to Raffaello Busoni, 18.6.1921.
4. Busoni's diary, 23.12.1914.
5. Busoni: Sketch for an introduction to Book II of *The Well-tempered Clavier*, 1914.
6. Letter to the bell foundry H. Rüetschi, Aarau, 30.5.1919.
7. Letter from Schoenberg to Busoni, 24.8.1909.
8. ibid.
9. Letter from Schoenberg to Busoni, Aug. 1909.
10. Guido Guerrini: 'Ferruccio Busoni Maestro', *Rassegna Musicale*, Florence, Jan. 1940 (see Bibliography).
11. Letter to Hugo Leichtentritt, 9.1.1916 (erroneously dated 1915 by Busoni).
12. ibid.
13. Busoni: 'The new harmony,' 1911. Publ. in *The Essence of Music*.
14. Letter from Schoenberg to Busoni, 24.8.1909.
15. Hesse: 'Kurzgefasste Lebenslauf (1924)', *Neue Rundschau*, 36 (Aug. 1925), pp. 841–56.

16. Bernard Bromage: 'The Mysticism of Ferruccio Busoni', *The Modern Mystic*, London, Sept. 1938, pp. 340–3.
17. Busoni: 'The Essence of Music', 1924. Publ. in *The Essence of Music*.
18. Busoni: 'Kunst und Technik', 1909. Publ. in *Wesen und Einheit der Musik*.
19. Letter to Gerda, 8.11.1908.
20. Kenneth Clark: *Leonardo da Vinci*. London, 1935.
21. Dimitri Mereshkovsky: *The Romance of Leonardo da Vinci. The re-birth of the gods.* St Petersburg, 1901.
22. Vasari: *Le Vite*, trans. George Bull. Harmondsworth, 1965.
23. Busoni: *Outline of a New Aesthetic of Music*, Trieste 1907.
24. Bernard van Dieren: *Down among the Dead Men*. London, 1935.
25. Busoni: 'Über die *Parsifal*–Partitur' (undated). Publ. in *Wesen und Einheit der Musik*.
26. Letter to Hans Reinhart, 15.4.1917.
27. Letter to Hugo Leichtentritt, 12.11.1915.
28. Letter to Egon Petri, 22.5.1913.
29. Unpublished section of letter to Gerda, 19.9.1913.
30. Letter to Egon Petri, 14.5.1921.
31. Letter to Paul Bekker, Jan. 1920, op. cit.
32. English translation by J. B. Leishman and Stephen Spender, London, 1939.
33. ibid.
34. Letter from Rilke to Josef Hulewicz, Feb. 1922. Trans. J. B. Leishman.
35. Erich Heller: 'Rilke und Nietzsche', op. cit.
36. Iannis Xenakis: *Formalized music*. Bloomington/London, 1971.
37. ibid.
38. ibid.
39. Busoni: *Outline of a New Aesthetic of Music*.
40. Xenakis: ibid.
41. ibid.
42. Karl H. Wörner: *Stockhausen, Life and Work*, trans. Bill Hopkins. London, 1973.
43. ibid.
44. Letter from Ronald Stevenson to the author, 29.3.1978.
45. ibid.
46. Wladimir Vogel: 'Busonis Einstellung zur Erforschung neuen musikalischen Materials', *Schriften und Aufzeichnungen über Musik*, ed. Walter Labhart, Zurich, 1977.
47. ibid.
48. Wilfrid Mellers: 'The problem of Busoni', *Music and Letters*, 1937, pp. 240–7.
49. Busoni: 'Self-Criticism', 1912. Publ. in *The Essence of Music*.
50. Letter to Raffaello Busoni, 6.2.1922.
51. Bernard van Dieren: op. cit.
52. Letter to Gerda, 4.9.1905.
53. Busoni: 'Remarks about the proper order of the opus numbers of my works', 1908. Publ. in *The Essence of Music*.
54. Busoni: 'Self-Criticism', 1912. Publ. in *The Essence of Music*.
55. Letter to Hugo Leichtentritt, 15.8.1915.

Section Two: From the Rubinstein Prize to the *Outline of a New Aesthetic of Music* (1890–1905)

I BEGINNINGS

1. *Musikalisches Wochenblatt*, 16.1.1890.
2. Letter to Anna Busoni, 10.1.1890.
3. *St Petersburger Herold*, 19(31).8.1890.
4. *AMZ*, July 1894, p. 401.
5. Ronald Stevenson: *Busoni e la Gran Bretagna*. Empoli, 1958.
6. Letter to Anna Busoni, 24.4.1894.
7. Letter to Henri Petri, 9.3.1897.
8. Letter to Martin Wegelius, 26.10.1893.
9. Josef Szigeti: *With Strings Attached*, New York, 1947.
10. Letter to Gerda, 11.7.1898.
11. Letter to Isidor Philipp, 13.1.1920.
12. *NMZ*, 1897, no. 21, p. 261.
13. *Musikalisches Wochenblatt*, Dec. 1897, p. 692.

II IN MEMORIAM

1. Letter to Gerda, 1.2.1897.
2. Letter to Hjalmar von Dameck, 29.5.1898.
3. Letter to Anna Busoni, 26.7.1898.
4. Letter to Egon Petri, 2.12.1915.
5. Letter to Arrigo Serato, 10.6.1916.

III THE PIANO CONCERTO

1. Trans. W. M. Clement, BBC London, 1936.
2. Letter to Hugo Leichtentritt, 16.12.1920.
3. Letter to Gerda, 17.7.1902.
4. Letter to Gerda, 21/22.7.1902.
5. Letter to Gerda, 12.7.1903.
6. cf. Edward J. Dent: *Ferruccio Busoni, a biography*, p. 149.
7. Letter to Gerda, 1.8.1902
8. 'The tale of Ala-ed-Din and the magic lamp', *1001 Nights*.
9. Letter to Gerda, 15.2.1911.
10. *Tägliche Rundschau*, 14.11.1904.
11. *Vossische Zeitung*, 15.11.1904.
12. *Deutsche Zeitung*, 13.11.1904.
13. *Signale für die musikalische Welt*, 23.11.1904.
14. Alfred Brendel: *Musical thoughts and afterthoughts*. London, 1976.
15. Letter to Gerda, 6.4.1910.

IV THE MUSIC FOR *Turandot*

1. Letter to Anna Busoni, 21.8.1905.
2. ibid.
3. An excellent account of the various stages of the Turandot legend is to be found in

Fritz Meier: 'Turandot in Persien', *Zeitschrift der Deutschen Morgenländischen Gesellschaft*, Leipzig, 1941, Vol. 95, pp. 1–27.

4. Goethe: *Noten zum 'West-östlichen Divan'*, Stuttgart, 1819.
5. *The Mask*, Florence, April 1914, pp. 286–96.
6. Busoni: 'The *Turandot* music', 1911. Publ. in *The Essence of Music*.
7. *Blätter des Deutschen Theaters*, Oct. 1911, pp. 81–3.
8. Letter from Schiller to Körner, 16.11.1801.
9. Letter to Gerda, 26.7.1905.
10. Nezami: *The Seven Tales of the Seven Princesses* (Haft Peiker).
11. Letter to Anna Busoni, 21.8.1905.
12. *Der Tag*, 27.10.1911.
13. *Berliner Zeitung*, 28.10.1911.
14. Letter to Gerda, 19.1.1913.
15. Edward J. Dent: 'Music in Berlin', *Monthly Musical Record*, Feb. 1909, pp. 31–2.

Section Three: *Outline of a New Aesthetic of Music*

1. *Birmingham Daily Post*, 24.8.1907.
2. *Monthly Musical Record*, Sept. 1909, pp. 197–8.
3. *AMZ*, July 1908, pp. 541–6.
4. Letter to Gerda, 3.3.1910. Publ. in *The Essence of Music*.
5. Letter to Gerda, 25.3.1911.
6. Unpublished section of letter to Gerda, 25.3.1911.
7. Letter to Edward Dent, 10.5.1911.
8. Magda von Hattingberg: *Rilke und Benvenuta*, Vienna, 1947.
9. Letter from Rilke to Anton Kippenberg, 8.3.1914.
10. Henry van de Velde: *Geschichte meines Lebens*, ed. Hans Curjel, Munich, 1962.
11. Letter to Gerda, 30.3.1904.
12. Quoted in Leo Kestenberg: *Bewegte Zeiten*, Wolfenbüttel, 1962.
13. Hans Mersmann: 'Busonis Entwurf einer neuen Aesthetik der Tonkunst', *AMZ*, Feb. 1917, pp. 79–81, 95–7.
14. ibid.
15. W. Nagel: 'Ferruccio Busoni als Aesthetiker', *NMZ*, May 1917, pp. 239–40, 253–4.
16. Hans Pfitzner: *Futuristengefahr*, Stuttgart, 1917.
17. Letter to the *Vossische Zeitung*, June 1917. Publ. in *The Essence of Music* as 'Open letter to Hans Pfitzner'.
18. Letter to José Vianna da Motta, 29.5.1917.
19. Paul Bekker: *Futuristengefahr?*, Frankfurt, 1917.
20. Hans Mersmann: 'Pfitzner und Busoni', *AMZ*, June 1917, pp. 447–8.
21. ibid.
22. Hans Mersmann: Article in *Melos*, Oct. 1930, p. 421.
23. Busoni: 'What is happening at the present time'. Publ. in *The Essence of Music*.
24. Letter to Gisella Selden-Goth, 7.2.1921.
25. Herbert Gerigk: Article in *Die Musik*, Dec. 1934, p. 189.

Section Four: The Radical Years (1907–15)

V ELEGIES

1. Letter to Gerda, 1.12.1907.
. 2. Letter to Egon Petri, 2.12.1907.
3. Letter to Gerda, 16.1.1908.
4. Ovid: *Tristium*, Book 1, II, 55.
5. Letter to José Vianna da Motta, 27.9.1916.
6. Translation by J. B. Leishman and Stephen Spender.
7. Leo Kestenberg: op. cit.
8. *Signale für die musikalische Welt*, 18.3.1908.
9. Letter to Egon Petri, 2.5.1908.
10. Letter to Robert Freund, 7.5.1908.
11. Letter to Gerda, 30.4.1908. The sentence was later incorporated in the 'Foreword to the studies by Liszt'. Publ. in *The Essence of Music*.
12. Letter to Hugo Leichtentritt, Feb. 1914.
13. From the programme note for the first performance of the *Berceuse élégiaque*, New York, 21.2.1911.

VI *Die Brautwahl*

1. Undated entry in a notebook of Edward Dent.
2. Letter to Gertrud Draber, 21.5.1918.
3. Hans von Müller: *Nachwort zur 'Brautwahl'*, Berlin, 1911.
4. G. B. Shaw: *The Gospel of the Brothers Barnabas*, London, 1921.
5. Letter to Gerda, 23.6.1908.
6. Letter to Gerda, 30.4.1908.
7. *The Times*, 14.4.1912.
8. Bernard van Dieren: op. cit.
9. Letter to Gerda, 16.7.1906.
10. Letter to Gerda, 13.7.1907.
11. Letter to José Vianna da Motta, 22.4.1912.
12. Letter to H. W. Draber, 10.3.1911.
13. *The Times*, 14.4.1912.
14. From a sketch for Busoni's libretto.
15. Letter to Egon Petri, 9.5.1911.
16. Letter to Gerda, 2.4.1912.
17. Letter to Egon Petri, 9.5.1911.
18. ibid.
19. Letter to Robert Freund, 8.11.1910.
20. *Vossische Zeitung*, (?) 15.4.1912.
21. *Hamburger Nachrichten*, 14.4.1912.
22. *Frankfurter Zeitung*, 15.4.1912.
23. Bernard van Dieren: op. cit.
24. Busoni: 'Simplicity of music in the future'. Publ. in *The Essence of Music*.
25. Letter to Edward Dent, 30.8.1923.

VII   EPITAPHS

1. From Busoni's edition of Book II of *The Well-tempered Clavier*.
2. Letter to Anna Busoni, 28.6.1909.
3. *The Times*, 18.10.1909.
4. Letter to Arrigo Serato, 2.2.1920.
5. Thomas de Quincey: *Suspiria de Profundis*, London, 1851.
6. Translation by Henry Meyer, Copenhagen, 1960.
7. From Busoni's programme note for the first performance of the *Berceuse élégiaque*, New York, 21.2.1911.
8. ibid.
9. Bernard van Dieren: op. cit.
10. Hugo Leichtentritt: 'Ferruccio Busoni', *Music Review*, Nov. 1945, pp. 205–19.
11. *New York Times*, 22.2.1911.
12. Letter to Gerda, 22.2.1911.
13. Busoni: 'Self-Criticism', 1912. Publ. in *The Essence of Music*.
14. Arnold Schoenerg: *Berliner Tagebuch*, ed. Josef Rufer, Frankfurt am Main, 1974.

VIII   NEW BEGINNINGS

1. Letter to Gerda, 28.7.1909.
2. Busoni: 'Biographical and critical study drawn up as a foundation to the proposed Collected Edition of Liszt's pianoforte works', 1900. Publ. in *The Essence of Music*.
3. Ludwig von Köchel: *Chronologisch-thematisches Verzeichnis sämtlicher Tonwerke Wolfgang Amadé Mozarts*, ed. Alfred Einstein, 3ᵉ Auflage, Leipzig, 1937.
4. Letter to Gerda (unpubl.), 26.7.1909.
5. Letter from Schoenberg to Busoni, 24.8.1909.
6. Bernard van Dieren: op. cit.
7. Busoni: 'An die Jugend', 1909. Publ. in *Wesen und Einheit der Musik*.
8. *Musical America*, 20.12.1909.
9. *Evening Standard*, 18.10.1909.
10. *AMZ*, 7.1.1910.
11. *Nationalzeitung*, Basle, 2.10.1910.
12. *Basler Nachrichten*, 2.10.1910.
13. Letter to Robert Freund, 8.11.1910.
14. *Musical America*, 24.12.1910.
15. Letter to H. W. Draber, 21.1.1913.
16. Letter to Egon Petri, 29.8.1909.

IX   THE *Fantasia Contrappuntistica*

1. Busoni: 'Die Gothiker von Chicago', 1910. Publ. in *Wesen und Einheit der Musik*.
2. Letter to Gerda, 20.1.1910.
3. Letter to Gerda, 19.2.1910.
4. Letter to H. W. Draber, 26.2.1910.
5. Letter to Egon Petri, 30.4.1910.
6. Letter to Egon Petri, 29.8.1910.
7. Busoni: 'Self-Criticism', 1912. Publ. in *The Essence of Music*.
8. *Nationalzeitung*, Basle, 2.10.1910.
9. Letter to Egon Petri, 29.8.1910.

10. Letter to Frida Kwast-Hodapp, 26.5.1920.
11. Letter to Egon Petri, 24.8.1911.
12. *AMZ*, 1.9.1911, p. 838.
13. Letter to Gerda, 4.9.1911.
14. Letter from Schoenberg to Busoni, 22.1.1912.
15. Ronald Stevenson: 'Busoni's Great Fugue', *The Listener*, 3.2.1972, p. 157.
16. From Busoni's edition of Book II of *The Well-tempered Clavier*.

X   THE OCCULT

1. M. D. Calvocoressi: *Musicians' Gallery*, London, 1933.
2. Busoni: 'Schoenberg matinée,' 1912 (not 1911 as usually cited). Publ. in *The Essence of Music*.
3. Schoenberg: *Berliner Tagebuch*. Entry for 29.1.1912.
4. Letter to Gerda, 18.3.1912.
5. Translation by Hugh Shankland in: *Futurism in literature and the theatre*, catalogue of the Futurist Exhibition, Newcastle upon Tyne, 1972.
6. From the diary of Edward Dent, 20.4.1912.
7. Jean-Paul Sartre: *Les Mots*. Paris, 1964. Trans. Irene Clephane, London, 1964.
8. Letter to Egon Petri, 7.9.1912. Busoni possessed the 1890 edition of Meyer's *Konversationslexikon*.
9. Letter to Gerda, 26.2.1913.
10. From Busoni's diary, 28.6.1912.
11. From the programme-book for the first performance of the *Sonatina seconda*, Milan, 12.5.1913.
12. Ronald Stevenson: *Busoni e la Gran Bretagna*, op. cit.
13. E. T. A. Hoffmann: *Die Automate*, Berlin, 1814.
14. Dimitri Mereshkovsky: op. cit.
15. Letter to Irma Bekh, 16.11.1912 (collection Fischer–Dieskau).
16. cf. Edward J. Dent: *Ferruccio Busoni, a biography*, p. 272.
17. Letter to Gerda, 19.11.1912.
18. Faubion Bowers: *The new Scriabin*, New York, 1973.
19. Letter to Harriet Lanier, 4.5.1915.
20. Letter to Gerda, 18.7.1913.
21. ibid.
22. Letter to Egon Petri, 13.5.1913.
23. *Neue Preussische Zeitung*, 14.3.1914.
24. *Deutsche Zeitung*, 15.3.1914.
25. *Vossische Zeitung*, (?)14.3.1914.
26. Nietzsche: *Beyond Good and Evil*, trans. R. J. Hollingdale, Harmondsworth, 1973.

XI   THE INDIANS' BOOK

1. Edward S. Curtis: *The North American Indian*. 20 vols., Cambridge and Norwood, Mass., 1907–29.
2. Edward S. Curtis: *Portraits of North American Indian Life*, introduction by A. D. Coleman and T. C. McLuhan, Outerbridge and Lazard, 1972. Natalie Curtis: *The Indians' Book*, Dover Publications Inc., New York, 1968.

3. Letter to Gerda, 22.3.1910.
4. Letter to Gerda, 9.3.1911.
5. Letter to Gerda, 15.3.1911.
6. Natalie Curtis: 'Busoni's Indian Fantasy', *The Southern Workman*, Oct. 1915.
7. Letter to Gerda, 18.6.1913.
8. Letter to Gerda, 22.6.1913.
9. Natalie Curtis: *The Indians' Book*, op. cit.
10. ibid.
11. Letter to Egon Petri, 18.1.1914.
12. Letter to Hugo Leichtentritt, Feb. 1914.
13. *Vossische Zeitung*, (?) 14.3.1914.
14. *Münchener Neueste Nachrichten*, 18.3.1914.
15. Natalie Curtis: 'Busoni's Indian Fantasy', op. cit.
16. *The Times*, 24.6.1920.
17. Natalie Curtis: 'Busoni's Indian Fantasy', op. cit.
18. From a programme note by Gisella Selden-Goth, Berlin, 27.1.1921.
19. Letter to Natalie Curtis, 22.2.1915.
20. Letter to Edith Andreae, 23.6.1915.
21. *Neue Zürcher Zeitung*, 10.11.1917.
22. Natalie Curtis: *The Indians' Book*, op. cit., pp. 41–4.
23. Letter to Hugo Leichtentritt, 27.6.1916.
24. Letter to Volkmar Andreae, 1.1.1919.
25. Busoni: 'The Essence of Music', 1924. Publ. in *The Essence of Music*.

Section Five: La nuova Commedia dell'Arte

XII   BEFORE *Arlecchino*

1. Letter to Gerda, 3.3.1909 (unpubl.).
2. Letter to Egon Petri, 3.5.1912.
3. Letter from Jakob Wassermann to Busoni, 12.6.1913.
4. Letter to Egon Petri, 19.6.1913.
5. Letter to Harriet Lanier, 18.8.1915.
6. Letter to Max Reinhardt, undated (probl. 26.10.1914).
7. Letter to Edith Andreae, 23.6.1915.
8. ibid.
9. Letter to Egon Petri, 12.4.1915.
10. Letter to Edith Andreae, 23.6.1915.
11. From the preface to the score of the *Rondò arlecchinesco*.
12. Letter to Arrigo Serato, 23.11.1915.
13. Letter to Egon Petri, 17.3.1916.
14. ibid.
15. *Neue Zürcher Zeitung*, 31.3.1916.
16. ibid.
17. Letter to Hugo Leichtentritt, 27.6.1916.
18. Letter to Edith Andreae, 10.1.1916.
19. Letter to Edith Andreae, 6.8.1916.
20. *Neue Zürcher Zeitung*, 10.11.1917.

XIII   *Arlecchino*

1. Letter to Harriet Lanier, 18.8.1915.
2. E. T. A. Hoffmann: *Prinzessin Brambilla*, Breslau, 1821.
3. Letter to José Vianna da Motta, 15.4.1917.
4. From Busoni's diary, 24.10.1914.
5. Translation by J. B. Leishman and Stephen Spender.
6. *The puppet-play of 'Faust'*, trans. Karl Simrock, ed. Alfred Sternbeck, Berlin, 1914.
7. Rilke: *Zu den Wachs-Puppen von Lotte Pritzel*, Leipzig, 1914.
8. ibid.
9. Edward Gordon Craig: 'Gentlemen, the Marionette', *The Mask*, Florence, Oct. 1912, pp. 95–7.
10. ibid.
11. Busoni: '*Arlecchino*'s Evolution', 1921. Publ. in *The Essence of Music*.
12. Letter from Rilke to Marianne Goldschmidt-Rothschild, 28.7.1915.
13. Busoni: 'The Meaning of *Arlecchino*', 1918. Publ. in *The Essence of Music*.
14. ibid.
15. Dante: *Inferno*, Canto V, 135–8, trans. Dorothy Sayers, Harmondsworth, 1949.
16. Dante: *Inferno*, Canto V, 133, ibid.
17. Busoni: '*Arlecchino*'s Evolution', op. cit.
18. Letter to Gerda, 25.1.1913.
19. Evaristo Gherardi: 'Introduction to "Le théâtre Italien"', trans. D. Neville Lees, *The Mask*, Florence, April 1911, pp. 164–8.
20. Busoni: 'Apropos of *Arlecchino*', 1922. Publ. in *The Essence of Music*.
21. Letter to Edith Andreae, 8.9.1916.
22. Busoni: 'The Meaning of *Arlecchino*', op. cit.
23. Letter to Egon Petri, 28.3.1916.
24. Letter to José Vianna da Motta, 15.4.1917.
25. Busoni: 'Autobiographical Fragment', 1909. Publ. in *The Essence of Music*.
26. Letter to Gerda, 25.11.1919.
27. Busoni: 'Apropros of *Arlecchino*', op. cit.
28. *Neue Freie Presse*, Vienna, 5.4.1918.

XIV   BEFORE *Turandot*

XV   *Turandot*

1. Letter to Gerda, 21.1.1913.
2. Letter to Egon Petri, 1.11.1916.
3. Mosco Carner: *Puccini, a critical biography*. London, 1958.
4. ibid.
5. *Neue Freie Presse*, Vienna, 5.4.1918.
6. Letters to Franz Ludwig Hörth, (a) 26.5.1921; (b) 15.10.1921.
7. Letter to Arrigo Serato, 29.12.1916.
8. Letter to Egon Petri, 4.4.1917.

XVI   *Arlecchino*, PART II

Section Six: Zurich and Berlin (1917–24)

XVII   *Faust* UNFOLDS

1. Letter to Isidor Philipp, 9.1.1918.
2. *Neue Zürcher Zeitung*, Jan. 1920.
3. Goethe: *Noten zum 'West-östlichen Divan'*, op. cit.
4. Edward J. Dent: *Ferruccio Busoni, a biography*, p. 239.
5. Letter to Volkmar Andreae, 21.12.1918.
6. Bernard van Dieren: 'Two studies for *Doktor Faust*', *The Listener*, 15.4.1936, p. 749.
7. Letter to Mario Corti, date unknown.
8. The original letter from G. B. Shaw is untraceable. This is a retranslation into quasi-Shavian English of Busoni's German translation in a letter to Albert Biolley, 4.8.1919.
9. Letter to Volkmar Andreae, Jan. 1919.
10. *Neue Zürcher Zeitung*, 4.4.1919.
11. *The Daily Telegraph*, 24.11.1919.
12. Letter to Gerda, 25.11.1919.
13. Reproduced on pp. 278–9 of Edward J. Dent: *Ferruccio Busoni, a biography*.
14. Reproduced on p. IX of *Wesen und Einheit der Musik*.
15. Letter to Albert Biolley, 4.8.1919.
16. Letter to Gisella Selden-Goth, date uncertain.
17. Letter to the Marchese di Casanova, 7.8.1920.

XVIII   IN SIGNO JOANNIS SEBASTIANI MAGNI

1. From Busoni's diary, 20.9.1912.
2. Letter from Schoenberg to Busoni, 24.8.1909.
3. Letter to Egon Petri, 19.6.1913.

XIX   LIGHT RELIEF

1. Magda von Hattingberg: op. cit.
2. Letter to Philipp Jarnach, 10.3.1920.
3. Letter to Philipp Jarnach, 22.3.1920.
4. Busoni: 'Mozart's *Don Giovanni* and Liszt's *Don Juan* Fantasy', 1917. Publ. in *The Essence of Music*.
5. Nietzsche: *Der Fall Wagner*, Leipzig, 1888.
6. Letter from Nietzsche to Carl Fuchs, 27.12.1888.
7. Bernard van Dieren, op. cit.
8. Letter to Egon Petri, 29.6.1920.
9. Retold by Robert Craft in: *Retrospectives and Conclusions*, New York, 1969.
10. Artur Schnabel: *My Life and Music*, London, 1961.
11. Letter to Edith Andreae, 13.6.1921.
12. Busoni: 'Die Bekehrte', 1921. Publ. in *The Essence of Music*.
13. Letter to H. W. Draber, 9.4.1919.

xx *Faust* PROGRESSES

1. Letter to Isidor Philipp, 26.8.1920.
2. Letter to Isidor Philipp, 7.9.1920.
3. Letter to Isidor Philipp, 17.9.1920.
4. Letter to Philipp Jarnach, 1.10.1920.
5. *Vossische Zeitung*, 20.11.1920.
6. Alfred Brendel: op. cit.
7. Letter to Gerda, 19.9.1920.
8. Letter to Albert Biolley, 1.10.1920.
9. Roman Vlad: 'Busoni's destiny', *The Score*, Dec. 1952, pp. 3–10.
10. *Berliner Börsen-Zeitung*, 14.1.1921.
11. Letter to Frida Kwast-Hodapp, 13.6.1921.
12. Letter to Jella Oppenheimer, 5.3.1924.

xxi THE *Klavierübung*

1. Letter to Egon Petri, 14.9.1912.
2. Busoni: 'Chopin', 1916. Publ. in *Wesen und Einheit der Musik*.
3. Letter to Isidor Philipp, 15.10.1922.

Section Seven: *Doktor Faust*

1. Letter to Gerda, 14.7.1907 (unpubl.).
2. Dimitri Mereshkovsky: op. cit.
3. Letter to Gerda, 19.2.1909.
4. From Busoni's diary, 9.12.1910.
5. From Edward Dent's diary, 19.4.1912.
6. Letter to Edward Dent, 20.5.1912.
7. Letter to Gerda, 25.1.1913.
8. Letter to Gerda, 26.2.1913.
9. Letter to Gerda, 23.6.1913.
10. From Busoni's diary, 3.7.1914.
11. From Busoni's diary, 21.12.1914 (trans. cf. Dent, p. 295).
12. From Busoni's diary, 2.1.1915.
13. Letter to Egon Petri, 19.1.1915.
14. Busoni: 'The Score of *Doktor Faust*', 1922. Publ. in *The Essence of Music*.
15. ibid.
16. Kurt Weill: 'Busonis Faust und die Erneuerung der Opernform'. Berlin, 1926. In *Ausgewählte Schriften*, ed. David Drew, Frankfurt am Main, 1975.
17. *Weimarer Landeszeitung*, 31.5.1920.
18. Letter to Gisella Selden-Goth, 28.6.1920.
19. Letter to Gerda, 31.3.1915.
20. Busoni: 'The Score of *Doktor Faust*', op. cit.
21. E. T. A. Hoffmann: 'Die Serapionsbrüder', 5. Abschnitt, Berlin, 1819–21.
22. Vladimir Vogel: 'Impressions of Ferruccio Busoni', *Perspectives of New Music*, Spring–Summer 1968, pp. 167–73.
23. Busoni: '*The Essence of Music*', op. cit.
24. Ludwig Rubiner: *Die Gewaltlosen. Eine Legende*, Potsdam, 1919.
25. Busoni: 'The Score of *Doktor Faust*', op. cit.

26. *The Athenaeum*, 17.12.1920.
27. Goethe to Eckermann, 12.2.1829.
28. Busoni: 'The Score of *Doktor Faust*', op. cit.
29. Letter to Alicja Simon, 13.9.1916.
30. Letter to Hugo Leichtentritt, 21.9.1918.
31. Letter to Volkmar Andreae, 18.8.1919.
32. Letter to Gerda, 25.3.1922.
33. Letter to Volkmar Andreae, 22.12.1922.
34. Recounted by Vladimir Vogel in: 'Eine Begegnung', in *Wesen und Einheit der Musik* and in Vogel: *Schriften und Aufzeichnungen über Musik*, ed. Walter Labhart (see Bibliography).
35. Letter to Jella Oppenheimer, 5.3.1924.
36. Letter to Gerda, 18.8.1918.
37. ibid.
38. H. H. Stuckenschmidt: *Ferruccio Busoni, Chronicle of a European*, Zurich, 1967 and London, 1970 (trans. Sandra Morris).
39. J. E. Cirlot: *A Dictionary of Symbols*, trans. Jack Sage, London, 1962.
40. Letter to Gerda, 23.7.1921.
41. Letter to Philipp Jarnach, 7.10.1923.
42. Letter to Egon Petri, 7.9.1912.
43. Letter to Albert Biolley, 20.1.1920.
44. Quoted by A. W. Ambros in: *Geschichte der Musik*, Vol. I, p. 317 (second edition, Leipzig, 1880).
45. Letter to Albert Biolley, 25.10.1918.
46. *NMZ*, July 1925, Vol. II, pp. 476–7.
47. *Die Musik*, July 1925, pp. 760–4.
48. *Musikblätter des Anbruch*, June/July 1925, p. 323.
49. *AMZ*, 29.5.1925, pp. 481–2.
50. *La Revue Musicale*, July 1925, pp. 76–7.
51. Bernard van Dieren: op. cit.
52. Busoni: 'The Score of *Doktor Faust*', op. cit.
53. Kurt Weill: 'Busonis Faust und die Erneuerung der Opernform', op. cit.
54. Letter to Hugo Leichtentritt, 10.2.1921.
55. Busoni: 'The Score of *Doktor Faust*', trans. Edward J. Dent, but last line altered (see p. 97, footnote)

Index of Busoni's works

Figures in *italic* refer to illustrations.

General Index

Figures in *italic* refer to illustrations.